Thomas Wilson
Introit: Towards the Light

© 2011 Margaret Wilson and David Griffith
Published by Queensgate Music
Glasgow, Scotland 2011
Cover Photograph: Eric Thorburn
Print Production: More, Glasgow
Book Design and Typesetting: Johanna Larson
www.larsondesign.co.uk

ISBN 978-0-9569529-0-5

www.thomaswilsoncomposer.co.uk

Thomas Wilson

Introit: Towards the Light

A biography of Scotland's great composer
by Margaret Wilson and David Griffith

ACKNOWLEDGEMENTS

My thanks go to Agnes Walker to whom I turned when the idea for this biography came to me, as she suggested I contact Lesley Duncan. I am indebted to Lesley who read and re-read the first draft of the manuscript as it evolved, and was of unfailing help and encouragement, and to Professor Karl Gwiasda of Iowa (retired Professor of English Literature) who corrected text, and gave me the 'international slant' on the manuscript as well as further editing. My thanks also for proof-reading to my friend Patricia Holmes who did some editing, and to Stuart Harris-Logan who completed the final edit. I am also very grateful to Celia Stevenson, Head of Corporate Communication at Scottish Screen, for her faith in the biography, and for introducing me to David Griffith, my friend and co-writer in the final version.

My thanks also to Martin Baillie, John Currie, Martin Dalby, John Maxwell Geddes, Adriene Khoury, James Loughran, Mary Millar, Jane Smeaton, Phillip Thorne, Stefan Grasse, Allan Neave, Michael Tumelty and Conrad Wilson, for permission to reproduce articles and interviews; and to Sandra Craig, and Flora Stagg. Thanks also to Andrew Whettam who was of great help when I was struggling to learn how to use the computer.

CONTENTS

INTRODUCTION

My husband Thomas Brendan Wilson not only wanted to be a composer, he said that he had to be one. There was an inner compulsion - he felt as though he had no choice in the matter. Composition was something that gave him great satisfaction. He said that when it went right there was no feeling like it in the world. Tom believed that it was the composer's duty to continually stretch his horizons since the process of composition did not stop with putting notes on paper. For him music was a form of communication between the composer and his audience, so if it was not performed, then there was no point in it having been written. He was more fortunate than most in that his work was, and continues to be, performed frequently.

When Tom received a commission for a new work it initiated a process of preparation that lasted at least three weeks. During that time Tom said he thought about many things: sometimes philosophical, sometimes related to the specific commission, sometimes purely abstract. He once told me he had imagined a wave starting on the coast of Ayrshire and heading out across the wide Atlantic. Once the wave had reached the far shore Tom seemed to have cleared a space in his mind so that he could just think about the music. At this time he would become very restless. It was a very physical process and quite strange to observe. You could almost see the tension around the area of his stomach as he paced pensively in his study. Finally, he would sit down at the piano and play a phrase. The phrase would usually be made up of three bars; sometimes seven but never more than ten – and this phrase would be the first musical idea. Then he would play with the phrase to see how it could be developed. He would turn it upside down, back to front, and inside out. He would check to see if it was capable of having good variation within it, and he would place the notes to see if they would make good chords.

When he had written maybe half a dozen bars, he would ask me to come in to listen. And I have to say I was usually fairly hard on him at this time, since this is what he wanted. One time particularly, when he was working on a musical idea during the composition of *Passeleth Tapestry* I remember commenting, "I've heard that before in the Hosanna from the *Missa Pro Mundo Conturbato*" (1970), to which Tom immediately replied, "Yes. But

1

this time it's there for a different reason. Before I was using the phrase as a paean of praise, the idea is now being used to indicate the avidity of mankind." It was being used ironically.

I mention this here not just to show that Tom was very conscious of the emotional and intellectual effect of his music, nor that he never wasted a good musical idea, but by way of introducing my husband, the composer Thomas Wilson, and my reasons for wanting to write this biography.

Although Tom taught musical appreciation at Glasgow University for nearly forty years he always said that did not believe that composition could be taught. He of course knew musical technique could be learned, but not that inspiration at the beginning of a new work, nor the point at which a composer knows in his heart that he has created a work of value and integrity. He believed more in developing an appropriate compositional attitude, as he explained in a lecture on composition broadcast on Radio Clyde in 1983:

> It's part of my philosophy that composers should take risks. That to some extent you should be living at the outer edge of your capabilities – and trying to extend the limits of your capabilities – at all times.

I hope, however, that through this biography, I can shed some light and insight onto the life and working methods of my husband to whom I was married for almost forty-nine years.

Throughout our life together Tom worked from home. Though I played very little part in his musical work, our paths would cross at regular intervals throughout the day when he came downstairs from his study to replenish his ever-faithful pot of tea. I would also hear his compositions developing as he worked through the composing process on the piano. I also attended almost every first performance of his work, and dozens of other concerts besides. As a result, I believe that I do have something to say about his life and music, and his hopes and dreams, something that will be of interest to the general reader, and of use to music students and musicologists in years to come. As you would expect, this biography is not only composed from memory and the transcripts from the diaries and press-cuttings I kept throughout our marriage, I have also included interviews with my husband as well as the anecdotes, quotes and reminiscences of friends and fellow musicians who knew him well.

Though Tom did not regard himself as a Scottish composer in the narrow sense, he was undoubtedly one of Scotland's most important musical voices of the twentieth century whose works were, and still are, played all over the world. His opus embraces orchestral, choral-orchestral, chamber-orchestral, opera, ballet, brass band, vocal music and works for a wide variety of chamber ensembles and solo instruments. During his life he received many important commissions, including the Henry Wood Proms, Scottish Opera, Glasgow 1990, Scottish Ballet, Edinburgh Festival, Cheltenham Festival, City of London Festival and the BBC's Musica Nova.

Writing Tom's obituary for the Guardian on Tuesday June 19, 2001, his fellow composer and friend John Maxwell Geddes, wrote:

> The composer Thomas Wilson, who has died aged 73, was the central figure in Scotland during the renaissance of 20th-century music. Recently described as 'the father of Scottish music in the Twentieth Century', he encouraged and inspired the generations of composers that followed. His prodigious output transcended national boundaries, and his legacy established him as a composer of the first magnitude.

While it is for future generations of musicians to judge his true level of importance and place in the history of music, it is nonetheless left to me to ensure that they know something of the man as well as his music. For Tom was not only a great composer, he was also an exceptional human being who believed in gentle persuasion and teaching through example.

Soon after Tom died in June 2001, I woke up at five one morning convinced that I had to write the story of his life as a composer, and of our life together. When I first began to write this biography I seemed to be driven - I do not think that inspiration is too strong a word - and I worked for eight hours each day for the first year and for shorter times thereafter. It did not feel like work to me and I believe it was a huge help in coping with my bereavement. In fact, I am continually grateful for the work that Tom has left me to do to keep his music alive. As John Maxwell Geddes concluded in his obituary for the Guardian:

> Wilson was the architect of much that enhances the human condition; he leaves us the blueprints; now it is over to the builders.

Notes from Childhood

> The artist is the grandchild of God.
> Leonardo da Vinci

Some claim that composers are born, some that they are made. I would not judge the matter. What I can say is that music so much filled the mind and soul of my husband, Thomas Brendan Wilson, that I cannot conceive his having pursued any other life but that of a composer. For him the world was much more a place of sounds than of sights. Tom suffered from colour blindness, which meant that although he could make out the shape of the berries on a holly bush, he could not distinguish the red from the green. What he could not see however, he heard; the colours, he said, were in his ears instead of his eyes.

He heard music everywhere. "Every sound," he would often remark, "is a musical sound." I am not saying that he thought every sound was a *beautiful* sound. The world, he knew, was not always a beautiful place, least of all when men marred it with cruelty and violence. Just the same, it was filled with an appropriate kind of music. To Tom even a pneumatic drill gave forth a musical sound.

Besides his sensitivity to the sounds around him however, Tom had the added good fortune to grow up in a family of music lovers. He was born on October 10, 1927 to Scots-Irish parents, Thomas and Mary (Maureen) Wilson, who were at that time living in the USA in a Colorado mining town called Trinidad. He did not have a birth certificate since only baptismal certificates were routinely issued in the town at that time.

When I first suggested to Tom that we visit his birthplace he showed little enthusiasm, having no conscious memories of his first year. However, when we finally visited the town in 1988, he was visibly moved by the experience. Located near the border between Colorado and New Mexico where the Great Plains meet the Rocky Mountains, Trinidad had been founded in 1842 by Mexican traders as a staging post on the Santa Fe Trail and like smaller western towns was constructed almost entirely of wood. In 1862, coal was discovered, which opened new opportunities for trained miners from Europe and the town grew rapidly to accommodate a wide mix of cultures including, Spanish, Italian, Greek, Polish, Lebanese, Slavic, Scandinavian, Scottish and Irish. The church where Tom was baptised remained the tallest building in the town, though even it was not very tall. Unfortunately the house, indeed the whole street where Tom had lived had been demolished and was now replaced by scrub, and the Kia Ora Mining Company where Tom's father had worked was long since closed, as were many of the mining companies in the surrounding areas.

These disappointments apart, Trinidad still looked much as it had in the photographs his parents had taken around the time of Tom's birth. Trains still rolled on the single railroad track that passed through the middle of the town. No warning gates or barriers separated the track from the land around. The railway lines were just something to be stepped over to get from one part of town to the other. However, it would be almost impossible for anyone to be caught unawares by approaching trains as they started to hoot about half a mile out of town, and continued the racket right through the town and for half a mile after they had left. None of the trains actually stopped in Trinidad while we were there, and the ones that rumbled through did not really bother us except for the three that came by during the night. I expect that the townsfolk got used to the noise and slept through it, but we certainly did not.

While there we asked the parish priest about Tom's godfather George Doherty, who was mentioned on Tom's Baptismal Card and were told that he had owned the local supermarket but had unfortunately died two years previously. We did however manage to meet the photographer Glenn Aultman who had taken the pictures that we had of Tom as a baby, and this was quite exciting. He was a bent old man of more than ninety years, and his workshop, which was in East Main Street, was up a flight of rickety old wooden stairs. He looked through some ancient wooden drawers that doubled as a filing cabinet and after quite a wait he reckoned that "yes", he had taken the photographs.

Being in this small western town was quite an eye-opener to me; I had thought that such places existed only in cowboy films. Perhaps because of those movies, we were not altogether surprised by what we saw when we went out to dinner on the night we arrived. When the local men ate dinner, we discovered they did not remove their Stetsons — or their guns. During the days we were in Trinidad, I couldn't help wondering what type of person Tom would have become had he grown up in this craggy

Western town instead of industrial Scotland. I wonder, too, if he would have heard music in the clatter of those nocturnal freight trains.

Tom's mother, Mary, was born on October 24, 1893 in Newry, Ireland. I have several certificates that belonged to her in which her name is variously recorded as Mary O'Doherty (birth certificate), May O'Dougherty (Certificate of Baptism), Mary O'Docherty (copy of the baptismal certificate), Mary O'Doherty (marriage certificate), Maria O'Docherty (Testimonium Status Liberi), this last to prove that she was a spinster and free to marry, and Maureen Wilson (death certificate). It seems that the approach to naming and spelling was rather freer then than it is now. Although several of Tom's forbears on his mother's side were born in Scotland I had the distinct impression that his mother's relatives thought of themselves as Irish. His maternal grandmother Annie O'Hanlon from Denny (whose father was an iron miner) graduated as a teacher in 1886. On July 18, 1887 she married a millwright, John O'Doherty in Bonhill, Dunbartonshire Scotland. After their marriage the couple went to live in Brazil where Tom's grandfather worked as an engineer in the city of Santos, while his grandmother worked as a teacher. Prior to the birth of their daughter, Annie and John had a son, John, who did not survive childhood. I think it is likely that he died in infancy in Brazil. That possibility would explain why his grandmother returned to Ireland for the birth of her second child, the daughter named Mary while Tom's grandfather remained in Brazil to earn money for the family.

Mary (now called Maureen) became a teacher like her mother and, in 1915 she took a job at St. Aloysius School in Springburn, Glasgow, where she remained until 1925, when she went to America to be married.

Tom's father, Thomas Joseph Wilson was born on June 1 1891 in Waterford, Ireland. Little is known about his family, save that he had a brother John, and that his mother's maiden name was Hannah Kneiff. Tom's father never liked to talk much about his early life, though he once mentioned that they never wore shoes in summer, which suggests that, though well educated, his family was not particularly well-off. Around the time of the Easter Rising in 1916, Tom's father, like many idealistic young Irishmen, became involved with the struggle for independence. He was friends with James Connelly and Eamonn De Valera, whom he used to call Dev, and he was a colonel in the "old IRA" during the Irish War of Independence. During the Civil War that followed the creation of the Irish Free State in 1922, Thomas was sent to Scotland to collect small arms from those sympathetic to the anti-treaty IRA. It was a dangerous assignment given the sectarianism between Protestants and Catholics in the West of Scotland and the level of bitterness that the Civil War had generated within Irish communities. In fact Tom's father later told me he used to walk around with a rifle hidden down the inside of his trouser leg for his own protection. It was in Glasgow in 1923 that Thomas met his future wife Mary O'Doherty whose family was sympathetic to the Republican cause.

The Civil War in Ireland went badly for the anti-treaty IRA and it was borne upon Tom's father that, for his own good, it would be prudent for him to leave Scotland rather quickly. Unable to return to Ireland where he might well have faced execution, he left for America and went to live in Dacona (now Dacono, 20 miles north of Denver, Colorado) and Mary followed the next year in 1925.

I see from their marriage certificate that Mary first went to live in Florence, Colorado, possibly to stay with relatives, some 140 miles south of Denver on the edge of the Rocky Mountains. Mary also had cousins in California and she was visited by her brother Father Camillus, who was a Franciscan friar living then in the Western United States. The couple were married in Florence on February 9 1925, and then they moved to the town of Trinidad, Colorado when Thomas got a post as a mining engineer in the office of the Kia Ora Mining Company. In his spare time he studied law, but he never advanced far enough to seek admission to the bar.

The couple's home, and Tom's birthplace in Trinidad, was made of clapboard, as were all of the buildings in the small town including the church. A typical house had a fenced off garden with a lawn and trees. Not so typical of the times, the family also owned an Essex car, no doubt more out of necessity than luxury. In November 1926 Tom's sister Thérèse was born, and eleven months later he arrived on October 10 1927. Unfortunately Thérèse died during the late summer of 1928. His mother always believed that Thérèse had eaten some poisonous berries that had blown into the garden. However, the cause of death was never determined since the couple lived too far from any hospital where tests could have been carried out, and diagnosis was not always reliable in those days. Many years later Tom's mother told me that she could never cry for the loss of her little girl, and I think that perhaps she was afraid to love Tom too much in case she lost him too.

Soon after Thérèse's death Tom's father had a bad accident to his knee in the mining office. I was told that he was rocking back and forth on his chair when it slipped and he hit his knee on the underside of the desk.

With no real medical provision in the town the knee became infected and he had to be driven to a state hospital further afield. During the operation, the surgeons did not remove the kneecap, but instead moved it to the side of his leg. As a result Tom's father walked with a stick, and he had a stiff right leg for the rest of his days.

Struck by two catastrophes in less than a year, Tom's mother understandably wanted to return to Scotland where she would have the support of her extended family. So when Tom was seventeen months old his parents left Colorado and made the long trip back to Scotland. She told me that the first time she saw rain in Scotland she ran out into the street, spread her arms wide and looked to the heavens, she was so glad to see it. Tom's father brought with him the compensation benefit he had received from the mining company for his accident: a lump-sum payment plus some shares in the company. The part of the lump sum remaining after the deposit on a house was paid was put into the British Linen Bank. However this was eventually lost at the onset of the Second World War as Tom's father was unaware of a requirement under newly introduced Defence (Finance) Regulations that foreign monies be registered with the government. Ignorant of this legislation he did not report his holdings until the allotted time had passed and, as a result, the government confiscated the lump sum. As for the shares, they became worthless when the pit closed.

During their first months in Scotland Tom and his parents lived with one of his mother's friends in Kings Park on the southern edge of Glasgow while they waited for a builder to complete the construction of the bungalow they had bought in Calderwood Road, Burnside, a suburb of the small town of Rutherglen. This town is the oldest Royal Burgh in Scotland and it is said that Mary Queen of Scots watched the Battle of Langside from what is now known as Queen Mary Seat on Cathkin Braes just outside the town. The church on Main Street, where she most certainly worshipped, is located diagonally opposite the modern Roman Catholic church of St Columbkille where Tom was choirmaster until we moved to the West End of Glasgow in 1970. The bungalow, which was named 'Maresa' (a combination of Mary and Teresa), was laid out like a square box, divided into four rooms with a kitchenette tacked onto the back. There was a formal front garden filled with roses, and a lawn, vegetable garden, and apple tree in the large back garden.

The family was soon joined by a new addition – an Alsatian dog. Although the dog allowed Tom to tease and play with it, it became aggressive whenever anyone else tried to enter the front gate, and because of this menacing behaviour, the dog had to go to live elsewhere. Tom was heartbroken. I think that this in fact was probably his first brush with grief.

One favourite family story was about three year old Tommy who, I was told, was invited each Saturday to the next door neighbours for lunch. A garden gate separated the two bungalows and an occasion was made of the meal. One Saturday he got angry with Mrs Allison who was a very good cook. Perhaps she had not made what he was expecting to eat. He stomped over her garden into his own, turned around and shouted "you big, fat...." (in all fairness she was big and fat but she and her husband were lovely people with no children of their own) - there was a long pause while he searched for the worst word he knew, then shouted "you big fat cook".

It was decided that since Tom's father was now partly disabled, he would look after Tom, while his mother returned to teaching. Since the Roman Catholic Church did not approve of married women working, and since it would not then have been possible for a Roman Catholic teacher to work in a Protestant School, Mary had to apply for a special dispensation from the diocese before she could secure a post. She taught first in St Joseph's Roman Catholic girls' school and then in St Francis' primary school in the Gorbals in Glasgow, where she stayed until she retired.

The family was very devout. His father went to mass daily and the family prayed at seven o'clock every night. His father sat on the chair by the fireplace because of his disability, while Tom and his mother knelt on the rug in front of the fire going through the Joyful, Sorrowful and Glorious Mysteries of the Rosary together. Tom's father was regarded as something of an authority on the works of St Thomas Aquinas within Catholic circles in Glasgow, and he gave talks on Thomistic teachings to different societies. He was at different times the first president of the Aquinas Society, a Prior of the Third Order of St Dominic, and a Master of the Catholic Evidence Guild. In fact, both of Tom's parents were members of the Third Order of St Dominic who said an 'office' daily, and they wore scapulars, small pieces of cloth about two inches square, attached by ribbons and placed over the head to rest on the back and chest. These were supposed to be symbolic of the hair shirts worn by saints in former times.

It was a calm and serious household where the word of Tom's father was law. The family ate regular meals at regular mealtimes and you could tell the day by what was being served: Sunday started the week with a roast;

10

Monday, we ate cold meat; Tuesday, mince; Wednesday, lamb chops; Thursday, gigot chops; Friday, fish; and Saturday, a mixed grill. His parents of course made sure that Tom served as an altar boy and there was certainly nothing of frivolity to be seen when I lived there in the early Nineteen Fifties. That said, I once watched his father preparing his own poteen from potatoes and raisins in an old terracotta crock, though I never saw him drink the resulting brew. His father and mother would occasionally take a thimbleful of Benedictine, Chartreuse or Aromas de Montserrat but as far as I was aware, never more than that.

Although Tom came from a large extended family, his relatives were dispersed widely across Scotland, Britain, Ireland and America. The only close relatives who lived nearby were Tom's mother's sister, Aunt Grace, who was too wild for Tom's father's liking, and their cousin 'Aunt' Jeannie. There were also a few distant cousins dotted around the Central Belt of Scotland, but they did not visit often. As a result the family lived a fairly isolated existence. In the years I came to know Tom, I was always aware that the family was two units – one of father and mother, and the other of son. This may also have been the result of him spending his formative years, from 13-18, at boarding school and from 18-21 in the RAF. After our own children were born we were both in agreement that we would never send any of our children away from home to boarding school – not that we could have afforded it anyway. Tom had missed the emotional warmth of a home and did not want this to be repeated.

Despite my own sense that Tom's mother held her emotions in reserve, Tom said that he never felt unloved. His childhood treatment, he held, had been strict but fair. In support of this, I know his father read him the Uncle Remus stories, and his memories of Brer Rabbit's antics amused him even as an adult. "Born and Bred in a briar patch Brer Fox. Born and bred in a Briar patch!" Though his parents did not allow Tom to read comics, his 'Aunt' Jeannie would provide them for him to read upstairs in her home while the adults played cards below.

Outside the family home Tom's childhood was much like that of any other Rutherglen boy of his time and class. During his Requiem Mass in 2001, his childhood friend Martin Sweeney (now Father Sweeney) remarked, "We were not angels – we just never got caught." Tom was not exempt from thoughtless pranks. He told me once of the day that his class from school was taken to a small menagerie in Argyle street in Glasgow - it always struck me as odd to have a menagerie in the middle of the city - and one of his classmates had thrown a *cheugh jean* (a chewy

11

caramel) into the cage of a parrot. The boys doubled up with laughter as they watched the bird struggle with the sticky sweet. Two hours later, when the boys again passed the parrot's cage on their way out of the building, they laughed when they found that the bird was still chewing.

Tom started smoking behind the toilets in the local primary school when he was nine years old, and during his teens he took up a pipe for a while. When he reached his sixties, he reverted to it because smoking a pipe was thought to be less harmful than smoking cigarettes. However, he inhaled the pipe so I didn't see that it made much difference. His friends tell me that once, when Tom was 16 his friend Jim asked for a puff on the pipe Tom was smoking. Reluctantly Tom handed over the cherished possession. Jim, a delicate young man, took a few puffs and quickly turned green. Tom took him from the park where they had been playing bowls to the nearby home of the third member of their gang, none other than Martin Sweeney, whose sister Roma was a nurse. Nothing, of course, was said to her about the pipe, but she had her suspicions.

From his earliest years Tom grew up listening to classical music in his home. His father had a large collection of gramophone records which he would play on Sunday afternoons. Neither of his parents could sing or play an instrument; however they enjoyed listening to Enrico Caruso, Richard Tauber and John McCormack and were not entirely uncreative. His mother wrote poetry, and indeed some of Tom's very first serious attempts at composition when he was fifteen were settings of her poems.

As Tom remembered in an article from 1983, his 'wake-up' call to the world of music took place when he was five years old while listening to Mozart's *Eine kleine Nachtmusik*. It was a sunny summer's day when his father put the record on the gramophone, and, after a few moments Tom looked out of the open window to see that the wall at the top of the front garden was lined with passers by who had stopped to listen. I think that he reckoned something important was happening, and his interest in music stemmed from that day.

His father noted this growing interest and took Tom, aged six, to hear the Scottish Orchestra, later the Scottish National Orchestra and now the Royal Scottish National Orchestra. The opening piece in the programme was Schubert's great C Major Symphony and at its end, his father asked him what he thought of it. Tom replied that it was "rather noisy" so his father took him home at the interval. It would be a number of years before his next visit to an orchestral concert.

When he was seven he was sent for piano lessons to Miss Julia Kelly who lived close by. At that age though he preferred to play football and had, in his own words, "a healthy resistance" to learning scales. When he left home aged 13 to go to boarding school in preparation for training for the priesthood, he was allowed to stop piano lessons. In the course of time this was something that he came to regret. He thought that the familiarity with the piano keyboard learned during the teen years could never be acquired later when one's fingers became less dexterous.

Tom started to compose when he was nine or ten and would deviate from the pieces he was given to learn into his own compositions. He never spoke of being chided for his departures from his lessons, so I think that Miss Kelly was indulgent towards him; after listening a while however she would gently lead him back to what he should have been playing. Years later Tom commented on his substituting his own pieces for the ones he was assigned:

> It seemed like a natural thing to do. I don't think it was anything to do with giving myself an alternative to what I'd been set to play, although I wasn't over the moon with a lot of the things I did play. These first things I composed were awful, very simple and 'folky', and quite untutored of course. It was a kind of intuitive composition. I didn't really know what I was doing, except that I wanted to do it.

By the time he reached his late teens Tom was composing piano pieces for his own performance. These works showed a good grasp of composition and indicate that he was no mean pianist despite having given up his lessons.

In 1938 he passed his eleven plus examination and was sent to Our Lady's High School in Motherwell which was the designated Secondary School for Roman Catholic boys from the Rutherglen area. His friends Jim Clayton and Martin Sweeney also passed the selection exams and the three of them travelled by train every day from Rutherglen to Motherwell.

One year after the war started he went away to school at St Mary's College on Royal Deeside. The reason for this evacuation had less to do with his safety than with his spiritual development. In those days, Catholic parents felt especially honoured to have a son become a priest, and Tom's parents encouraged him towards that vocation. There were several rôle models for this vocation as two of his father's friends were priests and his mother's brother, Uncle James, was a Franciscan Capuchin friar, so in line with his parents' hopes Tom applied to go to St Mary's College, a junior seminary on Royal Deeside near Aberdeen.

In the 1940's candidates for the priesthood were plentiful and selection to St Mary's, or Blairs as it was commonly known, was achieved through academic qualifications and a recommendation from the parish priest that the candidate was of suitable character. Following this the boy would be called to an interview with his Bishop and the Vicar General. The purpose of the interview was to try to ensure that it was indeed the boy's own determination to become a priest and that he was not applying under pressure from family and friends.

The college is a large, imposing neo-Gothic building constructed in the grounds of Blairs estate, a Catholic stronghold for many centuries. The National Junior Seminary was originally founded at Morar in the West Highlands when Roman Catholicism was proscribed in Scotland following the Reformation. The Junior Seminary moved several times to avoid detection before settling on the Blairs Estate in 1829 after the passing of the Roman Catholic Relief Act which emancipated Catholics throughout the United Kingdom. Blairs estate was donated to the Bishops of his Church by John Menzies of Pitfodels, the last member of an old Aberdeen Catholic family, who extended his mansion house to provide a suitable environment for the training of priests.

When Blairs first opened there were at least 240 students, but the roll had dwindled to 101 in 1986 when the college closed. It is now being converted into a hotel and conference centre, but the small museum still contains many important Catholic artefacts, including the full-size portrait of Mary Queen of Scots that used to hang in the college library. During its one hundred and fifty seven years of service, the college trained hundreds of young men from all kinds of backgrounds who went on to become priests in places ranging from the Glasgow slums to the far corners of the world. One of them was the future Cardinal, Thomas Winning, who had known Tom from their time attending Our Lady's High School, Motherwell, although he was three years older. Cardinal Winning later recalled that while Tom had been the tidiest boy at Our Lady's High School, he became the untidiest at Blairs. No doubt parental guidance, and the subsequent lack of it, had something to do with this.

The atmosphere at Blairs was friendly, but unsurprisingly quite restrained and not specifically comfortable even for a young man raised in a strict and austere home environment. With its long corridors, large classrooms,

14

vaulted ceilings and neo-Gothic facade, it must have been a far cry from the family's small blacked-out bungalow in Burnside. One of Tom's contemporaries at Blairs, Ed O'Donnell, recalled the experience of being a student to me in vivid detail:

> The dormitories on the top floor were divided into Spartan cubicles by wooden partitions, with a cloth hanging instead of a door. There was just room for a bed and a bed box. When the first bell went at 6.00am, we were still in the Grand Silence from evening prayers the night before. There was a dash downstairs to the 'ablution' for face and hand washing. Mirrors were provided only in the area allotted to the sixth year students so that they could shave! One shower a week at a scheduled time was mandatory. However I can't remember anyone ever volunteering for one since the water was cold! After washing, we had to return to our cubicles to make our beds. Then down to the "hall" to one's place, strictly regimented - no running or talking. At 6.30am we went down to chapel for morning prayers and meditation - led by "Big Steve", Fr. later Bishop, Stephen McGill, - and Mass, then on to breakfast in the refectory.
>
> In the refectory there were a number of long tables. Each refectory table was divided into three, with six sitting at each section. The six were classified according to order of seniority. The senior boys sat on the wall side. The oldest was known as the "divider", the second the "sub-divider" the third the "sub-scrub". On the front there were the three juniors - the senior one was known as the "tea-man". It was wartime food; occasionally it was even edible! The favourite was bread pudding - of which the senior side of the table ensured a division that favoured the elder.
>
> Each day was very structured and full: classes, midday meal with reading of lives of the saints, recreation; classes unless there were sports; then more classes, evening meal, recreation, evening study in the study hall, late recreation, evening prayers and Grand Silence, then bed. There were plays performed by the boys in the theatre, and regular singsongs.
>
> Blairs was run as a public school, with two sets of rules, as in almost every institution. There was the rule of the seminary which was designed to produce, and in great measure did, men who could pass themselves off in "polite society", and yet would be accepted in the single ends in Glasgow slums. They were educated, devout and

disciplined, used to obedience. Among the rules was one prohibiting the "laying on of hands." This I believe was initially to prevent bullying or demonstrating "particular friendships". In practice it meant you didn't touch another except on the football field – and there anything short of maiming was ignored.

Then there were the inmates' rules. For example, first year boys could only put their hands in their pockets when their jacket was unbuttoned. A second year lad could keep his jacket buttoned, but only one hand in his pocket showing one flap. Third year and up could button their jackets and put both hands in the pockets showing both flaps. Certain paths in the college grounds were sacred to certain forms.

Each Sunday evening in the study hall the Master of Discipline read out the report of all breaches of the rules noted by the monitor, prefects and the decano. Being on report meant a visit on Monday morning to the Master of Discipline, Mgr. Breen. Repeated breaches almost inevitably meant a "domi" – being sent home.

Male teenage energy was spilt in sports. It was rumoured the tea was laced with bromide to prevent build up of excess hormonal activity. Football was the main sport, but woe betide the weakling who came down from the dorm wearing more than a shirt and pair of pants over the underpants. Aberdonian weather was not allowed to interfere with this toughening routine. In the winter there was tobogganing on the hills around the college. The sledges were home made; some were built by the "Prof" Father John Sheridan, Mag. Agg. His sledges were for multiple passengers and the runners were steel shod. There was skating on the artificial pond, made from a flooded tarpaulin, usually with blunt, old skates which clipped insecurely on one's shoes. There was cricket in the summer. In the alternative, there were long crocodile walks to Maryculter, Peterculter and Cults across the "Shakin' Briggie" over the Dee. The shoes incidentally were provided by the college and were very sturdy; they were known as 'baps'.

Tom was a natural athlete who also grew to love the countryside of Royal Deeside. I tried many times to recreate the glories of the Blairs Bread Pudding without success. I also learned from Robert "Bobby" Grant, who was at Blairs just after Tom, that every October the boys would take part in the annual "tattie howking" on the Blairs estate and surrounding farms. This meant backbreaking work walking behind the tractor to pull out the potatoes.

Another contemporary, John A. Foley recalled that their professors at Blairs were of assorted and sometimes eccentric character:

> There was the Rector, Monsignor McGonagle, a formidable figure; Father, later Mgr. Breen the headmaster who taught English; Father Donnelly who taught Latin and was famous for continuing to speak in Latin, in a realm of his own, when discussing the poems of Horace and Ovid; Father McKinley who taught French and was considered very 'with it' for using an electric shaver; Father McKee from Oxford, who taught History, using Lingard as his main reference; Father Kilpatrick who taught Mathematics and could say Mass in one of the side chapels inside twelve minutes; Father Duffy the organist and choirmaster who also taught English; Father, later Bishop McGill who was our spiritual director; and another Father, whose name I cannot recall, who was a veteran from World War One with a gammy leg that used to trouble him and made him rather short tempered. He used to bawl out pupils running in the corridors with, "Walk, ye wee buggers!"

The educational curriculum was similar to that followed in most Scottish secondary schools, and included Latin and Greek, though Tom said that he felt that the fine arts were sadly neglected. Prior to 1939, it was customary for students at Blairs College to go to a Scots College in Europe after they had passed their 'Highers' to study philosophy for two years. They would then study theology for a further five years, before their ordination to the priesthood. Clearly this was not possible during the war, and in 1940 the Scots 'Philosophers', around forty in number, arrived at Blairs from Rome, France and Spain. They set up a course in Philosophy based mainly on the lines of the one taught at the Gregorian University in Rome, complete with textbooks in Latin. So from 1943 to 1945, Tom studied cosmology, criteriology, ethics, logic and ontology. Fortunately the cosmology was studied in English to accommodate the latest ideas! Tom's professors during this time included Father, later Monsignor Philip Flanagan, a friend of the family who lectured in ontology and ethics; Father Cahill who lectured in logic and criteriology; and Canon Dr. Sheridan who had a doctorate from Cambridge, lectured in cosmology, and apparently also found time to design new types of beehives.

Though many students clearly enjoyed the spiritual and educational life of Blairs, I do not think on balance, that the time Tom spent there was a particularly happy one. This may have been due to homesickness or the fact that he was becoming increasingly unsure about whether he was really suited to the priesthood. That said, he was very impressed by the attitude of his teachers and was always complimentary about them. Tom said he learned a great deal about humility and integrity, and how to teach by example rather than instruction, as I was to learn during the early years of our marriage.

Father Hanlon, one of Tom's contemporaries who now lives in Falkirk, remembers Tom as a very distinguished musician during his time at Blairs. He also told me that Tom was probably taught to play the organ by either Father Duffy or Canon Dr. Sheridan. Fr Duffy was an accomplished musician and composer himself, who as Vicar General wrote the Bellahouston Gloria for the visit of Pope John Paul II to Scotland in 1982, and probably had a key influence on Tom discovering his true vocation. I asked Fr. Hanlon if Tom ever played the organ for services but apparently this was always left to one of the priests. At this time, Tom also developed a love for plainsong, as can be seen from the Missal he used at College dated 1942, where he put emphasis marks over some of the plainchant notes in prayers that the priests intoned during the mass. The Psalms and other religious music he heard at Blairs were to have a great influence over his compositions throughout his life.

At every stage of their college life the boys at St Mary's were assured that if they had any doubts about their vocation, they should feel no shame about leaving. Many did choose to leave after their first or second year. Tom, however, remained there until June 1945 when he finally decided that he didn't want to be celibate and that he wanted to compose. I do not think that he had a sudden moment of musical epiphany when his true path was revealed to him, but it seems rather that his true calling had revealed itself to him gradually over the four years.

It must have taken a great deal of courage to break this news to his parents, who fully expected him to become a priest. Intriguingly I received a letter fifty years later from Doris Scott who went on to become Sister Mary of the Nativity and joined the enclosed Carmelite Order at the convent in Dumbarton. Having recently graduated with a music degree, she clearly recalled being asked to come along to Tom's home by Nancy Morrow (nee May) – presumably this was at the request of Tom's parents, "to judge if his musical talent was worth making a career of. Sister Mary went on to write "In fact he was infinitely better than I was; I who had gone through all the musical hoops!"

I believe that Father Philip Flanagan, Tom's philosophy teacher at Blairs and later Rector of the Scots College in Valladolid, played a large part in helping Tom convince them, and to their lasting credit, from that moment on they always supported Tom's choice. Tom already had a very kind and benevolent character and would have made a marvellous priest, but then, had he gone on to ordination, the world would have lost a lot of marvellous music. In any case, Tom always said that he did not choose to be a composer – composition chose him.

Though he missed the worst of the Glasgow blitz, many of the German bombers flew over Aberdeenshire en route to Glasgow from bases in Norway, and he was home from Blairs during the Easter holidays in 1941 when raids also took place. Although the German bombers were focussed primarily on destroying the Clydeside shipyards and the city's power stations, Colville's steel works in Cambuslang was an important secondary target – and Burnside was in their flight path. The family often had to take refuge in the Anderson Shelter in the back garden, and one night a stick of five incendiary bombs was dropped on their street. The first bomb hit the first house and every sixth house thereafter. Had there been six bombs in the stick, Tom's home would also have been destroyed. I had a similar experience of the German bombing in my home town of Newcastle upon Tyne. So though we grew up far apart, we both remembered vividly the nightly air raids when we heard the sounds of anti-aircraft fire and bombs destroying buildings. Like Tom, I also knew people who died in the bombing and I even had friends who lost their fathers from shrapnel wounds sustained while they patrolled the streets as members of the ARP (Air Raid Precautions).

Tom seldom spoke about it, or ever referred to any direct wartime influence over his life but I believe that the nightmarish experience of the bombings had a profound effect upon his philosophical outlook, his sense of commitment to the city of Glasgow and his music. Tom was a very kind, generous and humorous man who loved life but he also despaired at the state of the world and could not see any lessening of savagery, cruelty and viciousness between past ages and the present.

The Song of Youth

Tom left Blairs College at the end of June 1945 when he was seventeen years and nine months old. The war in Europe was only recently won and the war against Japan was still raging in the Pacific. Tom was therefore drafted directly into the RAF to carry out his National Service. During his physical examination, the doctors discovered to Tom's surprise that he suffered from red/green colour-blindness. Having grown up with the condition, he had hitherto been unaware of any problem, though it probably explained his total disinterest in fashion and flowers.

I never knew of Tom's difficulties with colour until shortly after our marriage when I asked him to bring me a pink blouse from the wardrobe, and I got a yellow one! Having recently purchased an old van, I asked him how he managed to drive, and discovered that he distinguished traffic lights by the position of the lens that was illuminated from behind. This method was unreliable in strong sunlight, but the problem did not arise often in Scotland. Later, when we travelled abroad, it was my job to keep him right whenever the sun masked the signal light.

The RAF doctor in England was quite matter-of-fact about the condition, told Tom never to play snooker for money, and recommended that he be assigned to ground staff. In the autumn of 1945, after three weeks of square bashing, Tom was shipped off to Provence in the south of France. Billetted in Bandol, his destination was an isolated aerodrome near Istres, where the local girls were to complete his education! His duties at this small RAF airbase in the Camargue were not too demanding, leaving him plenty of time to explore the historical towns of Southern France; to swim, which he always enjoyed; and to go eating and drinking with his friends in nearby Arles.

After four years of austerity at Blairs, Tom was amazed by the French cuisine and clearly enjoyed his newfound freedom. Money ran out of his pocket like water. After he received his first pay-packet, he was induced into a game of cards and he lost everything; it was a good lesson as he was very wary of playing cards from then on. When asked where he was from, he would of course reply "Glasgow". This meant that his fellow airmen wouldn't take any liberties with him since the city's tough reputation was well known. No one ever deserved the label of 'hard man' less than Tom; however, this, along with his good humour and his gift for music, helped keep him out of trouble. National Service threw young men together from all backgrounds and it was important to be liked, particularly when one of his fellow messmates, a Polish airman, went on to become a notorious London gangster who was rumoured to have been involved in the theft of the Jules Rimet World Cup in 1966.

In those days radios were expensive and hi-fi had yet to be invented, so Tom's ability to play the piano made him very popular in the RAF mess and central to most social gatherings. He was not a musical snob and did not play only well-known classical pieces from composers like Chopin and Mozart, but also big band music and other popular tunes of the day, such as *In the Mood, White Christmas, and The Foggy, Foggy Dew*. He could reproduce any song that was sung to him even though he had not heard it before, and would have happily played along to the more raucous drinking songs that are always popular with young men separated from the civilising influence of women. As a result, despite his lack of luck at cards, troubadour Tom was never short of a complimentary beer during his airforce days.

Istres occupies a central location in southern France, north of Marseilles and close to the Camargue region. This meant that off-duty airmen were always able to hitch a lift to the many other RAF airbases around the South of France and Northern Italy. Tom had a keen interest in history and the opportunity to explore an area so rich in history and natural beauty was a godsend. In 1971, we visited Le Lavendou in the Camargue on a camping holiday, and we often stayed overnight at Les Routiers establishments in the area on the way to and from Italy and Spain. Tom showed himself to be very knowledgeable about the places we visited, which included Arles, Aix en Provence, Avignon, Carcassonne and Montpellier, and the Val d'Enfer which impressed him greatly. He talked a great deal about Van Gogh and Cezanne, and showed us where the two popes had lived in Avignon, as well as where Picasso had painted Les Demoiselles. So clearly his time in the airforce was not solely concerned with rolling out the barrel.

Given his interests and pastimes, it is perhaps unsurprising that Tom became fascinated with the troubadours or travelling poet-musicians who flourished in the areas of Languedoc and Rousillon during the early mediaeval period. These troubadours wrote their verse using the langue d'oc (which had developed out of common Latin) and created new musical forms that incorporated the informal language of the people. They became identified not only with the development and spread of Courtly Love and the Chivalric Ideal through verse and song, but also with the Cathars, a heretical Christian sect who believed that Jesus was a man rather than the son of God. This heretical notion eventually led to their persecution by Pope Innocent III who launched the twenty year long Albigensian (or Cathar) Crusade against them in 1208. This crusade on European soil devastated much of Southern France and destroyed a flourishing culture. It is said that the cruelties inflicted on the people so horrified the church that it was forced to abandon further warfare as a method of curbing heretical thought in favour of the far gentler Inquisition!

Though Tom did not believe in the heresy, he couldn't help but be inspired by the creative and civilising power that the troubadours' music had over the development of European culture. And I think it was this aspect of the tradition that provided the inspiration for his virile and energetic composition for French horn, *Chanson de Geste* in 1991. This work was named after an epic poem that would have originally been sung at court by a troubadour to the accompaniment of a viol or lyre and in some cases, as in the Song of Roland a battle horn.

After a year in the service, Tom was promoted to the dizzy heights of corporal. However he soon lost one of his stripes when he went out on the town with some of his mates. On the road to Arles the driver of their 'borrowed' jeep missed a turning onto a bridge and demolished part of its wall. Tom ended up with a broken jaw and big toe. This was bad enough; but one of the other passengers was found the next day a mile along the road with two broken legs.

Unfortunately his time in the airforce was not all fun and games. On one occasion, a plane crashed onto the airfield, and Tom was one of the ground crew sent to help remove the burned and broken bodies from the wreckage. This proved a very traumatic experience, which he never liked to talk about. It also explains why he was never at ease when he travelled by plane.

During his stay in Istres he became enthralled with every aspect of southern France and dreamed of one day living there again. We visited the region many times during his working life, and when he retired from teaching we seriously considered buying an apartment to use as a holiday home in Provence. However, we were persuaded by our friend Malcolm

Rayment to buy an apartment near him in Sotogrande in southern Spain instead.

For all the attractions of Provence however, Tom's time there may have had one very serious downside. Many years later when I went into hospital for the removal of a mole, I asked the surgeon to look at a discolouration on Tom's face, and, after examining the mark, the surgeon said, 'Come in tomorrow, and we'll operate on both you and your wife'. The subsequent biopsy determined that Tom had had a squamous cell carcinoma that would have become very serious if it had been left any longer. The doctors believed that the damage to his skin could have occurred either during his early life in Colorado, when it was thought healthy for babies to be outside in the sun, or during his sojourn in the south of France.

When Lance Corporal Wilson was demobbed from the Air Force in 1948, he hitched a lift in an aeroplane back to London as he had done whenever he had leave. On this occasion however he had spent all his money celebrating and he arrived in London without a penny to his name. To buy a train ticket back to Glasgow he asked the Jesuits to lend him the fare, but they turned him away. Fortunately, he found a Good Samaritan in the form of an American Lieutenant and borrowed the money from him instead. He returned to his parents' home in Burnside and in October of that year he enrolled at Glasgow University.

Glasgow University was established by a Papal Bull of Pope Nicholas V in 1450-1, but the real founder was William Turnbull who was Bishop of Glasgow from 1447 to 1454. It was the second university in Scotland, the first being St Andrews. Glasgow University was originally very small as it only had one Faculty, that of Arts. In 1453 a building for it was erected at the top of the High Street on the northeast side of the city, but it was not until the 17th century that a college of any size was built. In the 19th century this also became too small for the number of students who wished to attend and so it was sold to the City of Glasgow Union Railway Company. The money raised, along with a government grant and public contributions, was used to erect in 1870 the present marvellous building on the commanding site of Gilmorehill in the West End of Glasgow. Cream sandstone was used in its construction along with the rest of Victorian Glasgow. It must have looked stunning when it was new. However, air pollution from coal burning and chemicals soon laid a fine patina of dirt on the building and this makes it look as though it has been there for centuries.

The Department of Music is situated close to the central campus in the heart of Glasgow's West End area. At the time Tom enrolled the department was much smaller than it is now, and an Honours Music Degree was not offered until 1951, which meant that he was one of the first three students to take the degree. In order to do this, he first needed to secure an MA degree. He studied Zoology, French and Music in his first year, then Scottish History and Music in his second year, and Moral Philosophy and Music in the third year. This allowed him to transfer to a BMus Honours Degree course which he completed in his fourth year.

He travelled from Rutherglen to Glasgow University by tramcar, a journey of 45 minutes whether he took the 18 green tram to its terminus at University Avenue, or the 26 white tram which carried on to Clydebank. Thanks to his father's record collection, Tom had developed a thorough knowledge of the work of many classical composers including: Bach, Brahms, Chopin, Khachaturian, Mozart, Rachmaninov, Schubert, Strauss, Stravinsky, Verdi and Vivaldi, as well as some jazz music and lots of Scots and Irish folk music. And he had been made aware of great singers like Victoria de los Angeles, Elizabeth Schwarzkopf, Enrico Caruso, Feodor Chaliapin and Paul Robeson. During his time at Blairs he had developed a great love of the organ and choral music as well as plainchant, while his time in France had made him familiar with the works of many of the modernist composers, including Claude Debussy, Manuel de Falla and Les Six, whose broad membership included Durey, Honegger, Milhaud, Poulenc and Satie. During his early years at Glasgow University he became particularly influenced by the works of Bartók, Berg and Webern, who were to have the most influence over the development of his own musical voice.

To assist with his university studies Tom's father lent him money to buy a boudoir grand piano, though Tom was told he had to pay it back. Half the cost was covered by the demob money he had received from the Air Force on his return to Glasgow and the rest he paid off by working during the university holidays. One holiday job involved working in the cellars beneath Glasgow's Central Station Hotel where he said there were "miles of cheeses", and another one consisted of packaging sliced bread at a commercial bakery in Bridgeton on the south side of Glasgow. Sometimes, to relieve the monotony of the job he, or one of the others, would slip a loaf in sideways to stop the wrapping machine. Then they could take things easy while they waited for the works engineer to clear the blockage.

During the summer of 1949, Tom went to Blackpool to work as a barman in a pub called Uncle Tom's Cabin. It was here in Blackpool that we first met, on July 20 1949 when I was eighteen and he was twenty-one. I was on holiday from my home in Newcastle upon Tyne with my mother, Aunt Gladys, and Cousin Sylvia, who was only fourteen but much more streetwise than I. My mother was suffering from a tired heart so why she would have chosen to go to Blackpool is puzzling. Probably she was just glad to be able to go anywhere. During the war holidays had been out of the question as fuel was scarce and food was rationed. Since the end of the war we had been away from home only once, in 1946, when we spent a week in London at the home of one of my father's younger brothers.

From what I have been told, I do not think that the seafront in Blackpool has changed much since the time Tom and I were there. Though our memories of the place were sweetly nostalgic, neither of us ever had any desire to go back. I was fascinated, though, by one place that I went to with my mother, aunt, and cousin – a huge pub named Yates' Corner House. My mother rarely visited public houses, but she had been told that we really should see this one. As I recall, the inside was split into lots of small bar counters, each one specialising in a particular type of spirit. I had not seen anything like it before, nor have I since.

On the July evening that I met Tom, I had gone to Blackpool Tower Ballroom with my cousin Sylvia as my chaperone. I was wearing a black moiré watered silk skirt and a white voile peasant blouse with red embroidery, and my aim was to meet up with a Welshman whom I had met at a dance two days previously. However, when Tom asked me to dance, I accepted. I loved dancing though Tom later said he usually found it boring. Not surprisingly, I liked him, though I never dreamed that this was the man I would marry. He was six feet tall with hazel eyes that sparkled with laughter. He was easily made to laugh and found things hilarious that I found only mildly amusing. His hair was very dark brown, but there was already the odd white strand (his hair would turn totally white by the time that he entered his forties - as had his mother's). He asked me what kind of music I preferred and fortunately I said 'classical', though he did not tell me he was a music student at Glasgow University until we met again two days later. At the time though I made a mental note of the music we first danced to. It was '"A" You're Adorable…' I do not know what happened to the Welshman.

My holiday stay soon came to its end, but Tom promised to visit me in Newcastle upon Tyne during the last two weeks of his summer vacation. He arrived without a penny, and wearing a pair of winkle picker shoes that he had bought in a second-hand shop in Blackpool when his previous shoes had worn out. They didn't suit him at all and hurt him so much that one evening he walked back to his lodgings in his socks. Next day I bought him a new pair of shoes – and paid for his lodgings. Neither money nor fashion meant much to Tom, but I was happy to see him.

Our courtship continued by letter. However, after about six months, Tom began to take longer and longer to reply. Once after waiting three weeks for a reply I became slightly annoyed and wrote to tell him that if he couldn't write more often he need not bother at all. To my horror he didn't! Of course I did not realise until after we were married just how much homework the lecturers in the music department of the university expected from their students. So Tom truly had little time for writing letters. Five days each week he left his parents' house at eight in the morning to arrive in time for the first lecture at nine. He was back at home by five in the evening, when he had dinner, and then got down to his homework, which took him until 10 p.m. This was the term-time pattern of his days. Over the Christmas holidays he worked as a postman and during the summer took whatever jobs were available.

After a few weeks of postal silence, I realised that unless I did something about the situation Tom might drift away, and I used the occasion of my reception into the Catholic faith as an excuse to write to him. He wrote back to say that he was delighted to hear from me and our courtship was resumed – much to my relief.

In the summer of 1950, Tom went to Paris with Jack Williams, a friend from his Air Force days, for what was meant to be two weeks. Before he left, he asked me what I would like him to bring back for me. I said, 'Just bring your self' and once again that was exactly what I got. He came home after only one week, broke, with no gifts for anyone. So that he would at least have something to give to his mother, I took him in to Newcastle where we purchased a glass ornament of a bird on a branch with flowers that at a stretch might have come from Paris. Fortunately, she was delighted by her son's thoughtfulness and no questions were ever asked regarding the provenance of the gift.

Tom had already begun his serious efforts at composing before he started his formal training at the university. I have his settings of some of his mother's poems, written when he was seventeen, a number of songs written in 1946 during his time in the RAF, as well as several other piano pieces from those early years. These include a set of twelve Preludes for piano, one in every key. I think this demonstrates quite clearly that, untutored though he was at that time, he already relished a challenge.

Tackle me if you dare (circa 1933)

Happiness (1936)

National Service in Istres (1945)

Our Wedding, Newcastle Upon Tyne (1952)

Graduation, University of Glasgow (1954)

The beginning of the journey (1956)

Tom and students meet Pope Pius XII at the Vatican (1958)

The family with three sons, Brendan, Martin and Stephen, and their maternal grand-parents (1959)

Circa 1960

Tom returning to work yet again on his *Second Symphony* (1963)

Moving to the West End (1970)

Attending Glasgow
University's conferment
of an Honourary Degree
on Watson Forbes, Head
of Music at the BBC
(1970)

Composing his
Sequentiae Passionis
(1971)

During our courtship and engagement between 1949 and 1952, Tom and I met each other twice each year, either in Glasgow or Newcastle. On one of his visits to my home he saw a piece of sheet music on the piano for the folk song *The Waters of Tyne*. It was one of his favourite folk songs from that moment on, and he often played it for his own enjoyment. Tom had a keen interest in folk music and the first compositions that he played for me were a series of folk-inspired piano pieces. Although it was not obvious, you could recognise the folk music influence in the three repeated notes at the ends of the piano pieces. It was just as well that he let me know. At that time I could not have differentiated an Irish folk tune from a Scottish one. Indeed while I enjoyed music I did not live and breathe the notes like Tom, and my musical education was really just beginning. I remember being shocked when he said that he would give up music if I asked him to. Of course I think that he knew I would never ask such a thing, but it underlined the feelings we had for one another.

Although I had taken my mother to see Stravinsky's *Petrushka* when I was eighteen years old, my real introduction to twentieth-century classical music came when Tom asked me to listen to the six *String Quartets* by Béla Bartók. It was a baptism of fire for me and I have to say I wondered at the time how I was going to cope with the commitment I had made. Fortunately he then put on a record of *Belshazzar's Feast* by William Walton and I remember thinking, "Maybe things are going to be all right after all". These days my ear is better attuned to the greater range and wider vocabulary of modern classical music, but I do understand from my own experience why some people find it difficult to accept at first.

Once a student at Glasgow University, Tom was given numerous exercises to complete, most of which I still have, and from then on he composed fairly constantly until his final illness. Tom Johnstone, a good friend from Tom's university years, told me of a conversation that took place between the students in the department after the Christmas holidays. Everyone recounted their experiences during their break. When someone asked Tom what he had done, he replied, "Oh, I wrote a piano concerto." Although Tom wrote prolifically throughout his life, he subsequently withdrew most of his pre-1960 works and considered that his first major composition of the 'new phase' was *Variations for Orchestra* written in 1960.

At the end of his first year in 1950, while his head was filled with music, he wandered absentmindedly into a room where students were sitting the second year French exam, At the time he did not realise his mistake, he took the exam, and passed it with flying colours – as he certainly should have done after three years in France.

We became officially engaged on my visit to Glasgow in the summer of 1951. I had gone to Scotland to hear a concert performed by Tom's fellow students in the attic of the building that still houses Glasgow University's music department. They performed a chamber work, a nonet called Sinfonietta written specifically for them by Tom who tailored each part to the strengths of the individual student performers. This was the first time I had heard his work performed in public, and though I was pleased for him, I did not then appreciate how highly his music was already regarded by other musicians. I was more excited about our engagement.

Years later Tom wrote of what the concert came to mean for him:

It was an exciting event. Hearing your own work in performance is the most exciting and nerve-racking thing. Everything depends on so many variables. The composer in this sense is less happily placed than the artist, because the artist is his own performer. The composer's ideas of what a piece should be like rest with the performers, who in turn have their own ideas. It's a kind of amalgamated view that emerges. The composer provides a blueprint, which is subject to a series of hazards in performance, and over which he has no control. There's no way of changing it; it's part of the excitement.

I kept the programme from the concert and told Tom that I intended to start a scrapbook. He was embarrassed that I would want to do this, but those scrapbooks have proved very useful over the years. They now occupy over two metres of shelf space in his study and without these cuttings and my diaries this biography would not have been possible.

On one of my visits to Glasgow, the Roman Catholic Church mounted a vocations exhibition in the Kelvin Hall in which the stalls were taken by various religious orders like the Dominicans, the Franciscans and the Benedictines – and for women; the Helpers of the Holy Souls, the Sisters of Notre Dame and the Bon Secours Sisters. When I expressed a desire to go to see it, Tom was a little concerned, and while we were there he was distinctly on edge. He held firmly onto my arm, and when I stopped to speak to the nuns at a couple of the stands, a gentle pressure was applied to ensure I did not tarry too long. He was not taking any chances!!

A Time of Exploration

In 1950, a year after we first met, Tom asked me to marry him, but he said that he would like to keep our plan secret for a while as he had so long still to study at university. So we waited to be officially engaged until August 20 1951 during my summer visit to Glasgow. By this time he had completed his general MA and the first part of his BMus degree, and we had protracted discussions by post as to how soon we could marry. We decided not to set any definite date until the next June when we would know whether he had obtained his BMus. It was a great relief to find out that he had, and we agreed on a September wedding.

I suspect that Tom's parents were initially horrified at the thought of having a daughter-in-law who came from a Protestant background and, even worse, one who came from England. I often wondered whether any pressure was brought to bear upon Tom at that time, or how the news of my reception into the Catholic Church had been perceived, but he never said anything about it and I never asked. I made sure, however, that I never mentioned to his parents the fact that my father, having lied about his age, had joined the army when he was sixteen and had then been sent to Ireland to serve with the infamous Black and Tans. Were it not such a familiar story, it might seem ironic that the children of such bitter enemies should fall in love and marry.

As it happened, I had in fact been baptised a Catholic as a baby, my Catholic mother being separated from my nominally Protestant father at the time. After re-uniting with my mother when I was two, my father would not allow me to be raised as a Catholic, but once I had completed high school I began to attend Mass with my mother. Then when Connie, a friend and colleague at work, asked me to be godmother to her expected baby, I started to take instruction in Catholicism. While I was talking with her one day about birth, she chided me for believing that babies were lifted from the mothers by some sort of natural caesarean process. When I asked her to put me right, she said, 'Well, they get out the way they got in.' It seems hard to believe in this day and age that girls of eighteen could be as naïve as I was, but my lack of knowledge of such matters was not at all atypical.

We were married on September 20 1952. Twenty became an important number in our life, as we met on July 20 1949, and our first son Brendan, (named after the Irish saint who supposedly sailed to America before Columbus) was born on March 20 1954. Up until our marriage Tom and I met only sporadically, and had spent in total just seven weeks in each other's company. In spite of this neither of us doubted our decision to spend our lives together. My aunt Laura loaned me two sovereigns, one for each shoe, so that I would walk on gold to my wedding, which took place in St Teresa's church, a small wooden Catholic Church in Heaton, Newcastle upon Tyne. Having obtained permission to leave the monastery, Tom's uncle James was the celebrant of the Nuptial Mass, and as a wedding gift, Tom presented me with a *Trio for oboe, clarinet, and piano* that he had dedicated to me. There were approximately thirty guests in attendance including our parents, my brother, his wife and daughter, and many friends. My mother made me a beautiful wedding dress to my design out of silver and blue material, while my aunt Laura made the bouquets and arranged flowers for the church. Our wedding day was absolutely the happiest day of my life and the gold I walked on worked! Everything was perfect. Sunlight filled the church and the choir sang beautifully. In those days the only time that a woman was allowed onto the altar was during her wedding, and as I came to that solemn moment in the Mass, I resolved to make our relationship the centre of my life. We may not have had much money, but I felt that what we had in our relationship was beyond the riches of the world.

The reception that followed the wedding was a happy one too. The wedding cake was square, with two tiers and rosebuds around the edges. During the dinner Tom's best man, John Donegan, gave a highly amusing speech laced with musical allusions, and later we returned with a small group of guests to my parents' home for tea and to prepare for our departure.

We had arranged to spend our honeymoon in the Red House Hotel in Aberdour, Fife, and when we left my parents' house to go to the station, our taxi had the obligatory tin cans tied to the back. My Uncle Bill and my bridesmaid Jean, secretly they thought, followed us in his car with boxes of confetti. Fortunately, we realised what was happening and managed to hide from them in the train, while they went up and down the platform searching for us. In my excitement, I travelled the whole way from Newcastle to Edinburgh with my hat on back to front, but luckily it was the kind of hat where it didn't really matter. When we arrived in Aberdour we made the mistake of going down to the bar for a drink after dinner, only to be corralled by an 'elderly' couple (in their fifties) who insisted that we play charades with them and some other guests – on our wedding night!

Aberdour is a small town on the south coast of Fife across the Firth of Forth from Edinburgh. Before the war Tom had gone on holiday to the town with his parents, when his boyish imagination had been captured by the holy island of Inchcolm and its deserted abbey. The island lies just offshore, across a stretch of water known as Mortimer's Deep, and Inchcolm had been home to a religious community linked with St Colm or St Columba, the 6th-century abbot of Iona. Later David I founded a priory there for monks of the Augustinian order, and in 1223 the priory was raised to the status of an abbey. Though Aberdour sounded like a suitably romantic location for our honeymoon when Tom first mentioned it to me, I remember writing to ask him what we would do if it rained all the time we were there. Tom replied that he would teach me how to play chess. It was only later that I learned exactly what he meant. He was the most wonderful teacher!

When we returned from our honeymoon, we went to live with my new in-laws in Burnside. We had a room that had been created out of the attic space, for which we paid £1 per week rent out of the £2 17s 6d grant received from the Scottish Education Department. We also paid half of all the bills such as food, electricity, gas, and even half the cost of the load of manure used in the garden. I also did my fair share of the household chores and shopping. To ease our financial situation I wanted to continue working as a secretary, but Tom's father pointed out that every penny I earned would be deducted from the grant from the Scottish Department of Education. I thought about it for a while and concluded that supporting Tom in his career as a composer would be of more worth to mankind than any career that I might pursue. This may sound strange but it was what I believed, and time has done nothing to change my mind.

Whatever I could do to give him the space he needed to fulfil his vocation, I would. Everyone who knew Tom as a student at school and at university remarked that there was something more than a little special about him. It was not only that he was very gifted musically, but also that his own conviction about his future career was so strong that others couldn't help but be impressed. Though still only a student he was completely focussed, determined and hard-working, and was already greatly respected by his fellow students.

Following our wedding, Tom had still one more year of study at the university and then he would have to undertake six months of teacher training. After paying our wedding and honeymoon expenses, we had £10 left in savings. Not a large amount even in those days. We had our own bed (a wedding present from my brother and his wife), and Tom had his piano. We also had a Westminster chiming clock from my Aunt Laura and Uncle Bill, but it quickly became the bane of Tom's life because the chimes interrupted his concentration when he was working on a composition. They could be switched off, but I'd sometimes switch them on to tease him. I said that God should have fitted every composer's head with a light bulb that they could switch on to let others know when they were 'thinking music.' Reluctantly, I learned not to sing in the house, although it took me two years to stop. Contrary to what one might think, a composer's home is most often a quiet one.

Our pleasures during this time were very simple and cheap because Tom had lots of homework from his teachers. Wednesday evenings and some Saturday afternoons were his only respite from counterpoint and double fugues. Saturday afternoons were spent watching Celtic football team when we could afford it. One weekend he decided that he would teach me how to play bowls on the free bowling greens in the local park. He omitted to say that the bowls had a bias, and my first bowl ended up as part of the game being played next to us. I didn't get much farther in my lessons before Tom decided that we should return home. He was a natural athlete and very good at most sports. When we played tennis in Armstrong Park during Tom's first visit to Newcastle, he put a top spin on a ball that left me standing, so there was absolutely no way that I could compete. Despite his ability, however, he was not very interested in playing competitive sports and preferred to watch.

Although our life was certainly not an easy one, we were ecstatically happy. Fortunately I had a good 'bottom drawer' as my mother was a dressmaker. Clothes were still scarce so it was a very good thing that she was able to make my wedding dress to my own design, and underwear from silk and lace that she bought at the market, which did not cost precious clothing coupons.

Early in our marriage a regular visitor to Calderwood Road was Tom's best man, the schoolteacher John Donegan, (uncle of the famous skiffle player Lonnie), who had been introduced to Tom by their mutual friend Jim Clayton. Jim, you may remember, was made ill by Tom's teenage pipe. John, who was about ten years older than us, was a handsome man with beetling brows and somewhat stern features. He had dark wavy hair and an aquiline nose and I can well imagine that one look was enough to subdue any unruly schoolboy. However he had a wicked sense of humour, and words and deeds were delivered with such a straight face that it needed a double take sometimes before the hilarious remark or act was appreciated. He came each Wednesday evening and there was a ritual to the beginning of the evening. First John removed his clarinet from its case and took it apart. Brushes, dusters etc. were pulled through the parts before they were carefully re-assembled and the instrument was put to one side. His cheeks were massaged quite violently, though whether to stop the flow of saliva or to stimulate it I never found out. Then the clarinet was put into his mouth and the mouthpiece wetted with the tongue. When this was completed to his satisfaction Tom, who was seated at the piano all this time, handed him the latest composition, and the music making began. At least it usually did. But one evening, after three false starts when the most terrible sounds came out, rather than admit to any mistake, John simply leaned forward and peered at the score, turned it the correct way up, and the music making resumed.

In 1953, Tom enjoyed two pieces of good fortune. First, the BBC asked the Music Department to recommend a student to write arrangements of nursery rhymes for the Children's Hour programme and Tom's name was put forward. He could do this sort of thing very easily and the arrangements brought Tom's compositional skills to the attention of programme producers. Later that same year it was proposed that Glasgow University award Tom the Goudie Prize and the Senate agreed. This prize had been established in 1936 by William John Goudie, Professor of the Theory and Practice of Heat Engines 1921-38. It is awarded to the university candidate proceeding to the degree of Bachelor of Music who has attained the highest standard of excellence in the final year of the Honours curriculum.

Encouraged by these early successes, I decided to send off his *First String Quartet* to Sir William Walton shortly after it was written in 1953, and got a flea in my ear for doing so. However Sir William replied that he thought it very effectively written. Maybe Sir William was being kind as Tom later withdrew the work.

In April Tom went to Dundee to be interviewed for a Caird Scholarship which would enable him to go to Paris to study with Nadia Boulanger, but he was turned down. We were disappointed until Sir Ernest Bullock's daughter Mary said that the Caird Trustees did not think that they could do much more for a person who would shortly have an Honours BMus. In the end the rejection was a blessing in disguise as two months later I became pregnant and this could have caused problems if we had been living in Paris when the baby was due.

Music students were required either to sing in the university choir or play in the orchestra so Tom taught himself the oboe. On one occasion a part-time lecturer in the university asked him to play the oboe in an orchestral concert the lecturer was conducting at Stirling's Albert Hall. Tom did so and was paid. This was one of his few appearances as a performer though, being self taught, he never felt he was up to professional standard.

Although Sir Ernest was the Gardiner Professor in the Music Department until his retirement in 1951, Tom was largely taught by Fred Rimmer, who was his supervisor. Rimmer was very strict, and to everyone's shock and surprise he rejected Tom's first composition thesis for his Honours degree, which was submitted in the spring of 1953. This was the *Trio for Clarinet, Oboe and Piano* that Tom had presented to me on our wedding day. We were astonished by this, as other members of the panel, Dr Herbert Howells, Professor of Composition at the Royal College of Music in London, Dr Herbert Wiseman, one-time Director of Music to the Edinburgh Education Committee and Head of Music for BBC Scotland, and Ian White the Scottish conductor and composer, held that the work "had freshness and interesting ideas". Rightly or wrongly his fellow students thought it a very good work too. However Mr Rimmer and Dr Andrews, a scholar of Caius College Cambridge and the Royal College of Music, did not agree. Eric Stapleton, who took his BMus at the same time remembered the incident well and he told me in 2006 that, "Tom's first thesis was not accepted because it was too *avant garde* – two hundred years ahead of anything that I could have written". Unfortunately, the knock-on effect of Rimmer's conservatism was to undermine Tom's confidence in his musical voice for some time to come. That summer Sir Ernest retired and Rimmer was made acting head of department. The Chair was not filled until 1956 when Robin Orr was appointed.

In July Tom's parents bought a small flat, so we had to find somewhere else to live. We found rented rooms in a council house in Knightswood on the west side of Glasgow. However we didn't have much space as the grand piano took up most of one room, and the other had our bed in it. I used to buy four pennies worth of spare ribs to make soup and the meat on them was then eaten with vegetables for our dinner. Another weekly buy was a packet of ginger Perkins. These biscuits were Tom's favourites but the packet had to last a week, as we couldn't afford more.

We didn't have a kitchen but we had a small electric fire with an element that was wound three times along the front. This was covered by protective wires so that it was impossible to touch the element by accident. However, if the fire was laid upon its back a pan of water could be placed on it to boil for a cup of tea. It was some time before we could even afford an electric kettle.

Our comparative poverty worried Tom less than me. He had been brought up in spartan conditions at home and at school, so this was nothing new to him. For example he cared nothing for how worn out or out of date a garment might be. When, later in our life we could afford such extravagance, and I could persuade him that he really needed some new clothes, I would buy him three suits and five sets of informal clothes on one shopping spree as I knew that I would not get him into a clothes shop for another ten years. Shopping for shoes was another nightmare. When he tried on the shoes in a shop he would say that they fitted very well. When we got home, however, he wouldn't wear them complaining that they hurt his feet too much. I'm convinced that he would agree to purchase any shoes just to get out as quickly as possible from a place he hated to be.

In order to pay back the second half of the loan his parents had provided for the piano Tom worked in the reservations department of Glasgow's Central Station during the summer vacation. It was a very difficult time for us living as we were in rooms; my pregnancy was not going well due to my having high blood pressure, and we had so little money. Tom used to come home very tired and start to work on his second thesis, a more traditional oboe quartet.

One of his fellow students, Alan Graham, said that Tom was obviously holding himself back in this composition and, unfortunately, this thesis was also turned down. This setback really depressed Tom as it confused him about whether he should follow his instinct or the direction of his professor.

The one year teacher-training course at Jordanhill College Glasgow was shortened to six months because Tom had fulfilled his obligations to the National Service Scheme. However it was not possible for him to qualify as a teacher because Rimmer had turned down his theses. If one of these had been accepted then he could have graduated. So in December he went to London to take the examination to become an Associate of the Royal College of Music. This allowed him to be certificated as a teacher when he completed his course at Jordanhill in March 1954, and he graduated in May. During his teacher training Tom taught at Glasgow High School for Boys for five weeks, and after leaving Jordanhill he went on to teach at Queens' Park Secondary School which is also in the city. He surprised himself by liking to teach there more than he had anticipated.

I was admitted to Stobhill Hospital four weeks before our baby was due as I was suffering from pre-eclampsia and on March 20 1954 our first son, Brendan, was born at 7.30am. He was premature and the birth was induced because of my high blood pressure. Nonetheless, the labour took four days so we were all very relieved when he finally arrived. On the afternoon of his birth Tom came to visit us in hospital. His mother told me that later that day he returned to Rutherglen and shouted from the garden gate "IT'S A BOY".

I haemorrhaged a week after the birth and was kept in hospital an extra two days, so was there eight days in all. When I was allowed to go home I learned from another young mother that two hours after I was released the ward I had been in was put in quarantine. Puerperal fever had been diagnosed in one of the mothers who had looked the healthiest of us all. I realise now that her rosy cheeks were due to fever. Sadly, she died.

Since I was not well enough to return to our lodgings, we stayed for the first two weeks with Tom's parents where Brendan slept in a drawer. Then we returned to Knightswood where Tom and his father had built a crude but strong cot out of builders lumber. This work of creative carpentry was placed on the landing outside our bedroom as this was the only space available. We had a third-hand pram, and I had to cut up bath sheets we received as wedding presents for nappies, but we were a very happy little family. However I was very relieved when Tom brought home his first month's pay packet at the end of April when Brendan was five weeks old. Having lived off his tiny grant of £2.17.6d per week throughout our marriage so far, it was a great relief to finally receive a cheque for £46.

To celebrate the birth Tom began his *Concerto for Clarinet and Strings* on April 11 and completed it in July. Brendan's godfather was John Donegan and the *Concerto* is dedicated appropriately to "Godfather and godson". Between December 1953 and April 1954 Tom had also been writing his *2nd String Quartet*. This was the third work he would submit for his thesis, and it was with great relief that we learned it had been accepted. Because Rimmer had criticised his first thesis, according to a fellow student for being too avant garde, and his second thesis, the *Oboe Quartet* for being "too diatonic" Tom worked very hard on the *Quartet* to ensure that it was more chromatic. He graduated in May 1954 but I missed the graduation ceremony as I was in bed suffering from cystitis. I doubt if I could have gone anyway as there was no one to care for the baby. Now Tom took on lectures one evening per week in the Extra-Mural department of the university, and this further helped to ease our financial problems. At last we could afford a radio and an electric kettle.

In May 1954 we moved into a "partly furnished" house in Clarkston on the south side of Glasgow which in reality meant carpets, curtains and a stove. The rent was £11 per month, which we paid out of Tom's salary of £46: somehow we managed to scrape together the deposit for it. The next-door neighbour lent me a chair to sit on while Tom and his father went to the Crown auction rooms in Sauchiehall Street, Glasgow to buy a dining table and chairs. And of course we had our piano, bed, cot, pram and clock! I had a lot of cleaning to do as the old lady who had lived there was moving into a home, and she had enough pills in the cupboards to stock a chemist's shop. What bliss it was to finally have our own home, with more space and a garden back and front – even if it was rented. The back garden was separated from Williamwood Golf Course by a railway line but unfortunately this was no defence from the rabbits who insisted in feasting on everything I tried to grow.

Following on from the success of his nursery rhymes Tom received a call from the BBC asking him to write incidental musical for a play by the Scottish playwright Ian Dallas called *The Face of Love*. The terms were very good, and he immediately accepted. The play is based on the story of Troilus and Cressida, and the cast included the famous actors Jill Balcon and Bryden Murdoch.

Word must have got around Broadcasting House that Tom's work was good, because the well-known producer Finlay J. Macdonald said that he would ask very few composers to write for him, and Tom was one of them. To the best of our knowledge he had not heard any of Tom's music at that time, so the other producers must have praised him highly. Finlay asked him to compose music for *Witchwood*, John Keir Cross's highly atmospheric adaptation of scenes from the novel of the same name by John Buchan. It is set in seventeenth-century Scotland during the religious and political upheavals of the Civil War period. Of all his books this bleakly powerful novel was apparently Buchan's favourite. Finlay J. Macdonald produced the play and the main parts were performed by Iain Cuthbertson and Robert Urquhart. One reviewer said the music was "full of fearful fury and scarifying irony, but rhythmic and beautiful".

Early in 1955 Tom received a telephone call from Robert Oughton the conductor of the Scottish Co-operative Wholesale Society Brass Band. Robert said that he had heard some of Tom's work on the radio and he would like to commission him to write a work. A first commission for an original work is a great moment in any composer's life and Tom of course said yes, though I am sure he had not anticipated that this would come from a brass band. Tom generally had a low opinion of much of the *Colonel*

Bogey style music that was then prevalent, and believed that the expertise of the brass band players deserved more challenging music. The work he produced is called *Processional*, and it was widely performed at the time. Unfortunately I do not have a recording of this particular piece, though it was to be the first of four innovative pieces for brass band that could be described as classical.

Shortly after receiving the cheque for the completed commission, Tom asked me what he should write next. Still a little ignorant of the demands of different types of composition, I replied "a symphony", but he said that he thought he was not ready for that. Nothing more was said but, nonetheless, he started work on his *First Symphony* on April 1. He may have changed his mind just to please me. Having written *Processional*, his *Second String Quartet*, a *Concerto for Clarinet* and a *Concertino for Piano and String Orchestra*, as well as his incidental music for radio plays for the BBC, Tom was confident now of his ability to write for a full orchestra. However, a symphony is more abstract than even a concerto, since the composer does not have the character of an individual instrument to focus on. I think the truth is that Tom relished a challenge, and he wanted to test himself. So he just put his head down and got on with it.

Then in June 1955 more music was needed for *The Castle of Mey*, a play about the Queen Mother's home in Scotland, to be broadcast in August. I was the chief clock-watcher as we timed each section of incidental music to the second.

Although Tom was always very methodical in the way he approached composition - he would not move on to the next bar until he was absolutely content with the one he was working on - he always took great delight in the way Beethoven would leave bars empty to be completed at a later time. Though this mode of working was alien to Tom, he couldn't help but admire Beethoven's ability to pass through a series of key changes while building a bridge from one musical idea to the next, or, in some cases, return to the original idea in the same key as before. He'd say to me, "Listen to this, Margaret, listen to this", and the next time we heard the piece, a quiet smile would pass between us during the bars before the expected episode in anticipation of the pleasure to come.

Despite Tom's preferred method of working, the offer from BBC Scotland of more incidental music was too opportune to refuse. The money from the commission would also mean that he could hire a copyist to write out the parts of the symphony when it was completed – parts that would be needed if the symphony was ever to be performed. So in July 1955 he put the symphony to one side and devoted his evenings instead to writing the music for a forthcoming BBC Scotland Radio Play entitled *The Battle of Glencoe*. The script was in the form of a cycle of ballads by Douglas Stewart, and Tom had to write 16 minutes of music in seven weeks. The music was later described as "graphically creating the pages and tradition of one of the most harassing events of Scottish history".

This was followed in September by a James Crampsey production of the play by James Bridie, *Susannah and the Elders*. All of this incidental music was written for the BBC Scottish Orchestra. It was a great training ground for Tom's orchestral skills as each play demanded music using different resources, and so he accumulated a great deal of experience in the sound worlds of different combinations of instruments. He could hear his ideas realised almost immediately; sometimes a mood had to be set in only a few bars, and the value of this discipline was incalculable.

The favourable reactions to his score led to further commissions from the BBC; and so, throughout 1955, Tom did not have as much time to focus on his *First Symphony* as he would have liked. I am sure the interruptions to his work on the symphony are partly to blame for his later dissatisfaction with the score, which he eventually suppressed along with others of his earlier compositions.

Eventually he made up his mind to turn down many of these requests to write incidental music as they were taking up time that he wanted for his other compositions. But he found it hard to say no, and in spite of this decision he went on to write incidental music for more than twenty other radio and television plays; it was good for a young composer to be able to hear his musical ideas translated into performance and the money certainly came in handy. It should also be said that some of the motifs and fragments of musical phrases that he used in these incidental commissions were developed in different ways in some of his early compositions. For instance elements of his *Fourth Quartet*, and another chamber work *Mosaics*, were later "extended, or pruned" (as he put it) for reformation in *Symphony No. 5*. This is of course a time-honoured practice amongst modern composers: Ralph Vaughan Williams transformed some of the ideas from his score for the film 'Scott of the Antarctic' into his *Sinfonia Antarctica*, and William Walton redeveloped some of the musical ideas for the Laurence Olivier film of the Shakespeare play Henry V into a Suite.

CHAPTER 4 (1955 - 1957)

Finding One's Voice

From the proceeds of Tom's teaching, his lecturing, and his incidental music, we had managed to save enough to put down 10% of the £1200 purchase price of a three room flat in Rutherglen in the street where his parents lived. We moved from Clarkston in January of 1955, and were glad to have a place of our own. The flat formed part of a building designed to a plan called "four in a block". Our flat was on the ground floor right; it had a sitting room (for the grand piano), one bedroom, a living/dining room, and a kitchenette and bathroom.

Most of the *First Symphony* was written at the kitchen table of the flat with family life going on around him. Since Tom was working as a school teacher during the day, his compositional time was restricted to evenings, weekends and the school holidays. He was quite happy for me to feed the children and for them to play football around his feet, but no extra curricular musical sounds – not even the drone of a vacuum cleaner - were allowed while he was working. If I started to sing he would lift his head slightly and shoot me a pained look from under his eyebrows and I'd know to stop and take the boys for a walk. Fortunately there was a park at the top of the street and the swings were a great attraction.

The *First Symphony* was the most complex piece of work he had yet undertaken. After six months he became very dissatisfied with it and his restlessness became so pronounced he threw the manuscript into the bin. Fortunately, I rescued the sketches and the draft for the first movement and suggested that he put it to one side for a while. In later life he told me that he sometimes went to bed with a musical problem in his mind only to find the next morning when he woke that it was solved. Unfortunately in this case the solutions were slow in coming.

After a few days he tried to get down to composition again, but then, just as he seemed to be hitting his stride, he received a call from Kemlo Stephen asking him to compose more incidental music and he had to put the symphony aside once more.

Normally Tom liked to finish whatever piece he was working on before he started on another but at this time teachers were not as well paid as they are today and family finances took precedence. This was a time of great hope, but we had very little disposable cash and any extra went into the savings account. A few months after Brendan was born I began to develop rheumatism in my hands and my elbow joints and the doctor said that I must stop scrubbing nappies, so my aunt Laura put down a deposit on a John Bloom "Fairy" washing machine and I paid up the rest monthly. The machine had a wringer; no spin dryers in those days. However it was a great help. As a child of the Thirties and the Second World War, I had been brought up to 'mind the pennies so that the pounds would look after themselves'. My mother had made sure that by the time I was twelve I could pluck a chicken and skin a rabbit and could prepare nourishing cheap meals. During the war pig's trotters, chittlings and tripe were not strangers to our menu, so having to be careful with money was not something that ever overwhelmed me. For his part, Tom lived in a more rarefied world where thoughts of money seldom entered his consciousness. I remember on my first visit to Glasgow I found a halfpenny on the floor of the top deck of the Number 18 Tramcar. When I handed it to Tom, he flung it the length of the car as though it was worthless. I was shocked! However, he grew to understand that I had been taught by my mother to 'cut my coat according to my cloth' and throughout our long marriage he was quite happy to leave that side of things to me.

I soon learned that as long as Tom had a few shillings for cigarettes, he was happy. He hardly ever asked for material things, though when he did they were usually very expensive – such as a better piano! Tom's first piano wasn't really as grand as its name sounded; so during the mid Fifties we were saving to buy a Bechstein boudoir grand piano. Indeed throughout the first twenty years of our life together we always seemed to be saving for something. After the piano we began to save for a car, so that Tom would have an easier time travelling to work. Our first car was in fact a van. The garage installed a window in one side and we re-painted it by hand. The next year when May came round Tom got the itch to change the car, and so it went on every May until 1968 when we could afford to buy a brand new car. He would always know the model he wanted, and the first one he saw he had to have. I used to tell him that there were more to look at but in his eyes the first one was the only one. He hated shopping around.

October 13 1955 saw the first public performance of Tom's composition *Prelude*, at a concert arranged by the Glasgow Society of Organists in

Renfield Street. The work was originally written for piano but it had been reworked for the organ. Not all piano music transfers well to organ, but this piece did. It was a very exciting moment for Tom to hear the work performed by Douglas Gillies. Unfortunately I was unable to attend since I had to care for Brendan; however, I do remember Tom was very happy when he came home. He also told me that Douglas had discussed twelve-tone music with him after the concert. Pioneered by Arnold Schoenberg in the early part of the Twentieth Century, the twelve-tone system was becoming increasingly popular amongst young composers at the time in the form of serialism or serial music. Tom told Douglas that he didn't think that the strict form conceived by Schoenberg had much of a future. Despite these early reservations, Tom would eventually incorporate the twelve-tone system into his compositional style, though he never became a strict serialist.

Tom's progress on the troublesome *First Symphony* was further impeded in the autumn of 1955 when he was transferred from teaching at a school in the city to a newly built, very modern school called St Augustine's in the recently constructed housing scheme at Milton on the northwest edge of Glasgow. Most of his pupils had little interest in classical music, and Tom became deeply frustrated. Some classes at the school were graded as "M". These children were slow learners and modified courses were created for them. All that Tom could do with them was to tell them stories about great composers. He came home one day to tell me that he had been describing horse-drawn carriages in the time of Mozart and one fellow put up his hand and said in all seriousness: "Please sir, horses werenae invented in thae days". Of course most of the pupils were of higher intelligence than this but I think that it was being borne in upon him that school teaching was not where he wanted to spend the rest of his life. He said himself that he had been trained to teach music at a much higher level and that at St Augustine's "I just felt that I never got out of first gear." In fact he grew increasingly depressed over the futility of trying to instruct students who would rather play than study. The students noted this too and gave him the nickname of "Sad Sam". Finally, Tom told me that he would rather do anything than teach there, and we even contemplated moving to Canada where my brother Lawrence lives.

As the Christmas Holidays approached Tom was once again making strong headway with the symphony and I remember recording in my diary that he was looking forward to travelling to my parents' home for Christmas. He had previously composed a number of shorter works in Newcastle and after the rigours of the school term he relished the prospect of different surroundings and the opportunity this would afford him to finish the fourth movement. With my mother helping to look after our baby, Brendan, and our financial affairs eased somewhat, Tom spent much of Christmas and Hogmanay composing, and completed the work before the new term began.

Though completed, the *First Symphony* was not performed until 1957. The delay was not due to any difficulty in finding an orchestra to perform the work. Instead, many months were needed to prepare the orchestral parts. In those days there were no computers or software to facilitate producing pages of music. Every sheet had to be written by hand and copyists were kept busy extracting parts from a full score and writing out each note. The process was laborious and time consuming. For his copyist Tom turned to the young composer Edward Maguire, who was a student at the time and probably glad of the extra money. Eddie's hand was, and remains, immaculate. In fact, he still prefers to do his own copying of his works rather than use a computer.

In the spring of 1956 Tom heard that the Extra Mural Department of Glasgow University was looking for a music lecturer and he applied for the post. At the interview he learned that they were also looking for a lecturer in Geology and could only offer one appointment at that time. However, they did promise Tom a permanent post beginning in October 1957 and this saved his sanity and kept us in Scotland.

In terms of public performances of Tom's larger-scale pieces 1956 proved a breakthrough year. Very early in January Harold Thomson, the Head of Music for BBC Scotland and a great admirer of his incidental music, wrote to say that the Corporation would like to devote a half hour programme to Tom's original compositions to be broadcast on January 8. Naturally Tom was delighted.

At the concert Wight Henderson, the distinguished Scottish pianist, played the *Sonatina* and the *Four Piano Pieces*, while tenor John Tainsh sang the *Five Shakespeare Songs* written in 1952.

In March Tom's *Suite for Piano* was played by Sheila Lessells in the British Council Rooms in Glasgow. The review in The Glasgow Herald next day read:

> ...with its short movements, effectively laid out for the keyboard and with contrasting rhythms and not unpleasant harmonic clashes, the work held interest for the listener and performer alike.

Yet again Tom was busy writing more incidental music for the BBC, on this occasion another historical play called *The March of the '45*. Shortly thereafter, he was commissioned to write incidental music for a film about a Norwegian ship for a company called Elder Film Productions. This score was given to the company who commissioned it and so it is unfortunately lost to us. This also happened to a score for cello commissioned by Educational Films of Scotland for a film about Charles Rennie Mackintosh in July 1964. I do have a video of this film though and while watching it I realised that Tom had used some of its musical material in his *Fantasia* for solo cello.

In April, thanks to money that Frederick Rimmer had discovered lying in the University's coffers, Glasgow University inaugurated a three-day series of concerts called the McEwen Memorial Concerts. These were enabled by a bequest made by Sir John Blackwood McEwen to encourage the performance of chamber works of composers living in Scotland. Fred had at this time been acting head of department for three years and was keen to encourage interest in modern classical music at a time when audiences were dwindling. As one critic observed: "The incentive and the platform are there to encourage them (composers) to spread their creative wings." These concerts later became a triennial institution and certainly helped to sustain popular interest in classical music in advance of the major audience renaissance of the 1970s. Wight Henderson played Tom's *Piano Sonatina* in the first series on April 5 1956, and Tom's music appeared in nearly every McEwen Concert that followed, until the money to fund the series was exhausted. The *Sonatina* was described as "clean, lean, and athletic" in a review in The Scotsman newspaper on the day following its performance. Tom was also awarded the McEwen prize that year for his *Second String Quartet* written the previous year.

Then the contralto Maria Moscardini sang Tom's songs *Most Holy Night* and *Auvergnat* at a concert given by the Dunedin Society in the British Council Rooms and recorded by the BBC for future transmission. The programme cost 3d which is just a tiny bit over 1p today! Tom's *Mass in D Minor* was transmitted on the BBC Home Service on April 20, performed by the BBC Singers conducted by Leslie Woodgate, who thought it "one of the finest of contemporary masses". This is one of the few pre-sixties works that Tom would always acknowledge as "a good work".

I remember Tom's Uncle James (Fr. Camillus) coming to visit us during this busy time. One morning he held out pyjama trousers in one hand and the cord in the other and asked me plaintively, "Margaret, how do I get that back in there?" It was just the sort of question that Tom would ask. I hope that the friary benefited from the instruction on how to use a safety pin as a slotting implement. If I needed anything to be done around the house, decorating, or maybe a shelf put up, Tom used to say, "Employ the man whose job it is." Money was in short supply so I became the "man" whose job it was! Of course, I couldn't trust him with electric plugs anyway because of his faulty red/green perception.

In May 1956 Tom was commissioned to write music for the play *Full Fathom Five*, and the first episode of *Ogg's Log* was broadcast. The latter, in six parts, was written by John Wilson (no relation) and Alastair Phillips. The lead part was taken by the legendary comic actor Duncan Macrae. Roddy MacMillan and Molly Urquhart were also in the cast and smaller rôles were performed by students from the Glasgow College of Dramatic Art, now part of the Royal Scottish Academy of Music and Drama. This was followed by *Storm*, a play by Fitzgerald O'Connor, produced by Archie Lee, in which the actors were James McKechnie, John M Bannerman, Bryden Murdoch, Leonard Maguire, and Arthur Boland. Archie P Lee wrote to Tom to say that James McKechnie (who was the storyteller) remarked that the music gave him a wonderful lift, and how he as producer was delighted with how well the music was fitted to the speech. In fact he doubted that Tom would stay in Scotland as the "fillums" would lure him away. However, barring his brief flirtation with the idea of Canada in 1955, Tom's heart, as well as his feet, were firmly rooted in Scotland.

Having spent most of the first half of the year writing incidental music Tom found little time for non-programmatic composition. Nevertheless, he was always hard working and did manage to write a number of very approachable masses for our local church St Columbkille's in Rutherglen, and for St Augustine's School. He also wrote a school song called *Magne Pater Augustine* but unfortunately this was lost when the school was demolished and all the papers became scattered. Maybe one day it will turn up again.

In January 1957 our second son, Martin, (named after Saint Martin de Porres, a Dominican monk in Peru) was born in Rottenrow Hospital in Glasgow. He was three weeks overdue and by that time I was really tired of waiting for a baby who seemed to be quite content to stay where he was. I was very bored too as I was too big to move around easily. Tom suggested to me that we do something together while we were waiting for labour to begin. He thought that it might be an idea for us to make a rug as his parents had done. So, I went to Lewis's Polytechnic, affectionately known to Glaswegians as "The Poly" and bought canvas, wool, and a progger, and we started on the rug. To encourage me Tom did the first row, then I was left to finish it! With blistered palms I went for a check-up to the hospital and asked them if the baby should have stopped moving. The ruse worked. They kept me in and broke the waters. When this didn't bring on the labour, they began to prepare me for a Ceasarian section. At this point however Martin finally decided it was time to investigate the outside world and was born at 11pm. He was a very contented baby who went to sleep at seven o'clock every night – unlike Brendan who never slept before midnight at that age.

In October 1957, Tom was finally able to give up teaching in schools and apply himself to the challenges of adult education. His duties in the Extra Mural Department required that he give four lectures each week in the history and appreciation of music. In the beginning this meant a great deal of work for him as often a lecture took 16 hours to prepare. His conscience would not allow him to give anything less than his best.

Of course every job has its drawbacks. In this case it was not the work, which Tom loved, but rather the social obligation of having to attend the departmental Christmas Party held at the home of the head of the Extra Mural Department, Harold Trump. Harold was an avuncular man who enjoyed Victorian party games such as charades, Chinese Whispers, and picking up grains of rice with knitting needles. Tom cringed!

When he was not teaching, he was composing, so he usually wanted to relax when he had a spare evening and not think about music. However, we would sometimes have fun playing transcriptions of Beethoven Symphonies (four hands at one piano). Needless to say he was a much better player than I. My piano lessons had stopped when I was fourteen, because my brother had married then, and my mother said that she could no longer afford the weekly fee of 2/6d. Nevertheless I struggled along, with Tom trying to persuade me not to stop each time I made a mistake. Other times he would accompany me while I sang Schumann songs. My previous experience of solo singing had been in the church choir at home in Newcastle where I was sometimes asked to sing motets during the collection. Having heard so many professional singers over the years I am well aware how far short I fell, but I think that Tom enjoyed these evenings as he was always the one who suggested them.

Building on the previous year's breakthroughs, Tom's reputation as a composer continued to grow throughout 1957. In February the Barry Ostlere and Shepherd Band performed his brass band work *Processional* for BBC Manchester to excellent reviews. And Tom was especially pleased when the Edinburgh conductor Eric Roberts took his String Orchestra on tour to New York to perform his *Clarinet Concerto* with Henry Morrison as soloist. This was the first international performance of one of his works, and though he was unable to be present it was a great boost to his confidence. He was able however to hear the work when the concert was later repeated in Edinburgh.

At this time he was composing more incidental music, this time for the plays *All in Good Faith*, and *For Tae Be King*, and he would continue to do so until the 1970s. However, from 1957 onwards these commissions would no longer have the same importance for Tom's development as a composer and I will therefore not mention them in subsequent chapters unless they are of particular significance. For those who are interested there is a full list of these commissions in the appendix.

In 1957 Harold Thomson arranged for the BBC to present the first performance of Tom's *First Symphony* completed the year before. At the time three composers working in Scotland were getting their music regularly performed: Ian Hamilton, Thea Musgrave and Tom. A good deal of the credit for this must go to the two conductors of the main orchestras in Scotland in the mid 1950s, James Loughran at the BBC Scottish Symphony Orchestra and Alexander Gibson with the Scottish National Orchestra. Whenever either of them performed a contemporary work that he thought was very good, he would recommend it to the other, who would then programme it as well, and sometimes they would even take Tom's works abroad. This meant that young composers often got the opportunity to hear their works at least twice. In these dedicated and gifted musicians Scottish music had at last found able champions. Tom held both men in high esteem and was grateful for their efforts on his behalf. They were very different personalities though, and I once asked Tom: "Alex's version and Jimmie's version of the same work are very different, which is the true version?" Tom replied: "Neither of them is the version that I heard in my head when I was composing the work, but each of them is valid." Now thanks in part to these pioneers, and the conductor Bryden Thomson who came later, we have many Scottish composers whose works are being heard.

Furthermore, with Harold Thomson as the Head of Music at the BBC, getting performances of new music was made much easier. Tom never had a problem getting his music played, though paradoxically the financial return for a substantial original piece was never as good as that for the shorter incidental music.

The transcription of the *First Symphony* was completed in July 1956 and the work was premièred by the BBC Symphony Orchestra in BBC Scotland's Studio One, Queen Margaret Drive, in Glasgow on a warm summer evening in August 1957.

A letter from Fred Rimmer dated July 30 1957 reads:

Dear Tom,

I am very glad that you let me know of the broadcast of your First Symphony on August 15. I have made a note of it and look forward to hearing the work. It is a great achievement to have a major work like this performed at this stage and I do congratulate you. Knowing you, I am not surprised that you have had second thoughts about some of it, but the experience of hearing it played by a professional orchestra will give you the opportunity of satisfying yourself about all this.

We hope to see Mary and you before very long and I shall write to you again about the middle of the month. My kindest regards as always.

Yours sincerely,
Fred

I obviously had not made much of an impression on Fred as he could not even remember my name!

The piece is forty minutes long and it was conducted by Colin Davis, who quite possibly didn't like it, as he has never again performed any of Tom's works. I must add though, that I cannot remember our ever approaching him with other scores. The concert, which was also a live transmission, began at seven o'clock and was completed by nine thirty that night. I thought that the performance and recording went very well, and the orchestra expressed their approval by applauding Tom. However, Tom was quiet and thoughtful on our drive back home, and I sensed he was not entirely happy with the work. The reviews the next day were generally good, one critic saying that "Those who have had the privilege of hearing this fine work feel that the symphony, in the contemporary manner, will gain many new admirers from the broadcast."

Despite the favourable reviews, Tom did indeed have concerns about the *First Symphony* and allowed it to be performed only once more - in 1960.

After that he refused to send tapes of the performance to people who wrote saying that they would like to add the recording to their collection of Wilson works. The most recent request came in 2006 from a music-lover in the United States.

Tom never went into detail about the reasons why he thought it was a bad work, but I know that he thought that the symphony went on too long. For a composer as well as a painter it is important to know how and when to stop. He said that Fred thought the work "fell between two stools". I think that Fred was probably right and that Tom really needed to shrug off Fred's influence before he could write a big work in his own voice. The lack of consistency of style was hampering the satisfactory exploitation of his ideas.

Of course it may simply have been, as he had told me in 1955, that he wasn't ready yet. Tom already had a clear vision of what he was capable of, but felt that this *First Symphony* did not live up to his own high expectations, and it was this realisation that informed his final decision to withdraw this and other early works. As it transpired, it would be another eight years before he would return to the symphonic form, by which time his work had developed and matured greatly.

CHAPTER 5 (1957 - 1962)

A Dalliance with Serialism

In 1957 Tom was appointed to the post of lecturer in the Extra Mural Department of Glasgow University. The department was set up to provide lectures to adults who, in the main, had not had the opportunity to go to university but who wanted to broaden their knowledge. No examinations were held at the end of the year, and the students did not graduate; they attended classes simply to learn more about a subject of particular interest to them. Tom told me that it was his rôle to increase the understanding of classical music outside the narrow confines of the music department. The courses in music ranged from studies in harmony and counterpoint, and the analysis of scores, to the study of musical style across the ages. He thought that explaining the context in which different styles of music came into being was of great importance. Of all styles however, he felt that those of the Twentieth Century were the hardest for people to understand. Society had been radically changed through conflict and technology and similarly its artists had undergone revolutionary changes in thought and methodology – changes that seeped only slowly into the consciousness of the general population. Tom recognised that "One of the greatest problems for the modern composer is that audiences may lose touch with him."

He had a unique position in a Scottish university at that time in that he was the only full time lecturer in music in an Adult Education Department (as it was then called). On the face of it his work at the university did not sound particularly taxing – four two-hour lectures each week. But often a lecture took sixteen hours to prepare and he also revised his courses and lectures year on year. Sometimes he prepared an entirely new lecture on a work that he had analysed just a few years before. When I asked why he was redoing material he had already prepared he said, "My ideas may have altered slightly over the years." The classes were not only held in Glasgow, but in other larger centres, so Tom's weekly duties included travelling with the painter and lecturer Martin Baillie to such places as Oban and Dumfries. Their territory was a large one – from Argyll to Galloway, and they had to bring in tutors from the university internal staff in the first instance, and then from colleges and schools, which involved them in interviewing prospective tutors and discussing proposals for courses. For all that, the larger part of the work was lecturing, and certainly for Tom and Martin this was where their real interest lay. When delivering evening classes far from Glasgow they stayed overnight and came home the next day. In Oban Tom always stayed with two of his class members, Canon Douglas Muir, the incumbent of Oban Cathedral, and his wife Eve who was a Newcastle girl like me. Although they were much older than us they became great friends of ours and they truly loved and admired Tom.

I once asked Tom what he and Martin talked about on their journeys and after a long pause, followed by a weary sigh, he replied, "Food". Martin grew his own vegetables and was very interested in the various properties of different foods and their effects on the human body. Tom on the other hand ate to live rather than lived to eat. He enjoyed a good meal, but his interest in its preparation was minimal. Toasted cheese was the height of his culinary skills. Of course Tom and Martin were also good friends who talked a great deal about the arts, and this made it all worthwhile.

During Tom's career at the university students who had attended the winter sessions were offered the opportunity the following summer to visit a music festival in Europe. Martin Baillie accompanied him as the art lecturer, and the group would also visit the local museums and art galleries. As our children were young I was unable to join the group, but on his return Tom used to describe to me the places they had seen and the concerts they had attended. The students had lectures about what they were to hear and see before concerts, operas and gallery visits, and afterwards there were discussions. On one of the trips, this time to Paris, an elderly lady who had attended Tom's lectures over several years bought tickets for them both to go to hear Verdi's *Falstaff*. It was not an opera that Tom cared for but the tickets were expensive so he felt duty bound to attend, and in the event he admitted that he had enjoyed the performance very much. To Tom there was no place like home, and he was always glad to be back. In later years he said that he had always enjoyed his work at the university as it provided the perfect foil to the isolation of composition. Not only did it commit him to re-examining his own musical values, but it also forced him to communicate and justify these values directly to an audience. He had great respect for the intelligence of the ordinary working man and said that people liked to be "intellectually stretched".

In December 1957 a publisher whose name I cannot recall asked Tom to write a light overture. At the end of it Tom said to me "Well the overture is finished, but it isn't what one would describe as light music – however we'll send it off as he's asked for it." Another work lost, as it was never returned – and Tom was never paid.

The next spring Tom started his *Third String Quartet*. As the composition developed he told me he felt that significant changes were taking place in his writing, and that he was refining his compositional language. After the experience of writing the *First Symphony*, it was very important that this piece should translate more successfully from page to performance. Though Tom was a modest man, he had a great belief in his gifts and was troubled by the thought that his work might be difficult to interpret and the audience would not properly understand his musical intentions. Around this time he said to me, "Margaret, I know how good I am even though others at this time may not appreciate it". Of course he would never have said this to anyone else, but it was just an expression of his honest and assured belief.

Publishers we approached often praised Tom's works, but still found reasons not to publish. Here are some quotes from letters Maurice Jacobson wrote at that time:

> I have faithfully gone through the scores that you sent. I have, in fact had to divide myself in two. As a musician may I say how stimulating I find your music; it is vital and really has something to say,

But he goes on to say why they cannot publish it.

On another occasion the same publisher wrote:

> These seem to me excellent pieces, but I have to say with regret that they are not within Curwen's field of publication. But I am glad to have seen them, and wish you all success with them elsewhere.

The reasons for rejection were that Curwen was a publisher who specialised in music for schools and amateurs so it seems now that the company had a point, although some of Tom's works have been performed very well by youth orchestras.

Another wrote:

> Thank you for sending Refrains and Cadenzas, which I find admirable altogether.

But in a later letter he rejects it due to:

> a)...our very full publishing programme, and b) unfortunately the market for brass band music is not large enough to justify the financial outlay.

The work in question was later published by Boosey and Hawkes who used it as the test piece for the European Brass Band Championship in May 1984.

Again when Tom submitted his *Te Deum*,

> As you have been so patient in awaiting a decision about your Te Deum, I apologise for having to tell you that we do not feel able to accept the work for publication. This has nothing to do with the musical quality of the work. We have such a large publishing programme in hand that we have not the facilities to handle or promote the work effectively.

Yet again:

> I did in fact hear the performance of Soliloquy Julian Bream gave in London, and much enjoyed the piece. Unfortunately however, our commitments in the field of contemporary guitar music are rather heavy at the moment. Please do not take this as a reflection of the quality of the writing, which both Julian Bream and we ourselves recognise as expert. It is I am afraid a question of economics. I am sure you would have no difficulty in placing it elsewhere.

Sometimes works were taken into a publisher's hire library, put on the shelves, and left there until a conductor wanted to give a certain work a performance. Then they were taken down, dusted off and sent out only to be put back on the shelves on their return. The publisher took his 50% and it was hard for me not to suspect that there was an anti-Scottish agenda at work in the cavalier treatment shown to the submitted scores. Novello actually managed to lose the original manuscript of *Variations for Orchestra*. The copy that they returned is a mirror image of the original. This is yet another original manuscript that is probably at the back of someone's cupboard – in Germany I believe. Fortunately the copyrights for most of the works from this period – if not the original manuscripts - eventually came back to our own hands. Tom said to me that music was only worth writing if people hear it but he sometimes doubted in the 1950s whether he would make that all-important breakthrough outside of Scotland.

Around this time, we posted a work called *Supplications* to Michael Howard, choirmaster at Ely Cathedral, but it was not acknowledged. From the Post Office we learned that it was definitely delivered, but despite repeated requests for the score's return (we said that we would send the postage), we never got it back. Eventually Mr Howard said that as he had not asked for the work he did not feel under any obligation to return it. In 2002 I contacted the librarian at Ely Cathedral who searched for the manuscript without success. As Michael Howard is now dead I think I must accept that it is lost. This was a risk that composers took in those days. In fact there are at least four original scores that have been lost by publishers and others. Nowadays of course, when copying is so easy, original scores are never sent.

Our third son Stephen (named after the first Christian Martyr) was born in Glasgow in St Francis Nursing Home, in June 1958. I awoke at 3am when Martin, who was teething, began to cry. His crying and my first labour pain came together. I waited until 7am before I woke Tom, or should I say attempted to wake Tom. I think that after two babies he was becoming blasé. After trying for half an hour, he managed to stir himself and drove me to St Francis Maternity Unit where Stephen was born three hours later. As a young man Tom was never very good at early rising, and it was just as well that his lecturing took place either in the afternoons or evenings. Nuns staffed St Francis maternity home, and they were very kind to me. However the building left a lot to be desired in that I had to climb two flights of stairs one hour after the birth. I knew that the staff room was at the other end of the building from the ward where I was, so when after-pains started at midnight I waited until the nursing staff came at 5am to ask for pain relief. The nun then told me that I "should have rung for us at midnight as the good Lord does not mean mothers to suffer in childbirth." However, overall my stay at St Francis was better than those in Stobhill and Rottenrow where Brendan and Martin were born. Stephen was a happy baby, perhaps because I was more relaxed after two babies and didn't worry so much about him. That said, all three children suffered from serious bouts of juvenile asthma which concerned us both greatly. But while Brendan was diagnosed at sixteen weeks, the others didn't begin to suffer from it until they were three years old. With the new addition, our one-bedroom flat was now filled to overflowing, and after having three babies in four years we bought our first TV, deciding that it was probably less hassle than a larger family!

While we were living in Dryburgh Avenue, Canon Rooney asked Tom to become choirmaster of our local Roman Catholic Church, St Columbkille's in Rutherglen. With Tom at the helm the choir and the congregation were introduced not only to Tom's original masses (many of which remain), but also works by Palestrina, Byrd and Ockeghem. I joined the choir in 1969, when the younger boys were old enough to be left in Brendan's care, and I would have to say that our choral efforts were a bit like the curate's egg – good in parts. Nonetheless Tom showed great patience and the standard of singing steadily improved even though Tom's good friend Jim Clayton, who sang in the bass section, followed the soprano line!

Tom greatly enjoyed working with the choir, many of whom he had known all his life, and he became deeply involved over a twelve year period. In addition to Jim Clayton, Arthur McCaffrey and Pat Holmes, there were Rose and John McCann, Peter McLaughlin and Maureen Carter who later married, Ann and Eddie Dunn, and his old primary school teacher Miss Kane who played the organ. There were several marriages within the choir over that period and generally it was a very close-knit group. The choristers would sing at High Mass at twelve o'clock every Sunday, practice for an hour for the next week's Mass, and afterwards go for coffee. At Christmas they would sing carols for an hour before Midnight Mass and after the service come to our home for a party. During the early years they had a New Year outing at a local hotel where Tom became a little merry and proceeded to introduce the members of the choir to Canon Rooney, quite forgetting that they were part of his congregation. Although I looked on in consternation, Canon Rooney obviously found the moment quite humorous and smiled politely.

In January 1959 the Music Department submitted Tom's *Third String Quartet* for Glasgow University's McEwen Competition for Composition without telling him. We were therefore very surprised when we received a letter saying that Tom had won; apparently there were twelve other entries. The prize money was £60 - not a lot even in those days, but I expect that the committee awarding the prize thought that it was the glory that counted. The Goudie Prize, which was awarded to him in 1953, and the McEwen Composition Prize were the only prizes Tom won, but as he said, "he had not entered into competition for either of them". It is most likely that he gave the music department a copy of the score for their library, and, without his knowledge, it was submitted for the competition.

One needs to remember that the late 1950s were a time of considerable musical ferment. The turmoil stemmed from Schoenberg's radical rejection, earlier in the century, of traditional harmony, the system of tonal relationships that had been the bedrock of European music from Bach to Brahms. In Schoenberg's scheme all twelve notes within an octave stood as equals. Such once-central distinctions as major/minor or consonance/dissonance were dissolved. No longer were certain chords, like the triad, accorded a privileged status. By enabling composers to take music in new directions rather than follow along well-worn paths, Schoenberg intended his revolution to have a liberating effect. In some ways it did, but it also threw up a barrier to listeners, who often felt that twelve-tone compositions lacked structure and clarity. From the 1920s through or until the 1940s twelve-tone music remained on the edges of the musical mainstream despite its adoption and development by two of Schoenberg's most gifted students, Alban Berg and Anton von Webern. Following World War Two, however, it swept across Europe through the proselytising efforts of Pierre Boulez in France and Karlheinz Stockhausen in Germany. A less strict form of the twelve-tone technique then passed to the United States through such composers as Milton Babbitt and Elliott Carter under the new banner of 'Serialism'.

When revolutionary new ideas are introduced to any arena of artistic endeavour they always cause intense debate. Some embrace the ideas in their totality, others become increasingly conservative and trenchant; some bury their heads in the sand and pretend that the world does not move, while others seek compromise positions in the midst of battle. In these conditions it is extremely difficult to not only find one's true voice, but also to find an impartial audience.

The entry on "Harmony" in the Ninth Edition of the *Oxford Companion to Music* 1955 conveys a sense of the turbulence produced by the spread of serialism at the time.

> There is one gross anomaly about the rules of harmony today. In every other age the rules have been based more or less upon the music of the time. The essentials of music from Bach to Brahms were the same and hence the rules remained practically unchanged. We are still teaching on the basis of these rules (as every published harmony textbook shows - even Schoenberg's). Yet not merely the idiom but the very principles of the art have changed. We are still teaching rules based on the major and minor key system and the triad to students who, if they become composers, will perhaps write atonally and take no account of the triad. We are compelled to this because the rules for the new periodic-style of music are not yet formulated - and perhaps not yet capable of formulation, the style itself being insufficiently settled (and, indeed we are not yet quite sure that it will ever be settled).

One of Tom's good friends, the composer Martin Dalby, who was a music producer at the BBC in London, explained the situation in this more practical fashion:

> The Schoenberg method became the established philosophy for twelve-note composing since it embraced all the texture of the music. It threaded its way through chords, it could be transposed (sometimes the transposition beginning midway in the row), could be played backwards, inverted and so on. In short it offered such flexibility that even the most enthusiastic student of it could lose his path during the course of a piece. Even Schoenberg's later pieces don't use the method. It was the Americans who subsequently went absolutely and stupidly crazy with it. Tom never went anywhere near that and nobody that I know of composes by the American method any more.

In this turbulent artistic climate, that also saw the arrival of Neo-Dadaism, Action Painting, Beat Poetry and Cut-up Writing, it was inevitable that confusion about the future direction of music should occur on a general and individual level. Something of this uncertain state of affairs appears in Fred Rimmer's later responses to Tom's *First Symphony* complaining that it "fell between two stools," having judged an earlier trio to be too avant garde, and an oboe quartet to be "too diatonic". I think that because the Glasgow University Music Department was no longer teaching 'rules' by this time, but 'styles', Fred probably had a different vision for Tom's music than Tom had himself. However, neither of these criticisms necessarily meant that he did not appreciate Tom's talent and potential.

Fred, I believe, felt that there were clear choices to be made in composition. On the other hand Tom was of a more eclectic disposition, seeing in the differing systems opportunities to select whatever best suited his purposes and met his ends. For Tom this was not about compromise, but about defining his own personal musical integrity.

Tom said later, that in the 1950s and 1960s there were two types of composer: those who wanted to break completely with the past and develop a wholly new musical vocabulary for the post-war world, and consolidators who sought to adapt new techniques to expand upon the range of musical possibilities. Clearly Tom felt that he was of the latter camp; however it was not an easy time in which to compose with such theoretical and stylistic battles raging around him.

Controversies over musical styles were not the only difficulties that a young Scottish composer had to contend with. Another was getting his music out into the world, to be played and heard. The McEwen Concerts at Glasgow University were a godsend, and the BBC was faithful to its responsibilities. However, as Professor (and composer) Robin Orr pointed out in remarks made to The Glasgow Herald in April of that year, Scottish composers were ill-served by another of the country's musical organisations:

> The generous help given by the BBC with the BBC Scottish, Orchestra is familiar to all. But the situation in which a national orchestra practically never plays a work by a native composer is without parallel in any country. It arises from a combination of prejudice, ignorance and timidity.

The situation lamented by Robin began to improve when, later in the year, Alexander Gibson became the conductor of the Scottish National Orchestra.

At one of the McEwen series concerts, Tom's *Two Mediaeval Lyrics* were sung by the distinguished soprano Joan Alexander, accompanied by Elspeth Low. The reviewer said, "The songs worked up a fine and freely rhapsodic exuberance." Although I have a set of *Three Lyrics* written around that time, the scores for the *Two Mediaeval Lyrics* are lost. Not surprisingly Tom's prize winning *Third String Quartet* also received its first performance in that year's series on April 2. Unfortunately the violist of the Lyra String Quartet fell ill and Herbert Downes bravely agreed to take over the part only ten hours before the performance. One reviewer said that the performance was badly lacking in spontaneity – can one wonder!

A few weeks after this performance, Tom sent Downes two copies of his *Viola Sonata* to get his opinion of it. Herbert wrote to say that he had sent one copy to the BBC and hoped that an early performance would happen. In the end the performance did not take place, nor did we get back either score, so this work is also lost.

Depressed by the number of his works that were being lost around this time, Tom began to write his music on a fairly new paper called Symphax so that copies could be printed. Because the system uses Indian ink, using it is much slower than writing on ordinary manuscript paper with a pencil. However changes could be made by scraping off errors with a razor blade. The alterations that Tom needed to make were minor, and were to dynamics as a rule. Dynamics for those who don't know are the instructions to the performer, such as *fortissimo, decrescendo* and *rallentando*. Performers have told me since that there is never any doubt as to Tom's intentions.

During 1959, Tom took his extra-mural students on a study trip to London at Easter and then another to Vienna in the summer. On his return from Austria in August we went camping in Cornwall for our family holiday. We enjoyed a very sunny week on the beach, but were then hit by a monumental downpour. On returning to the campsite we found all our possessions floating out of the tent. This forced us to sleep the next night in the van and then abandon the holiday. The rain only stopped when we reached Gloucester! As soon as we got back to Glasgow Tom had to travel on to Newbattle Abbey College, south of Edinburgh, to teach for two weeks. Unfortunately, the night sitting in the front seat of the cold van had taken its toll and I became ill with pneumonia and viral meningitis, and so Tom had to come home immediately to take care of the children, aged five, two, and fourteen months, while I was placed in isolation in the polio ward of Ruchill Hospital. Tom's parents were on a coach tour of Israel at the time, and he was on his own for some days. Poor Tom went hollow cheeked again; I hadn't seen him look like that since his student days. Fortunately, once his mother returned, she was able to help with the children in the evenings when he had to lecture.

I spent our seventh wedding anniversary in hospital. Tom brought me eight red roses! Maths was never his best subject. In the early years of our marriage Tom had great difficulty in remembering birthdays and anniversaries and I would wait all day to see whether he would remember. Then in the evening I would ask "what day is this?" and wait for the stricken look that came across his face. I could almost see the silent prayer go up to heaven, "Dear Lord, please let me remember!" It was a good excuse for a cuddle when I eventually told him. Over the years, and with some carefully laid hints, his memory did improve, and in later years I even got some poems on the cards. Though I was released from hospital after three weeks, it took me more than four months to recover physically, and four to five years before I could easily find some of the words that I knew were in my brain but couldn't locate. Tom used to say, "Well tell me a word that is close to what you mean," but unfortunately I feel the same way about words as Tom did with musical notes, only the exact one will do.

Despite the ups and downs of the year, we struggled on, and Tom completed the composition of his *Toccata* on September 26 1959. The piece starts with what could be described as an "orchestral fanfare" and ends, unusually for Tom, *fortissimo*. A reviewer, after an SNO concert in 1963, described the work as "Brilliantly colourful, live and accomplished, the nature of the scoring and counterpoint had in fact close links to Hindemith". While Tom always said that "comparisons are odious", he also understood that no work exists in a vacuum, and since he admired Hindemith, he took no offence at the comparison. As soon as *Toccata* was finished, he made a start on the *Piano Sonata* which was completed the following month (though he revised the work in 1964). In October the BBC broadcast some of his *Scottish Songs*. Altogether it was a very busy autumn and winter.

In March 1960 Bryden Thomson conducted the *First Symphony* with the BBC Scottish Orchestra. This was the first time Jack had conducted one of Tom's pieces, but he said that he had been a player in an orchestra when one of Tom's earlier works had been performed. Though the performance was very good, Tom remained dissatisfied with the work and this was the last time he allowed it to be played.

Variations for Orchestra was composed between March 18 and June 26 1960. This was an eighteen-minute set of variations on a musical theme taken from the second movement of his *Piano Sonata* (where it also forms part of a set of variations). *Variations for Orchestra* shows him experimenting with the twelve-tone technique though not using it in its strict form (serialism). Tom always maintained that though he would like to write at least one work for every genre in classical music during his lifetime, the precise choice of what he wrote at any one time depended on a number of factors: his desire to undertake a challenge, what he had written in the recent past, and his other work commitments. While each compositional form presents its own specific technical challenges, a set of variations was perhaps easier to fit into his busy schedule at this time. In his notes Tom wrote:

> The piece takes the form of a theme first heard on the solo horn, followed by twelve continuous variations which present a widely contrasted range of moods. This theme itself is formally straightforward. Clearly divided into two main parts, the beginning of each part is melodic in character, scored for solo horn and violas and oboe respectively, while the end of each part consists of a brief comment by other sections of the orchestra. The first of the twelve variations might be described as a 2-part invention and is scored mainly for woodwind and strings. This variation reduces the rather expansive theme to its basic essentials by extracting from it a much terser melodic outline which is then treated in a contrapuntal

antiphonal manner. In this piece the initial theme and variation are in G. Thereafter eleven different keys are used, one for each variation (including a dirge and nocturne, a waltz and a French overture) before the restatement of the main theme in the coda.

In October and November Tom's incidental music featured in two programmes. The first, produced by Robert Reid, was called *Enquiry*, during which the presenter Fyfe Robertson looked into "issues of importance to Britons in 1960" – specifically those of "the Wild North West". The second was the play, *'The Wallace'* by Sydney Goodsir Smith.

On November 3 1960 *Toccata* was given its first performance by the conductor Michael Steyn and the BBC Scottish Orchestra. It was repeated in November 1961 and May 1962 and many times since. Apart from playing at the Proms Concerts in the Albert Hall in London and at the Edinburgh Festival, the BBCSO was, at this time, mostly confined to the studio. It was an orchestra whose main raison d'être was to broadcast; however it did occasionally venture forth to places like Ayr and Inverness. Eventually foreign tours became part of the itinerary, but in the early days there were rarely, if ever, reviews of their concerts.

On November 20 we moved a few streets away to a house in Stonelaw Drive as our one-bedroom flat was becoming too small to accommodate the growing family. Located at the top of a hill, our new home had seven rooms which provided lots of space for the three boys. Here they were able to play cricket in the big back garden using a washing pole as a rather large middle stump. We also had a visiting tortoise that was a great source of interest and was watched very carefully so that he did not get in the way of their game. Brendan also had a shed at the bottom of the garden from which noxious smells emanated when he was "doing his chemistry experiments" and lots of fun was had by all. After years of composing at the kitchen table Tom at last had a study which, even though it was too small to house a piano, was a great relief to him. The dormer windows of the upper floor jutted out of the roof space and the low campsile ceilings made the three bedrooms and study difficult to furnish.

We used to talk about what Tom thought was happening to him during the two or three weeks before he began to compose a new work. We both recognised the restless simmering period that gradually came to the boil and burst forth into a musical idea (sometimes it was only a motif that was played over and over again until it blossomed into a musical phrase), but neither of us had the psychological knowledge or vocabulary to explain it satisfactorily. It did involve a lot of floor pacing. He said that before he began to put together his musical ideas, he thought about such things as philosophical matters or natural phenomena. Though these reflections often had very little to do with the work that followed, they helped him to form a picture of the overall shape that he wanted the composition to have. I think that once the picture was in place, the ideas seemed to grow out of it. Our eldest son Brendan also paces while thinking about the books he writes on philosophy, but whereas Tom paced back and forth, Brendan paces in a circle. I have carpets that are worn in some very funny places! I once met a seer in the BBC who had come to talk on the Jimmy Mack Programme and asked him about Tom and he said: "I see a man who paces". I thought it very strange.

Early in 1961, the publishers Ricordi invited Tom to write three pieces for piano to be used as examination pieces. There was some discussion before Ricordi finally accepted *Reverie* (which had been originally called *Chaconne*), *Valse Viennoise (homage à Alban Berg)*, and *Tzigane*.

In his programme note Tom writes, "*Reverie* needs no explanation – *Valse Viennoise* is a little tribute to the music of Alban Berg, while the more Bartokian *Tzigane* acknowledges another important influence felt during my early career."

In the programme notes for Johannes Wolff's later recording of Tom's piano works, the German pianist elaborated on the structure of the three pieces:

> *(Reverie)* First a monophonic, later a yearning two-part melody, is followed by a dramatic Allegro part. When the harmonic constellations of the beginning return with only tiny alterations, the Perpetuum Mobile of the left hand seems to continue. But then the connection with the preceding process becomes evident, as both major chords overlap each other very softly, resulting in a surprisingly consonant impression.

> The twofold charm derived from spontaneous listening and analytic reflection can also be discovered in *Valse Viennoise* as the title does not only refer to a well-known rhythmic model, but also to the twelve-note technique of the Second Viennese School. The tonal final chord indeed points to Alban Berg. The preceding monophonic material, however, is reminiscent of Anton Weber, as Wilson forms his undogmatically used row from a three-tone interval sequence as well as its mirror and transposition.

The dominant characteristics of the third piece, *Tzigane*, are the shifts of a motorically accompanied minor-like melody with contrasting triads, which following each other in fourths, spread and condense at the end, while the motoric process breaks off suddenly.

In the spring of 1961 we watched a Monitor programme on TV in which the young composer Peter Maxwell Davies was interviewed. Tom and I talked about it afterwards and both agreed that we were a bit puzzled by composers who gave the impression that they fill every spare minute composing. Tom said that, "They seem inhuman – as though they can't take time off to have a pint of beer or go to a football match. As though they compose because they want to, but without having the overwhelming need to". He felt that he had short but definite barren periods when, if he made himself compose, he would be dissatisfied with the results. When the urge to compose was upon him, it could not be denied. Tom always pursued paths that he felt he must take, rather than those that were fashionable to follow. What a lot of soul-searching he did before he wrote his first strictly serial piece of music! Though even when he did, I think that he looked upon it as an 'academic challenge' rather than something he would necessarily wish to continue to pursue in future works.

Tom's first commission, apart from incidental music for the BBC, and the advance on future royalties of £45 from Ricordi for the *Three Pieces*, was from the Court of the University of Glasgow. When the commission offer arrived Tom agonised over what would be most suitable to write, but, as McEwen Concerts were limited to chamber works, his choice was somewhat limited.

He chose to write a *Sonata for Violin and Piano*, and composed it between June 1960 and February 1961. It is Tom's only strictly serial work in the public domain. Though he had no desire to follow fashion and had strong reservations about the serial technique in its strict form, he had nevertheless developed a healthy curiosity about its technical possibilities and ultimately it was this that swayed him to write the *Violin Sonata*. Tom's mother, who couldn't stand serial music as a rule, liked it, and I found the second movement beautiful – not an adjective that I had previously been able to use to describe any serial music - but on this occasion I agreed with her. The première took place in the Bute Hall of the University on May 3 as part of that year's McEwen Concert Series. The players were Louis Carus and Wight Henderson. This series also included a performance of *Rosa Mystica* sung by Joan Alexander and shortly afterwards the works were repeated in the Modern Composer

Series on Radio 3. Tom and I were very nervous beforehand and absolutely exhausted afterwards. We need not have been concerned; the critics were kind and the piece well received.

After the première, the Glasgow Herald critic wrote about the *Sonata* in a way which I think reflected many people's reservations about serial music at the time:

> The *Sonata*, though a tougher listening nut, showed that serial writing need not be wholly a cerebral soulless affair; it can approximate to music in the usual sense of the term and claim a response too.

Another critic, Christopher Grier wrote very perceptively in The Scotsman:

> This respect-worthy sonata will, I fancy, come to be regarded as a transitional product in the career of an interesting musician.

After another performance at a McEwen Memorial concert in April 1962 he added, also in The Scotsman:

> Mr. Wilson prefers a theme and variation for his slow movement. This was, I thought, the most distinguished part of the sonata, apart from its being the one in which his brand of near-melodic serialism is most prominent.

At the time Tom worked on the *Violin Sonata*, I think he regarded his turn to strict serialism as nothing more than an experiment. I doubt whether the favourable reception, especially following the third performance in 1962, caused him to think of changing the direction of his music. Ultimately I do not think that the reaction of others, whatever it was, would have any effect on his future composition. He came to his own conclusions, and made his own decisions irrespective of what others thought.

It was around this time that Tom decided to teach himself the rudiments of the guitar because he wanted to compose some pieces for the instrument. That way he could make sure that the notes lay easily under the hands. The *Three Pieces for Guitar* that resulted was originally better known in Europe than in Britain, having been published, and frequently performed there. But in more recent years they have become widely known here also. He said that although they are short they are serious in intention. Indeed they are pioneering works for guitar in the same way that *Sinfonietta* was for the Brass Band. They are never obvious or overt like many solo guitar works but explore a notion of musical subtext uncommon in compositions of the time. The breathing and use of time is very different from Flamenco or other classical Spanish guitar music, which is perhaps one of the reasons why Tom's works for guitar have such a strong appeal to performers around the world.

On January 22 1962 *Variations for Orchestra* received its première in a broadcast from Studio 1 by the BBCSO, conducted by Norman del Mar. The orchestra went on to perform it twice in June. The first public performance took place on May Day, at a concert given in Glasgow's St Andrews Halls, with the Scottish National Orchestra under Alexander Gibson.

Afterwards Anthony Hedges wrote in The Guardian:

> The music moves with purpose and certainty in that most testing idiom that hovers between free tonality and atonality without having recourse to the prop of serial structures.

In the same programme, John Ogdon played Bartók's *Piano Concerto No.1*. John's was a monumental talent, but he was painfully shy, so shy that when he came to visit he would talk to us but could not look at us for the first half-hour. Invariably he would later go to the piano and play for us, and then this very nervous man became a veritable lion. While Tom was not shy, they were very alike in many other ways. Both were gentle men and great musicians, and they got on very well together. I'm glad to say that John became a good friend.

Through his work as a composer and teacher, Tom met many composers and musicians. He spoke with Aaron Copland, Karlheinz Stockhausen, Luciano Berio, and Krzysztof Penderecki at the university, when they came here for performances of their pieces, and when they came to give lectures. Witold Lutoslawski was a frequent visitor and I remember the common language was French when he first came. Tom acted as interpreter when Fred invited us all to dinner in the university club. However it was not long before Witold could speak perfect English. Alas their visits were usually so short that Tom did not have the opportunity to talk at any great length with them.

On the family front, the boys were growing up quickly and as each of them reached the age of seven they were sent to the Ommer School of

Music to learn piano. The school, which enjoyed a very good reputation, was run by two sisters who lived in a big house on the south side of Glasgow - Miss Julia taught piano, and Miss Elsa taught violin - and they also employed other teachers. The different attitudes the boys had to this discipline were interesting. For the first two years of Brendan's tuition it was blood, sweat, and tears from both of us. Eventually, though, he began to buckle down and practise, and thereafter his musical training was not so much of a torture. Each year competitions are held as part of the Glasgow Music Festival, and when Brendan was eight years old, his music teacher at the Ommer school entered him in the relevant section for his age. Brendan won a book as a prize and subsequently took no further interest in the proceedings. We took Martin, who was five years old at the time, with us, thinking that it might prepare him for the time when it was his turn to compete. There were thirty entrants in Brendan's section, and after number twenty three Martin gave a huge sigh that was heard by all. The examiner, with a rueful smile said "Yes, we can all feel that way after a while." In the event however, Martin never entered the competition. He was so sick before, during, and after taking his first piano examination that we decided that pressure of that kind was not for him.

In contrast to Brendan's initial approach to practice, Martin took to the piano like a duck to water. He read music as I would read the newspaper, and practice was never a problem. Stephen, however, hated it! He has an exceptionally good ear and for the first two years he just copied what he had heard Martin playing the previous year. Then things began to get a bit more complicated and he had to learn to read music. From that moment on Stephen loathed the piano. He regularly begged to be allowed to give it up but Tom was adamant. "When you are sixteen years old and leave school, then you may choose to give it up or not. Until then, you do it!" I think that Tom's own regret at giving up piano tuition was showing itself and he was determined that Stephen would not repeat his mistake. It should be said that Stephen was playing keyboards as well as bass guitar in his pop group two years after his sixteenth birthday.

When Brendan was thirteen years old he began to study the violin too, but later he said that he could not cope with all the studying he had to do and also play the piano and violin. He was given the choice of which instrument he wanted to stop and chose to continue with his piano studies. His violin teacher, Salvatore Secchi, telephoned to ask us to beg Brendan to change his mind as he was so good, but as Brendan said: "There are only so many hours in a day." Nevertheless when Brendan was eighteen, he decided to write a string quartet. He was amazed at how difficult it was, and I could see his dad rising in his estimation daily. Eventually he gave up the unequal task.

This was also the month that I recorded in my diary that Tom was having a lot of trouble with the first movement of his *Second Symphony*. However he managed to sort the problems out before the end of the month

Tom himself was no stranger to anxiety and pressure and would sit with the fingers of his right hand crossed, which he then covered with his left hand, during every public performance. His *Violin Sonata* was played again at the McEwen Memorial Concerts on April 28 and it was also accepted for performance at the Cheltenham Festival on July 7 1962. This Festival performance was a very prestigious occasion, which while flattering, was also quite stressful for him. Audiences were there because they were interested in contemporary music, and critics came from far and near, so the publicity for a young composer was very important. Commissions could follow from these performances, and performers who heard their music would often ask for other pieces that they could perform in the future. Even to have works played at Cheltenham showed that the composer was regarded seriously by the profession as a whole. Altogether it was a satisfying time for a young composer. However on this occasion there was a downside.

After the performance Tom was invited to join a panel chaired by Richard Rodney Bennett, and including Harrison Birtwhistle and Peter Maxwell Davies, to talk about the future of classical music – and once again serialism was uppermost in many people's minds. Some composers embraced it wholeheartedly and completely at the time and denigrated those who dared to disagree with them – Tom was one of those who dared to disagree! Leading the discussion, Bennett attacked Tom's *Sonata* on the grounds that it had 'tonal implications' and therefore was not properly serial. Tom defended the *Sonata* as a successful work, and went on to say that though he had enjoyed the experience of writing it, he thought that "to keep strictly to the discipline of pure serialism causes people to create some very ugly sounds." And the lack of any tangible rhythm in so much music written at that time bothered him. This did not mean that he felt that music should be pretty, but rather that it must have a cohesive internal logic, and not seem to jump about without reason. This was not what the purists wanted to hear and the discussion became very spirited. Though Tom was angered by the personal aspects of the attack, he remained cool and serene on the outside.

Tom did make one further foray into the field of strict serialism – almost as if to test his words. This was the *Wind Quintet*, completed in December 1961 but never performed. It was consigned to the back of the cupboard with some of his other early works, and has stayed there ever since. He said it was a thoroughly bad work, because the serial idiom was not his language or proper medium of expression.

That Christmas I remember him saying that after two years (1960-61) of experimenting with strict serial technique, but being uncomfortable with it, he was returning to tonality. His decision was not based on an insistence that music have a tonal centre. He was prepared, in fact, to adopt serial methods, but very fluidly, when they served to mould a piece as he wished it to sound. But he had found that the rigorous application of the serial technique was a creative straightjacket. He explained to me that serialism could easily force him to make illogical choices that would compromise his musical integrity. He always accepted that music does not need to have a tonal centre, but hereafter he would use whatever idiom and syntax was best suited to the ideas and the emotions that he wanted to convey, moving between tonality and atonality, serial technique and chromaticism, plain chant and aleatory as he saw fit.

Tom would continue to use the twelve-tone technique during certain passages; "but just as another way to express myself, another tool". He made up his mind as always, after a great deal of thought. Once made up, he stuck with his conviction that the technique when applied rigidly was too restrictive. He was stung by the public personal attack at Cheltenham, but gratified that ultimately he was proved right, that the way forward was to modify and incorporate the technique. This cannot have endeared him to those purists on the panel he proved wrong, and who later followed his lead.

What the technique would allow Tom to do was to create rapidly interlocking musical patterns that could be used to express agitation, conflict, or uncertainty, or that permitted a change of direction without the need for such traditional devices as pauses, accelerandos, or crescendos, as were the more traditional routes in centuries past.

Tom told me many years later "there are lots of secrets in my music, lots of things to discover, but they are there for those who care to look." Tom's good friend, the composer Martin Dalby found this to be true when he was asked to contribute a chapter to the symposium Musica Scotica published in 2004. He chose to analyse two of Tom's works, *Missa Pro Mundo Conturbato* and *Sequentiae Passionis*. At the very end of the

68

Sequentiae Passionis he said that he could see eleven of the twelve notes in the final chord but had to search diligently before he found the twelfth hidden away, and he describes it thus: "Where is the twelfth, the B flat?" Eventually he discovered it! "It is there in the sort of parallel universe created by harp, piano and percussion. Their menace, though quiet, is unyielding."

During the preparation of a lecture, I discovered what I believe to be two of Tom's secrets. The first of them is present at the very end of the orchestral work *Introit: Towards the Light*. The final section of the work is very calm, but we find that there creeps in a suggestion of dissonance in the closing bars. This I believe indicates that one can never know why we are here or what our purpose is. The second secret is in the introduction to *Sequentiae Passionis*. This is written for percussion only and is very bleak and troubled, perhaps to indicate that Christ was contemplating the horror of what was to happen to Him – he was after all man as well as God – and the sorrow of the apparent rejection of His message. However we find two protracted pauses, and these, I believe, are there to indicate the two occasions when the cross fell from Christ's shoulder on the walk to Calvary.

A Stylistic Levelling Off

Early in 1962 Tom decided that it was time to write a second symphony. He felt that he had matured greatly as a composer over the previous few years and was now ready to undertake such a major project. He did not necessarily regard the symphony as the most difficult musical form. Indeed he held that a string quartet could be more testing to write since you have only four instruments to work with and each instrument is exposed. This means that any minor error of judgment in the writing for even one of them will be transparently evident. For him the scale of a symphony was its major challenge. Any composer writing for this form is inevitably judged on his ability to employ the full instrumental resources of an orchestra to creative effect. Of course the judgment will be based on more than conjuring up a splendid variety of noises. The formal demands for both genres should exhibit structure, logic and order. Given Tom's dissatisfaction with his *First Symphony*, it was clear from the outset that he intended to take his time to make sure that the *Second Symphony* was exactly right. It was not written to commission and he would have to fit it into an already busy work schedule. Nevertheless he wanted to prove something to himself and was determined to make a success of it however long it took.

Tom liked time to mull things over, and on this occasion he put the initial sketches aside and instead set to work on a series of shorter works: the *Fantasia for Solo Cello*, *Three Pieces for Piano*, *Carmina Sacra* (for high voice harp and strings), the revisions of the *Piano Sonata* (which was initially written in 1959), *Pas de Quoi* (a series of six little dances), *Six Scots Songs*, and the *Sonatina for Clarinet and Piano*. This prolific period was one of the very few times when Tom put one work aside to compose others. However, following his experiences at Cheltenham, he was determined to show that serial techniques could be used within a composition without also controlling it, and it seemed clear that he was using this time to consolidate his new musical vision. In this respect, I believe he was, if not the first, certainly one of the first composers, to attempt to use serial techniques in this way.

He also had his academic duties to attend to and he and Martin Baillie took the students from their previous winter's classes to Salzburg for two weeks during the summer of 1962. On his return his *Six Scots Songs* were performed in the Queen Elizabeth Hall, London, and they were subsequently sung in Glasgow, Edinburgh, Israel and the USA.

His *Third String Quartet* was performed in October at Aula University, Oslo, and was received enthusiastically by the audience, according to a letter from Bodil Russ of Norsk Komponistforening.

It was in October, too, that Glasgow's outstanding concert venue the St Andrew's Halls, burned down. The cause was never conclusively established, but rumour had it that the blaze began with a smouldering cigar butt that was left after a boxing match. In any case Scotland's musical community thought the loss nothing short of a tragedy. The hall's acoustics were superb, and we all suspected that it would be some time before the venue was replaced. We didn't dream that it would be almost thirty years!

At the beginning of November Tom announced that he had started work on the *Second Symphony* again. I was pleased but not surprised since I knew that once he had committed himself to a work it would not leave him alone. He went on to extensively alter the material from the sketches and I doubt if there was much to recognise from the initial efforts when it was finished. Even so, neither of us anticipated the trouble it would still give him, nor that the *Second Symphony* would not be completed for another three years. It seemed though that he had a new vision for his music which he was determined to make real.

His aim was not to be an 'original' composer for originality's sake. He believed that "The current obsession with 'originality' is a sign of a deep cultural malaise. Originality without knowledge of the history and traditions of music, and an understanding of how it affects audiences, is deeply flawed." More importantly perhaps, Tom said that he felt much happier now that he had decided to use whatever idiom and syntax he felt was best for the work. After the *Symphony's* première he wrote about what this meant to him:

> My first effort [i.e. his *First Symphony*] was diatonically dissonant in idiom, with overtones of Walton. Since then I've tampered with strict serialism but have regressed. I've worked a number of things out of my system, and my new work [i.e. the *Second Symphony*], represents what might be called a stylistic levelling off.

71

He also noted that not so long before he had been criticised for reintroducing tonality into his music. In doing so, his objectors charged, he was failing to be "modern". Now however, other composers were coming round to his way of thinking, in that they were putting concords into their works. Forty years on, Tom's effort to marry serial techniques with tonality appears to have been an innovative rather than a retrograde step.

Variations for Orchestra was performed in March 1963 by the BBCSO in Studio One Glasgow under the baton of Bernard Keefe. When the performance was broadcast the following year, the Musical Times described the work as "tremendously impressive". I have since discovered that for the *Variations*, Tom used a theme that contains all twelve notes, but as he repeated some before he had introduced the complete set, he was not following a strict serial technique. Even then, in 1962, he was already moving towards relaxing the reins of a musical system that he did not deliberately turn away from until he began working on his *Second Symphony*. It is almost as though he is having a bit of fun, saying, "Here are your twelve notes, but see what I can do with them". Whatever the reason, the *Variations* proved very popular with audiences and the BBCSO, and the SNO performed the work eight times between 1962 and 1964.

Also in March 1963 the BBC World Service broadcast an evening service from St Columbkille's Church, Rutherglen, where Tom was choir master. After this, Canon Rooney received letters from Nigeria and Peru congratulating him on the quality of the chorus. Tom certainly worked very hard with the choir each Sunday after Mass. They were all amateurs who had more enthusiasm than ability, and the fact that he was able to mould them into a fairly good choir was a minor miracle.

The next month *Toccata for Orchestra* was given a public performance by the Scottish National Orchestra conducted by Alexander Gibson. This was the first time one of Tom's pieces was performed by the SNO, and it was in a programme devoted entirely to music written by contemporary Scottish composers or by composers resident in Scotland. The critic Brian Newbould described Tom's work as 'brilliantly colourful" in The Herald. In The Guardian he described it as 'brilliantly effective'. Christopher Grier wrote in The Scotsman that while his neighbour deemed the piece to be much too modern, he found it to be "a lively and accomplished work".

We hired a tent and went to Spain during the summer because our three sons suffered from juvenile asthma, and we wanted to build up their stores of vitamin D. We took with us a primus stove, a kettle, pan, cups and lots of packet soups. Along the way we bought lovely crusty bread, ham, cheese and fruit, and dined splendidly by the sides of country roads in France and Spain. On the way through southern France we stopped overnight at a coastal campsite called Le Lavendou where we were caught in a spectacular thunderstorm with high winds, sheet lightning and torrential rains. The next morning we found that our car, a Humber Hawk, was bogged down in sand, and the more we tried to get it out, the deeper it sank. Men from all over the campsite appeared out of nowhere and bodily lifted the car onto firmer ground. We were both moved by the kindness as they were strangers to us.

Once our car was back on firm ground we resumed our journey to the small seaside village of Estartit on the Costa Brava in Spain, and arrived on the feast day of St Iago da Compostela. There the villagers and tourists danced in the streets to a band that travelled from one village to the next, spending about two hours in each. The instruments were brass and woodwind and made sounds that were most unusual to us. Most of them looked like oboes or clarinets that had small stands welded onto them to hold tiny sheets of music. The instruments seemed to take a lot of breath to play as all the players had very red faces. On mature consideration though, I suspect that the band had been well wined at their previous venues. The music certainly sounded Arabian to me and had obviously influenced music in this region since the time that the Moors ruled southern Spain. Tom was intrigued to hear quarter-tones used in dance music and he used them in *Ritornelli per Archi*, a work for strings completed in 1972. That afternoon Tom decided to have the beard that he had grown shaved off. I suspect he grew it to avoid having to join in the dancing. Even though he was only thirty-five, the beard was almost white, and I hated it. He had found it very itchy and he was further encouraged to let the barber remove it by the fact that the campsite had only cold water. The barber took an hour to shave him with a cut-throat razor as the work was regularly interrupted by visits to the shop door to watch the dancing. Though Tom went into the shop just to have the beard removed, he came out having had his hair trimmed and shampooed too – and all for 4p in today's money.

The *Second Symphony* was once again at the forefront of Tom's mind at the beginning of 1964. He said that the third movement was "fighting him every inch of the way." It was proving so difficult that he lost much of the joy that he usually gained in creating something new. I told him that nothing worthwhile comes easily and I also reminded him that even when he was very enthusiastic about something, he sometimes modified his opinion of it after two years or so. Though normally he would have been focussed single-mindedly on completing the piece, during this time he was glad of any distractions that would give him the opportunity to gain a little distance from it. Many years later, when I saw him frustrated while he worked on another musical problem, I asked him why he had chosen such a difficult career. He replied that he had not had a choice, but added that "when it goes right it is the best feeling in the world."

In February 1964 the *Piano Sonatina* was broadcast as part of the Modern Scottish Composers series of programmes. The performer, Julian Dawson, later became assistant conductor to Alexander Gibson at the Scottish National Orchestra. In 1971 he conducted the première of Tom's *Sequentiae Passionis* and made an excellent job of it.

On three successive days in February/March *Variations for Orchestra* was performed. The first of these performances was in Glasgow, the second Edinburgh, and finally there was a broadcast from Studio One in Glasgow which was part of the BBC Sunday Symphony Concert series. These performances were given by the Scottish National Orchestra conducted by Alexander Gibson in a programme which also included Barber's *Piano Concerto*.

The reviewer Brian Newbould wrote in the Guardian on March 2:

> The Scottish composer's Variations emerged as the more thoughtful and substantial of the two works. Each variation presents an attractive new characterisation of the distinctive theme, and at the same time fits aptly into a well ordered sequence that makes as much of the continuity as of contrast. By the end of the twelfth variation we have, without much difficulty, followed the opening few notes of the theme through some far-reaching transformations; when a solo horn recalls these notes in the coda we are given a last tangible proof of a unity of form and content which have already been implied strongly enough at earlier stages. Wilson's scoring is as lucid as his musical thought. He uses fairly normal orchestral resources sparingly and judiciously, and always in such a way as to clarify the musical structure.

In the Musical Times of April 1964 Conrad Wilson wrote:

The young composer who has an ear for the most softly shimmering orchestral colours is going to be worth encouraging. His *Variations*, twelve in number, and based on an original and coldly beautiful theme, had an overall character of their own that was tremendously impressive. But the temperature of the Variations themselves is by no means governed by that of the theme. It ranges from the icy to the white-hot. His ear for orchestral colour is extraordinarily delicate.

We had a lot of illness in the family and among friends during the years 1963-64. At one point we were going to three different hospitals each day. Tom's mother had a problem with her Achilles tendons and was in traction, Stephen was suffering from Status Asthmaticus, and one of Tom's oldest friends, Jim Clayton, though only thirty-nine years old, had been diagnosed with terminal cancer and was hospitalised. This made Tom very depressed. Along with Martin Sweeney Jim was an old friend from his primary school days. Whereas Martin had become a priest and was sent for a time to Nigeria, Jim had remained in Glasgow as a teacher at a private school in Glasgow's West End. Although Jim's health had been poor since childhood all his friends were shocked to learn of his illness. His desperate struggle inevitably made Tom also think of his own mortality and place in the world.

This was the time that Tom started to question whether he was only writing 'musicians' music' - music that would not connect to a wider audience. Tom was a very private person, and when such doubts arose he would often bottle them up for several weeks or cope with them himself. However, this time I could see that this process of internal questioning was not reaching a natural resolution, and I remember eventually telling him that as long as the music satisfied him intellectually, and emotionally, he must trust that others would feel the same. I can only hope that this helped calm his disquiet. He seemed to accept that this was the best that could be done.

At the end of October 1964 the BBC Scottish Orchestra gave the first performance of *Carmina Sacra* conducted by Norman del Mar, who said that it was a very beautiful work. The tenor soloist was Neil Mackie whose performances of it always pleased Tom. I agreed with Norman's description of the piece, but Tom later confided that he was uneasy about it because he felt that this kind of music was too easy for him to write. He felt the words almost set themselves and he had therefore not experienced the usual struggle that was the norm for his more abstract works. However I feel sure that Norman's praise gave

Tom the impetus to pick up his *Second Symphony* and start to work on it again.

The next month the *Fantasia for Solo Cello* was given its first performance by John McInulty in Paisley Town Hall. This rhapsodic piece is a complete re-working of some ideas which first appeared in a film score on the work of Charles Rennie Mackintosh which Tom had written the previous year. Tom described the work as "tonal and lyrical". The *Fantasia* has been played many times since and was described by Conrad Wilson (after a performance in April 1965) in The Scotsman, as: "Eloquent and handsomely written – a work of impressive narrative power and concentration." The Russian 'cellist Alla Vassilyeva has recorded this work on CD along with Tom's *Cello Sonata* from 1971 where she is accompanied by her fellow Muscovite, the pianist (and organist) Alexei Smitov.

Another première in November was a broadcast of *Reverie*, one of the *Three Pieces for Piano*. And yet another première, a broadcast of *Pas de Quoi*, was given in December by the BBC Scottish Orchestra conducted by Robert Irving.

Tom completed his arrangement of *Pas de Quoi* for string orchestra in December 1964. This suite of six little dances was originally written for piano as a wedding present for a friend in 1957. The title is a kind of pun on the French for a dance-step, and the idiom used to indicate something of no importance. As Tom put it, "It is a divertimento – music for fun". Though there are light-hearted moments in other works such as *Touchstone* and *Confessions of a Justified Sinner*, this is perhaps the most carefree composition in his opus.

These were all very satisfying events at the time but Tom's satisfaction was greatly tempered by the fact that Jim Clayton's condition had become critical. Tom visited him regularly during these final weeks and shortly before his death Jim asked that the choir come to his home after midnight mass to celebrate Christmas with him. Tom told me afterwards that the choir had sung several carols round Jim's bed and they all did their best to make it a happy occasion for him. Sadly, Jim died early in the New Year.

Very soon after the turn of the year the BBC asked Tom to write incidental music for a BBC TV programme about Robert Burns, to be broadcast on January 28 1965. The music had to be produced in a very short time but the project helped take his mind off his deep sadness at

Jim's untimely death. Along with background music for various scenes, Tom composed an introductory fanfare, and song settings of several of Burns' texts. Two of Tom's arrangements were premièred in the McEwen Memorial Concerts in April 1965 and at these same concerts, the *Piano Sonata* and *Cello Fantasia* were also performed on successive days.

January 16 saw the first performance by Thomas Rajna of the recently revised *Piano Sonata* in the Great Hall of Nottingham University. This is a major work in two parts lasting twenty minutes and shows some cross-pollination with the shorter piano works *Reverie* and *Tzigane*. In his programme note Tom wrote, "It is cast in two movements and seeks to develop a musical oak tree from an initial acorn – the "acorn" being the interval of a tri-tone. All the major facets of the work, melody, harmony, tonality reflect this interval."

Conrad Wilson, writing in the Glasgow Herald described the *Piano Sonata* as:

> ...a powerful and concentrated work in two movements framed by a softly tolling adagio of rich beauty. In the first movement this leads to, and alternates with, a fierce, rather chunkily written allegro. Then comes a set of seven variations, sinewy and sensitive, full of colours and phrases and rhythms that compel attention, leading to a reprise of the opening adagio, now sounding still more lovely.

Brian Newbould wrote in the Guardian:

> A power of utterance is achieved by an economy of idea and texture typical of this composer. After one performance the impression remains of a dramatic style. The slow variations near the end of the work were striking in their pureness of sonority.

The BBC Scottish Choral Society conducted by Bernard Keefe broadcast the Mass in D Minor from Studio One, Glasgow in April 1965. The programme producer Stanley Pritchard later wrote to say that, "the *Mass in D Minor* is certainly the finest music we have had so far in a studio Mass." Though a wonderful work for amateur choirs the *Mass in D Minor* has not been performed many times since 1965. This was because the Second Vatican Council, probably concerned at the declining number of church goers, ruled that masses were to be held in the vernacular. Fortunately this ruling has now been relaxed.

Tom's next assignment was to compose incidental music for a programme called *"Brush off the Dust"*, a 'retrospective look by Fyfe Robertson at unrelated events in history', for BBC Scotland in July. Shortly after that he was invited by the publishers Bayley and Ferguson to arrange six Scots songs of his own choice, for a series that they were contemplating, to be called the *Kelvin Series*. The other composers involved were Robert Crawford, Robin Orr, Iain Hamilton and Kenneth Elliott.

The songs that Tom chose to arrange were *Adieu Dundee, Auld Robin Gray, A Highland Lad My Love was Born, The Piper of Dundee, The Wee, Wee German Lairdie* and *Willy's Rare and Willy's Fair*. Talking about the process of arranging *The Wee, Wee German Lairdie*, he said:

> I have taken it upon myself to suggest certain minor rhythmic modifications in several places where the difficulties of articulating the amusing text at the required speed are quite considerable. If I may be permitted an Irishism in this context – some of the mouthfuls would otherwise be a bit of a handful.

Two of these arrangements by Tom were performed during the McEwen Memorial Concerts in April, and the *Piano Sonata* and *Cello Fantasia* were heard on successive days. Four of the songs were sung by Patricia MacMahon at a memorial concert given for Tom in the Royal Scottish Academy of Music and Drama on June 26 2002.

Tom spent a few days in London that July to attend the Annual General Meeting of the Composers' Guild and while there he met George Rizza who was on the reading panel of the Park Lane Group. This Group, founded in 1956, provides a platform for outstanding young musicians be they composers or performers. Also at the meeting were Alan Frank, Head of Music Publishing for over twenty years at OUP and Howard Hartog, owner of the agency Ingpen and Williams. Howard Hartog was obviously used to composers "making their pitch" and said to Tom; "You have been here fifteen minutes and you haven't mentioned your own music yet". Tom replied: "I hope that my music speaks for itself". This was very outspoken for Tom, and is a measure of his confidence at the time.

At this time Tom was asked by the Extra Mural Department of Glasgow University to write an article for a forthcoming book, 'Approaches to Adult Teaching'. He submitted the article explaining his approach to musical pedagogy in late April, prefacing it with a quotation from Robert Browning's *Abt Vogler*:

And I know not, that save in this, such gift be allowed to man, that out of three sounds he frame not a fourth sound but a star.

And at the end of the article he wrote:

The wonder of music will remain, for ultimately it is beyond our understanding. But it is important that a sense of awe should proceed as it does in Browning's Abt Vogler from informed insight rather than from ignorance.

Throughout the spring and summer of 1965 Tom was still working on his *Second Symphony* and by the end of September it was finally completed. He always took at least a year to write a major work such as a symphony, and each note was carefully thought about, but this one had been particularly difficult. It bears repeating that during the three years that he struggled with the *Second Symphony* he also wrote *Six Scots Songs*, 1962; *Sonatina for Clarinet and Piano*, 1962; *Sonata for Piano*, revised in 1964; *Three Pieces for Piano*, revised in 1964; *Fantasia for Solo Cello*, 1964; *Pas de Quoi*, 1964 and *Carmina Sacra*, 1964. As a rule he was so obsessed with the work in hand that he could not concentrate on writing anything else, so this was quite a departure for him.

Not all composers shared Tom's preference for working on one piece at a time. The composer Robin Orr, for instance, once told us that he and Benjamin Britten worked on two or more compositions concurrently. With Tom, however, he would typically become so engrossed in the work at hand that he couldn't put his mind to another piece until that one was completed. Composers such as Beethoven left bars empty, to be dealt with later, but Tom never did, he "through-composed". What I mean by this is that he started with bar one and worked his way through incrementally until he reached the end. He did occasionally make a note of a future idea, but that was unusual. This was not because he felt that his method was superior, it was simply his way of working. It was at this time too that he told me that he thought that he had reached an important point in his career. There was, however, no disruption of continuity in his development. He did not go off at a tangent. In fact he consolidated what had gone before. He was not interested in tailoring his style to the fashions of the day, but was open to adopting, and then making his own, methods that would help him towards the ends he sought.

He was kind enough to make me feel that I was involved in this side of his life by asking my opinion right at the beginning of a new work, when the idea was first formed, and at times during the evolution of it. I was very critical and would say, "I've heard that in your music before." But he would answer, "Probably so. Every composer has his own vocabulary, his own fingerprints as it were. That is how we distinguish Mozart from Beethoven." When he had a problem he would tell me that the difficulty was not in seeing a way forward, but that there were many ways forward and only one was the correct one. If he chose wrongly he would eventually realise it because he would come to a dead end. Then he would have to go back to the problem area and rewrite. On one occasion I watched him struggle with a passage for three weeks and so I began to make suggestions. Each one was rejected out of hand and I said, "Well, I wasn't much use there was I?" He disagreed. "You were a great deal of use, at least now I know some of the ways I do <u>not</u> want to go." I was puzzled when he once told me that F-sharp and G-flat were two different sounds, but after a good think I realised what he meant.

In the summer we learned that the BBC was planning to hold a *Festival of Music by Scots* in November and wanted to build one concert around the *Second Symphony*. This was a great honour for Tom but also an expensive one, for the BBC did not help with the printing costs for the orchestral parts. So the at-that-time significant bill we had to pay was between £50 and £100.

This financial inconvenience notwithstanding, the *Second Symphony* was given its first performance on November 29 1965 in Studio One of Broadcasting House by the BBCSSO conducted by James Loughran. (This was the year that the word Symphony was added to the title of what had previously been the BBC Scottish Orchestra). After the concert Jimmie said that he had not fully understood the logic of the symphony until he realised that some of the problems posed were not capable of solution. I remember clearly Tom replying: "Indeed some of the problems posed in the work are not capable of solution". I presumed at the time that he meant philosophical problems because he added, "You could write a book about God, but at the end you wouldn't have any firm answers, and the symphony's questions are like this".

I made some notes of a conversation Tom and I had about the *Symphony* a few days later. (I may say that he was unaware that I was keeping a diary). This is what he said:

> The first movement contains an idea that the orchestra tries to work out; it is dramatic and forceful, and fully orchestral, but ends, without the idea being brought to a satisfactory conclusion. The second movement is apathetic, sparse, and like the quiet centre at

the eye of a tornado. It is an essay in instrumental colour, and is the opposite of the first movement in every way - yet it uses the same basic material. It would be impossible for people to take the third movement straight after the first. The third movement also harks back to the first, but this time it is worked out satisfactorily and so leads to a triumphant conclusion.

The reviews were generally excellent. Kenneth Walton of the Glasgow Herald spoke of the "symphony's sparkling instrumentation and forceful dynamic expression." He said it was "the highlight of the programme - taut, truly symphonic in scale and intention." Writing in The Listener John Purser remarked that, "Wilson's tautly conceived and deeply serious music has recently gained a new and sustainable lyricism," while The Scotsman spoke of the work's "darkly powerful, forceful symphonic argument, immediately attractive and comprehensible."

After the setbacks and frustrations of the *First Symphony* Tom was delighted with the reaction of the audience and the critics. He was now 38 years of age, confident in his own abilities, and the *Second Symphony* was an assured announcement that he was now ready for any challenge.

Early in our marriage Tom told me that it was his ambition to write at least one work in every major genre. He did not want to write one symphony after another, or one string quartet after another, but longed for the flexibility to write what he wished when he wished. After the success of the *Second Symphony*, he found that an increasing number of musicians and organisations were now keen to commission new works from him. So for the rest of his creative life he was able to pick and choose among these offers in order to compose the pieces he wanted to write.

He was always happy to write to commission, not chiefly because of the money but because of the implied appreciation of his worth as a composer. But he knew the monetary worth of a commission and would not settle for less as he believed it was not doing a favour to other composers to do so. The money received was never the reason for accepting a commission. Commissions were to be welcomed because they helped him decide what to write next. The commissioner knew what he wanted, so the form of the work, the forces to be used, and more often than not a rough guide to the length, were stipulated in advance. Tom could therefore accept the commission or reject it as he saw fit.

Composition had to take place around his working week teaching at the university, but he saw it as a completely different kind of activity and so he did not tire of either. Going to concerts at the weekends however was something he did not normally enjoy. He said that he had enough music every other day - including choir on Sunday, so on Saturdays he would invariably spend the afternoon and evening watching sport on television and drinking endless pots of Indian tea.

Shortly after the completion of the *Second Symphony* in 1965, the pianist Audrey Innes asked Tom to write a piece for the Bernicia Ensemble, and so *Concerto da Camera* was born. This was his first commission from a group of fellow musicians. The work took the form of a theme and seven concertante variations with a final coda. He said that "two of the variations divide the ensemble into groups reminiscent of the Baroque concerto. For the others, each instrument is given one variation in which some of its special characteristics are exploited". Tom completed the composition without the protracted struggle that had attended his efforts with the *Second Symphony*, and the première, which was well received, took place in the National Gallery in Edinburgh in October.

The commission from the Bernicia Ensemble followed the typical process for obtaining new compositions. When a musician or a group of musicians wished to commission a composer, the usual process began with them asking what fee he would accept to write what they wanted. A first performance date was also a necessity in order for them to convince the Scottish Arts Council that this was a serious undertaking. A lot of form filling had to be done by the composer to assure the SAC that he wished to fulfil this commission; for example dates of completion, who was to pay for the printing of the parts, and whose property they would be afterwards. Tom always had his own parts printed so that the materials remained in his hands. Once the Scottish Arts Council was satisfied of the seriousness of intent, fifty percent of the fee was paid to the composer upon his acceptance of the commission. When the work was completed, the second half of the fee also came from the Arts Council. Sadly, this state of affairs did not continue, and after some years, when new music had been actively cultivated in Scotland, the Scottish Arts Council changed their rules and only provided fifty percent of the commission fee, leaving the commissioner to find the rest. This was always difficult and sometimes impossible for soloists who sought new works, because, for the most part, they did not have time to fundraise being already busy performing or teaching. However in Tom's case commissioners were always so keen to have their names attached to a new work of his that they made great efforts to find the money. As a major work like a concerto would take Tom a year to write, the remuneration was a fraction of the cost per hour paid to other professionals such as lawyers and accountants. Indeed at times too many requests for works came in at once (four were waiting to be started when he died), and he suggested names of other composers he admired to the commissioners. At the time when he was writing *The Confessions of a Justified Sinner* 1972-75, he was offered several commissions that he had to turn down, suggesting that the commissioners might like to come back when the opera was finished. Fortunately many of them did.

One of the commissions that Tom turned down at this time was a request for a folk opera to be performed on the Fringe at the Edinburgh Festival. Tom was genuinely too busy to meet the request, but I do not think that he was disappointed over having to refuse. He said that a folk opera was not his chosen idiom.

CHAPTER 7 (1966 - 1967)

Writing to Commission

During 1966 Tom's music continued to attract performers and audiences. In March he appeared on television as a conductor when he led a massed chorus made up from the choirs of several churches for a broadcast of Songs of Praise. He conducted professionally on only four occasions. Although he enjoyed conducting our church choir, I think that the performance of a major work was stressful enough without the added pressure of conducting – and besides, he hated wearing a dinner jacket. He had a great respect for the conductor's skill, force of personality, and powers of interpretation, but found conducting a daunting experience which ran contrary to his unassuming nature. Conductors without exception came to him for advice during rehearsals, asking exactly how he wanted certain phrases interpreted, and he came to regard every performance as an interpretation rather than a perfect realisation of his work. In fact, only once did I hear him saying that a performance gave him exactly what he had heard in his head, and this despite the fact that he had never met any of the musicians prior to the performance. That was the performance in Rostov on Don in 1989 when the Rostov Quartet played the *Fourth String Quartet*. Tom's eyes lit up and his delight was obvious to everyone.

Two of his arrangements of Scots songs – A *Highland Lad* and *The Piper of Dundee* – were used as competition pieces during the 55th Glasgow Music Festival that took place at the Highlanders' Institute between April 23 and 30 1966. This was quickly followed by a performance of the *Fantasia for Solo Cello* when Joan Dickson gave its Edinburgh première in the National Gallery of Scotland.

Malcolm Rayment, the London correspondent of the Glasgow Herald, came north at the invitation of the Glasgow editor to hear a performance of *Cosi Fan Tutti* conducted by Alexander Gibson. The performance by the Glasgow-based Scottish Opera which had been founded in 1962, impressed him very much, and he decided he would accept the position of music critic on the paper and come to live in Scotland. Except for official interviews Tom never enjoyed talking with critics about his work in case he might influence them. He particularly avoided them after a concert that had featured one of his works. However in this case he and Malcolm became very good friends and indeed, the first time that Malcolm came to our home in Rutherglen during the summer of 1966 he stayed until dawn. Thereafter he insisted that the tradition must be maintained, and so sometimes his wife Ann, who had to work the next day, took a taxi home, while Tom and Malcolm continued their conversation. They shared an all-embracing interest in music, particularly the work of twentieth century composers such as Stravinsky, Janácek and Bartók, and both men also enjoyed a drop of malt. This friendship was later to result in Tom writing a number of articles for the paper.

At the beginning of September, the *Second Symphony* was performed for the fourth time by the BBCSSO conducted by James Loughran at the Edinburgh Festival. Jimmie took the work the following year to Zurich where it was performed by the Zurich Radio Orchestra to further acclaim.

> For the more adventurous musical minds, Thomas Wilson's *Second Symphony* was the highlight of the programme.
>
> The Scotsman

> The estimable James Loughran piloted the orchestra through Thomas Wilson's thoughtful, purposeful and by no means inconsiderable Second Symphony.... the composer is a constructionist and can well afford to be
>
> Edinburgh Evening News and Dispatch

During the same Edinburgh Festival series, the *Concerto da Camera* was played at a late night concert by the Bernicia Ensemble in the Reid School of Music, Edinburgh University. Earlier in the evening we had hoped to hear Berg's opera *Lulu*, but the performance did not take place because the German conductor asked for his money 'up front' and the BBC said that they did not work that way. Alex Gibson was in the audience and was asked if he would take up the baton but he (very sensibly in my view) declined to do so. After all, he had not been involved in the production, and it could have been a disaster.

Over the next six years Tom had a work performed each year at the Edinburgh Festival. These were the golden years when Peter Diamand, who held Tom in high esteem, was director of the Festival. I'm so glad that we were young enough to enjoy them to the full. One time I blithely invited an administrator of the Scottish National Orchestra to accompany us to a supper after a concert which I thought would be a buffet, only to find when we got there that the table was set for twelve. Quickly I told the doorman we were just being shown the way, and, fortunately our friend took the incident in good humour. Some lessons in life are only learned at the price of a bit of embarrassment and a lot of laughter.

Later in September 1966, the *Variations for Orchestra* was performed again by the BBCSSO, conducted by James Loughran. In an article to accompany the performance Watson Forbes, who was Head of Music at BBC Scotland, observed:

> As each year passes the Scottish composer Thomas Wilson grows in stature and in reputation. Following the acclaim that the first performance of his *Second Symphony* received at the Edinburgh International Festival, the BBC Scottish Orchestra is now reviving the *Variations for Orchestra*. The work dates from 1961 when it received its first performance by this same orchestra. The *Variations*, founded on a theme taken from his own *Pianoforte Sonata* written in 1959, are not serial in composition, but the writing is undoubtedly influenced by that technique. There are twelve variations, strongly contrasted, plus a coda, which is really a re-statement of the theme in a different setting. The work calls for a full orchestra, the composer tending to highlight certain sections in turn, and even making use of chamber music texture – one particularly interesting variation is in the form of a Viennese waltz and is dedicated to Alban Berg, with scoring characteristic of that composer. During the coming winter we can look forward to several new works from Thomas Wilson. Mention should be made of a *Piano Trio*, and he is at present engrossed in a work tentatively called *Concerto for Orchestra*. His output is almost equally divided between chamber and orchestral music – with a bias towards chamber music, since, as the composer admits, (with a keen evaluation of present economic trends), 'It's cheaper to produce'.

The next pieces Tom wrote were *Three Orkney Songs* which were commissioned by the BBC for a radio programme for St Andrew's Day called *A Season for Mirth*. These were based on poems by George Mackay Brown called *The Horse, Our Lady of the Waves* and *The Wedding* (an extract from the poem '*The Finished House*'). On this occasion these very evocative pieces for voice and piano were sung by Joan Alexander (soprano) and Norman Clarke (tenor).

In a letter to Tom after the performance Mackay Brown wrote:

I have just been listening to the wireless programme 'A Season for Mirth', and I feel I must write to you at once to let you know how much moved I was, and delighted too, by your musical settings to three of my poems. None of my poems had had music put to them before, so I didn't know quite what to expect. I am very pleased, and I hope we may be able to collaborate in the future.

On Burns Night 1967 the *Piano Trio* was given its first performance by Wight Henderson, Louis Carus and Joan Dickson. The producer of the programme was Martin Dalby who Tom had met previously at a meeting of the Composers' Guild in London and here they renewed their acquaintance, and in fact they went on to become good friends.

Tom was asked by the BBC to give a talk on January 23 1967 to be included in one of a series of transmissions entitled "Composer's Portrait". He sent Martin a copy of the script that he had prepared and Martin, remembering the "tonal implications" controversy of the Cheltenham Festival in 1962, was keen to discuss how Tom's music had moved on since then. In an exchange of letters between them Martin wrote:

Perhaps it's my two-headedness, but I always feel that the antagonism of the two, if there are only two, stylistic camps is a dying battle, waged only by beings whose talents are on a lesser scale than their convictions. Does your statement that not only can serial and non-serial procedures coexist, but even interpenetrate one another successfully, have any meaning? Surely when foreign elements penetrate, the function of seriality is destroyed. Or do you use serial techniques to rationalise your own musical intuition? I always feel that Schoenberg did this. Perhaps it's the implications of the word "penetrate" that disturb me.

Tom replied two days later:

The antagonism of "serial/non-serial" is virtually dead, but only about five years ago it was at its height and was at times pretty outspoken. There seems little reason to suppose that once the current aleatoric and stochastic (etc., etc.) ideas are past the experimental stage, that battle will not be joined yet again. At the moment the conservatories don't take them seriously, but as soon as they show themselves as serious contenders the atmosphere will quickly change from indulgence to hostility. But it is remarkable how things change. In 1962 my *Violin Sonata* was performed at the

Cheltenham Festival at a concert arranged by the Society for the Promotion of New Music. Richard Rodney Bennett led the after concert discussion and criticised my piece on the grounds that it was tonal in its implications (as well as being serial). I doubt whether many people would advance the incompatibility of 'free' tonality with serialism nowadays, e.g. Crosse's recent works, Bennett's Symphony, Goehr, Henze, Uncle Tom Cobley and all. So you are quite right that the serial duck is dead, but controversy is simply flexing its muscles in the wings.

You are probably right when you say that I use serial techniques to rationalise my own musical intuition. For me methods in the abstract have no validity, i.e. serial theory for me is neuter gender. What I am interested in are the results of this theory passing through the creative consciousness of the individual composer. I have little patience with people who insist on the 'purity' of the system as if it were an ideal, whereas it is really only a tool, a means to an end, which if it is to be of any real consequence must be capable of elasticity and not applied with a sort of rigid orthodoxy. It must leave room for individual interpretation; it must be capable of leading to a variety of consequences. If this is true then the only "function" of serialism is to help music to cohere, to achieve an overall unity. Undue insistence on the grammar and syntax reduces it to the dangers of mere pedantry.

In my diary entry for February 27 1967, I noted "I do not remember Tom ever being so angry." William Glock (Controller of Music BBC London) had commissioned Tom to write an 18-minute concerto for orchestra, the full score to be submitted by Easter. Good Friday fell on March 26 and by late February the work was almost finished and ready for scoring. Then Tom received a telephone call from a member of the music department of BBC London asking for a 10-minute work instead. Meeting this demand in such a short time was almost impossible. After the call Tom exclaimed "Glock is a b......" a word I had never heard him apply to anyone before (or since I may add). The next day he went to see Watson Forbes in BBC in Glasgow. I wrote in my diary, "I hope that he has simmered down a bit because both Watson Forbes and James Loughran have argued with Glock about this, but apparently he is determined to have his own way." For all the protestations from different parties, Glock did have his own way and Tom took up the challenge of writing a wholly new piece.

Two weeks later Glock wrote to Tom:

Dear Mr. Wilson,

I do hope that my request to you that you should write a ten-minute Scherzo for your Prom commission instead of the Concerto for Orchestra, as originally suggested, will not cause you too much inconvenience. The chief reason is that the programme for August 7th, though excellent, is in danger of lasting till midnight. In addition, I have been longing for a new Scherzo, as Haydn always used to ask for someone to write a good Minuet. I am sure you will write a splendid piece, and I am most grateful to you for agreeing to change horses literally in mid-stream.

With best wishes,
Yours sincerely,
William Glock.

By the time Tom wrote back to Glock three days later, he had calmed down considerably:

Dear Mr. Glock,

Thank you for your letter of March 13. In fact things are going well at the moment. The new Scherzo is well under way and up to now I am pleased with it. Also the *Concerto for Orchestra* has fallen on its feet as it were, as it is planned to include it in the BBCSSO's Edinburgh Festival concert (an idea which Peter Diamand has approved). The result of the recent change has been to make me write a piece which otherwise might not have been written and I am enjoying myself immensely in the process.

With best wishes,
Yours sincerely,
Thomas Wilson

Whatever William Glock's reasons for his peremptory decision, the result made life difficult for Tom, but his perfectly polite reply was a lovely example of grace under pressure. And so *Touchstone: Portrait for Orchestra* came into being.

After completing *Touchstone* Tom set the Hilaire Belloc poem *The Moon's Funeral* for the second time to music. The first version, for soprano and piano, was written in 1949 while he was still a student, and there is a fair copy in my hand that dates from that time. I must admit that producing the copy caused me some eye strain and made me physically sick so I never undertook such work again. I was left with a great admiration for copyists who did this for a living. Later Tom mentioned this song to the young conductor of the a cappella group, The John Currie Singers. Keen to promote new music from Scotland, John decided to commission Tom to write a cycle of three songs. As a result Tom rewrote *The Moon's Funeral* and added two more *Night Songs*. In his programme note, Tom wrote:

> The first song is a setting of Lorenzo's speech from Act V, Scene 1 of 'The Merchant of Venice' – '*How sweet the moonlight sleeps upon this bank*'. The style of the music is spacious and romantic, using a rich harmonic palette. The second is a setting of the Edward Thomas poem, '*Out in the Dark*' and takes quite a different view of the night, seeing it as something sinister and hostile. The last, then, is '*The Moon's Funeral*' which is a dirge and sees night in a more visionary and contemplative way ('The Moon is dead, I saw her die') in which the overtones of a fey mysticism produce a weird, almost religious atmosphere.

The Moon's Funeral was premièred in the McLellan Galleries, Glasgow on March 7 1967. The complete cycle of *Night Songs* was first performed as part of the BBC Third Programme by The Aeolian Singers on the January 27 1969.

April saw the second broadcast on BBC Radio of *Processional* (for brass band) this time played by Broxburn Public Band. Broadcasts of classical music were of minimal interest to our children as they were growing up. Finding Tom and me listening to music they would stick their heads around the door and ask, "Is this one of yours, dad?" When told that it was, they would go back to play, apparently unaffected. Nevertheless their father's example must have made an impression, for they all grew up with a feeling for, and appreciation of classical music. Indeed Martin made classical music his profession, and Stephen is a songwriter.

In June the first rehearsal of the *Concerto for Orchestra* took place in the BBC Studio 1 Glasgow. Both James Loughran, (the conductor) and Malcolm Rayment expressed their pleasure on hearing it, while the BBC Scottish Symphony Orchestra tapped their stands to indicate their approval.

By this time Tom was well established as one of Scotland's leading composers, and the critic of the Glasgow Herald, Malcolm Rayment, asked him to write two articles for the paper. These were to be published asked him to write two articles for the paper. These were to be published in June and July, and the subject of the articles was to be about the direction of modern classical music, and the challenges facing the contemporary composer. In the first, titled "Bridging the gulf between composer and audience," Tom wrote:

> Much has been said and written about the "gap" which separates the present-day composer from his audience. In this century music has undergone a series of such fundamental upheavals that the public has found itself largely unable to follow what has been happening. Discouraged and bemused, many people have developed a prejudice against modern music, and have, as a result, tended to limit their musical interests to a period which begins with Bach, and ends with Brahms.

> However, there are signs that this isolationist attitude is in decline. The musical public is undoubtedly beginning to come to grips with the problems of modern music. For example, Stravinsky's *Rite of Spring*, given a riotous première, is now almost a popular classic. More recently I remember with particular pleasure an elderly lady enthusing to me about *Le Soleil des Eaux* by Pierre Boulez.

> Composers on the other hand are keenly aware of their isolation from the public. Their dilemma is that their commitment to the advancement of music often tends to be in direct conflict with their desire to communicate with the listener. (Perhaps composers whose natural mode of expression remains fairly conservative find this problem less acute and the chances of immediate success correspondingly greater).

> Like most composers, I am wholeheartedly in favour of progress. For example, the renewed interest of such composers as Luciano Berio in the spatial element of music (first exploited by the Venetian composers of the sixteenth and seventeenth centuries) may well yield results which will open the door to new and exciting developments.

> The world of electronic sound also looks promising, though I have yet to hear an electronic work which is wholly convincing in its realisation of the potential which is undoubtedly there.

> Again, Olivier Messaien's use of birdsong and other natural phenomena as a starting point for his musical invention may

conceivably encourage future composers to embark on a new and different type of naturalism to any which has been attempted before.

Music NEEDS an avant-garde to chart the path ahead. Composers who devote themselves to increasing the range and vocabulary of music have my unreserved admiration, provided always that I am able to discern in their work a vein of truly musical responsibility.

Unfortunately, progress, however desirable and necessary, often tends to increase the rift between the composer and his audience. Nevertheless it seems to me that the real problem which the public has to face is not so much how to understand what is happening now, but rather to come to grips with what first happened fifty or sixty years ago.

I am convinced that once the public manages to accept fully the music of Schoenberg, Berg, and Webern, and comes to feel completely at home with the serial atonal style which they developed, the capacity to enjoy the music of the present day will follow without much difficulty. For the real problem lies not in the harshness of modern dissonance, or the apparent demise of traditional melody, but rather in the changes which came about in the field of tonality at the beginning of the present century.

Slowly it will be perceived that music has not changed its laws or its expressive ideals, but has rather developed a new idiom, a new language with which to transmit its message. In other words, what has changed is not so much what is said, but rather the manner in which it is said.

The following week the second article 'A composer and his audience' appeared. In it Tom wrote:

In my article last Wednesday I stressed the importance of the fact that musical advances must always stem from musical, and not merely from technical or formalistic, thinking. Unfortunately the ever-present thinking has sometimes become obscured during the course of the present century.

Subsequent upon the first great phrase of serialism exemplified in the music of Schoenberg, Berg, and Webern, a brief period followed (known as total serialism) in which works were produced which sought to apply serial methods not only to melody and harmony, as had previously been the case, but also to all other facets of composition. This was the consequence of logical rather than musical thinking.

Appropriately enough the result of this misguided venture was a disastrous reductio ad absurdum. It soon became clear that a technique of such complete rigidity deprived music of the flexibility of expression which a work of art requires. Ere long, total serialism was abandoned. However, if those concerned had unreservedly concentrated their thoughts on the musicality of what they were doing, it would probably never have happened at all.

Abortive though this little episode was, at least it was distinguished by a positive intention, which made it possible to believe in the sincerity of the composers concerned. It was simply a regrettable but genuine mistake. It is less easy to take such a charitable view of some of the experiments of the present. Certain "composers" exhibit a desire to abdicate wholly from their creative responsibilities in favour of chance procedures. It is important to stress here that chance elements in music are neither new nor undesirable. The realisation of a Baroque figured bass is, within set limits, a highly variable factor which depends on the skill of the player concerned.

Furthermore, the classic composers of the eighteenth century were, for the most part content to leave the cadenzas of their concertos to the invention of the soloist. But in each of these cases (and one could easily quote others) the element of chance is peripheral rather than integral.

I can see no limit to the use of chance procedures as long as the overall framework of the music remains firmly in the control of the composer. Indeed, I have heard, and been impressed by, several modern scores which treat chance elements in this way. But when a composer directs (to give only one example) that the performer may play all, some, or none of the notes written, the situation has got out of hand. I am irresistibly reminded of Hans Christian Andersen's story about the King's new clothes.

Equally regrettable in its lack of musicality is the new pedantry which threatens to grow up around the music of the present day. For example, some critics will tend to take exception to the use in modern works of common chords and other tonal influences, on the grounds that these devices are incompatible with contemporary techniques. This is to elevate technique to a position of supremacy which it does not merit. Technique is the hand-maiden of music and not the other way round. If a composer wishes to incorporate diverse and seemingly alien elements in his work, the only criterion of success should be "does it work?" A score like Berg's Violin Concerto demonstrates that apparently incompatible materials can be reconciled with one another to produce a masterpiece. The extent to which a work adheres to or departs from an a priori set of rules does not constitute valid grounds for criticism. Good music makes its own rules from within rather than submits to them from without.

This is a notably eclectic age. Much of the best music of the present time draws upon a wide variety of dissimilar sources. Success or failure depends on the composer's ability to weld these diverse elements into an integrated whole. If he succeeds he will achieve a new and exciting unity; if he fails, that failure will be only too apparent.

I have mentioned only some of the problems which face music at the moment. Many other difficulties could be cited, but this is no ground for pessimism. On the contrary, I am convinced that the composer-audience gap is getting steadily smaller.

Moreover, once the majority of the musical public has managed to come to terms with the new language of twentieth-century music, and can perceive and appreciate more fully the great works which it has produced, the process of catching up with current developments will be a fairly rapid one.

Earlier in the year, the National Amateur Music Society had commissioned Tom to write a piece to be performed in Madras College, St Andrews University, by the National Youth Brass Band. The product of that commission was the *Sinfonietta for Brass Band*. It was quickly taken up by other bands such as the SCWS Brass Band (who recorded it) and the GUS (footware) Band. These two bands, along with many others such as the Black Dyke Mills Band, the Grimethorpe Colliery Band, the Royal Norwegian Brass Band went on to play all of Tom's music for brass, and each of the works has been recorded at least once.

The *Sinfonietta*'s première performance on July 14 was led by Bryden Thomson. Through this concert we came to know "Jack", as Thomson was familiarly called, very well. Both professionally, and personally, Tom and Jack shared a mutual esteem, and the two of them maintained a warm friendship until Jack's untimely death in 1991. The piece brought brass band music firmly into the later twentieth century. It acknowledges the traditions of the brass band, at the same time as it moves away from the clichés to create music that is, across its three movements, in turns grand, energetic and playful; sombre, nostalgic and melancholic; triumphal, extroverted and jazzy. It uses dissonance, syncopation and percussive brass arrangements in revolutionary new ways and was an immediate success amongst the brass bands that were hungry for something new. As Edward Gregson wrote in the New Music Review for the British Bandsman, "This is one of the finest pieces to be published for brass bands. The band repertoire is so lacking in truly contemporary works that this piece is like a breath of fresh air." It is also worth saying that his brass band music shows a different side of Tom's character which could be both exuberant and gregarious.

After many broadcasts and performances *Sinfonietta* was chosen in 1973 as the test piece for the Second Section of the National Brass Band Competition that was to take place in London. Along with the prominent teacher and conductor Walter Hargreaves, Tom had been invited to serve as an adjudicator for the competition. The prize is so fiercely fought for, and the lobbying before the competition so intense, that Tom and Hargreaves were protected from being "got at" by isolating them in a small room, out of sight of the bands, with some sandwiches, tea, and a bucket in the corner. They were not allowed out under any circumstances until the competition was over. That day he listened to his piece thirty times before they decided that Tredegar Town Brass Band and their conductor J Childs were the winners.

When the Scottish Music Archive was established in July 1967 Tom was invited to become a member of the advisory board, and he served on the six-man committee for the next ten years. The Archive, which was funded by five Scottish universities and the Scottish Arts Council, was to be a national centre where the music of Scottish composers could be collected for documentation and study purposes. A complete record of Scottish composers and their music both printed and in manuscript, as well as cassette recordings would be readily available.

Through the generosity of the University of Glasgow, premises were provided on campus in Lilybank Gardens and the work of building up the library began. I well remember Tom telling me of the lengthy discussion that took place in order to decide just who should qualify as a Scottish composer. In the end, common sense prevailed and it was agreed that the Archive should house the music not just of those born in Scotland, but also those who lived and worked here.

The scores donated by composers and publishers were mostly classical, and the first priority was to collect music composed during the period 1920 to 1968. By the time the Archive was officially opened in 1969, music by sixty composers had been deposited there. The first catalogue listed 1500 items. The Archive was of enormous help to composers, and when, in October 1972, Tom became the first of four composers commissioned by Scottish Opera, the Archive called me in to help with the copying of the parts for his opera, *The Confessions of a Justified Sinner*. The copying was a slow process in which the pages of the score were put through huge rollers that looked rather like an old-fashioned mangle, and were then hung up like laundry for the ink to dry. We literally pegged them onto a clothes-line in the office. Binding them was equally laborious. The modern means of producing parts by way of computers is so much easier and quicker, and the collection has become enormous. Newly named the Scottish Music Centre the archive now caters for all tastes in music.

The University of Glasgow gave Tom the McEwen Triennial Commission, but fortunately the work was not needed until 1968. The piece written for this commission was the *Sinfonia for Seven Instruments*. The BBC continued to broadcast his works too, reflecting his growing reputation.

On 7 August 1967, conductor James Loughran and the BBCSSO, gave *Touchstone* its first performance at the Henry Wood Promenade Concerts in The Albert Hall in London. The performance was simultaneously broadcast by the Third Programme and repeated in September by the Scottish Home Service. This prestigious première was enthusiastically received by the full house of nearly 4,000 people, and on this occasion Tom managed to find the stage to take his bow without any problem. Unusually, however, some of the critics had reservations about the work.

Hugo Cole wrote in the Guardian:

> The orchestra brought with them a new orchestral scherzo, by Thomas Wilson; a 10-minute portrait of Shakespeare's Touchstone. It is nicely scored in a non-extremist but up-to-date way, with contrasted themes that deserved leisured and expansive

development. The trouble was that the composer was always whipping us away to introduce us to the next theme, so the promised momentum never developed. Perhaps Touchstone himself was at the root of the trouble – he is not – like Falstaff, a fulfilled clown, but a withered clown (and even Falstaff needed to be placed in his environment, as Elgar saw, with a good dose of the young Henry). Mr Wilson does give us one fine expressive theme – orthodoxly presented by unison upper strings over heavy brass chords and ominous low tremolos; Rosalind or Audrey? Whichever it was, it vanished never to reappear. Touchstone himself would never have wasted a good line in this way.

Writing in the Times, Stanley Sadie remarked:

> The music has a lot of ideas, and attractive ideas at that, but it is too short for what it attempts to do. For instance, there is one passage of an impassioned elegiac character, which is strong and appealing; but it finishes the moment one has adjusted to it. The piece is scored for large orchestra, but is laid out with a light touch and a sharp ear for sonorities, particularly those of a gentle, evanescent kind.

Of course the critics didn't know that Tom had been given such a short time to write the piece, and that he was restricted by the commission to ten minutes. He felt that these critics had failed to understand his intention which was to portray Shakespeare's professional fool in an appropriately mercurial musical form. When William Glock had suddenly requested a scherzo instead of the work he had originally commissioned, Tom pondered the best way to approach such a composition. While he had written scherzos as parts of larger symphonic works, he had not previously attempted to write one as a self-contained concert piece. He told Adriene Khoury, his second cousin, how he had decided to address the form.

> Rather than write music which would simply be amusing, I felt drawn to the idea of a work in which humour, wit and general attractiveness would allow darker moments of mystery: my problem was therefore to find a subject which would permit of this broader spectrum of mood yet which would remain predominantly "Scherzo" in character.

Tom had long been fascinated by the contradictions within the rôle of the clown, and so it seemed natural that the solution to his problem should lie in making his piece a depiction of a Shakespearean clown. In the beginning he had no idea what he would call the piece. However, when he played a few bars on the piano to his friend Tom Walsh, who had been a fellow student at Glasgow University, the name Touchstone was suggested. The reference was to Shakespeare's character from *As You Like It*, and Tom immediately saw that this would provide the perfect inspiration to complete the work. He later wrote about the character of Touchstone in his programme note for the première at the annual Henry Wood Promenade Concerts:

> A clown whose fooling barely conceals profound wisdom, whose wit is precise, subtle and devious rather than simply hilarious. Whose humour is often edgy, and even boisterous, yet always essentially kind and humane; whose comments on life are invariably comic yet often melancholy and contemplative.

Ultimately Tom knew that the character of a clown is too complex to be captured in its entirety and wrote at the end of his programme notes

> Touchstone has escaped us. He remains an enigma.

The manifold aspects of Touchstone's nature inevitably called for a piece filled with shifting and contrasted themes. To underline his intent, Tom added a quotation to the cover of his score: "Motley's the only wear" (*As You Like It*, Act 2, Scene 7). In the programme notes Tom elaborated his aims:

> As people go, clowns are probably more complicated than most. Though their public task is to make us laugh, in private they are not necessarily funny or amusing. Touchstone, the fool in Shakespeare's *As You Like It* is such a man. My intention in this music has been to suggest some of the enigmatic and apparently contradictory aspects of this most interesting clown's character – his sudden, abrupt changes of mood; his acid wit, "dry as the remainder biscuit after a voyage," his sophistication (he had been a courtier himself), his moments of boisterous high spirits, his sardonic elegance. But perhaps most basic and pervasive of all is the strong vein of contemplative melancholy which runs deep in the man, and is to my mind his most essential characteristic.

Not all critics, however, were dissatisfied with Tom's realisation of his musical purpose. Malcolm Rayment wrote in the Glasgow Herald:

Deeper thoughts, in which there is nothing jocular, predominate, as was almost inevitable from the subject chosen. All the greatest clowns have their sad and wise sides and Shakespeare's Touchstone in *As You Like It* is no exception. This is most effectively brought out in Thomas Wilson's Portrait. Great use is made of rapid and strong contrast, but we are made to feel that they all belong to the same person, since all the material is related. Most of the composition is scored with restraint. This gives a feeling of great intimacy. It cannot be easy to get to the heart of a work such as this where the composer displays a Berg-like sympathy for an under-privileged being, and one whose true worth does not meet with its desserts – not that the composition is in any way programmatic. Both the conductor and the orchestra had obviously taken great pains in preparing this 10-minute piece, the interpretation being revealing and the playing assured.

Leslie Ayre in The Evening News commented:

The composer has set out to indicate not only the comicalities of Shakespeare's clown but also the more solemn and contemplative side of his nature. Indeed, while there are fittingly quirky little themes and rhythms, the overall effect is one of thoughtfulness rather than of fun.

This was a very perceptive comment that had significance beyond the character of the music. Thoughtfulness, rather than fun, was most on Tom's mind at the time. While his career as a composer was flourishing, life on the home front was much more fraught. His father had an operation for cancer, and his mother at this time was weak and unwell. Because they were unable to look after themselves properly in their flat in Rutherglen I suggested that they come to live with us in Stonelaw Drive as we had seven rooms. Though everyone did their best to accommodate each other's needs, it is difficult to look after one's own children and care for aging parents at the same time, particularly when the grandparents have definite views on how children should be raised and how the household should be run. Differences between the three generations grew steadily over the following two years and it was far from the happiest time in our lives.

We lived at the top of a hill and I did not drive at first so I was carrying shopping for a family of seven. Our car was a Humber Hawk without power steering. After Tom had taken me out twice to teach me how to drive, we agreed that I should go to a proper driving school to learn or there would be a divorce! Once I had passed the driving test I was not so dependent on Tom. However, the stress and strain of remaining respectful to his father was affecting me, and I was eventually prescribed Valium by our local doctor. Unused as I was to taking drugs this seemed to have a disproportionate effect because the first night's dose left me drowsy the next day. I do not think that the doctor believed I was in such a state, but after seeing me she told me to 'go home and sleep it off'. After my visit I proceeded to back the new Hillman Imp into a lamp post and when I got home I told Tom "I have backed the car into a lamp post and I don't give a damn!"

Tom was not immune to the tension in the household and some years later he told me that one day on the drive up to Oban for his lecture, he had pulled into a lay-by and wept from the strain of being placed between me and his father. Today one might say that Tom's father was autocratic, but in his defence he came from a generation where men thought it was their right to decide. Though Tom always stood firmly by me when conflicts flared up, usually over intergenerational childrearing issues, it was obviously a real emotional strain for him.

Though our marriage was never threatened by the situation, it was a very difficult climate in which to compose and for this reason I have to say that I regretted inviting his parents into our home. Eventually they moved to Dunoon to live with the Dominican nuns, and our lives returned to normality and a more easy-going regime. To give Tom's mother her due, she did write to me after his father died in 1969 to ask my forgiveness for what happened, and her part in it during that time.

Despite the difficult domestic circumstances he had been experiencing, Tom always had an amazing capacity to lose himself in his music. So while the *Concerto for Orchestra* which was completed in 1967 has its stormy moments, it is more romantic in its conception and execution than tragic or pessimistic.

On August 24, the BBCSSO under conductor James Loughran, premièred the *Concerto for Orchestra*, the work originally intended for the Proms, in the Usher Hall, as part of the Edinburgh International Festival. Peter Diamand, the Festival's Artistic Director, was as delighted with the piece as the orchestra had been during its rehearsal. In his pre-concert talk Tom spoke in his usual understated way about his intentions:

The term Concerto is used here not only to indicate a degree of orchestral virtuosity, but also, and more important, to underline the interplay and interaction of strongly contrasted musical situations upon one another.

Unlike the mixed reception accorded to *Touchstone*, the *Concerto for Orchestra* enjoyed an unqualified success. Malcolm Rayment observed in The Glasgow Herald:

This masterly work probably surprised many who, from the title, expected something of an orchestral display piece. Virtuosity is certainly called upon, but never as an end for its own sake. On the contrary, this is a composition of great emotional intensity and extreme sensitivity to texture and colour. Everything in this magnificent work gives the impression of inevitability coupled with individuality – the distinguishing stamp of a masterpiece.

In his review for The Scotsman Conrad Wilson wrote:

The Concerto is an effective, well-wrought piece. The orchestra is used in a skilled, musical, orderly fashion. Though it contains some strong effects, it is not just a show-piece; some of its most memorable and personal moments come in its softer passages – in its delicate gleams of celesta tone, in an eloquent cadenza for solo cello, in the sensitive woodwind writing. It is a telling, well-argued piece, which one hopes the orchestra will retain in their repertoire.

The Concerto for Orchestra was performed extensively between 1967 and 1970 and was very popular with both orchestras and audiences. When the Scottish National Orchestra brought the piece shortly after the première to the City Hall, Glasgow, the concert was sold out. After one of the 1970s performances Peter Stadlen wrote in the Daily Telegraph:

Thomas Wilson plainly refuses to put pen to paper unless he can think of something to say. Works of less cogent symphonic thought have been called symphonies.

Christopher Grier said in The Scotsman:

Well written and effective, Thomas Wilson's *Concerto for Orchestra* scored a trick with London audiences.

Malcolm Rayment wrote:

> Thomas Wilson's Concerto for Orchestra has already been highly praised in these columns, and this performance can have left little doubt that it is one of the finest orchestral works ever written by a Scottish composer. Indeed Wilson's work was most warmly received. It is this sort of response that can help to transform the dream of a full-sized concert hall for Glasgow into reality.

CHAPTER 8 (1966 – 1970)

Scotland's Musical Renaissance

By 1967 Tom was considered a major force in the Scottish musical scene. Writing about the vibrant climate for Scottish music and the rôle of Watson Forbes, Conrad Wilson the correspondent for The Scotsman wrote on Saturday August 5 of that year, "Now 40 years old, Thomas Wilson is one of the most exciting musical talents to emerge from Scotland in recent years and the BBC is rightly backing him hard." Despite this accolade from Conrad, Tom was disappointed that he had not achieved what he had set out to do in international terms. Though in interviews he was always positive about his decision to stay in Scotland, there is no doubt in my mind that his reputation as a composer would have risen faster had we moved to London or America.

During the Fifties and early Sixties public concerts in Scotland outside of the universities rarely included works by contemporary Scottish composers, or contemporary classical music in general. The most modern works would typically be from English composers like Delius, Elgar or Vaughan Williams. The late 1960s however witnessed a renaissance in Scottish music which has continued until the present day. The groundwork laid by Watson Forbes, the Head of Music at BBC Scotland, and by conductors James Loughran at the BBC Scottish Orchestra and Alex Gibson with the Scottish National Orchestra, were built upon through the formation of the Edinburgh Quartet in 1959. This was further reinforced by the creation of Scottish Opera in 1962, the Scottish Baroque Ensemble in 1969, and Scottish Ballet in 1974. Their support for contemporary music started to attract growing audiences to a greater variety of works. A large part of this new musical impetus was due to the formation of the Scottish Arts Council in 1967, which provided orchestras, ensembles and other musical groups, such as the John Currie Singers, the Bernicia Ensemble and the Glasgow Chamber Music Society with funds to commission and perform new works from the growing number of Scottish composers.

In June 1966 Tom attended a performance of his *Piano Sonata* at Gladstone's Land in Edinburgh, by the soloist Alexander Kelly. The programme also included *Three Antique Pieces* by a young composer John Maxwell Geddes. After the concert John approached Tom to say that he had enjoyed the *Sonata*. Tom replied that he admired John's pieces too and so was born perhaps Tom's deepest and most significant musical friendship. Though John was some fourteen years younger than Tom, they immediately hit it off and met with increasing regularity from that moment on to discuss ideas, music, and their current compositions, over a glass or two of single malt.

Tom and John came from very different backgrounds. However, they were both deeply serious musicians and shared an interest in history and philosophy. Whereas Tom grew up within a religious family of classical music lovers in Burnside, John was raised in Maryhill in a family with a background in vaudeville and popular music halls. As John puts it, "Tom came from the choir, I came from the pit. But we shared a similar approach to composition and found similar solutions to musical problems; Tom in plainchant, I in popular songs".

John was one of the new generation of composers and musicians emerging from the Royal Scottish Academy of Music (renamed the Royal Scottish Academy of Music and Drama in 1968). The Academy could trace its roots back to the Glasgow Athenaeum set up in 1847 when Charles Dickens had delivered the inaugural address. The college had expanded from teaching music to include dramatic arts in 1950 – and in 1962 it was the first UK College to open its own television studio. The product of this vision was to introduce a whole new generation of actors, directors, composers and musicians to the burgeoning television industry in which they would be able to make their living. Many of the fresh young composers and musicians who came out of the Academy looked up to Tom. This was not only because they admired his work, but also because he lived and worked in Glasgow and had never felt the need to migrate to one of the more traditional musical centres. Earlier in the century most successful Scottish composers such as Muir Mathieson and Hamish MacCunn had moved to London but Tom had proved that a composer could make a living (albeit as a music lecturer), compose, and remain in Scotland, even before the heyday of terrestrial television. As John Maxwell Geddes puts it, "Tom was an amazing musician, he was approachable, and he was here."

While the younger generation of composers saw themselves as rebels trying to remake the world, in Tom they found a quiet man who was always pushing his limits but never drawing specific attention to his originality. I think this impressed many of them and Tom is still held in very high regard by his successors. Though he was by no means conservative in his music, and was always striving to develop his language, he did not seek to innovate for innovation's sake. He felt it was better to occupy the centre ground: "When one is there one can view and consider the extreme right and the extreme left, whereas from the extreme outer positions it is impossible to see the whole spectrum of what is going on".

John Maxwell Geddes remembers him at this time as being both an inspirational figure for the new generation of composers and a very knowledgeable mentor, a composer who would always find what was good in another musician's music, who would always be prepared to discuss the work in minute detail, and who would always be prepared to suggest ways to solve any problems that might be there. He was in no way prescriptive in his comments but was good at helping others to find their own voice. John says that, "Even if a neighbour's twelve year old daughter was to turn up with a symphony Tom would have been prepared to help. Whereas I would have just told the parents she was too young to be writing symphonies. In this way he was a much better man than I." That said, Tom turned down many requests to provide individual tuition. While he believed that the techniques of composition could be learned through study, he did not believe that a good composer could be created; it was something that was inborn.

Tom was not an envious man and was always happy to promote others' work and inspire confidence. John Maxwell Geddes remembers too that it was Tom who suggested he should try teaching in the Extra Mural Department at Glasgow University. Having no prior experience in this area, John asked him how he knew he would be any good, to which Tom replied, "Because I like your music."

While Tom had friends like John who were younger than himself, he also had friendships with composers such as Bill Wordsworth who was nineteen years older. Bill was still a very active man who had worked on the land during the Second World War and loved outdoor pursuits such as fishing and hill-walking. Although Tom and Bill played golf together, and were comfortable in each other's company, they never discussed their own compositions in the same way Tom did with John. Instead they talked about developments in music in the twentieth century, as well as philosophy and religion and the deep-seated spiritual convictions they shared.

Bill's music was not as experimental as Tom's (or John's) but was very approachable and his works were played widely in the 1940s and '50s.

Indeed, his music was performed so often during that time that his nineteen-room Georgian house in Kincraig, near Kingussie, was bought entirely with money earned from his performing rights royalties.

Originally from London, Bill felt a little isolated in the north of Scotland, and I think he appreciated being able to communicate with like minds. So, in June, the 2nd Annual General Meeting of the Scottish Branch of the Composers' Guild was held in Bill and Frieda's warm and welcoming home. They were excellent hosts who had a spacious garden that was full of fruit and vegetables. They also kept bees so honey was plentiful. Bill made bread and many of the delicious vegetarian dishes that were served each day. It was inspiring for composers such as John Maxwell Geddes, Bobby Crawford, David Dorward, Kenneth Leighton and Tom to meet each spring and talk in a relaxed Highland setting; to go fishing in Loch Insh, and of course to talk about music, and the business of music.

So from that time Tom went to Kincraig twice a year: once in the spring with a small group of composers, and again later in the year with our family. These two visits book-ended the summer, so Tom and Bill saw each other at least twice a year, though they would also meet occasionally at concerts in Glasgow and Edinburgh, and in London for the meetings of the Composers' Guild. Bill and Frieda were kind enough to present us with silver salad servers for our silver wedding in 1977 and I will never part with them.

Our reason for spending many of our summer holidays during the 1960s motoring around Spain visiting sites of historical interest was because all our sons suffered from juvenile asthma, and the dry heat of mainland Spain helped build up their health for the winter. When we tired of camping we would stay in Paradors, which were in many cases magnificent Spanish castles. These were cheap and beautifully maintained and they cost about £10 per night for a family room. Nowadays they are quite expensive. Tom would seldom drive for more than a couple of hundred miles on any one day, except for the journey from Glasgow to Dover. We would also typically alternate between one week of sightseeing and one week of sea, sun and sand; so for the most part everyone's interests were catered for.

As the breakthrough year of 1967 drew to a close, the Glasgow University Chapel Choir performed Tom's a cappella composition *Ave Maria/Pater Noster*. In a review, Malcolm Rayment described the pieces as being: "Miniature gems with their subtle yet wholly personal harmony." Tom later made a version adding strings to this previously a cappella work.

Just before Christmas the Broadcasting Council for Scotland wrote to Tom to ask whether he would accept a commission to write an opera in one act, lasting an hour, to be broadcast in March 1969. This was one of four operas commissioned by them at that time. Tom accepted the commission, and suggested as librettist the well-known Scottish poet Edwin Morgan whom he knew from Glasgow University, who became Scotland's Makar (the Scottish equivalent of England's Poet Laureate). The subject he chose for the opera was to be the story of John Walford, a charcoal burner from the Quantock Hills area of the West Country who was publicly executed in 1797 for the murder of his wife Jane Stovey.

The idea behind the choice of this story sprang out of a conversation with Bill Wordsworth, whose ancestor the Romantic poet William Wordsworth, had written a poem after he came across Walford's body hanging on the gibbet while out walking with his friends Samuel Taylor Coleridge and Thomas Poole, in the Quantock Hills in Somerset in 1798. It is said that Wordsworth's original poem was destroyed by a later member of the Wordsworth family in 1931, since its subject matter seemed to differ so greatly from the poet's more celebrated later 'Lakeland' works. Indeed William Knight, who published an edition of Wordsworth's complete poems in 1896, is reputed to have declared that he had destroyed the copy he had of the poem, and wrote in his preface of this act of literary vandalism, "I rejoice, however, that there is no likelihood that the *Somersetshire Tragedy* will ever see the light." Such stern censure notwithstanding, some critics believe that Walford's tragic story had a powerful and lasting effect upon Wordsworth's poetry. It was also a story that attracted Tom because it not only had all the dramatic elements required for a good opera, but also it was a tale that demonstrated the best and worst in mankind - a concern that underlies the contrasting dark and light in much of Tom's work.

Because the commission was for an opera lasting sixty minutes, Edwin and Tom had to make some hard decisions on which elements of the story to focus on and which details to exclude. After much discussion they decided to centre the narrative round the question of how a handsome young man with good marriage prospects could fall prey to isolation and lust. The opera also demonstrates the piteous effect that these events induced in the mind and soul of the (unnamed) poet who appears as the narrator in the opera. From letters written at the time we can see that Tom and Edwin referred to Thomas Poole's contemporaneous account *John Walford* (written in 1797), as well as to the account of Wordsworth's missing poem given by F.W. Bateson in his book *Wordsworth: a Re-Interpretation* (1967), before deciding on the narrative structure.

The opera starts with the poet discovering the body on the gibbet and then goes back in time to relate the sad tale of John Walford's love for Anne Rice, and his fling with Jenny that resulted in the birth of an illegitimate child. Though Anne is able to forgive John his past indiscretions, his domineering mother refuses to help John raise the child and with the help of the parish officer forces her youngest son to marry 'the wild strange creature' Jenny, even though she knows they are not compatible and bear no real love for each other. After the marriage John discovers that Jenny is free with her favours and following an argument in the woods he kills her in a rage. After the court sentences him for 'Wilful Murder', John is visited in prison by the clergyman, his mother and finally his former fiancée Anne Rice. In a duet they declare their undying love for each other, before John is taken out and hanged, his body left twisting in the wind. The poet reappears in the epilogue to describe the execution in greater detail, and sings of how John Walford "gave a leap from the board and ran into eternity while the people wept".

Tom's arrangement with Eddie Morgan was that he would be able to modify the libretto as he saw fit in order that the words would lie easily with the notes. Tom had written many songs and so knew the pitfalls that could occur. Although the commission was for a radio production, Tom was careful to write something that could also be easily staged, while remaining effective when only heard. The opera's interlude – suitably revised – became the concert piece *Threnody*. Tom did not believe in wasting good ideas, and whenever he saw that he had not exploited the full potential of an idea in one work, he would use it again.

The Charcoal Burner was recorded in early March 1969 and was transmitted on the sixteenth of the month on Radio 4. The BBCSSO was conducted by James Loughran and many of the cast, who were mostly Scottish, were famous names in the operatic field. I refer to John Robertson, William McAlpine, Ronald Morrison, Johanna Peters, Noelle Barker, Patricia Purcell and William McCue.

The critic Malcolm Rayment wrote that:

> It would have been difficult to assemble a finer cast. The work as a whole gives a strong impression of a symphonic structure in which variation technique is the principle element. Last night's broadcast left no doubt that this is a major contribution to operatic literature. This is Wilson's first venture into the operatic medium but his touch is everywhere assured – and never more so than in the extraordinary aleatoric passage that accompanies the murder.

The approving reference to the extraordinary "aleatoric" passage testifies to Tom's ability to incorporate avant-garde techniques while making them serve his own needs and purposes.

After completing *The Charcoal Burner*, Tom said that he felt that he had reached another important point in his career. Tackling this hitherto untried genre forced him to expand his musical vocabulary. In taking this step, he was not renouncing his past development, but building upon it. He was not interested in tailoring his compositions to conform to the fashions of the day, but he was open to whatever methods would help him towards the ends he sought. Tom specified the notes that the orchestra was to play during the aleatoric passage, but not their individual duration. He specified where the increase in dynamics and tempo was to take place. The device was well-suited to intensify the expressive content of his work, to convey a sense of chaos, and he would use it again in later works.

On a later occasion I was reminded of the reason for Tom's careful attention to all the parts and elements of his scores. At the Edinburgh Festival, I attended an opera in which there was a section in the score where the composer had indicated that the musicians should just play whatever they liked. Afterwards, a trumpet player told me that he had chosen "Yes, We Have No Bananas." To me, this confession offered a good lesson for younger composers on the inherent dangers of allowing orchestral players a completely free hand.

The next summer, after the opera was completed, we travelled to the Quantock Hills in Somerset to visit the crossroads (or four lane ends as they were called), where the infamous gibbet once stood. It was a pretty spot, and we found it difficult to envisage how such a horrific punishment could have been carried out there just two hundred years before. We had similar thoughts in the 1970s when we drove through the fertile, rolling countryside surrounding Belsen Concentration Camp near Hanover in Germany.

I would guess that all artists of any worth go through a transition, when they cease to show how well they can handle the techniques that they have learned from others, and turn instead to defining a mode of expression that is theirs' alone. Herein is true originality – not in pursuing novelty, but in evincing personality; not in doing what is different, but in doing what is distinctive. Polonius had things the wrong way round: "the man is the style." Tom helped me to understand this point.

Early in March 1968, Tom's *Second Symphony* was given its seventh performance by the SNO, conducted by Alexander Gibson, in the Concert Hall, Glasgow. It was pleasing that this concert was a sell-out too. The Aberdeen Press and Journal called it "an interesting and important work." Then on March 26, the *Sonatina for Clarinet and Piano* was given its first performance in Houldsworth Hall, Manchester, by James Gregson and John McCabe. Since the première it has been played countless times, most often by Penny Smith and her husband Geoffrey Haydock, who were members of the BBC Scottish Symphony Orchestra. On the last day of March Tom's choral work *My Soul Longs for Thee My God* was premièred in the Good Shepherd Cathedral, Ayr, for BBCTV. Published by Cary and Co. for the English Holy Week Series, there are two versions of this piece, one for SSA and another for SATB.

A contributor to the Catholic National Church Music Commission of Scotland wrote:

> Thomas Wilson writes in a modern style, but very sympathetically for choirs. He has produced what must be the best music of all the choral settings of the new English liturgy so far. We could do with a lot more from composers of his calibre!

On April 25, *Sinfonia for Seven Instruments*, commissioned by Glasgow University the previous year, was given its first performance by the Bernicia Ensemble in the Randolph Hall as part of the annual McEwen Concerts series. This was one of the rare occasions where Tom conducted his own work. The fifteen minute 'mini-symphony' is scored for clarinet, horn, bassoon, violin, viola, cello and piano. It is an intriguing chamber work with an underlying sense of mystery. His sketches for the work are quite extensive, though, as was often the case, many early ideas were not followed through.

In his programme notes for the *Sinfonia* Tom wrote:

> Cast in one continuous movement the work divides itself into five main parts. The first section is a microcosm of the whole, presenting in quick succession a wide variety of different ideas, tempi and moods, which are later explored in greater depth in the rest of the work. The second section is agitated and dramatic, and more sustained both in mood and tempo than the first. The intensity of the music then declines, and a transitional passage leads to a Scherzo in which the colouristic and textural possibilities of the ensemble are more fully investigated. Simple melodic

phrases for 'cello and violin then open the slow movement and are commented on by the other instruments. The violin and cello then expand their ideas in free canonic style before reverting to the simplicity of the original statement. After this the Coda allows the music to end quietly as it began.

Commenting on its sprightly structure, Conrad Wilson said: "It is a virile, clear cut piece, tightly packed."

Malcolm Rayment wrote:

> One striking aspect of the piece is that the form is so lucid which is rarely the case with single movements in works on a first hearing. Another is that it shows the composer, who is normally unsmiling, and sometimes positively grim, in a new light; this *Sinfonia* could equally be called a serenade.

I would not agree with him that Tom's other works are either 'unsmiling' or 'grim'; however, the *Sinfonia for Seven Instruments* is certainly one of his more buoyant and playful works, with shades of *Touchstone*, written the previous year, and the *Cello Fantasia* from 1964. This mood is also evident in *Mosaics* written in 1981 and the *St Kentigern Suite* 1986. And of course there are comedic dances in both operas. Though the overriding impression of Tom's work is that he wrote serious music, particularly at that time, he did enjoy writing playful – if not light – music. He was deeply interested in the contrast between the Apollonian and Dionysian and he liked to explore these conflicts in many of his works, particularly the *Piano Concerto* from 1985 where he makes clear reference to this in the programme notes.

Glasgow University Chapel Choir gave the première of *A Babe is Born* in December 1968. And soon after this the Scottish poet and music critic Maurice Lindsay interviewed Tom for another BBC radio programme about the state of contemporary music, in which the opera was also discussed. Lindsay's first question was:

> Mr. Wilson, most people with musical training do not find it too difficult to read silently a score written up to about 1940. But a great many contemporary scores are so complex that they find it quite impossible as it were, to hear them in the mind's ear, to hear the sounds the avant-garde composer intended. Do you agree with this?

Tom: I think this is undoubtedly true. Whether or not this is a really serious difficulty is another matter because I think that as music progresses the possibility of performance also increases. There are certain difficulties of course placed in the way of public performance – public apathy perhaps being one of the main ones. But the recording, and the availability of recorded music in many different shapes and forms, also helps to some extent to negate this, what would be otherwise a very serious difficulty. No doubt however as the century progresses we will develop new techniques and new attitudes which will help us to cope with this problem.

Maurice: What I was really getting at was, Beethoven couldn't physically hear, and therefore wrote down all sorts of sounds that, had he been able to physically hear, he would have altered.

Tom: That's not true.

Maurice: I know that's not true, but on the other hand if a person who's really a fairly adequate conductor says he can't hear a complex score, how can the composer hear the score as he's setting down the sound?

Tom: Well I think a composer develops a language of his own. He develops a series of experiences in the composition of music. He develops mannerisms. He develops his own vocabulary. And while this vocabulary is subject to constant change as he himself changes, nevertheless he knows the sort of sounds that he makes, and his ear is particularly tuned in to this vocabulary of his own. Consequently as he writes at his desk, as I do, away from the piano most of the time, (although I use the piano to check the results obviously), one can be pretty sure, pretty exact in fact, as exact possibly as composers of the past have been, about what the results are going to be. It's very seldom that one has to make any serious changes once it has been sketched in this sort of way. I think the difficulty is not so much whether I can hear what I have written, but whether I can hear what someone else has written. This is the difficult part. What I mean is that when I write a thing, when I am sketching something, I can be pretty certain without checking it that it will sound the way I intend it to sound. If, on the other hand, someone puts a score by Xenakis or someone like that in my hand, I would find it difficult to arrive at a total aural appreciation of what was going on. I would be able to get a good idea of the textural factors, and the rhythmic factors, and the dynamic factors, and all the other various things, but it would be very much more difficult to put all this together into a composite impression.

Maurice: You said a few moments ago that you thought that techniques might be evolved to get over this difficulty. What had you in mind?

Tom: Well, it's simply that techniques have been evolving all the time and standards of instrumental performance are constantly going up. We always believe we've reached the threshold of what is possible but this is in fact not the case. I believe that our capacity for aural exactitude will increase also, and that as we meet the new problems, we'll find new ways of solving them.

Maurice: With which one might conclude that Spohr, instead of being one of the leading violinists of his day, might today find himself only in the back row of the BBC Scottish Orchestra's 2nd violins – if there?

Tom: A controversial question, but it's a possibility I think.

Maurice: Not that I'm casting any aspersions on them, one has to sit somewhere in the orchestra. You mentioned also earlier, public apathy – I heard an opera company manager saying the other day that on average the view in this country was that if you put on a new opera by a contemporary composer, instead of getting an 85% audience, that's to say apart from Britten, you run the risk of getting a 15% audience, and this was gradually going to discourage operatic performances. Now I know that amongst your most recent works you have written an opera. Is this a problem you've given any thought to? Do you think opera is in a worse position than ordinary music – I mean than orchestral music?

Tom: I wouldn't have thought so. I must defer of course to the more immediate knowledge of the people who are concerned with making ends meet in opera companies. It's not one of the things that primarily exercises a position in my thinking when I'm composing I must confess. At the same time composers must be practical and take some account of the ultimate state of what they are doing. But I do believe that the situation is not as bad as that. I was in London recently and I attended a performance of Wozzeck, which perhaps is not to be regarded as a modern opera. But in terms of the public, who are the people that we're talking about, Wozzeck is a modern opera, an opera which presents much greater difficulties shall we say than Don Giovanni would do – and the house was full. It may be that later offerings like Richard Rodney Bennett.....

Maurice: And Thea Musgrave, Humphrey Searle, or yourself......

Tom: I think that there is a resistance on the part of the public to acceptance of anything new, and this has been very clearly exemplified during the course of this entire century. The rift between the creative musician on the one hand, and his public on the other, is very serious. I do believe myself that the rift is slowly closing and that we are starting to arrive at a position now where people are beginning to recognise the fact that contemporary music is something vital to contemporary living. And that if they miss out on what is happening in the arts (if they're interested in the arts at all that is), if they miss out on what's happening on the contemporary scene – then the fact is that they are the losers in a sense, not simply the composer. They're missing out on something vital. I think that slowly people are beginning to recognise this fact.

Maurice: It is of course very much easier for the promoter of a concert to take risks, if risks have to be taken, than it is anyone staging an opera because the money involved is so vast. So I suppose the rift, if rift is the word, will always be wider so far as....

Tom: I think that it would be at its most acute in the theatre, yes.

Maurice: Well now, you talk about missing out on the contemporary scene. Where do you see yourself in the contemporary scene? How do you see yourself?

Tom: I hardly think about it. I think probably that the assessment made of my music by other people might well be that I was firmly middle of the road. I am, perhaps, a moderate in my thinking. My moderation derives not from any artistic cowardice but from what I believe is common sense. If you place yourself in the middle of a situation you're able to avail yourself of everything that's going on around about you. If, on the other hand, you adopt an extreme attitude, then you are to that extent out of contact with the other extreme. It seems to me that the emphasis nowadays is far too much upon the 'how' of music, questions of style and so forth. These are very, very important – people like the avant-garde, bless their hearts, are the people who in fact forge the vocabulary for the next generation. And I believe that they're absolutely indispensable and I much commend what they're doing. On the other hand, while I give full importance to the question of the 'how' in music, I'm very much more interested in the old, what I consider the much more important area, of the 'why'. I think it was Stravinsky who said: "There are only two kinds of music, good music and bad music". All I'm interested in doing is, to the best of my ability, writing good music.

Maurice: Well I wish some of our younger critics would take the same view and not print us so many essays in irrelevancy that I think we get. It's also true to say that I think historically, well, composers like Mozart and even to some extent Beethoven were not the avant-garde composers on the 'how' side.

Tom: Quite so. In fact, I would be tempted to take it a little further than that, although elevating concepts like this into generalisations is always dangerous. I would think that the lessons that can be learnt from the history of music would tend to reveal that the avant-garde composers, with certain very notable exceptions, have not been the great composers.

Maurice: Can I just take you up on something there? There's a lot of experimenting going on just now, trying to combine the arts, make them relate. Not the way that music and drama relate in opera, but in the way that poetry and bits of stone for instance are made to be tried in concrete poetry; music and, well, space, playing around with balances of space. Do you think the future of music will produce new situations of this sort or do you remain fairly convinced that music will always have to stand as it were upon its own artistic feet?

Tom: Again I take the moderate view. I believe that both of these are true. I don't believe that music ever develops something like the spatial arrangements and the spatial emphases, which have been arrived at during this century, in a sort of erratic fashion. I'm sure that some use, and positive use, will be made of this in the future. I'm sure that the visual element, which has been brought into musical performance, will be used in the future. I'm sure that things like electronics and aleatoric arrangements and so forth are here to stay. What I'm less sure about is that music in the old sense will disappear. I think that it may well be that some kind of fusion of the old and the new (again my moderation coming to the fore), will be arrived at. And indeed, clearly, the musical style now has sundered apart into such a sort of cult of personality, with everyone pursuing his own little avenue, that I think that it's very possibly, and indeed very likely this will in fact happen.

Maurice: Mr Wilson, thank you.

Tom went to Romania two months after the performance of his *Concerto for Orchestra* in January 1969 in the City Halls, Glasgow. This was to hear the work played by the Bucharest Philharmonic Orchestra, conducted by Mircea Cristescu, in the cities of Bucharest and Cluj. After the first concert he was taken to Mircea's home for dinner. Offered second and third helpings of the first courses, Tom gracefully accepted his host's hospitality unaware that there were a further fourteen courses! Never a big eater, poor Tom was faced with a terrible predicament. After the fourth course, he had to give up and just watched in amazement as the Romanians continued to the end of the feast without any seeming discomfort. While in Bucharest, Tom also met Thurston Dart, the distinguished harpsichordist, writer, and university teacher, who was very impressed by the *Concerto* and wondered why he had not heard any of Tom's music in London where he lived and worked. Dart was surprised to hear that only one of Tom's major works (*Touchstone*) had ever received a performance in London and said that he would remedy that omission when he got home. Sadly, he died shortly after his return to the UK.

Tom was invited by the Scottish Home Service to conduct the BBC Scottish Symphony Orchestra in a performance of *Touchstone* in April 1969. He remembered his traumatic experience conducting an amateur group when they played *Eine Kleine Nachtmusik*, and was not keen to dip his hand in that particular well again, particularly since they required him to wear a dinner jacket. He believed that conductors were trained for the job and that it wasn't his real area of expertise. Nonetheless, he was persuaded to take up the baton again. When it was over, he said that while it was not the unmitigated disaster that he had feared it might be, there were, in retrospect, things that he would have done differently.

During the spring, Tom also taught himself to play acoustic guitar. He had always been fascinated by the use of the guitar in the music of the Western Mediterranean, whether it was Classical or Flamenco. He was keen to explore the potential of the instrument and believed that the only way he could write for it was to learn how it was played. He never became a virtuoso; however he felt he had to explore its capabilities. Because the guitar does not fall among the standard instruments of an orchestra, he needed to know which sounds were possible and which chords would lie easily under the fingers. After one pre-programme talk, a non-musician asked him if he had to be able to play all the instruments he used in his compositions. Tom laughed and replied:

> No, no, though I must understand the quality and function of the instruments for which I'm writing. Far more important is an acute colour sense, for it is the composer's craft to know what will blend with what, and which sounds best suit an instrument. He must know what a player can do in the same way as an architect must dovetail his plans with what is practical for the builder.

The first fruit of this exploration, which he completed on May 28 1969, was *Soliloquy*, a work commissioned by Master Concerts Ltd, at the behest of their chairman, the lawyer John Boyle.

Having completed this work he immediately set to work on a short commission for Robert Oughton, the conductor of the Scottish Cooperative Wholesale Society (SCWS) Brass Band. This display piece, called *Cartoon*, was to be used to demonstrate the virtuosity of the cornet soloist. Tom started to work on the sketches in June, in full knowledge that we would leave on holiday in early July at the start of the school holidays. Unless he was facing a performance deadline, he never had a problem putting the manuscript aside for a few weeks, and would use the time productively to mull over the possibilities. That said he would always take manuscript paper, a pencil and an eraser with him in case he wanted to write. Though perhaps this was more as an insurance against such temptations.

During the summer we travelled as a family for six weeks' holiday to our favourite areas in Spain. We stopped at the Theatre of Carlos V in Granada to hear the Spanish National Orchestra rehearsing *Eine Kleine Nachtmusik*, and for a magical hour we stood in the open air in the curved upper gallery and looked down on the orchestra playing below. Later in the holiday, we spent a few days in Venice and while there we took a motorised gondola to visit a glass works built on an island in the lagoon. On a subsequent visit to Venice we passed by the island graveyard where Stravinsky was buried, and we saw gondolas draped in black for a funeral. I was able to picture the marvellous spectacle that the funeral of Stravinsky must have been, when the choir sang his *Symphony of Psalms* on the banks of the Grand Canal, as his cortège passed down it. Tom was eager to go into St Mark's Cathedral as he wanted to see where Monteverdi had worked, using the architecture of the great cathedral to create specific acoustic effects. Unfortunately we were not aware of the dress code: Tom was wearing shorts and I wore a sleeveless dress, so the guards refused to let us in. Tom was deeply disappointed.

Upon our return from our holiday at the end of July, Tom began to work again on the piece for brass band which he completed in ten days. Titled *Cartoon*, this five minute showpiece features unusual wayward rhythms and incorporates effects then unusual in brass band music. These included blowing though the instruments while trilling freely, striking the bell with the finger nail and clapping the palm of the hand over the mouthpiece. The piece falls into five parts – introduction, scherzo, a more lyrical central section, a repeat of the scherzo, and a short coda. Nigel Boddice has since arranged the piece for trumpet and brass ensemble, and Alan Duguid made another arrangement for cornet and piano.

On November 9 1969, *Soliloquy* for guitar was given its first performance by Julian Bream in the Concert Hall at Anderston Cross, Glasgow. The hall, a godforsaken place, was a converted cinema. After the performance Julian told Tom that he had practised the work for 72 hours, and for the first 43 hours he couldn't figure out what it was all about. Then suddenly it all fell into place.

Malcolm Rayment commented:

> Although not a guitar player Thomas Wilson made use of one when writing this piece thereby ensuring that his demands were practical. A highly specialised technique has not curbed his imagination. On the contrary, it seems to have stimulated it, for his work represents a novel approach to the instrument, yet one that does not go against its nature. On paper Soliloquy looks horribly difficult to play, but in performance it comes off tellingly.

Another critic that I can only identify as J.C. referring to Julian Bream wrote:

> One hopes that this world-famous player will keep the piece in his repertoire.

After the second performance of *Soliloquy* in the Queen Elizabeth Hall, London, in February 1970 Max Harrison wrote:

It was Thomas Wilson's *Soliloquy* that provided the evening's most encouraging moment; angular and dark-toned, but with a noticeably wider range of gesture than the rest of Bream's programme.

A stylistically original work, *Soliloquy* remained intimidating to guitarists for many years. However, it is currently enjoying a renaissance amongst a new generation of musicians such as Stefan Grasse of Nuremburg.

Mass for a Troubled World

During 1969 Tom also composed what I consider to be one of his most prescient works in that it perfectly captured the zeitgeist of the time. The *Missa Pro Mundo Conturbato: Mass for a Troubled World* was commissioned by the John Currie Singers, a group of twenty solo singers, who have performed it many times since, most recently in March 2002 when they performed it at a tribute concert for Tom shortly after his death. Sadly the Scottish Arts Council withdrew funding for the Singers in the 1990s, so Scotland has lost an ensemble of outstanding calibre.

The commissioner John Currie trusted Tom enough to give him the freedom to write what he wished in the knowledge that he would deliver a work of power and integrity. The *Missa Pro Mundo Conturbato*, which Tom started in August 1969 and finished in January 1970, reflects his fears for the future of mankind. Alongside the traditional verbal prayers to God that are part of the mass, we hear in the music the brooding horror of the state of the world as it was when the work was written. Though some people remember the end of the 1960s for the moon landings, it was also a time of global unrest which saw war in Biafra, the Mai Lai massacre in Vietnam, the invasion of Cambodia and the invasion of Jordan – as well as the rise of international terrorism. The *Agnus Dei*, the final prayer of the mass, is a plea to God for mercy for the folly, arrogance and cruelty of mankind. The actual translation of the prayer is "Lamb of God who takes away the sins of the world, have mercy on us."

Some listeners have commented that the *Mass* seems to fade away and have used this feature to suggest that the work showed Tom in a pessimistic mood. I hear the work differently. Despite the gloom of those times, when the world seemed to worsen by the day, Tom was all about balance and I believe that the ultimate message of the work is one of qualified hope for a new future. He was not a gloomy man, but did not shy away from reflecting the darker side of life in his work. He believed the only way to counter the ills plaguing the world was with hope, and trusted that sooner or later mankind would come to its senses. The *Missa* is a major work both in terms of conception and emotional range, despite the fact that it is written for chamber choir, strings, percussion and harp rather than for a full orchestra.

Shortly after New Year 1970, *Cartoon for Brass Band* was given its first performance on BBC Radio by the SCWS Band conducted by Robert Oughton, who commissioned the work.

On March 1, *Missa Pro Mundo Conturbato*, was premièred by the John Currie Singers, at the Reid School of Music in Edinburgh University. The work was conducted by John Currie. Malcolm Rayment commented:

> The immediate effect of the work is one of almost overwhelming expressiveness, but at the same time its formal logic cannot be missed. With this Mass Thomas Wilson, whose development in the last few years has been the most notable aspect of the Scottish musical scene, has taken another important step forward. It is not so much his explorations into aleatoric means that are significant, brilliantly effective though these have proved, but the ever-increasing depths and mastery of his music.

Conrad Wilson said: "The quality of the work and the performance were gripping and masterly."

Before he began to work on the *Missa*, Tom told me that he was going to leave out the Credo (the affirmative statement of belief in the Catholic faith that forms the third prayer in the mass), but we did not go into it in any detail as I did not want to pry. I thought that the reason might be personal rather than musical since Tom expressed doubts about the direction that the Catholic Church was taking at the time. After a performance of the Mass in 1996, however, Karl Gwiasda asked Tom if he had omitted the Credo in order to make the work less sectarian, and Tom replied "Partly, and partly to keep the work from being too long. But mostly because it doesn't seem possible in our time to say 'I believe.'"

Martin Dalby also asked about the omission of the Credo during a published interview with Tom, who said "I feel that its clear categorical, take-it-or-leave-it assertions would have been at odds with the sombre, questioning atmosphere of the work, and its inclusion would therefore have tended to disrupt the unity of the whole. In any case I take the view that the words of the Gloria imply the assertions of the Credo, but being implications, do so in an oblique rather than a direct way, which was better suited to my purposes." Martin Dalby goes on to comment: "Questioning atmosphere? Yes. But is there another if private question lurking discreetly somewhere beyond us?"

What is certain is that religion was at the forefront of Tom's creative consciousness during these years. During 1971 he wrote two other major works based on sacred texts: the *Sequentiae Passionis* (sequences from the Passion), which Malcolm Rayment described as "an extremely important work", and the *Te Deum*.

Tom had shared an office at Glasgow University with Martin Baillie, painter and lecturer in art history since 1957, and they noted that in their continuing discussions on art and music they were often enough using the same, or very similar, terms when describing their respective artistic disciplines. Words such as linearity, rhythm, colour and texture, and in considering historical development, Baroque, Romantic, Impressionist, were common to them both. This led them to the idea of preparing a lecture series that would trace the historical developments in style and form in both fields to see what other common terms and links emerged. The series eventually lasted six years, and the lectures covered the whole millennium up to the present time arguing that parallels existed. The courses were designed to show how developments in the different arts influenced each other. Martin Baillie kindly provided me with some examples of the type of connections they discussed in a recent 'phone call and letter to me:

> The latter part of the 19th century witnessed an erosion of the key system in the interests of chromatic colour, as was the perspective system so long established in painting. The development from polyphony into homophony as seen, or rather heard, with Ockeghem and Josquin, was compared to the step from Botticelli to Raphael where line has lost its independence in serving to define forms within space; the motor rhythms of baroque music paralleled in Pietro da Cortona's Barberini ceiling; the raw emotional attack of Goya and Beethoven, so different from the 'good manners' of the preceding century discussed in terms of changing structures.

> The moves of Chopin and Schumann away from tonality in the 'Prelude in E Minor' and Florestan respectively, prefigure Manet's movement away from Romanticism to a form of Proto Impressionism in the 1860s with Luncheon on the Grass. Contrariwise in the 1870s Cezanne introduced a change away from the "Impressionists" attention to light and shade in favour of a stark chromaticism, a shift later paralleled by the Post Impressionism of Claude Debussy. In this respect it was proposed that Debussy's La Mer should be related not to the Impressionism of Monet, but the Post-Impressionism of Cezanne landscapes, achieving both brilliance of colour and solid structure.

The closing lectures centred on two aspects of twentieth century music, primitivism and emphasis on rhythm, citing Stravinsky and Picasso – The Rite of Spring and Les Demoiselles d'Avignon, and 'analytical cubism' of the pre-war years. The brilliant colour and lack of strict perspective in the work of Van Gogh and Cezanne were compared to Stravinsky's use of polytonality. Likewise, the total disregard of perspective in Les Demoiselles d'Avignon and Cubist works like the Portrait of Daniel-Henry Kahnweiler (where the main colouristic element is rhythmic and the works monochrome) were compared with the dissonance and primitivism of The Rite of Spring which also disregarded many of the existing conventions of harmony, rhythm and form.

Tom said that sometimes music was ahead of art, and sometimes the reverse was the case, and he made some fascinating notes for his lectures on the subject of 'Style and Idea'. Of course stylistic change is a fluid process and the cross fertilisations are not always easy to spot; however, they provide an illuminating area of study. These comparative courses were groundbreaking for their time, and the students found them very interesting. I do wish that the lectures had been recorded and I once suggested that this would make a good idea for a TV programme to an arts producer at the BBC. Unfortunately neither Tom nor I had time to prepare the synopsis he asked for, so the opportunity was missed.

During his career in the Extra-Mural Department Tom always looked forward to his summer trips to the cultural capitals of Western Europe. Now that the boys were growing older, I sometimes wished that I could join him in visits to places like Salzburg, Vienna and Hanover. Whilst we travelled widely in Southern Europe as a family, these were sightseeing trips, and I would have dearly loved to hear his talks on music and art. When he was younger he felt reticent lecturing in my presence and asked me not to go to his classes but surprisingly he did not feel the same about the fore-talks he gave to an audience before a performance. However, after twenty years of marriage he felt more confident and I was able to go along to some of the lectures in Glasgow. But a family matter or something else always seemed to get in the way when it came to the foreign trips. One of Tom's dearest wishes was for us to go together to Vienna and Salzburg when the boys were old enough to look after themselves. Sadly we never did so. In fact I travelled only once with him, and this was to an Easter course in London, where I came down with a bad case of 'flu. Fortunately there was a doctor and a surgeon among his students so I was well looked after.

Of course the trips with his students were not all work. 'Discussions' after concerts often took place in bistros, bars and beer gardens, and though Tom never gossiped, one or two amusing tales did get back to me. As his fellow lecturer, Martin Baillie recalls:

> One summer in the late sixties, Tom Wilson and I were conducting a study tour in Rome, and sharing a room in the student hostel of the university. We were relaxing in the late afternoon after a visit with our thirty odd students to some museum when a knock came to the door. At our "Come in" it was thrown open to disclose a young man in slacks and white shirt, who pulled himself up to his full height, almost drew in an over-generous tummy, paused while we waited expectantly, then sang out in a voice that seemed to spread us against the wall, Viva la Musica! He was in fact a trained opera singer who had apparently not yet made it professionally. Having learned that there was a musician from Britain in residence he had come to pay his respects. I waited all week for someone to knock at the door with Viva la belle Arti.

Though adult education and 'lifelong learning' are now accepted there was a certain mystique about adult education at that time, with frequent conferences to discuss the special needs and problems of adult students. Again as Martin Baillie recalls:

> It seemed that some very particular approach had to be made to motivate the adult student (motivate is a word I remember), who was clearly a special breed: human certainly, or very nearly so, but suspicious of academics, wary of condescension and highly susceptible to boredom, liable moreover to run into the thickets at the first wrong move, but capable of great things, for he was after all mature, experienced, and a lover of learning. The unique problem of teaching adults seemed to find its way onto every agenda. Meanwhile the working tutors studied in their various fields in the naïve belief that knowing their subject was of the first importance. Certainly I have no recollection of Tom and me ever discussing the thorny problem of the adult student, but I am sure that we did appreciate that one had to alter stance a little as between adult and child; knew instinctively that Mr Smith could not be given the belt, Mr Jones made to stand in the corner, or Miss Brown sent home with a note to her parents.

Being a composer, and an increasingly distinguished one over the years, gave Tom's teaching a special character and authority; though it should be

124

said that this does not necessarily mean that specialists always have the knack of teaching. On the contrary, it may be more difficult for the creative musician, painter or writer, who is deeply involved in the craft of his art, and who must work for the most part intuitively, to give conscious rational voice to his inner thoughts. Fortunately Tom had the ability to see his subject from the standpoint of his adult students, who though they had an obvious interest in musical appreciation, often came to the courses with little ability to read a score. Tom realised that it was not that the students were in any way deficient, but rather that they had never been taught how to listen to music on an intellectual as well as an emotional level. He did not minimise the student's difficulties, recognising how formidable and intimidating these must seem, but he believed that the overwhelming desire to learn, and the appeal of the music, would carry the student forward; that here lay the necessity of good tuition – informing the student as the need arose, of symphonic structure, the nature of counterpoint and harmony, and chromatic colour, as elements to be responded to and recognised in the music. He believed that musical ideas were the building blocks of the composition, but one also needed to understand the different ways they could be developed – wherein lies the genius of the composer. As Martin Baillie remembers:

It is worth remarking too that Tom was never dismissive of a student's opinion, however ill-judged. He said: "This is the basis on which we have to build so we must respect it as we seek to change it." He was patient with students' foibles, though having to swallow hard on occasion, as when a student confided that she didn't much care for strings. Students on his courses were obliged to learn to read scores, not as a musician does, but at least in such rough and ready fashion as would help sustain and concentrate his listening; the eyes would be in harness with the ears. This he felt was essential to a proper study of music which was not the accumulation of knowledge but a sharpening of response, an extension and development of the students' tastes, not their abandonment in favour of the tutor's, in a misguided willingness to learn.

A propos of this last point one might add that while recognising the need for the tutor to project, Tom set his face against a performance by the tutor which could come between the student and the work being studied – in this respect "always the song and never the singer".

In this outlook I can once again detect the persuasive influence of Tom's religious education at Blairs College.

More as result of his growing status as a composer than his long service, Tom was offered a senior lectureship at the university. However, he turned it down because he said that it would involve him in more administration and so leave less time for composition. Wanting to recognise him in some way, the Extra-Mural Department took the problem to the Principal, Sir Charles H Wilson who suggested offering Tom a Readership. At the meeting of Senate to discuss the matter, however, Professor Rimmer tried to block Tom's promotion by putting forward one of his own staff – knowing quite well that two Readerships would not be granted at the same time. Tom learned of this manoeuvre from a member of Senate who had been at the meeting. Neither Tom nor I could explain Fred's behaviour, though over the years Tom was not the only member of staff to be treated by him in this way. Fortunately Fred's objection was overruled and Tom received his Readership.

In other respects too the new decade augured well with the radio broadcast of six of Tom's works between January 8 and 22, including *The Charcoal Burner*, the *Second Symphony*, *Touchstone* and *Cartoon for Cornet and Brass Band* - the last piece performed by the SCWS Band conducted by Robert Oughton.

In February 1971, Joan and Hester Dickson gave the first performance of Tom's *Sonata for Cello and Piano* in the Merchants' Hall, Glasgow. These famous sisters taught in the Royal Scottish Academy for many years, and indeed at the time of writing Hester - now in her eighties - still does so, regularly travelling to Glasgow from her home in Edinburgh. At one point in the *Sonata* Tom calls for the cellist and the pianist to become quite confrontational and each one reaches across to play the other's instrument. He called it a "sight piece as well as a sound piece", and this is the only time, apart from the operas, where Tom invites the audience to draw amusement from the visual impact of something happening on the stage. I am not sure what Joan and Hester made of this theatrical request in those more conservative times; however, they performed the required action with bemused *gravitas*. I remember two girls of about eleven sitting in front of us who laughed and were shushed by their parents. Tom remarked to me afterwards that it was "such a pity that people expected all classical music to be serious, intellectual, and so by implication joyless. The little girls were right to laugh. At that point it is meant to be funny".

Tom was aware at this time of changes coming over his music, that since writing *The Charcoal Burner* he had "turned a corner somewhere along the line". He felt freer to experiment, to incorporate avant-garde techniques in his works, and the *Cello Sonata* was a case in point.

In their respective reviews Conrad Wilson and Malcolm Rayment both praised the work, Conrad speaking of the "many striking features, a few of which deserve special mention: the splendid declamatory opening, the occasional (conscious or subconscious?) tributes to Béla Bartók", (whom Tom admired greatly), "the nervy, splintery scherzo which forms the centre-piece of the work; and the cello's slow powerful song towards the end". While Malcolm Rayment expressed his delight at the unconventional instrumentation:

> Much use is made of unorthodox sounds, especially by the pianist who is required to play on the strings, tap metal parts of the frame, and produce gamelan like sounds by sliding her fingers along the strings at the same time as the strings are being struck by the hammers. All of this may suggest an avant-garde type of work in which novelty of sound is the sole aim, but Wilson is not that sort of composer; instead he utilises the discoveries of others for genuinely expressive purposes. Above all else Wilson is a lyrical composer with great sensitivity to colour, and these aspects of the Sonata were extremely impressive. But the work also shows a light-hearted touch that is a new development in his musical make-up.

Since its first performance, the *Sonata for Cello and Piano* has been performed across the world on many occasions. In the 1990s the famous Russian cellist Alla Vassilyeva, and the accomplished keyboard player Alexei Smitov, recorded it in Moscow. The *Cello Fantasia* also features on the same CD.

At the age of forty three, Tom was at the stage when he could accept only those commissions he really wanted to write. Though we were not rich, and though he was frequently offered more lucrative work on films, radio and television, he was very careful about whom he would write for and what he would write. He had reached a point in his life where he knew absolutely the road that he wanted to follow in his compositional career.

Most of his incidental music was written at the beginning of his career, music where the discipline of conveying an atmosphere with relatively few instruments – and sometimes only one – was a challenge. However he did not want to continue giving time to it when he would rather be writing abstract music. So he began avoiding fresh commissions for incidental music. Nonetheless some of the offers he received were tempting, particularly those for TV plays based on works of great literary merit, like *Sunset Song*. Apart from these, however, he rejected most invitations to provide incidental music explaining that he simply did not have time to fulfil them.

Ideas rarely evolved out of his incidental works. However, they could sometimes spring out of a work previously written. Though in most instances, the ideas were reworked so radically that it is often difficult to recognise their original placing unless you listen carefully to both works. One example of this is *Threnody*, which was written between January and March 1970 and grew directly out of ideas developed in his opera *The Charcoal Burner*. As Tom wrote in his programme note, "The work is not simply a series of extracts from the opera, but rather a reworking or synthesis of some of the opera's orchestral music." While this symphonic composition mirrors many of the dark and passionate moods that occur in *The Charcoal Burner*, *Threnody* relates only to itself and is in his own words "simply music".

After the first performance and Radio 3 broadcast of *Threnody* by the BBCSSO conducted by James Loughran in Glasgow City Hall on May 17 1970, Malcolm Rayment, realising that *Threnody* derived from material in the interlude for the opera, remarked:

> The work is eminently suited to presentation in a concentrated form as "absolute" music in the concert hall. It made a memorable impression. James Loughran left no doubt about its merits, getting right to the heart of the score.

Writing in The Scotsman, Conrad Wilson described the work as "a strongly wrought symphonic poem, dramatic and impressive."

Remarkable for being written out of an inner compulsion rather than to commission, *Threnody* was played widely at the time. I think that Tom needed to clear these ideas out of his head, ideas that obviously were left behind from the opera, before he could continue with his trilogy. The fact that *Threnody* was written in only two months also reveals that the piece had already been worked through before he put pen to manuscript.

In June 1970 we moved house. I had always wanted to live in the West End of Glasgow but Tom had been reluctant saying that he did not want to be too close to his work. He was afraid that he would not be able to compose undisturbed, that the department would call upon him as a replacement tutor whenever the need arose. In fact this did not happen. I put forward the idea that it would be much easier for the boys if they went to Glasgow University, which seemed to be more than likely. This would save one and a half hours travelling time each day since the Kingston Bridge had not yet been built and the tram cars were a very slow form of transport. Tom saw the logic in this and so we bought a spacious

Edwardian townhouse in Dowanhill. The mortgage cost us every penny that we could afford, but neither of us ever regretted it and I knew that things would get easier as Tom's salary increased year on year. The West End of Glasgow is like a little village surrounded by a big city, and here Tom was near a lot of his composer and musician friends. There are composers, conductors, artists, writers, actors, and even film directors within one square mile. We were within easy walking distance of the University, and the BBC studios were also close, so it was easy for people of like minds to get together. Perhaps best of all, though, Tom at last had a large study in which to work. We placed his desk near to the bay window and had shelves built round two walls of the room to house his scores, orchestral parts, stereo equipment, and so on. The furnishing was completed with filing cabinets placed along another wall next to his upright piano. This would be his workplace for the rest of his life and is now where I am writing his biography.

Built in 1900, the house has very thick walls so it is very quiet; exactly what a composer needs. Tom was now also more accessible to young musicians and composers who frequently came for advice and help. Although he would never give lessons in composition, he would often give them practical advice before telling them: "Go away and listen to as much modern music as you can. Then write something and bring it to me, and we will go over it together". They all, metaphorically speaking, sat at his feet, and went away encouraged. That said, few of them ever came back with a composition, having perhaps understood through the process of listening, that while you can teach history, principles and techniques of music, the true composer has to have the intuition to know how his or her musical ideas should be developed. Musicians who were preparing to perform his works would also come to discuss matters of technique with him as well as the underlying ideas and emotions that Tom was trying to convey. This was particularly important for a soloist preparing a concerto where so much rests on one instrument.

Surrounded by musicians, and with the BBC just up the road, the whole atmosphere was much more exciting, and though we would always miss the warmth and personality of Rutherglen and the Southside, we never considered returning.

For our summer holidays that year we drove to Italy to visit Rome, Florence, Assisi and the towers of San Gimignano. We usually alternated our six weeks abroad with art galleries and the seaside, but on this occasion it was art galleries all the way and the boys were growing more than a little restless. However they have all grown up with an appreciation of fine art. On arrival at the hotel in Assisi, Tom went for a siesta to recover from the long, hot and dusty drive from Rome, but no sooner was he settled than the boys came back from their exploring to tell us that there was a brass quintet playing in the town square in front of the Temple of Minerva. Naturally we went to listen. The players were students from North Carolina and were part of the university orchestra that was visiting the town to give a concert in the local church. On the evening of the concert I was surprised to see mothers with babies in prams wandering in for a short listen. There was nothing of the formality of a British concert. We all enjoyed the performance and the relaxed manner in which classical music was approached in this part of Italy. Having not heard classical music for a month it was like manna from heaven.

Our holidays were done on a shoestring and we stayed in some really weird places. We really lived it up though if we had money left over towards the end. Once we arrived home with only one penny left but at least I knew that there would be a salary payment from the University in the bank on our return.

During the autumn Tom was approached to compose the title music for a TV dramatisation of *Sunset Song*, the first part of the classic trilogy *A Scots Quair* by Lewis Grassic Gibbon. He not only admired the work, which is set in the Mearns to the West of Aberdeen, not far from Blairs College, but the fee also helped pay for additional furniture and redecoration in the house. In later years he was again commissioned to compose the incidental music for the second and third parts, *Cloud Howe* and *Grey Granite*. As Tom had already been commissioned by Musica Nova to write *Sequentiae Passionis* he really did not have time to compose the incidental music for the whole of *Sunset Song*, and it was agreed that he should only write the music to begin and end the programme. Though he never regarded these pieces of incidental music as 'high art', he took great care over them and took quiet satisfaction in their musical merits. Several years later, a woman from Aberdeen telephoned to ask Tom for permission to use some of his incidental music for *Sunset Song* at the memorial service of her brother, an Aberdeen artist and pilot, whose 'plane had crashed into the sea. Tom was very touched by this request, which he freely granted.

In January 1971, the SNO and the John Currie Singers, conducted by Alexander Gibson, performed Tom's *Missa Pro Mundo Conturbato* in the Usher Hall, Edinburgh, and the City Halls, Glasgow.

In his review for the Glasgow Herald Malcolm Rayment wrote:

> If the first part of the evening was musically slight, the second immediately assumed a very serious note with Thomas Wilson's *Missa Pro Mundo Conturbato* (Mass for a Troubled World), written just over a year ago for the John Currie Singers.

> This work represents an important stage in Wilson's development, which, in the last three or four years, has been as rapid as it has been impressive. He is one of the relatively few composers who have been able to absorb the discoveries of the avant-garde and turn them to truly musical purposes.

> In this work, besides aleatoric passages for voices and instruments, there are un-academic methods of producing sounds, such as playing tremolos on wooden parts of stringed instruments.

> But effects are never used for their own sake and the music can never be called "experimental." On the contrary, it is individual, the composer's personality being stamped on every paragraph.

Alexander Gibson, who had never conducted one of Tom's choral works before, was tremendously excited by the *Missa* which created incredible tension through the use of choir, strings, harp, piano and percussion. After the Glasgow concert we went to his home for drinks and he said to me, "Your husband is a most remarkable man." I replied, "I've known that all along." It seemed to me that it had taken him a long time to recognise Tom's true worth, even though he had conducted many of Tom's orchestral works, and obviously admired them.

Up to this point it had annoyed me that lesser composers were commissioned by the board of the SNO, while Tom was ignored. However, following on from the performance of the *Missa*, Tom was commissioned to write a work for Musica Nova, a festival of new music held in Glasgow and organised by the SNO and Glasgow University. He had complete freedom to choose what this work might be.

Originally the commission from the Scottish National Orchestra was for a short piece but Tom told the general administrator that the piece might last twenty minutes. I imagine they were expecting an orchestral work, but his mind quickly became fixed on writing *Sequentiae Passionis*, the second part of his religious trilogy. Tom always held that form preceded expression, and he needed to have a clear picture of the form the work would take – even before he thought of musical ideas. So when he decided that he wanted to make settings from the Passion, it seemed unlikely that he would be able to hold to the agreed time limit. I remember telling him that he would never do it in twenty minutes but he replied: "Well, it may last twenty nine – it will take as long as it takes!" In fact it took sixty minutes and I think that he always knew it would. Robert Ponsonby did not understand this, and he was not well pleased that the length of the piece would upset his programme schedule. However as I said to Tom, he was getting a good deal more for his money than he asked for, so he should be well content. This was the only time that I can recollect that Tom allowed a work to overrun to this extent, and unfortunately, he would pay for it later.

I don't think that many people who are uninvolved in the creative process realise that once begun, a work of art takes on its own impetus and imposes its own demands, even though its creator applies his own discipline in that he needs to know when the work is complete. The ideas demand their own time in which to make their point. In any great composition the length is exactly right: great composers know when to stop.

Sequentiae Passionis was written between April 1970 and March 1971 during a very busy time for the family when we had many house guests, and our attic was used as a storeroom for second hand clothing collected to raise funds for the visit in 1972 to Israel of the SNO Chorus. Separating himself in his study from the turmoil in the rest of the house, Tom managed to maintain his calm in order to reach deep inside to depict both the horror of the Crucifixion and the rapture of the Resurrection.

In February 1971 shortly before the completion of the work, Conrad Wilson interviewed Tom for a piece in The Scotsman to be entitled "One Man's Music". He started by mentioning a recent article in The Guardian that attempted to survey composition across the UK but made scant mention of anything happening "north of the Tweed". Conrad went on to catalogue the broad range of activity on the Classical scene and stated that "of the home-grown pieces none should be awaited more eagerly than Thomas Wilson's *Sequences from the Passion*." He wrote:

> Wilson has recently, in his forties, begun to reach his full stride as a composer. In work after work he has been showing new strengths, new ideas, a richer command of musical expression, a productive exploration of the sounds of today. His orchestral output was first to benefit: the *Concerto for Orchestra*, the *Second Symphony*, the

Threnody, based on music from his opera *The Charcoal Burner*, all showed how fertile was the soil he had started to till.

Then last year he turned his attention to choral music. First, for the John Currie Singers, came the *Mass for a Troubled World*, a vehement, direct, affecting resetting of the old Latin words, which struck an obvious chord of sympathy in the audience who heard it in an SNO programme last month. Next, for the same forces, comes the new Passion, and then, for the much larger Edinburgh Festival Chorus, a *Te Deum* which Alexander Gibson will probably conduct at the opening concert of this year's Festival.

That he should be willing to tackle, one after another, three pillars of the European choral tradition – not only a Mass and a Te Deum, but a Passion, if you please - says much for the present state of Wilson's inspiration. Dozens of composers, it is true, have dabbled through the years in Masses and Te Deums, and made a fair success of them. But Bach's Passions, the Matthew and John, not to mention those of his predecessor Schutz, are such fundamental masterpieces of the choral repertoire that there has been an understandable reluctance among composers to trespass on the same ground.

Conrad Wilson further observed that Tom's Sequences from the Passion would incorporate aleatory passages just as the Polish composer Krzysztof Penderecki had done in his widely admired and popular *St. Luke Passion*. The works would however differ in other respects. In particular, Conrad Wilson pointed out, "….instead of basing it on a single gospel, Wilson has decided to use extracts from all the evangelists, interweaving these with a number of plainsong antiphonies".

Tom explained that he chose his texts so that the drama would unfold in three parts: first the Betrayals, then the Passion itself, and finally (because he feels that "to end with the Crucifixion would be profoundly negative") the Resurrection. He also played some of his initial sketches for the work prompting Conrad to write:

Musically the piece looks like being a logical follow-up to the *Mass for a Troubled World*. The vividness of the writing has been increased. Even when tried out at home on the piano its impact is shattering. The orchestra, slightly larger than for the Mass, will include such exotica as bongo drums, anvils, and a wooden clapper such as is used in Catholic services during Holy Week. The so-called "screaming cymbal" effect already used in the Mass will be doubled in intensity, and will be the first sound the audience hears – to quote the composer, "a screaming noise from nowhere."

Soloists, as in the Mass, will be drawn from among the John Currie Singers – God is to be performed by three basses, singing either in unison or in three parts, representing as it were the Holy Trinity. Gimmicks, gimmicks some people may say, but Wilson hopes his audience will think his methods for creating a Passion to be both musical and justified, and will not be deterred by the boldness – starkness even – which has been creeping steadily into his music in recent years.

Putting together the parts for such a large-scale work was daunting. On one day I remember eight of us collating the twenty choral parts that were spread out on the edge of a very large round table in John Currie's home in Glasgow. We marched round and round it like a game of musical chairs, each adding our own pages until the scores were complete and ready for binding.

Commissioned for the 21st Birthday celebrations of the SNO, *Sequentiae Passionis* was performed for the first time on April 30 1971 in the Chapel of the University of Glasgow by the SNO and the John Currie Singers conducted by the newly appointed young conductor Julian Dawson.

As I mentioned earlier the length of the work did upset programming somewhat, and caused extra work for the SNO administrator Robert Ponsonby. The work required that the orchestra pre-record the taped passages that introduce the three sections of the Passion. Ponsonby demanded that we pay for the audio engineer and the labour costs of his porters to transport the percussion instruments from Glasgow University's Bute Hall to the Chapel where the recording and the subsequent performance was to take place – at most a distance of 500 yards. He later sent us, what was at the time an exorbitant bill, for £108, for the transfer of the instruments from one building to the other. However Professor Rimmer approached the University Senate who donated £50, while the Music Department donated another £30, so we only had to find the remaining £28. Mr Ponsonby's attitude seemed to be that Tom was commissioned to write a work for the John Currie Singers and an orchestra, and that the tapes were an unnecessary luxury that he would have to pay for himself. Tellingly, the SNO could afford to pay the Italian composer Luciano Berio £2000 for a fifteen minute work for the same event while Tom's commission fee was £300.

Ponsonby further displayed his irritation by making rehearsals as difficult as possible. His decision to use the University Chapel as the venue for the première meant that the concert would not be broadcast. (He placed the other four commissioned works in a City Halls concert that was broadcast.) Furthermore, he allotted so little time for rehearsals that the first complete run-through took place just one hour before the performance.

During the rehearsal, Tom grew concerned that the pauses in the score would make the work appear disconnected, and thought that it would help the piece to hang together better if he reduced or removed some of them. After the première however, he restored them, having become convinced that his original instincts were the correct ones. Rather than interrupt the music's continuity, the longer pauses act as needed resting places along the Passion's dramatic journey. His error confirmed my feeling that he was under a great deal of stress.

The work made new demands of the orchestra and some unusual sound effects were required. One of the percussionists said that she could not play what was written, so Tom took her gently back to her place saying, "Come along, and I will show you how to do it". He never wrote things solely for effect; his integrity as a man and as a musician would not have allowed him to do so. If his scores called for unusual sounds, they were there because he thought them to be absolutely necessary. And always, they were playable. He also included an optional passage which calls for the participation of the audience at the point of the death of Jesus. This is a direct reference to a ritual that used to figure in the liturgy of the Catholic Church during Holy Week, in which the congregation, at a given point, banged their books on the stalls. This he said "produced a sound which always impressed me as both elemental and terrifying". During the Mass of the Pre-Sanctified on Good Friday, clappers are always used at the Sanctus instead of bells, and Tom used this device in the score of *Sequentiae Passionis* to indicate despair at the death of Christ.

In the end, as I had forecast, *Sequentiae Passionis* did give the SNO board much more than their money's worth. Malcolm Rayment said that he "found the music more inventive than Penderecki's much lauded St Luke Passion".

My anger over the whole affair could not have helped Tom, who was now busy composing his *Te Deum*, the third part of the trilogy of religious works written during 1970 and 1971. My anger was assuaged however when the BBC later did Tom proud by recording *Sequentiae Passionis* for broadcast on April 19 1973. On this occasion the John Currie Singers and the BBC Scottish Symphony Orchestra were conducted by John Currie.

Tom completed the *Te Deum* on June 20 1971. The shortest part of the trilogy, it is unusual in being one of the few works whose ending he conceived before writing the full work. Here he knew that he wanted to have a particular ending that would challenge audience perceptions. In February, during the course of his interview with Tom about the Passion, Conrad Wilson asked Tom about his intentions for the still unwritten *Te Deum*.

> Though he (*Tom*) has thought about the music so far "only amorphously" his mind is already working on how he should end it.

> "What would you say," he asks, "to 250 singers producing a powerful, sustained note-cluster which would gradually contract until only one note is left?"

Commissioned by the Edinburgh Festival to celebrate its 25th anniversary the *Te Deum* was originally scheduled to open the Festival in 1971. It was performed at successive concerts on August 21 and 22 by the Scottish National Orchestra and Chorus directed by Alexander Gibson. In the programme the festival organisers wrote: "One would hazard a view that the three sacred works of 1970-71 are Wilson's most telling and successful creations so far." In the event, however, the Festival's inaugural concert went differently than planned. Because Igor Stravinsky had died the night before, the orchestra and chorus began the opening concert with performances of his *Ave Maria* and *Pater Noster*. In its own way, the *Te Deum* also served as a tribute to one of the twentieth century's masters.

John Currie wanted to hear the new work but could not get a ticket as the concert was a sell-out. So Tom said, "Take my ticket; they cannot keep the composer out". His generosity meant that he sat on the steps of the aisle between the seats for the performance! From any seat, however, the music made a wonderful sound – there were over 100 singers in the Festival Chorus, and they gave of their very best.

We were told many years later that Peter Hemmings, an administrator in the SNO offices, had been disappointed in the work because he had expected a triumphant ending, not the quiet one written for the final verse.

O Lord, let Thy mercy be upon us
Who have hoped in thee.
O Lord, in Thee have I hoped;
May I never be confounded.

Tom told me that he deliberately closed the *Te Deum* to leave a question in the minds of the audience – not because he questioned God's mercy, but whether mankind deserved it. The only other Te Deum I know of that could arguably be interpreted in this way is that of Verdi. It was at this concert that I first heard, and took note of, the fine bass voice of John Shirley-Quirk when he sang the solo bass part in *Belshazzar's Feast*.

Writing in the Glasgow Herald, Malcolm Rayment had this to say about the *Te Deum*:

> This is the last and most straightforward panel of a trilogy of settings of religious texts that has occupied the composer over the last two years. It differs from other Te Deums in that it both begins and ends quietly.
> Wilson has avoided returning to the first part of the text towards the end, and a consequence of this is that the dynamic climaxes are almost entirely confined to the first third of the piece.
>
> For its germinating ideas the work draws on its two predecessors – the *Mass* and the *Passion* – but there is no need for the listener to know this. Even on a first hearing there is no mistaking the play of motifs, shared by the chorus and the orchestra, while the overall form is thoroughly convincing. The choral parts are cunningly laid out to avoid unnecessary difficulties. This fine work was given a splendid performance.

Though compositions based on religious works or using religious motifs were to thread his creative life, Tom was not overtly pious. However, he loved the beauty and simplicity of the words of sacred texts, and often turned to them when he was looking for inspiration. In some cases he regarded poetic texts as so perfect in themselves that he could add nothing to them and he rejected them for that reason. This is something that is discussed at length in Vivienne Olive's essay, '"Perfection of Form within Simplicity of Substance": An Analysis of Thomas Wilson's *The Willow Branches* for Mezzo-Soprano and Piano.'

As the concert was at the beginning of the Festival we could then relax and enjoy the next three weeks. We went to hear Messiaen's *Cinq Rechants* which we found very moving. I was particularly impressed by Phillip Langridge's fine voice, and when Tom was thinking of casting an opera the next year, I was able to suggest him as the lead".

CHAPTER 10 (1972 – 1973)

A Trilogy

During the latter part of 1971, the Scottish National Orchestra Chorus and the John Currie Singers began raising money for a trip they were to make to Israel the following year. Coffee mornings were held, and the top floor of our home was filled with clothes for a huge sale to be held in town. Charity shops were unheard of at that time, so the clothes sold well. Tom was also asked to write an essay for the tour programme on the subject: "What's it like to be a Scottish composer?" This is what he wrote:

'Unguarded Moments...'

Unguarded moments hardly ever turn out well. There I was one Wednesday evening quietly sipping my orange juice when Libby McLean, James Moultrie and George Eastop (nice people all), hove to and told me how they planned to issue a magazine to mark the occasion of the SNO Chorus's impending visit to Israel. "All sorts of articles", they said. "Great", I said (in all innocence, not yet getting the message). "Well," they said, "you won't mind doing a piece for it, will you? Tell us what its like to be a Scottish composer" they said. Outnumbered and outmanoeuvred, the only course left open to me was unconditional surrender.

Now the general tenor of this magazine (no reference to James Moultrie intended) is supposed to be "amusing", and that's a real problem, because when composers start talking on this kind of subject the results are usually (to paraphrase a friend of mine), as funny as Brahms' Requiem without the jokes. However they asked for it........

Questions, Problems

People often say "How do you compose? What starts you off?" The answer to the second question is fairly easy – a melodic phrase, a texture, an instrumental colour, a rhythm, a formal pattern of some sort, an image, a deadline – in short pretty well anything may start the juices flowing. But the first question is harder. The real answer is, I suppose, that I don't know (which is not very helpful). The point is that each new piece is like a new beginning, creating new problems to which you have to find new answers – there is no general recipe or formula for composing.

"What's it like to be a composer?" is a bit easier to answer. When things are going well, it's exhilarating, intoxicating, marvellous – when they stick, it's very trying indeed. As a good deal of the time things get stuck, it is necessary to dredge up unsuspected reserves of patience and tenacity to enable you to do unremitting battle with a single recalcitrant bar or note 'til it does what you want. What makes for "explosions", is, that the answer when you finally find it, tends to make what previously was right, become wrong. Then the hostilities begin again and the logical question to ask would be, "Are composers easy people to live with?" (Anyone who cannot guess the answer is recommended to read Madame Stravinsky's account of life with the great man).

One way of looking at composing is that it is a fantastically complex balancing act. A composer must be able to mould his material into a sound formal structure which will not prevent the expressive qualities of the music from developing freely and fully. He must be able to integrate variety of content with overall unity of impact. He must make every note count without ever losing his focussed view of the whole piece. And if that is not enough, he must communicate something "meaningful", he must touch a nerve, awaken a response, say something relevant to his day and age. But here we get into deep waters which cannot be plumbed in one thousand words, if they can be plumbed at all.

Scots music on the move
"What's it like to be a Scottish composer?" My answer would simply be – exciting. Great things are afoot here, a new musical tradition is in the making. One need only look at the success of Scottish Opera, the increasingly high standards of our orchestras, the birth in recent years of many excellent new ensembles. But where does the composer fit into all of this? Again my answer would be simple – his rôle is absolutely central. The basis of a healthy musical life rests not simply on how well we perform, but on how well we create. The composer is vital. More than that, he is the key to the whole situation.

Fortunately this is becoming more widely understood. The composer is now more actively encouraged than he used to be in terms of performances, and financial and administrative support. But the situation is far from perfect and much more needs to be done. Nevertheless, the barometer seems to be swinging firmly in the direction of "Fair". Even now our best music has little to fear from comparison with that of other countries (which is not bad going if we remember that apart from our folk music, we have no continuous musical tradition to build on, and what has been achieved since the war started virtually from scratch).

What we need to do now is aim for the bull's-eye. Let's get rid of our national conviction that the home-grown product can't be much good, and abandon for evermore the "I know his faither" syndrome. Hungary has its Bartók, Czechoslovakia its Janáček, Finland its Sibelius. It could be Scotland's turn next if we help it to happen.

"Communications gap"

The composer today lives and participates in a world of ferment. Inside and all around him new stylistic experiments are taking place, new formal concepts are emerging and new aesthetic views on what music is about are evolving. As a result a communications gap has arisen between the composer, and the listener and the performer. Plenty has been said about that and there is not enough space to go into it here. But make no mistake about it, contemporary music is not something that the musical public or any musician, amateur or professional can opt out of with impunity. It is THEIR music – it speaks to them of their own times. It is relevant to their lives in an immediate way that the music of the past, however great, can never be. If they cut themselves off from it THEY are the losers. But there are problems. What about the amateur musician (in many ways the salt of the musical earth)? What about the large mixed chorus (like the SNO Chorus), for example? If we take it that such a chorus ought to be doing some contemporary works, the question remains as to how they are going to do them. Such works may contain great difficulties, they may use a new, unfamiliar language, and they may increasingly use the choir in ways which differ entirely from the "traditional" things one finds in the big choral works of the normal repertoire.

To be or not to be……..?

The inevitable result is that the amateur will have to develop or adapt his skill to allow him to cope with works using so-called "advanced techniques." That may sound a bit peremptory or even arrogant, but it has always been so. It is a question of evolution, or even ultimately of survival. The large chorus will always be necessary to sing those great works which already exist. But if this repertoire does not continue to expand to accommodate new works, if the large chorus fails to evolve to meet changing musical needs, then it stands in danger of becoming a kind of musical dinosaur. Nobody wants that to happen, and I for one don't think it will if we go about things the right way.

But enough is enough. Anyway, I've just about had my 1,000 words. As "amusing" articles go, I suppose this one will seem to make a splendid funeral address. But there is no need for gloom as long as we always think forward and set our face against stagnation and complacency in our musical doings.

Well, there you are. They asked for it, and they got it (such nice people too)! Come to think of it, I wonder if on that Wednesday evening I was the only one to have an unguarded moment? Even if I promise to include the "jokes" the next time, I wonder if my orange juice and I stand in any danger of being out-manoeuvred again?

The Scottish Branch of the Composers' Guild decided to hold their Annual General Meeting (preceded by a lunch) at Houston House at the suggestion of Bobby Crawford. Situated roughly halfway between Glasgow and Edinburgh the site seemed fair to most of the composers who lived near one or other of the conurbations. We arranged to take John and Lily Geddes and Martin and Flora Dalby in our car. As we were driving John told us all a joke that left us laughing hilariously, with the result that we missed the turn off to the venue. We arrived – very flustered – mere minutes before the lunch was to begin. The guest speaker was Hans Keller, the much-respected music critic. He was also a football fanatic and as Celtic and Rangers (both Glasgow teams) were playing each other that day, Tom bet him a fiver as to who would win. When Celtic did, Hans insisted on honouring his bet, so we had the cheque pinned to the wall of Tom's study. We had promised to take Martin Dalby to the airport on our return to Glasgow. Once again, we got lost, and a very nervous Martin barely managed to make his plane. I don't remember Houston House being used again for an AGM.

During the final months of 1971, Tom received a second request from the Italian guitarist, Angelo Gilardino, to write a work for solo guitar. In response Tom composed *Coplas del Ruiseñor (Songs of the Nightingale)* which is an evocative portrait of the nightingale and the night. Since writing

Soliloquy for Julian Bream in 1969, Tom had composed the *Three Pieces* for Gilardino in the early part of 1971 and these had obviously impressed him as he later referred to *Coplas* as having: "an aura that is personal, deep and mysterious". *Coplas* is an eight-minute work whose core musical idea was drawn in part from incidental music Tom had written for a BBC documentary about the Spanish architect Antoni Gaudi; more particularly the music he composed for the section dealing with the Cathedral of the *Sagrada Familia*. In his programme notes, Tom wrote:

> "Copla" is a term associated especially with Mediterranean music, signifying a measure of freedom or improvisation. The nightingale (el ruiseñor) is the universal symbol of the night – seen here not only as a time of peace, but also of furtive dramas and sudden alarms.

Premièred by Angelo Gilardino in Borgo d'Ale in November 1972 the work has been performed and recorded many times.

The virtuoso German guitarist Stefan Grasse finds *Coplas del Ruiseñor* "a very physical piece where you can almost feel the bird suspiring and fluttering in the notes as they are played. There are so many dramatic moments, moments of silence, a pause for breath then moments of poetry. There is a certain truth in the work, a direct relation between each individual note and the whole composition. Tom pays so much attention to every note, every idea, the development of the music, the dynamics. At the same time as it flows out you can feel the attention to detail and the work that he put into every aspect of the piece." Stefan went on to say that he did not know of another piece that moved him in the same way except perhaps the compositions of J.S. Bach. In talking of Tom's work more generally Stefan offered the insight that Tom's great ability was to combine an almost traditional sense of musical structure with self-determined tonal material and rows of notes that are distinctly late twentieth century. He says he feels that Tom's compositional style reminds him of William Turner's later paintings of ships – rays of lucidity emerging from the fog and smoke – and that like the great painter he too is a master of atmospheres.

In February 1972 we were approached by Geoffrey Brand of R. Smith and Company who wished to purchase the work *Sinfonietta for Brass Band* for £50. Though this was not a great deal of money Tom agreed, hoping that the work would get more performances, since Geoffrey was a well-known conductor within the world of brass. This led to the piece being recorded by City of London Brass for an LP in 1974. In later years we regretted the decision as Tom preferred to keep his works in his own hands, feeling that publishers often did little work to promote performances.

In April, Witold Lutoslawski came to Glasgow to deliver two lectures at the university, and we had dinner with him and his beautiful wife. We all got along famously. Witold was a quiet, gentlemanly man whose English was now excellent. The talk was wide ranging and I remember him speaking of his son in Norway of whom he was very proud. Tom and he shared an admiration for the work of Bartók, but music certainly did not dominate the time we all spent together. I got the impression that Witold, like Tom, was retiring when it came to talking about his own compositions.

During the late spring Tom had a few weeks free from composing before he had to start work on his next commission so we had time to ourselves without the attentions of his 'muse'. He told me that he felt so close to me that he found it odd to have to tell me things, and constantly asked himself; "Why am I having to put this into words?" He felt that I should know things simply because he knew them, although he realised that this was absurd. Nonetheless, I would often say things 'out of the blue' as it were, and he would say "But that is exactly what I was thinking." These telepathic moments happened so often that they ceased to be a source of wonder.

In June, as part of the Clyde Fair International Season at the City Hall, Glasgow, the Lennox Ensemble premièred *Canti Notturni*. Apart from special occasions like premières, we did not always know when and where Tom's works were being performed. Once, for instance, we happened to hear a broadcast of Touchstone, conducted by Irwin Hoffman, who was for a while an associate conductor of the Chicago Symphony Orchestra. This was a transmission of a concert that had been recorded two weeks previously. Another time Professor Graham Hair told us that he had heard a broadcast in Australia of one of Tom's works as it was being performed at a Proms concert in the Albert Hall in London.

Brendan was to begin his degree course at Glasgow University in October so he stayed at home to study during the summer holidays. His chosen subjects were English and Philosophy. He was miffed when he only came second after his first year exams. However he said, "I now know what they are looking for" and he came top thereafter. At the same time, Martin was busy with his O level examinations, while Stephen who was fourteen formed a pop group with three of his friends. A local policeman was their manager and they played at old folks' homes. There is a tradition in

Glasgow that the drivers of the city's black taxis set aside one day in June to take children with special needs to the seaside. The taxis are bedecked with balloons and streamers, and the children are treated to entertainment and refreshments at the coast. Stephen and his group went with the children to play for them. He came home shocked. He said to me: "Mum, I never knew that there were children in the world who suffered like that." It seems to me now that this early experience helped form the caring man that he is.

In July, we flew with the John Currie Singers and the SNO chorus to Israel. At least I flew with the chorus. We decided that Tom should go on the flight that left the next morning. We thought it better that we did not travel together in case anything happened to the plane. Our caution was due to the fact that there had been a recent spate of plane hijackings. The preceding May fanatics from the "Japanese Red Army" had killed 24 people at the Tel Aviv airport we were flying to. Airport security measures were so strict that before our departure even cameras were opened to make sure that nothing was hidden in them. As a result, a lot of film was spoiled. Armed soldiers accompanied us on the El Al flight to Israel, and when we arrived there were army snipers on the roof of Lod (now Ben Gurion) airport. While Tom's later flight was uneventful, the plane that I travelled in went through a quite spectacular storm as we were flying over the Alps. The turbulence buffeted the airplane so I did what I usually do in situations where I am unhappy: I went to sleep.

Israel in 1972 struck me as a strange mixture of ancient and modern, East and West. It seemed hotter than Morocco, and was full of surprises. On my arrival at the hotel in Tel Aviv, I went into the restaurant for breakfast and helped myself to a glass of what I thought was a strawberry milk shake only to find out that it was chilled borscht. I don't think that my taste buds have ever had such a shock. After this, I returned to my room to rest, and I poured myself a very small whisky diluted with tap water. I am not a whisky drinker, and after taking a sip I decided that I would try to do without it after all. Having however been brought up to "waste not, want not", I poured the whisky and water back into the bottle. When Tom arrived I told him that I had bought him a bottle of duty free whisky. He was pleased until we looked at it and found that there was some fungus growing in the whisky and obviously loving where it was! The rest of the bottle was poured down the sink.

The SNO chorus had come to Israel to give performances of Brahms' 'German Requiem' in Tel Aviv and Jerusalem, with the Israel Philharmonic Orchestra. The Prime Minister Golda Meir attended the concert in the

Mann Auditorium in Tel Aviv for the opening of the Israeli International Festival. These were the first performances of the '*German Requiem*' in Israel and they were stunning. The conductor Daniel Barenboim allowed the music to breathe, and during the magical opening bars the hairs stood up on the back of my neck.

Every concert that we attended was full – even those that had no previous publicity. For example, at a recital given by Jacqueline du Pré, Daniel Barenboim, and Pinchas Zukerman, they announced a further concert to take place two days later and within hours there was not a ticket left unsold. Tom and I were royally treated by our hosts. During our visit we had a chauffeur-driven car and guide, and we stayed in an air-conditioned hotel in Tel Aviv. Unfortunately the accommodation for the chorus was not air-conditioned and was overcrowded, and I felt very sorry for them. They slept six to one small room on bunk beds, and the heat was overpowering. It seemed though that nothing could dampen their spirits.

When we were in Tel Aviv and Jerusalem we were somewhat cosseted, meeting largely with people of culture and wealth. The only time we really came into contact with some of the contradictions currently affecting Israel was during the first week when the John Currie Singers gave a concert of their own in the crypt of the Knights' Hall in Old Acre. Tom's *Night Songs* was included in the programme, as well as his *Ave Maria* and *Pater Noster*. The crypt had low ceilings, was pillared, had a sand floor, and was – what a relief – cool! In Old Acre the ground floors of the houses were used as space for the animals. The town appeared at that time to be predominantly Palestinian, and we couldn't help but be troubled by the comparative poverty of these people. On our return journey I asked our official guide, Gideon, what he thought of the Palestinians; he replied that he thought they were all right. But when I probed a little further and asked if he would allow his sister to marry one, he replied with a very definite "no".

During the trip Tom was putting the final touches to *Ritornelli per Archi*, a work for eleven solo strings commissioned by Leonard Friedman and the Scottish Baroque Ensemble. In this work, Tom incorporated the quarter-tones he had heard in the muezzin's call. Because he needed to complete the commission during the first week in Tel Aviv, in time for the Edinburgh Festival première, Tom had been reluctant to make the trip to Israel at all. He acceded only after the conductor Gary Bertini offered him the use of the piano in his flat in Tel Aviv. This kindness enabled Tom to finish his composition. Though he never wrote at the piano, he did use it as a tool to make sure that he was properly translating the sounds that he heard in his head onto the manuscript paper. The work, subsequently described as a 'tour de force', was brought back to Glasgow by Conrad Wilson, so that the copyist, composer Edward McGuire, could get on with writing out the parts. Tom worked hard during that first week and once his commitment was fulfilled we were able to relax and spend the next two weeks sightseeing.

At our request we were also taken to see Bethlehem, Nazareth, Calvary, the Sepulchre of the Rock, and the room where we were told the Last Supper took place. We also saw the crown jewels of King David, the Wailing Wall, and the Dome of the Rock where Abraham took his son Isaac to be sacrificed. Another day, en route to Massada, we stopped at Qumran, the place where the Dead Sea Scrolls were found. When we got to Massada, I suffered from heat stroke and fainted at the top of the cliff where the Essenes had killed themselves rather than be taken by the Romans. As a result, Tom and I did not see the remains of Herod's palace, nor did we swim in the Dead Sea. However, our friends told us that the swim is not a pleasant experience – "a bit like swimming in castor oil". The following evening we went to a Roman amphitheatre to hear an outdoor performance of Saint-Saëns' opera *Samson and Delilah*. Even though we sat on the top seats, the acoustics were so marvellous that we heard everything clearly. The visual effects were amazing; at one point a troupe of horsemen rode over the table rocks onto the stage.

The day before we were due to fly back to Scotland, Tom bought me a diamond ring in Tel Aviv to celebrate our coming twentieth wedding anniversary. When one of the diamonds proved to be flawed, we decided that early the next day we would take the ring back to the Hilton Hotel where we had bought it, to have the stone replaced. However, the next morning at breakfast, we received a letter from our Spanish friends who had been hosts to Martin and Stephen while we were in Israel. Martin had become so ill that he had been hospitalised. He had recovered, and returned to Glasgow with Stephen, but our friends had been within 24 hours of sending for us because of the severity of his illness. I was still tearful when we returned to the diamond merchant. He misinterpreted my tears and tried to console me by saying, "It is only a diamond." I had to explain that my tears were not for the ring but for my son!

In November Alexander Gibson conducted *Touchstone* in the Powell Hall, St Louis, Missouri, during a guest appearance with the St Louis Symphony Orchestra. Throughout his career Alex strove to bring the music of living Scottish composers to his audiences, a cause that he was able to pursue with particular vigour when he became conductor of the

Scottish National Orchestra in 1959. Three other fine Scottish conductors – Bryden Thomson, John Currie and James Loughran, were also strong advocates of Tom's music. However it should be recorded that at the last count there have been 86 conductors involved in the performances of Tom's works over his lifetime, the most devoted of them being Jerzy Maksymiuk.

During the autumn and winter of 1972-73, Tom was commissioned by the Clarina Ensemble with the support of the Scottish Arts Council to write *Complementi*. This fourteen minute piece for clarinet (doubling bass clarinet), violin, cello and piano is in one continuous movement and is concerned with the development of ideas and how they complement and interpenetrate each other. Tom always strove to find titles that would not just identify a piece but describe it. For example he said that he chose the title *Complementi* to indicate "something added to something else". It is also a good example of the way he would experiment with unusual combinations of instruments, working with balance and contrast to create a satisfying whole. I remember him telling me at the time: "In a drama of sound the ideas are brought together till they form a unity. This is a plot you might find in a novel or a play. It is an expression of the same human instinct."

He completed *Complementi* on February 3 1973 and it was performed for the first time by the Clarina Ensemble on February 22 in the Fore Hall of Glasgow University. Malcolm Rayment supplied the following commentary on *Complementi* in an article in The Glasgow Herald:

> When writing programme notes for his works Wilson usually speaks of several sections, but this is only part of the truth. His one-movement compositions have the contrast and emotional range we associate with works of three or more. Moreover their construction incorporates elements of variation and sonata form. Taking *Complementi* as an example we find an exposition made up of four contrasting groups of material, each associated with a different instrument and indeed stemming from its natural character. In all that follows these basic elements interweave with each other in complementary ways, hence the title of the piece, which would be equally applicable to most of the composer's non-programmatic works. By making much use of small motifs, which can consist of as few as two notes, the listener can readily perceive the connections between the various sections, and consequently the unity of the whole. Also helpful in this direction is the textural clarity that is one of the hallmarks of this composer.

Another reviewer afterwards hailed it as "a superb new work".

During the spring of 1973, Tom was commissioned to write a score for Scottish Theatre Ballet using only two percussion players. The artist George Devlin designed the set, and the choreography was by Walter Gore, a famous figure in the world of ballet. Titled *The Embers of Glencoe*, the ballet was performed 29 times during September and October, in Glasgow, Stirling, Aberdeen, and Nottingham. Then it sank without trace! At the time it was the only ballet created in its entirety for Scottish Ballet. One reviewer expressed reservations about the choreography and overall production but noted that: "The music has oblique strength which could supply the backbone for a moving Celtic ballet." Another noted that it was "a strong and interesting score" that featured wood blocks and temple blocks, as well as drums, tambourines and cymbals." This was the only ballet score that Tom composed and I think he enjoyed this novel collaborative experience. I think it also provided creative preparation for the bigger challenge of the commissions that lay ahead.

CHAPTER 11 (1972 - 1975)

Writing an Opera

Shortly after our return from Israel, Scottish Opera approached Tom with a commission to write a full-length opera. It was to be one of four that they planned to commission from Scottish composers at that time, and Tom was delighted to be asked. Curiously, he had been talking with John Currie about the idea of writing an opera after a concert at the Glasgow City Chambers the week before, so it was surprising that the approach should be made so soon after. Tom's previous opera *The Charcoal Burner* had been commissioned by the BBC for radio (although he wrote it so that it could also be staged), and it had to be just less than one hour in length to allow for opening and closing announcements. The idea of writing a full length opera was therefore a new challenge to be relished.

Tom was allowed a chamber orchestra of forty-five players, three main singers, and a chorus limited to twenty. He said that because he had other commissions to fulfil, he could not have the opera ready before the end of 1975, and Scottish Opera accepted that condition and scheduled the première for 1976.

The first choice he faced was to select the right librettist. Since he had conducted many of Tom's choral works in the past, Tom knew that John Currie understood his music very well indeed, and felt that he would be the right person to undertake an adaptation if the appropriate work could be found. However, as John explained to me recently, this is not always an easy matter:

It is quite difficult to find an appropriate text to adapt for a new classical opera, and for this reason composers frequently ask publishers to commission writers to come up with appropriate original stories. It was especially difficult for Tom since he had not written a long work in English before apart from *The Charcoal Burner* and sections of *Sequentiae Passionis* and he needed to find a work with suitable character-driven subject matter and a style and metre suitable to his artistic voice.

Though Tom claimed in one interview to be no literary scholar, he was a great reader with a wide range of interests. His memory for the names of characters in classical novels amazed me – it was as much as I could do to remember the plots! One of the books that impressed him most at this time was *Bury My Heart at Wounded Knee*, the story of a Native American massacre, though this did not strike him as the appropriate subject for a Scottish opera.

It was John who first suggested adapting *The Private Memoirs and Confessions of a Justified Sinner*, the remarkable novel written by the poet James Hogg in 1824 when he was fifty-four years old. Having read the work Tom immediately agreed. *The Private Memoirs and Confessions of a Justified Sinner* is one of the most singular works of Scottish fiction. Written in two sections from two different viewpoints, it is a tale that concerns the Calvinistic belief in, and the implications of, "predestination" as a theological idea. An anti-hero narrative, it has often been hailed for its contemporary sensibility by modernists such as André Gide (and more recently the post-modernists). That said its subject matter is first and foremost Scottish Presbyterian, and was therefore familiar to both John Currie and Tom. I think the sheer strangeness of the tale, yet the familiarity of the characters attracted them. As John explained:

> My parents were 'cheerful' Calvinists and so I had an instinctive understanding for the material, whereas Tom was part of a strict Catholic family whose ethos was of a quite different nature. It's not a realistic story, but rather a psychological and spiritual study. I therefore think Tom was attracted because, firstly, it is a completely character-driven piece and, secondly, he realised he would be able to work on two levels at the same time.

The idea of predestination is that since God is omnipotent he can choose the 'elect' because he knows who they are going to be, and they in turn can be very sure of their spiritual position. It's a bit like the Bertrand Russell limerick:

> *There was a young man who said, Damn!*
> *I learned with regret that I am*
> *A creature that moves*
> *In predestinate grooves*
> *In short, not a bus, but a tram.*

The central idea that drives the novel is that because the main character Robert Wringhim is told that he is one of the elect, he comes to believe that this gives him a licence to do what he wants.

John went on to talk more about the process of adaptation:

> The novel is structured in a very interesting way as a diary within a diary, though we decided early on to adapt the work only from the second book, the Sinner's (Robert Wringhim's) diary. We agreed that we should write the libretto based solely on the Sinner's version of events. We also decided that it should be written in the muscular language of the Orthodox King James Bible, which was the bible used by the Calvinists; not beautiful language, but strong.

> The psychology of the book is very interesting since it also features the enigmatic character of Gil-Martin, who can be seen as either Satan or as a satanic alter ego 'imagined' by the Sinner. There was a great deal of talk about other similar operas like *Don Giovanni*, (to which Tom makes a direct musical reference in Act 3) and the available ambiguities in the text and story of the Sinner. I remember we talked endlessly about the notion of Satan in literature in works like *Paradise Lost*, and how often he is represented as suave and interesting.

Tom's view was that Robert Wringhim was both a perpetrator of terrible crimes, and at the same time an easily swayed victim of his religious upbringing, who was shamed by his family and society. (There was always the covert suggestion that Wringhim was illegitimate). Tom was struck by the extremities of good and evil as presented in the work and their musical implications. It was a work that was on one level really clear cut, and on the other very complicated, with lots of factors bearing on it from every direction. The principal characters are very complex and devious. The narrative is also surprising in the way it twists and turns and subverts the expectations of the audience.

For Tom, it was this complex interweaving of the psychology, philosophy and social conditioning within the compulsive (some might say 'schizophrenic') main character that made the project so interesting. The music would have to reveal the interplay between these conflicting forces if the opera was to convince the audience of Robert Wringhim's early self-deceptions, his growing sense of doubt about the validity of his actions, and his final sense of despair and remorse. I think he also liked the sorrowful resolution of a man who finally realises that "his hour of repentance has passed" and seems resigned to death's approach; who realises his life has become a lesson.

Tom said that he would need to have John's permission to change the wording if he felt it necessary, as he had done with Edwin Morgan, and John accepted this proviso. However, John's background also meant that he knew how to avoid words that were difficult or ugly for singers, and in the event Tom made very few changes – though he did write the words of the Houghmagandie song himself. John was very respectful of the relative provinces of librettist and composer and they therefore developed a working method that would suit the evolving music, as John explains:

> The way we worked was first to discuss the story in detail. From that we were able to produce an outline of each of the scenes. We would then agree how the conflict should progress in each scene, whether through monologues or a duet, and then it was over to me. All the hard structural work was done in advance. I'd write a few scenes and then hand them over to Tom, who would compose them immediately.

The composition of the opera developed into three years of obsession for Tom. A symphony generally took a year to write, but an opera takes much longer since each act is almost equivalent to a symphony.

John Currie puts it this way:

> The Sinner became his whole life. The whole idea of the book is so challenging, and the idea of whether he could pull it off probably began to play on his mind. Verdi was also obsessed with writing character-based opera, but it's a very difficult way to work, I'd rather write ten librettos, than one opera.

The words in one sense make the writing of the music easier than it would be in a truly abstract creation. As Tom put it "the words led where the music needed to go". However, the sheer size of an opera presents a major challenge in coming up with new ideas that maintain the integrity and inventiveness of the music – as well as ensuring that the audience is rewarded with an emotionally satisfying conclusion to the work. And, unlike a symphony, the mood of the music in an opera has to be able to change instantly to reflect the drama and the words.

By now Tom had a reputation to maintain and he felt that he would have to come up with something extraordinary that would do justice to this prescient novel. He was aware that it was a canonical work, but his sense of commitment to the story would have been equally great if it had not been so well known. An opera is not just music. He needed to become involved with the character and he felt that he had to get inside the Sinner's mind. He felt that the intensity of the piece went to the core of the human experience, as Tom explained at the time:

> What I find is beginning to happen here is that since the nature of the subject is schizophrenic, I'm entering into a musical style which is also schizophrenic. What one might call the norm of the piece is 20th century chromatic style, if you can understand what I mean by this general description. But on the other hand, the piece is able to embrace much more traditional elements (I suppose they would be seen as such), modal things for example. One of the main cornerstones on which the musical structure rests and from which the musical structure as a whole is derived is the hymn-tune Martyrs. I have found it desirable and necessary from time to time to create a musical situation in which the unreality and the demented nature of what is going on is represented by unrealistic almost collage-like techniques, in which for example the chromatic style which is the norm is suddenly confronted by a simple, beautiful, gorgeous, coloured diatonic style.

Tom and John also wanted to reveal the blackly comic side of the narrative and the opera features moments of ironic wit and musical levity that underscore this point. Early on John Currie noticed that the novel features numerous profane versions of Christian rituals. Both he and Tom were able to ensure that these ironies would also be presented to the operatic audience.

Obviously Tom still had to lecture; however, the commission changed his way of life in that he began to compose late at night as well as during the hours of daylight. It was his usual practice to make a pot of tea after breakfast and retire to his study with it, only appearing for another one when the first was empty. This second one generally lasted until lunchtime, which was brief. Then the same thing took place between lunch and dinner. In the evening he relaxed by reading or watching television. All this changed, however, during the three years it took to write the opera. He had always been a 'night person' rarely going to bed before midnight, but now he went to his study and worked from 11pm until 2 or 3am. This was the time when the house was quietest, when there were no telephone calls or doorbells ringing. He had complete peace to concentrate. He was very quiet and careful not to disrupt my sleep, and

I joked with him that anyone could have got into bed with me at that time and I would not have known.

Early in 1973, Tom was commissioned by the Cheltenham Festival to write a piece for brass band. He thought about the form that he wanted the piece to take, and quickly settled on the working title *Refrains and Cadenzas*, which became its established name. The commission fee was £200 and we had to provide the parts for the performance. Though the fee was not great in those inflationary times, Tom saw it as a challenge, and worth doing to show that brass bands were capable of playing in an exciting, modern, classical idiom. As he wrote at the time:

> There are certain pieces of melodic material in the piece which do not develop, but simply recur in the manner of refrains, alternating with bouts of demonstrative music. The cadenzas, which have a display element - although it's not in my judgment a terribly technically difficult piece, are the places where the music actually develops. Having written Sinfonietta some years before, I had certain notions about brass band sound. I wanted to add a dash of pepper and vinegar to the plum duff sound – thin it down and make it more athletic. I used muted effects of various kinds and tuned and un-tuned percussion. A little tap on a wood block adds a touch of rigour to a chord. In short I wanted to widen the colour vocabulary of the brass band. However, I accept the constitution of the brass band, and, believe it or not, I see myself as a lyrical composer and I think in strongly melodic terms. The musical difficulties of the piece are quite acute. It's a question of getting across what the music means – whatever THAT means! The music is in a 20th century idiom (I have been influenced at various times by Bartók and Berg, although by now they're things remembered rather than things actually present) which some bands will still think of as a foreign language, although others won't have any particular difficulty. In addition to that there's a continual jostling for position between the static elements and the developing elements. The performer has to make his mind up what's going on at any given time. That's more difficult than handling the actual notes. Such is the virtuosity and brilliance of many brass bands that they'll do that without any difficulty at all. I thoroughly enjoy the brass band world.

However, his enjoyment was put to the test when *Refrains and Cadenzas* was given its first rehearsal in a tiny upstairs room in Bradford. The Black Dyke Mills Band, who had been asked to première the work, slotted itself in with difficulty, and the decibels were shattering! I remember Tom coming back to the hotel with his ears still ringing. However, he was heartened by the presence of a figure sitting at the back of the room – one keen supporter who came both to all the rehearsals and all the concerts. He said to me: "It's hard not to warm to that sort of thing."

Whenever we could combine the family summer holiday with a foreign performance of Tom's music we did so. So in September 1973 we travelled en famille to Roasio Sant' Eusebio in Italy, where some of Tom guitar works were being studied at the Summer School for Guitar. We spent a most enjoyable week, which culminated in a concert, where Angelo Gilardino performed *Coplas del Ruiseñor* (Songs of the Nightingale). After the concert we found a long-stemmed red rose tucked into the windscreen of the car. I was pleased for Tom that his music was so appreciated. The following week we turned south to continue our holiday in Pisa, Florence and Siena. When we arrived in Siena we parked the car outside a church opposite the local maternity hospital, and made our way down a very narrow street to the main square. The singing students at the music academy halfway down the hill were in great voice and when we returned from our wanderings we saw an immaculate figure in white with a beautiful pith helmet, who had just issued us with a parking ticket. I asked him if, now that we had the ticket, we needed to move the car, or could we go and have dinner first. I was assured with a wide smile that indeed we could leave the car and have dinner. A family of three obviously very hungry boys was a great asset at times.

Now the boys were growing up, and having spent the last twenty years as a full-time mother I felt that it was time to show the family that I was up to a little more than washing dishes. Before I was married I had worked in the Laing Art Gallery as a secretary and always felt that I would have been capable of continuing my education to university level had my father allowed it. Since I did not have the time to go back to college, I decided to take the exams to join Mensa for my own self-esteem. I did not tell anyone when I sent in the application form, but when a date was set for me to go to the Caledonian University to sit the exams I asked Tom to take me. He was delighted that I was doing something for myself, and so was I when the results arrived and I found that I was in the top two to three per cent of the population. More recently I have come to reassess the value of such tests; however, this was just the confidence boost I needed at the time.

Refrains and Cadenzas received its première at the Cheltenham Festival July 14 1973 when Geoffrey Brand conducted the Black Dyke Mills Band at a concert that was also broadcast on Radio 3. After the performance, the distinguished English composer Elizabeth Lutyens told Tom that she was "unaware that a brass band could sound like that". She was most complimentary to Tom, and I think that the piece was a revelation to her. The Glasgow Herald reviewer remarked that: "This is a work of which the composer, the commissioners, and all those interested in good music for brass bands can be justly proud." Though some of this might sound like critical hyperbole, the brass bands did genuinely take to this innovative work. At the close of a quite exhaustive analysis in The British Bandsman, Ray Steadman-Allen stated that *Refrains and Cadenzas* was "a well constructed work, the craftsmanship of which is impressive on close study." And in retrospect I think that Tom was something of a trailblazer where brass band music was concerned.

The following month *Ritornelli per Archi* received its première at the Freemason's Hall as part of the Edinburgh Festival (August 23, 1973), when Leonard Friedman directed the Scottish Baroque Ensemble. Leonard was an exemplary musician and a real rôle model for younger members of the Ensemble since he practised every day - even when they were on tour.

From its challenging, discordant opening bars to its uneasy ending, *Ritornelli per Archi* is one of Tom's most forward looking works. Although in the first instance it does not set out to please, and is in many ways a dissonant work for a dissonant time, it rewards repeated hearings, offering a sophisticated emotional and intellectual experience. In a radio talk from 1973, Tom described the work in his typically cerebral way that belies the music's emotional impact:

> The piece is in one movement and is written for 11 string players; 6 violins, 2 violas, 2 cellos, and 1 bass. These instruments are each treated in a solo manner (with an especially prominent part for Leonard). Apart from the aleatoric passages the piece makes use of quarter tones, and in particular features a number of recurring refrains (or ritornelli) which appear from time to time during the course of the work.

Describing the work in a later programme note from 1979, Tom added:

> The work functions on two levels. On the first level are the main source materials of the piece which can be recognised by their dynamic and developmental character. On the other hand the second level is a more static network of refrains, which punctuates

the work as it unfolds. So the work begins with the symbiosis of these two elements and works progressively towards their fusion into one.

The piece was described by The Glasgow Herald as "a striking major work by a composer whose rapid development has been most impressive .... a work of altogether exceptional merits"; and by The Scotsman as "a taut compelling drama." The Glasgow Herald went on to report that the performance was "undoubtedly the most adventurous Scottish contribution to this year's official festival", and was described by the performers as a "tour de force". Not that Tom was always adventurous in his own tastes outside music. That year as always he went to Edinburgh to hear many of the Festival concerts with John Maxwell Geddes. They went to hear recitals in the morning and afternoon, and in the evening they went to see cowboy films!

It often strikes me as strange that the same ideas can occur to people at the same time who are quite a distance from each other. In March 1973, Tom and Martin Dalby discussed the idea of asking the Scottish Arts Council for funds to set up a group of chamber musicians. Then they learned there was already a Trust - recently set up in Edinburgh - for the same purpose. A group of eight Glasgow musicians met to discuss whether or not there was room for two new music groups, and they reached the conclusion that it would be better to join forces if the Edinburgh group agreed. Then, at a meeting of all the parties the following month, it was agreed that the committee already formed in Glasgow would have the function of acting as an executive committee to the already established Trust. Edward Harper became the Musical Director and Tom was Chairman. The New Music Group of Scotland went on to give some fine concerts and many composers have much to thank them for.

John Currie delivered the libretto for Act One of *Confessions of a Justified Sinner* in the week before New Year. One of the most striking differences between the libretto and the novel is that the Sinner's mother and his 'adopted' father 'The Reverend Wringhim' are given a more central rôle, and young Wringhim's religious indoctrination is presented as a sinister form of psychological manipulation over an impressionable young man, underpinning his meeting with Gil-Martin and his ability to rationalise his subsequent crimes.

To achieve the right tone and ironical counterpoint Tom looked for musical inspiration from Scots hymns from the time when the Sinner was supposed to have lived, most notably *Martyrs* from the Scottish Psalter of

1615, whose harmony was composed by T L Hately. After months of eager anticipation he wrote the first five minutes on the first day of 1974. He was like a dog with two tails. He had been so excited about the project that to get his teeth into it at last was tremendously satisfying for him. However he was soon interrupted, as a few days later the publishers Chappell asked him to write a carol "immediately" as they were bringing out a book called a *Garland of Carols*. We thought that perhaps one of the composers originally asked had not completed his carol in time for inclusion, so Tom wrote *There Is No Rose* in one day. It has been performed many times, and is universally liked. Though at the time, its speed of composition worried Tom as he wondered if he had over-simplified his usual style and asked me if I thought it was déjà vu. However I reminded him that he was asked to write it for amateur choirs. King's College, Cambridge included it in their annual worldwide TV broadcast of Twelve Lessons and Carols in 1975, and the university invited us to Cambridge for the performance, but I preferred to follow our usual custom and spend Christmas at home with the family. This was a decision that I have since regretted, having heard that Christmas services there are very special. The BBC Singers also performed the carol in St John's church, Smith Square, London, on December 14 1975. Since then it has been sung countless times, and on two occasions in Glasgow we dashed from one church to another to hear it performed by different choirs.

In February we went out to lunch with Martin and Flora Dalby after the BBCSSO had recorded Tom's *Second Symphony* for future transmission. The talk turned on death and Tom said that he'd like to die after he had written the last note of what he felt to be a really great work. Martin Dalby's witty reply was that he'd see what could be arranged when Tom had finished his new opera! Unhappily, Tom's health began to fail in 1997 shortly after the completion of his *Fifth Symphony*, which many people regard as one of his finest works.

In the spring of 1974 my Aunt Laura died, so instead of travelling abroad that summer we decided to take Uncle Bill on a holiday to 'Constable Country' in Suffolk. The boys were older now and were not interested in accompanying us on a "boring" holiday to England; however, we had an enjoyable time in and around Barton Mills even if Tom was not quite as enthused as he was in some of the great cities of Europe. He was less interested in nature for its own sake and was most fascinated by places that revealed the cross-fertilisation between cultures and the sweep of human activity down the ages, such as a Roman pavement in the medieval village of Carcassone in the South of France or the University of Fez in Morocco. It was therefore little surprise that at Tom's suggestion we went to see the historical towns of Colchester, Bury St Edmunds and Flatford Mill where 'The Hay Wain' and many of Constable's most famous works were painted. Even though Tom and Martin Baillie had lectured about the relationship between art and music for fifteen years, Tom never talked much with me about painting, perhaps because he realised his perception of colour was faulty. He could take in the overall composition, texture, contrast and brush technique within a work; however, with his red-green colour blindness he would have been pressed to fully appreciate Constable's adroit use of red within these celebrated paintings to create colour contrast and pictorial depth.

Having worked on the opera all summer and into the early autumn, Tom finally completed the first act of *The Confessions of a Justified Sinner* in October. Apart from his lecturing commitments, he said that he was going to be a complete vegetable for a week, but it was impossible. He couldn't leave it alone and was forever tidying it up, making tiny changes in dynamics and the like. He was still being offered commissions but had to turn them down, saying, "Come back to me in 1977". Fortunately, most people replied that they certainly would be returning then.

From time to time – especially during Edinburgh Festival weeks – we were 'wined and dined' by the current Secretary of State, and various other VIPs. I could not suppress the feeling that we were getting some of our taxes back at these 'do's'! But we did meet some interesting people – among them Arthur Rubinstein, and the confirmed bachelor Ted Heath, who was Prime Minister at the time. Arthur Rubenstein was a charming conversationalist though Ted Heath ignored me completely and spoke only to Tom!

Around this time Alexander Gibson suggested to Tom and John Dankworth, the famous jazz band leader, that they should collaborate on a work. As they lived so far from each other, and so could not easily collaborate, Tom came up with the idea that the Canterbury Tales might be a possibility. That way they could each set tales turn and turn about, but unfortunately they were both too busy with other undertakings to pursue the idea.

When we travelled outside of Scotland for performances we were often asked where we lived, and I noticed that when we said 'Glasgow' the faces of the enquirers would change. The city's hard-man reputation from the 1930s still lingered. My response to this prejudice was to say that I came from a city with two universities, an Academy of Music and Drama, two symphony orchestras, chamber orchestras, an opera company, a ballet company, and many art galleries. A place where there are lots of parks and where there is even a book written about it called *The Dear Green Place*. They would then ask with some awe "where's that?" to which I replied, "Glasgow." I hope that I changed some people's perception of the city. I remember how amazed Brendan's Japanese fiancé Makiyo (now my daughter-in-law) was when she first visited us in 1980 and saw the number of trees and parks in the city.

In May 1975, the artist and journalist Emilio Coia came to our home to interview Tom for an article for the magazine Scottish Field and he made sketches of Tom as he recorded what was said. The published interview ran as follows:

> A creator of "the least disagreeable of all noises" – to quote in fun Dr. Johnson's churlish definition of music – Thomas Wilson may not be to The Scotsman-in-the-street the country's Irving Berlin or Cole Porter, but to the cognoscenti, who may be dimensionally detached from such melodists, he is a composer of first quality and real distinction. In my presence certain musicologists have suspected he is Scotland's best living composer.

> Although temperamentally disposed to agree heartily with Carlyle's assertion that music is "the speech of angels" (Dr J. must be firmly rebutted) I was well aware that the angel I located in Glasgow's West End was very much a human being. We had met before but not in his house. His pleasant study on the first floor is neatly equipped with piano, hi-fi, business-like desk placed against the daylight, books, small pictures of Mozart and Beethoven, comfortable chairs and a dozen pipes or so, which to an uninitiated eye looked well smoked.

> Mightily articulate, and patently of equable temperament, one soon discovers that he is utterly incapable of parvanimity - Boulez, Stockhausen, John Cage...he expounds on all three, and brings sweet reason to bear on any attempt to disparage, either by some oblique reference, or by a stiff silence made noisily overt, their honest endeavours - which is not to suggest for one moment that Thomas Wilson is adopting a patronising attitude. Far from it, he greatly admires much of their work; and apropos of Boulez ("a very fine composer at his best") and my feeble attempts at kite-flying, he is ready to retort: "Would you commit yourself to Michelangelo's Last Judgement from a distance of four feet, or would you wait until you were forty feet from it?" Point of course taken - but anticipated.

He readily admits he is influenced by things going on around him and is "very much aware of contemporary music and of different stylistic factors as they appear." He finds them "interesting or useful" and, he goes on, "I will take due notice of them and incorporate them; but I will only try to use them after I have thought them through again from the beginning. I won't simply go to the works of X and lift his technique, his approach...what I am ready to absorb must be consistent with MY approach, MY style, MY way of operating."

Discussing trends and the manner of some modern composers (Tom Wilson is reluctant to criticise them and gently but firmly declines to name names), he admits "there is a tendency to become reliant on matters of technique and on purely intellectual qualities. It is true that one can become preoccupied with the WAY that one does things rather than WHY one does them in the first place. It's all a question of ends and means, and I cannot deny there is certainly evidence of too much concern for the means and too little for the ends. At the same time the qualities of structure, of techniques, are extremely important because without them the expression would not exist; but again if the expression is non-existent all the technical expertise in the world will not compensate for its absence."

I asked him, why did he think that so many composers were turning to conducting? Was it perhaps because it is a more glamorous and easier pursuit? He didn't take time to ponder the questions.

"Do you know, for some time I have also been wondering why composers are conducting, but I cannot pretend I have come up with the answer. Boulez, for example, has been most successful in this regard, and in recent years Tippett has taken up the baton. It could be they simply think it is a good thing to splinter off one's activities, to indulge in a separate but related experience; it could also be that they discovered within themselves a real talent for conducting. I would NOT agree that conducting is a second best; I have conducted my own music in the past and, in my opinion, done it unsuccessfully. But I would want to do it again sometime, having learned a thing or two from, so to speak, previous misdemeanours.... Yes, I think every composer has experienced what he considers are inferior performances of his work, and some that he cannot help comparing with those by such and such. But usually, in fairness, there are a number of very good reasons for what are considered indifferent performances. Economics, for instance, can be an important factor. Rehearsing music is a very costly business, and often enough the conductor finds himself in the position where he has to extract the most music from, so to speak, the least money, and this situation obviously operates AGAINST the complexities of modern music which tends to take rather a lot of rehearsals if it is to be performed properly...and so errors occur."

Tom Wilson's current monumental task is the writing of a full-scale opera commissioned directly by Scottish Opera, of James Hogg's acknowledged classic *Confessions of a Justified Sinner* which was first published in 1824. Tom said: 'It is a fascinating story, and seems to me to stem to some extent from Faust (although I cannot speak as a literary critic) because there is a diabolic element, and also leads on to Stevenson's Jekyll and Hyde. At the same time it is unique to itself. It is really about fanaticism – about a person whose ideals become disordered to an extent that he forgets humanity around him, regarding people as pawns in the realisation of his own ideals.'

To the qualities of his librettist (and close friend) John Currie he pays considerable tribute, and rightly considers it an extraordinary coincidence that both of them should be discussing at a party the possibility of creating an opera from Hogg's work just one week before receiving the totally unexpected invitation to proceed. Truly Scottish Opera doesn't miss a trick.

On October 16 there was a grand opening of Glasgow's refurbished Theatre Royal. Everyone that the powers that be thought important was invited, except the composer who was writing the new opera for the next season. I was very angry about the continuous slights that Tom had to bear from people who are really of no importance in the grand scheme of things, and I was worried about the change I could see in him because of their treatment. He had borne it with patience for so long. But now that he saw the years passing and little encouragement from the British musical establishment, I saw a tinge of bitterness creeping into him and it was heartbreaking. I remember the occasion when, during a pre-concert talk, at one of his infrequent outings at the Proms, the BBC executive John Drummond told the audience that Tom's works were rarely performed because he frequently wrote for triple woodwind. Tom was fuming and afterwards said to me, "I've written only one work that calls for triple woodwind." And I replied, "Well you should have said that!" But Tom would never humiliate anyone publicly in that way.

In 1973 Tom had been commissioned to write a hymn for the Third Edition of The Church Hymnary called "*I greet Thee who my true Redeemer art*" and when the hymn was scheduled to be performed during a Songs of Praise TV transmission in 1975, he was asked to submit a short note for the Radio Times. With the themes of the opera obviously at the forefront of his mind, this is what Tom wrote:

> Music is more a religious experience than Catholicism, but, as a Catholic, I find it a nice ecumenical approach to set a hymn by Calvin to music for the new Church of Scotland Hymnary.

> You have to be slightly schizophrenic to capture the feel of the words, to be meaningful to your audience, and still to satisfy your own artistic standards.

> The music for a hymn like "I Greet Thee who my True Redeemer art" must be direct and simple. I'm not a do-gooder but charity and a revulsion against excesses from apathy to greed is a guiding principle. Music imposes its own morals.

Quoted in another article from December of that year, Tom said:

> Music is magic and we would do without it at our peril. Art in all its forms is more than ever necessary for the sanity of mankind. One man goes to a football match to see a good game, another goes to a concert to hear a refreshing performance. It is the same aesthetic instinct. It is important for a composer to be aware of his surroundings. Music doesn't happen in the study. It is a reflection of the life we live and the environment we live in, not an abstracted effusion. For the musician there is a great danger that he will become isolated in an ivory tower. Firstly this is because he writes what is right according to his own artistic standards and conscience, and can only hope that audiences will follow him. Secondly music requires an interpreter. The composer is not like a painter who is his own performer, and whose art has a quality of immediacy which music lacks. Throughout the ages musicians have had to avoid becoming detached from people. The ethics of the profession have remained constant even though styles have changed. One can only dimly understand, if at all, the honesty and integrity built into music.

Tom would have composed come what may. He couldn't help himself. But the continual performances of his works gave him a great lift. His scores were being heard even more often than either of us realised at the time. While some performers notified us when they played Tom's compositions, others did not. Consequently, only later – sometimes much later – would we learn about performances that had taken place not just in Britain but elsewhere. I have been able to identify more than eleven hundred performances of his music which took place in his lifetime involving eighty six conductors.

He was always happy that all his sons had a great appreciation of music and he was quietly satisfied when our son Martin chose to study Music at the Royal Scottish Academy of Music and Drama in Glasgow. Martin was there until 1978 and in the final year of his studies he was offered a part-time post on the teaching staff which he accepted. After this he went on to study for his Honours BMus at Glasgow University for a further four years.

Before commencing his studies in September 1975, Martin decided that he needed a better piano than the one that we had, so we asked friends to tell us of any good pianos that came on the market. Wight Henderson, the celebrated Scottish pianist, said that he knew of a Steinway boudoir grand for sale that belonged to a former fellow student of his at the Academy. When we went to see the owner at her home in Spean Bridge in the Scottish Highlands we found that the piano needed a new soundboard and new felts, but it was basically a good instrument, so we bought it and sent it off to Steinway to have it brought up to standard. At the time we did not know of the sad story attached to the sale. We learned, when the piano was delivered to us six months after we bought it, that the owner, whose father had had it built for her 21st birthday, was dying of cancer, and she was going to spend her last months with her son in Canada. She told us that she was so pleased that it was going to a home where it would be played, and not regarded as just a piece of furniture. It sounds so much better than the old workhorse in Tom's study, and the whole family use it from time to time.

Martin wished to study the harpsichord as his second subject at the Academy. He was 6ft 4in so we had one built that could accommodate his long legs. Lionel Gliori made us a copy of a beautiful double-manual French instrument by Taskin, and special plinths were made to go under the feet to raise the height of the keyboards. The original instrument is part of the Russell Collection at Edinburgh University. On the inside of the lid Lionel painted a copy of a Poussin picture, and the soundboard is covered with paintings of flowers around the names of Thomas and Margaret. The original Poussin is housed in the National Gallery of

Scotland in Edinburgh. Unfortunately, harpsichords are large instruments that need to be tuned daily and after Martin graduated from the Academy it was rarely played, so it was sold to a retired BBC executive who lived in the Borders.

The Sinner

It was a great relief to me when in February of 1976 Tom completed *The Confessions of a Justified Sinner*. He was emotionally drained after writing the music needed for the final flight of the Sinner from the Manor House at Dalcastle pursued by outraged villagers and vengeful apparitions. The final bars portray the Sinner in a prison-like bothy on the moors where he finally recognises his inevitable end. The opera had already occupied Tom for two years and ahead of him were weeks of preparing and attending rehearsals of the production. Alongside this was the usual preparation and delivery of lectures. Despite being very tired he did not complain about this workload, because to him music was work of the most enjoyable kind. Although composition was never easy it was his life. In the spring he added to this workload when he accepted an invitation to join the Board of the Royal Scottish Academy of Music and Drama. The letter from the Scottish Education Department stated that: "The Secretary of State will, I know, be pleased to learn that you have agreed to undertake this public service."

A BBC broadcast in May of *Threnody*, which was conducted by James Loughran, gave Tom a real lift. He was further buoyed by a letter from his old friend Campbell MacLean, who was minister of Cramond Kirk and erstwhile minister of St Giles Cathedral in Edinburgh. On the rare occasions when Campbell was in Glasgow he would join Tom and John Geddes for a wee dram. After hearing the broadcast, he wrote to Tom to say:

Dear Tom,

THRENODY is a truly stunning piece. Fortunately I was able to record it and will have the pleasure of many re-hearings. I hope you enjoyed the performance.

Love to Margaret,
As ever,
Campbell.

Another letter that gave Tom great pleasure was from the Austrian-born British composer Joseph Horovitz:

Dear Thomas Wilson,

Allow me to congratulate you on *"Threnody"* which I heard in a car this morning. It is so rare for me to listen to music composed these days without an immediate compulsion to switch off, that I feel I must write to you and express my delight at my new sensation – i.e. a desire to keep my ears glued to the radio in order not to miss anything!

The question of idiom is hardly worth mentioning; it is the musical ideas, and above all a clearly felt rhythmic drive, which I found truly exhilarating. I wish very much to know how I can listen to your piece again – if you have a moment, do drop me a line and tell me if it is recorded, or about to be, or if I can get hold of a tape somewhere.

With my best wishes and much admiration,

Sincerely,

Joseph Horovitz

As I think about it now, Tom had an ambivalent relationship to praise. Like every creative person he enjoyed a good review or a personal compliment, especially from a fellow musician whom he respected. At the same time however, being praised left him a bit uncomfortable, and he never allowed it to go to his head. Even after having spent a night at an after-concert dinner celebrating the performance of one of his new works, Tom was back to 'business as usual' the next day. I often thought that he did not draw enough satisfaction from his successes and perhaps did not even realise his own greatness in the way that others might. On reflection, however, I think it was the combination of his natural integrity as well as his classical education that encouraged him not to tempt fate and perhaps jeopardise the wellspring of his own creativity. To me this was a form of superstition, and I do think that it caused Tom to hide his light under a bushel when he was young to the detriment of his career. If I had asked him, he would have simply responded, "I just want to get on to the next composition." The process of creating was the focus of his attention and praise was simply a fleeting by-product. On the rare occasions when he received an unflattering review, he could not help but take it personally, even if the shortcomings weren't in the composition itself. This was not because the review damaged his ego, but because it made him question whether he had communicated his intentions successfully. So perhaps his matter-of-fact view of fame helped him to remain focussed on the work at hand, and he would not allow the rare poor review to keep him down for long.

After all the trials and anxieties of writing *The Sinner*, Tom decided to dedicate his next work to me as a thank-you for my support. Completed on June 23 and commissioned by the Baccholian Singers *Ubi Caritas et Amor* is a work for five solo male voices and percussion loosely based on the plainsong *Ubi Caritas* which was usually sung during the Solemn Evening Mass of the Last Supper on Maundy Thursday. It is the final antiphon sung during the ceremony of the Washing of the Feet and it may not be omitted.

At the beginning of June we went on holiday for ten days to Islay, an island off the west coast of Scotland, famous for its golf course and its distilleries which produce whiskies having a distinctly peaty quality. Islay is also known for its round church in Bowmore, built like that so that the devil would have no corner to hide in! One can go from the north to the south of the island in an hour by car, but even so, its attractions left us with lots to see and do. The weather was warm and sunny, so during the day Tom played a lot of golf with our sons Brendan and Stephen. Martin played rarely as he wanted to protect his hands for his piano playing.

Tom went into the bar of the local hotel each evening for a nightcap as it was only yards away from where we were staying. He told me that the local policeman came to the hotel at closing time to make sure that the shutters had been put down over the bar. But fifteen minutes after he left, the shutters went up again, and the evening's festivities continued. One evening I accompanied him, and we met a German sea captain who told his fellow drinkers that he had been on board a submarine in the Sound of Jura (a stretch of water that flows between the islands of Islay and Jura) for the duration of the war. He asked the farmers if they did not wonder what was happening to their disappearing sheep as there had been regular sorties to the mainland for fresh meat.

Confessions of a Justified Sinner was given its first performance on June 15 1976 when Norman Del Mar conducted the Scottish Opera Orchestra, Chamber Chorus, and a superb trio of singers: Phillip Langridge in the rôle of the Sinner, John Shirley-Quirk as Gil-Martin (the Devil), and Thomas Hemsley as the Reverend Wringhim. Tom worked closely with

Norman and producer Michael Geliot and assisted with the casting of the opera as well as the arrangements and stage direction.

The collaboration between conductor, producer and composer worked well and the performers did us proud, but Tom was especially fortunate in his soloists. It was interesting to watch such fine singers growing into their parts. I was amazed in particular by the baritone John Shirley-Quirk who had the particular good fortune to possess a photographic memory and perfect pitch, two great assets in a singer. This meant that when Tom asked: 'Would you go back to page 91 bar 383 and sing that again please' John could sing it immediately without referring to his score, and in perfect pitch. No mean feat since some of the intervals in the opera are quite challenging. He truly excelled in the rôle of Gil-Martin the satanic mentor.

The first performance took place in the Theatre Royal, York, and was broadcast live. Unfortunately the power failed one minute into the performance and so the whole opera had to begin again two minutes later. The problems were not over however. The conductor for the offstage chorus that sings at the beginning of the opera was supposed to follow Norman del Mar's beat in the pit via a television screen, but when the power was restored the TV no longer worked. So a third conductor was hastily placed in the wings to beat in time with Norman, and the chorus master took his cues from there. Amazingly it all worked though Tom kept his fingers tightly crossed throughout the rest of the performance and was drained afterwards.

Tom had specified electronic "surround sound" which was something new at that time, and in old theatres it presented something of a challenge. When describing this device to Martin Dalby some time later Tom said: "I had this multiple stereophonic loudspeaker arrangement in which the Sinner, in a visionary fit, sees himself as being Emmanuel, and all the wonderful sort of quasi mythical biblical figures, and the chorus of voices, is redounding in his head. The idea was to have all this relayed to the audience, so that they were part of the confusion going on in his own mind, as the different names for Satan bounced off the walls and ceiling."

In the end everything went beautifully, though the sword that had to appear out of thin air at one point was never successfully managed and instead it was lowered rather obviously from above on a wire. I found this embarrassingly awful, but none of these problems of production would give a moment's concern these days: having said that, creative artists of any age always push the limits of the technology of the time.

The York performances were followed by others in the Eden Court Theatre, Inverness; the King's Theatre, Edinburgh; The Grand Theatre, Leeds; His Majesty's Theatre, Aberdeen; The Theatre Royal, Newcastle-upon-Tyne; and five performances in the Theatre Royal, Glasgow. The thirteen performances took place between June 23 and October 30 and they were well attended, some people returning more than once. Tom and I were invited to the home of a lady potter who had been so inspired that she had gone from the Inverness performance straight to her workshop and stayed up all night making a pottery collage of scenes from the opera. It was very impressive if somewhat gory, and was installed above the fireplace in the bar of the hotel she and her husband owned in Nairn.

Tom and I attended every performance not out of vanity, but because his perfectionism demanded that he check and recheck his artistic choices, his orchestration and his dynamic markings. We were asked many times when there was going to be another production of *The Sinner*, and as recently as 2001 the composer Robert Crawford wrote:

> It is high time that Scottish Opera took the hint from the BBCSSO's performances of Wilson and Leighton to revive Thomas Wilson's fine opera *Confessions of a Justified Sinner*, as well as the one-act opera *The Charcoal Burner*, both unjustly neglected works by Scotland's finest composer bar none.

Despite such appeals however, Scottish Opera has done nothing. The reviews at the time were very good and the music always received particular praise. The Seventies blend of historically realistic costumes and the modernist set design, with its geodesic dome representing the sinner's brain, might now be seen as a little dated, though it worked well at the time. But in my opinion the opera should not be judged on the basis of scenography or choreography and production matters that are so easily changed. This is one of very few operas based on a great work of Scottish literature and its central subjects of the dangers of religious fanaticism and the belief of some people that they are beyond the law are timelier than ever. Though modern programmers are often rather conservative and risk-averse, I feel sure that sooner or later the work will be rediscovered as a masterpiece of the twentieth century. I did in fact send a score of *The Sinner* to Scottish Opera's music director in 2000. His rather perfunctory reply was: "The repertoire of our own time is a casualty due to the present financial climate, and there is no possibility to consider your late husband's work for performance." On top of the "economic" complaint (which isn't justified given that *The Sinner* only requires a chamber orchestra, three main voices and chorus), I was taken aback by the reference to my "late" husband. At this time, Tom was a very sick man, but he did not die until June 2001. I would have expected anyone from Scottish Opera to be more knowledgeable about a prominent composer living within three miles of the opera theatre.

The excitement and stress of the months between June and October exhausted Tom, and he said that he would take a rest for three months. I agreed that it was a very good idea, but when the three months stretched into four, and then five, I began to worry a little, but said nothing.

And then Tom got a telephone call from a young mezzo-soprano, Marilyn de Blieck, who said that she would like to commission him to write a song cycle for her. He invited her to come to the house to sing for him. I listened from the steps between the front and back halls as Marilyn performed a marvellous selection of Schumann's songs while Tom provided the piano accompaniment. When the recital was over and Marilyn left, I said to Tom: "You must write something for that most glorious voice." Marilyn told us later that she was receiving lessons from the great diva Elizabeth Schwarzkopf, who was obviously also very impressed with her voice. Though Tom would have loved to oblige, he had just accepted a commission to write for another fine mezzo-soprano, Josephine Nendick, so the work for Marilyn had to be put on the back burner for the time being. The song cycle *One Foot in Eden*, written for Josephine and chamber orchestra, consisted of settings of three poems by Edwin Muir (*The Refugees*, *The Horses* and *One Foot in Eden*). The next year Tom wrote a piano version for Marilyn. Then, some years later, he fulfilled Marilyn's commission with the song cycle *The Willow Branches*.

Hard on the heels of this request came another commission, this time from the John Currie Singers, to write a work to be premièred the following February. All this meant that he needed to get his mind back into the discipline of composition: what was the subject of the work to be? Where would he find the right words, ones that would fire his imagination? In the end he chose to freely set music to words from the Psalms. The work he chose to write is about emergent faith and hope, and the intention behind it is to be symbolic rather than literal, moral without being moralistic, religious with a small "r". As he described the work at the time:

> Faith and hope are not simple states – they imply their own opposites, doubt and uncertainty. So the music begins hesitantly ("out of the depths...") the anxious momentum generated by the predominant male voices being constantly dissipated by ritual

incantations by female voices (Kyrie eleison, Christe eleison). But such continuing uncertainty is intolerable, and brings in its wake an eruption of fearful and angry complaint. The catalogue of reproaches mounts, but gradually the recognition grows that most of man's troubles result from his fallibilities ("Man is sunk deep in the pit he has made, in the net he has woven his own foot is tangled"). Unable to save himself Man must look outside of himself for deliverance, believing and hoping. Moments of doubt and anxiety continue to recur, but the tentative beginnings of new confidence persist.

He completed the work *Songs of Hope and Expectation* on February 7 1977 and regarded it as a sister piece to *Ubi Caritas* which was about love. Though Tom had composed three major religious works between 1970-71, (*Missa Pro Mundo Conturbato*, *Sequentiae Passionis*, and *Te Deum*), and a number of shorter sacred pieces, he had grown increasingly disenchanted with Roman Catholicism during this time. To him, music offered a far greater spiritual experience, and provided a quality of refreshment and inspiration lacking in the rather sterilizing power structure of the church. His real concern lay with basic human values, and religious works make up a minor part of his total output. Tom was led to write *Ubi Caritas* as a countering statement to the disbelief, scepticism, and superficiality that seemed increasingly prevalent during the 1970s. And I remember him saying to me: "There is self-seeking at every level and there is inequity in the distribution of things that are too important to leave to chance."

He said of *Songs of Hope and Expectation*:

> Religious in character, and about faith and hope, and meant to lock on to "*Ubi Caritas et Amor*" written last year, which is about love, it is my intention, that while both of these works exist independently of one another, they can be performed in sequence. The text is freely adapted from the Psalms. The intention behind it is symbolic rather than literal. Matters of religious orthodoxy played no part in my choice. I selected these words because for me they crystallize Man's age-old hopes and dilemmas with a power that remains undimmed by the passage of time.

He thought that this spreading Philistinism was reflected on another level in that school music was perceived by many students as an hour of relaxation between practical subjects like maths and physics. Tom felt "one could do without oil, but without the arts we would go mad." Perhaps unsurprisingly he was not greatly impressed by the musical talents of many popular musicians of the day, defining their work as "exploitation of a pretty base nature" since so much pop music seemed to sacrifice almost everything to a simplistic beat. He was not envious of the attention given to pop music; he just felt that ninety-five percent of these compositions were harmonically dull and of little musical interest. Every now and then he would ask about a tune he had overheard on the radio or television that sounded "quite interesting", and our son, Stephen, remembers in particular Tom expressing a passing interest in the bands Cream, Weather Report, Steeleye Dan, and Sting (in his middle period). Early in our marriage I had often suggested that he might dip his toe in these waters to alleviate our economic situation; however, the answer was always a firm 'no' because he felt that there was a danger he might never be taken seriously if he'd made a name in that world. At the same time, however, Tom did like the freewheeling spirit of jazz and sought to capture that spirit in his passing use of syncopation in some of his works such as *Carillon* and *Mosaics*.

In the summer of 1976, Brendan graduated with a double first class honours degree from Glasgow University in English and Philosophy, and he took himself off to Oxford, to St Edmund Hall, fondly known as Teddy Hall, for further studies. We missed him. Martin continued his studies at the Royal Scottish Academy of Music and Drama, and Stephen went to live in London with the other members of his pop group. For my part I was asked by Martin Dalby, Head of Music at BBC Scotland, to step in to help the department organise the insurance of the instruments, and the vaccination programme for the BBCSSO and all those who would accompany them to Hong Kong later in the year. Given the fact that all 86 orchestral members were never available at the same time, and each one needed three vaccinations one month apart, this was no simple assignment. Fortunately, I managed the task and no one died on the tour. As a result I was offered a full-time post; however, I was only prepared to work part-time and so I started work as a librarian in the Gramophone Library. I worked for BBC Radio Scotland on short-term contracts for the next fifteen years until my retirement.

The Annual Cheltenham Festival in July 1976 featured two of Tom's works for brass band, *Refrains and Cadenzas*, and *Cartoon* for cornet and brass band, both played by the GUS (Kettering) Band. A few days later they were recorded by the BBC in Gloucester Cathedral. The cathedral's echoing acoustic left us hearing the work three times, and I worried about what the broadcast would sound like. However the BBC sound engineers had placed their microphones so well that the transmission was perfect. *Cartoon* makes humorous use of the 12-tone technique (hence perhaps the title) and is quite jazzy. *Refrains and Cadenzas* was later chosen as the test piece for the 1984 European Brass Band Championship Competition held in the Usher Hall in Edinburgh, and we were presented with a brass plaque with the first page of the score engraved on it to commemorate the occasion.

Three days after the recordings of these performances in Gloucester Cathedral, the Baccholian Singers premièred *Ubi Caritas et Amor, Deus Ibi Est* in a concert given in St Giles Church, Cripplegate, as part of the Festival of London. Tom wrote the following about it:

> The theme of the work is Love – represented here by the simplicity and purity of the plainsong melody which acts as a refrain, and gives the work its name. Our attempts to achieve Love in these terms have only fragile success, and the poems I have chosen to set begin by suggesting some of the reasons for our failure – the self-absorbed detachment from life of "Lucy Ashton's Song" by Sir Walter Scott, and the hypocrisy and malice of "The Old Women" by George MacKay Brown. But short extracts from the celebrated description of Charity given by St Paul, and the Gradual for Holy Thursday, "Christus factus est" reiterate that selflessness is within our reach. The last setting (from Edwin Muir's 'The Transfiguration') offers hope that our frailties may, one day, be transcended. Finally the plainsong re-establishes the ideal.

Writing in the Sunday Times on July 18 1976, Felix Aprahamian described Tom's piece as:

> ....a masterly musical homily on various aspects of love, beginning and ending with a plainsong refrain, enclosing a fascinating division of solos and ensembles.

In October we were invited to a private concert at the Palace of Holyroodhouse, Edinburgh, where Leonard Friedman and his chamber group played Scottish airs. Afterwards there was a reception where we met the Queen who was attended by her Company of Archers. I remember that sugared almonds, champagne, cigarettes, and cucumber sandwiches were laid on tables around the room. This struck me as a strange combination even before the rise of the anti-smoking movement.

Commissioned by the John Currie Singers, *Songs of Hope and Expectation* was first performed on March 21 1977 at a concert held in the McLellan Galleries, Glasgow.

John Purser wrote in his review:

> There is no doubt as to its musical stature. The vocal textures were
> tremendously compelling and the shape of the work clearly
> imagined.

In May 1977 Tom and I were again invited to the Palace of
Holyroodhouse this time for the Royal Garden Party. It was a cold, damp,
and miserable day, and we did not enjoy it. I felt sorry for the women who
were wearing fine shoes, as the car park was a very muddy field. We
received another invitation the following year but Tom had rehearsals that
he could not miss so we had to refuse. I was very glad as once again it was
a very wet day.

In the early summer and unbeknownst to Tom, the head of his
department Norman Dees approached the University Principal Sir
Charles Wilson asking that a Personal Chair be given to Tom. A Personal
Chair is given to a staff member who has achieved eminence in their
chosen field. The principal Sir Charles Wilson (no relation) supported this
idea and so it came before Senate and was approved by them. Over the
years Tom was sounded out for a variety of academic posts, such as
Principal of the Royal Northern College of Music in Manchester, and
Principal of the Royal Scottish Academy of Music and Drama in Glasgow.
I felt rueful when I thought of the salaries that went with these positions
but each time Tom was adamant and said that he was not an administrator,
but a composer. He wanted to be true to himself, and was not interested
in the money or the "kudos" that went with such appointments. By
accepting a Personal Chair, however, he would not have the responsibility
of a department so nothing would encroach on his 'composition time', and
life continued much as it had before.

While Tom could quite happily say 'no' to positions that would involve
greater administrative responsibilities, it was a different matter where
compositional challenges were concerned. So when his colleague, the
artist Martin Baillie, asked him to write a piece for an amateur guitarist,
this was a walk into a new countryside. Though he was asked to write a
simple piece, the resulting work, *Cancion*, which means song or lullaby in
Spanish, took on a life of its own and proved to be not quite as easy as
Martin had hoped. Indeed it was selected in 1983 as the set piece in the
RSAMD Guitar Challenge Prize Competition. The winner of that
competition, Stefan Grasse, rang me yesterday (April 4 2008) to say that
the CD with his recording of it was now complete and that although
Cancion is a short piece he regards it as a masterpiece. "It has everything.

It is like an essence or distillate. In some ways it is like a sketch but the drama is all there with a clear beginning, middle and end. It is therefore able to encompass the range and movement of a far longer piece. Chords develop from the initial two note idea then build to a dramatic point; then there is a rethinking and finally a reworking of the initial phrase." While recording the work Stefan went on to say, "The structure presented no technical problems, and the beauty of sound developed so much that it felt like a poem." When Stefan came to prepare it for the recording, "it was like a meeting of friends" and made him feel very emotional. He also remembered that when he first played it as a young graduate student at the RSAMD, Tom told him that part of the inspiration for this deceptively simple piece came from a work by Mozart, the *Adagio for Glass Armonica*.

After its first public performance by Alan Crocker at a Festival Fringe concert on August 25 at St Andrew's & St George's Church, Edinburgh, Conrad Wilson called the three-minute piece "beautiful," while in 1983 the Italian guitarist Angelo Gilardino wrote a letter to Tom saying:

> May I disagree with your suggestion that '*Cancion*' is only a little piece: it is a short piece, but, as to musical value, it is as high as '*Coplas del Ruisenor*' or '*Dream Music*' and its power of fascination with an audience is magic… I am convinced that your pieces will make a milestone in the literature of the instrument: they have an aura that is personal, deep and mysterious. When guitarists will realise that, is another question, but I am sure that sooner or later the best among them will open their eyes and ears. It happened in Zagreb – during my seminar I performed so many passages of your pieces to the class that everybody was seeking for the music.

In an article for an Italian magazine, Gilardino, who had commissioned *Coplas del Ruiseñor* in 1971, had more to say about Tom's compositions for the guitar:

> In Wilson can be discerned a composer, who, although gifted with an excellent professionalism, does not care to repeat himself, and requires in each of his creations qualities which are absolutely new and personal. He works therefore with a rhythm dictated by spiritual rather than professional needs, and this aspect of his personality is clearly revealed in a comparison between his recent works and those – for example – of ten years ago.

Tom wrote only eight works for guitar, but these are all well known and are still played throughout the world by such eminent guitarists as Julian

Bream, Phillip Thorne, Stefan Grasse, Alan Neave, Timothy Walker, and Gerald Garcia.

On October 10 the Scottish branch of the Composers' Guild threw a party for Tom's fiftieth birthday. Because Tom and our sons were keen on homemade wine, the composers were invited by the Guild to contribute their own efforts in order to make the party go with a swing. They all had to give their wines a name, and one guest called his wine *Clos de Bussi*. As a family we made a peach perfection wine which was supposed to take nine months to ferment, but ours rarely lived that long. After soaking the fruit for three days, we squeezed it through pillowcases and left it to ferment in very big plastic bins. When Martin Baillie dropped around each Wednesday for his dinner prior to their regular lectures, a jug was lowered into the peach perfection and Tom and he left the house with sparkling eyes. Their students reckoned that these lectures were terrific and they came back year on year. Once we tried to make rhubarb wine and found most of it the following morning on the ceiling!

It was around this time that Tom and many other composers in Scotland first became involved with Scotus Publishing, a company formed by James Douglas. The aim of the company was to promote and sell Scottish contemporary classical music, an obviously very seductive idea to Scottish composers. Unfortunately the company had little success and was liquidated some ten years later.

On December 20 *One Foot in Eden* was given its first performance by the New Music Group of Scotland directed by Edward Harper in BBC Studio 1, Edinburgh. Josephine Nendick (mezzo-soprano) was the soloist.

Conrad Wilson wrote in The Scotsman:

> *One Foot in Eden* was the centre-piece of last night's chamber invitation concert. Based on three poems by Edwin Muir, is seemed in some ways a spin-off from the composer's recent opera "The Confessions of a Justified Sinner". Certainly the strange oscillating sonorities that accompany the second of the poems, the eerily scrabbling strings and the wavery flute evoked the hallucinatory world of Hogg's novel but seemed equally appropriate to Muir's death-conscious lines; the musical colouring – generally subdued, yet striking – as always, lucidly made its point.

Ian Robertson wrote in The Herald:

Miss Nendick commissioned as well as performed the centrepiece of the programme, a new cycle of three Edwin Muir settings by Thomas Wilson. Muir is Wilson's poet, and many of T.S. Eliot's famous remarks on the sincere and serious nature of Muir could well apply to Wilson. The largely unaccompanied setting of Muir's great poem, "The Horses" is possibly the most impressive marriage yet of words and music in the Scottish experience.

For the concert, Tom provided some comments on the choice of poems:

> "*The Refugees*" reflects on our indifference to the sufferings of others, and the social crisis and decay which stems from such injustice. The consequences are seen in the second poem '*The Horses*' ('that great terrifying poem of the nuclear age' as T S Eliot called it), which describes in chilling terms the aftermath of the 'seven days war that put the world to sleep.' However, towards the end of the poem the return of the horses prompts the first attempt to build anew. Finally, *One Foot in Eden* sounds a note of hope, but warns that the answers to our problems depend on our ability to resolve the contradictions of our own natures – 'Blossoms of grief and charity bloom in these darkened fields alone.'

The New Music Group, which sadly has now disbanded, performed Tom's music frequently. When they made their first appearance in London in 1979, the group included *One Foot in Eden* in a programme consisting entirely of works by composers either living or working in Scotland. Josephine Nendick was again the soloist. After this concert the reviewer Nicholas Kenyon wrote:

> Wilson has matched Edwin Muir's measured, carefully selected metaphors with potently evocative music. With eight instruments and voice he succeeds in creating crisply characteristic textures, especially in the interludes between the poems. The vocal writing is direct and communicative.

Josephine Nendick wrote to Tom in January 1978 saying:

Dear Tom,

Ever since I received 'One Foot in Eden' I wanted to tell you how tremendously moving I found the last song and how pleased I was with the whole piece. I wish I'd had the final draft earlier; it's possible to do it, of course, but not (as they say) to "get it in the voice". However I was glad that despite many shortcomings in performance it was hailed as an important new work. This makes me all the more pleased that we actually got it done after so long. I'm honoured that you should have written such a splendid piece for me.

Now it's imperative that it reaches a wider audience. There are people both in France and Italy who could now be approached. At all events I am looking forward to the next performance, and hope it will be soon.

All good wishes to you both, and for many triumphant performances.

Jo

Having largely written vocal works during the previous five years, Tom was keen to return to something more abstract. And once again the right commission materialised at the right time.

The Edinburgh String Quartet had played Tom's *Third Quartet* many times at home and abroad and felt that they wanted a new string quartet of their own. Tom had not undertaken a string quartet since 1958, and was at once excited by the prospect of returning to a medium that he held to be the "Mount Olympus of music making, demanding stringency and purity of discipline." He said that he "looked forward to the challenge of the limited colour palette and resulting ascetic texture. An opera offers a big canvas and grand display, but with a quartet it's all nitty-gritty."

The new quartet, he told me, would be different from its predecessor. *The Third Quartet* was heavily contrapuntal, but he felt he had moved away from that. "I don't know what stylistic slot my new quartet will fit into," he remarked, "but it will be in one movement, with contrasts of metre, tempo, style and texture – music choc-a-bloc with paradox."

In his sketches for the composition, Tom wrote the following reminders to himself which would act as his spiritual map for the work ahead:

Music is a language. Like a Sumerian script or code which no one has yet solved, it is clearly precise, yet its precisions are clouded because musical meanings are musical. Nonetheless the function of music is to communicate exactly, this it does through form and formal relationships.

CONCERTATI: - Baroque contrasts of form and idea.
Musically: Contrasts, oppositions of colours, idea, mood, texture, etc. etc.

Experientially: Reflections, human experience, art

More generally: - Paradox, apparent irrationality of life, art (yet its obvious rationality)

i.e. – Here the term concertati is used metaphorically as well as musically to indicate the ambivalences and apparent contradictions (yet stabilising certitudes) of being alive as well as placing myself as a musician within the content of established musical tradition by employing materials in a way which seeks variety (albeit often of a paradoxical kind) yet fosters the wider unity which is essential to any work of art. Where the metaphors lie, and what they mean to me are not apposite. I leave that to the listener. If the work speaks to people they will understand.

Written between January and August 1978, the work makes use of the Fibonacci sequence (for each number a different parameter: 2 – colours, 3 – moods, 5 – tempi, 8 – tones, 13 – rhythms, etc. etc.). Once completed Tom likened the result to a "study in oppositions". He qualified this by saying, "That at any rate is the basic idea, but I rarely seem to end up with the concept I started with. The material you work with tends to make demands not anticipated in the original plan."

With the *Fourth String Quartet*, Tom said he thought he had finally broken free from the influence of his opera *The Confessions of a Justified Sinner*. He confessed that: "When you have been on a trip for three years, it's hard not to remain on it."

Confessions of a Justified Sinner, *Ubi Caritas*, and *One Foot in Eden* had all been very intense emotional works with deep philosophical themes relating to the fall of man and what the individual might do to avert his destiny.

Music in the Abstract

Tom was now the pre-eminent Scottish composer of his time, completely secure in his rôle in life as well as in his art. This was not regarded as a reason to relax, and the idea of an empty sheet of manuscript paper was still a challenge that he relished. He was by now being offered more commissions than he had time to fulfil and when he was too busy to accept them he often suggested the names of other Scottish composers whom he admired. He would of course keep this information to himself and never alert the nominees in case the commissioners were to reject his suggestions.

As part of Tom's fiftieth birthday celebrations the New Music Group under their director Edward Harper, arranged a retrospective concert to be held in May of 1978. Tom had played a significant part in the foundation of the New Music Group, and Eddie was a great admirer of Tom's music - he also commissioned and performed many of his chamber works. The concert took place in the Concert Hall at Glasgow University, where members of the group performed a range of Tom's compositions including the *Violin Sonata* (1961), *Concerto da Camera* (1965), *Canti Notturni* (1972) and *Complementi* (1973).

A quote from the Spanish novelist, poet, dramatist and philosopher Miguel de Unamuno was used as a preface to the 'Thomas Wilson Retrospective Concert':

> There is nothing more universal than the individual, for what is the property of each is the property of all. Each man is worth more than the whole of humanity, nor will it do to sacrifice each to save all insofar as all sacrifice themselves to each.

Though he did not choose the passage, Tom would have wholeheartedly agreed with the sentiment. In his programme note Edward Harper wrote:

> Those who have known Thomas Wilson know how much these words typify the man. Those who only know the man from the music can be assured that the vision of the music reveals the man.

It was a wonderful occasion and Tom was very pleased with both the tribute and the performances. Sitting there amongst his friends, students and fellow lecturers, as well as other composers, music critics and members of the public, he felt very much at ease, though as always he held the fingers of his right hand crossed throughout the concert in case there was any technical hitch.

Our boys had now grown into men and they were all very busy during the summer months. This meant that rather than going abroad Tom and I decided to spend our annual holiday touring in England so that we would be on hand when needed. Our son Martin graduated from the RSAMD, and he decided to devote a year to studying something other than music before he began to study for his four-year Honours B.Mus. at Glasgow University. The following year, 1978, Brendan, who had been studying at St Edmund Hall, Oxford, and who was then twenty-four, chose to spend a year teaching English in Kagoshima (near Hiroshima), Japan. He ended up staying for two at the request of the university authorities there, and so did not resume his studies for his D. Phil until October 1980. Our youngest son, Stephen, was in London looking for another pop group as Cy Jack of Cuddly Toys had decided to stay in Glasgow. Another band member was working as a mini cab driver in London and Brian Fairweather, who shared a flat in London with Stephen, decided to move to Los Angeles. Eventually Stephen (or Paul as he was then known) joined the New Romantic pop group *Classix Nouveau* which played its first gig in 1979. Having travelled the world with the group, he eventually left as he was unhappy with the quality of the material they were playing. Moreover, he wanted to spend more time writing songs, some of which were being recorded in America.

Tribute performances of Tom's works continued throughout 1978. In August, Phillip Thorne played Tom's *Three Pieces for Guitar* at an Edinburgh Festival Fringe concert. Then in November a series of concerts took place in Glasgow and Edinburgh featuring works written by Scottish and Finnish composers. To go along with the series, a booklet was published, which had potted biographies of the composers. Tom's biography was so full of inaccuracies and unsubstantiated criticisms of individual works that he took the unusual step of sending a complaint to its author, Paul Hindmarsh. It went against Tom's nature to make such a protest, but on this occasion he felt that he had no choice. Hindmarsh replied with an apology and an explanation that Professor Rimmer had edited the text and had the final say in what was written. This revelation made it all the more inexplicable that the biography failed to mention Tom's current position as professor. After all, Rimmer was at the Senate meeting that had confirmed the appointment! That said, his behaviour towards Tom through the years had shown a strange ambivalence – one moment supportive and the next belittling – so we were not entirely surprised. Indeed, the previous year Fred had asked Tom to take over the post of Cramb Fellow in the Music Department for twelve months, teaching undergraduates (as well as carrying on his work in the Adult Education Department, and at no extra pay) so that he, Fred, could go to Canada for a Sabbatical Year. If Tom had not done this then the post would have been lost due to the economic squeeze. However, when Tom was asked to continue it for a second year I argued strongly against it, saying that his composition had to come first. So perhaps it was my intervention that prompted Fred's reaction.

The *Fourth String Quartet* was completed in August 1978, and in the run-up to the first performance Elizabeth Lyon interviewed Tom for an article to be published in the arts magazine Craftwork. When she asked him about the financial rewards of working as a composer he remarked: "This is a very dicey and risky profession. You have to be very lucky to end up with a reasonable supply of this world's goods. But so far I have been very fortunate."

Then she enquired where he found inspiration for his music, and Tom replied:

> I always find this a very difficult question to answer. I certainly don't get ideas from expected sources. A beautiful landscape doesn't do anything for me musically. I can respond to the beauty of the landscape and enjoy it, but it doesn't have any musical consequence. But possibly this isn't true of a poem or a piece of literature. I have always thought of poetry as a sister art to music, possibly because it participates in certain things which are essentially rhythmic. It is sound, it is rhythm, it is assonance and dissonance. These are all musical things. But, that apart, I wouldn't say that the musical ideas I get come from any outside sources. They are purely musical. The idea may take the form of some formal structure, I may become excited by the idea of writing something cyclic, or I may be excited by a kind of shape, even a geometric shape. You might write a piece in the shape of an arch. Other people have done that before, like Bartók. It might be a sequence of notes, or a rhythm, colour effect, or the idea of the combination of a trumpet and xylophone. Any of these might excite me to write.

One is obviously influenced always by the things one hears. If you admire the work of another person I suppose to some extent it has a bearing on what you do yourself. It's not a direct bearing, but something that sets your mind going in a certain direction. I listen to a great deal of music by very many composers. I've a very catholic taste in music. There is an awful lot of music that I don't like at all. I think that my own tastes favour a classical approach. I like things to be simple and clear, and to have a certain elegance, yet to be full of expressive qualities, passion and sentiment. Mozart, for instance, is one of my favourite composers. But I would find much to admire in the work of Dufay of the sixteenth century, Josquin des Prés, Palestrina, and Monteverdi of the seventeenth. In the twentieth century the influences that have been most direct for me have been people like Bartók, and, to a lesser extent Webern and Berg and Stravinsky; having said that, I would say that I take my music on a one at a time basis. Some of the works of these composers I like very much indeed, and others I'm much less enthusiastic about. There are things I respond to in Stockhausen, Boulez, Lutoslawski and Ligeti. Music at the moment seems to me in a crossroads situation. We have advanced at such a prodigious rate in this century that we now find ourselves out of breath, not sure where to go next. The options are many and various, and quite separate in the character of the solutions they offer.

My own philosophy in music is to seek a greater element of simplification. This process, if properly achieved, is an infinitely complex thing. It seems to me quite possible that all these optional avenues might offer a way forward. Having started myself without a classical background, I would say it was an essential to have a grounding in tradition. It's quite fashionable sometimes to pretend that the nineteenth century didn't exist, but that is manifest nonsense. We stand in a tradition of composers. That doesn't mean that you have to take the whole thing on your shoulders like Atlas and shoulder it forward a few steps. It's simply that you have to be aware of it. There is an element of music that is highly craftsmanlike, and that you have to learn. The intuitive or creative side of composition is something that will flower more fruitfully, given a measure of technical expertise.

It is a melancholy fact that we live in a society that is, near enough, musically illiterate. There is a wide measure of support for good music. People do go to the opera and they do go to concerts. But people do not hear new music and feel at home with it, the way they might with a new play or a new book or an exhibition of paintings. I suppose people can generally read, and they can look at paintings and discern shapes. People generally cannot read music. They have little idea how it is made or what kind of formal structure it employs. They simply accept the result as it were. They either like it or they dislike it. I think that it's inevitable that a composer today feels that his music gets something less than the audience he would like for it.

On January 15 1979, the *Third String Quartet* was broadcast on Radio 3, as a lead-in to the première of the *Fourth String Quartet*, by its commissioners the Edinburgh Quartet. The première - itself a studio recording - was held eight days later, and broadcast as the central feature of the 'Spectrum' arts programme on January 26 on BBC TV Scotland. The critic Malcolm Rayment interviewed Tom in the studio before the performance and Malcolm later wrote about this unusual experience in The Glasgow Herald:

Many musical works have, of course, been written specially for television, while others have been televised on the occasion of their first performances as outside broadcasts. But I cannot recall any composition having for its world première a performance built up in the TV studio until Thomas Wilson's new *Fourth String Quartet* was so treated by the Edinburgh Quartet. The recording took place on Tuesday January 23 and a long drawn-out affair it turned out to be – partly because there was a period during which the sound was lost. Jim Longmuir had designed a special set for the event, but viewers will not see it tonight. It is said to be brilliantly effective but, because of the lorry drivers' strike, it was impossible to transport it to Queen Margaret Drive from Kirkintilloch where it had been built. Only two days beforehand there was talk of a cancellation, but in a matter of hours Jim Longmuir improvised a new set using whatever came to hand. As will be seen he made a marvellous job of it. So did James Hunter the producer. A musician himself, he had learned the work in advance, and his presentation of it amounts to the equivalent of choreography. His treatment aids comprehension by underlining the musical structure. It is, however, essential to see this presentation in colour for this plays a very important rôle. This is a fine and typical work, again consisting of a single movement.

Perhaps because this was a new experience for both composer and critic, the television interview reveals a great deal about Tom's attitudes, not just towards the innovative structure of the *Fourth String Quartet*, but also towards chamber music generally.

186

Malcolm: Tom, not so many composers in our century have written as many as four quartets but you've now reached this number, and I believe there's a very long gap between the new work and its predecessor.

Tom: Yes it's about twenty years in fact between No. 3 and No. 4, but the explanation for that is really quite simple, I had other things to do. I've been very busy in many other areas; I've written operas and orchestral music, and music for all sorts of instruments, choirs and so forth.

Malcolm: ...and also quite a lot of chamber music.

Tom: Oh, a lot of chamber music, yes. But the point was that when I started out to be a composer, and I decided that's what I wanted to do, I wanted to confront the challenges of all the possible musical mediums, and that's really why it's taken such a long time to come back round to writing another string quartet. That's the reason there's been a long gap between them.

Malcolm: At the beginning you must have been fascinated to produce three string quartets very early in your career. It must have been a great fascination. Of course today the popularity of the medium is certainly growing as the number of string quartet combinations show. One of them is the Edinburgh Quartet, which has commissioned the new work with assistance from the Scottish Arts Council, and from various donors I believe.

Tom: Yes, well, the fascination of it is of course the fact that it really presents perhaps the greatest challenge that a composer can confront himself with, because it's one of the most pure musical mediums that have so far been devised. You're dealing with instruments of a like type, they are all producing relatively similar kinds of tone and colour, they are limited in number; there are only four of them, so the challenge to the composer writing in this form is a great challenge indeed. It's very demanding.

Malcolm: You can't get away with anything can you?

Tom: No, there's absolutely no excess fat on this arrangement at all. You've got to be absolutely precise about what you do. You can't produce the great washes of colour for example that are available if you were writing a symphony or something for a large orchestra. As you say you only have four instruments, and consequently you are down to basic rations as far as music making is concerned, and as a result therefore everything has to be absolutely in focus, absolutely precise, absolutely economical.

Malcolm: To go one stage further you've got 16 strings on the four instruments, and there's a limit to what they can do.

Tom: That's true.

Malcolm: I've had a very good look at the new quartet, and I'm very excited about it I must say. I can see that it's concise and all the rest of it, but the idiom, now this is very important, some listeners will not get all out of it – no listener will get everything out of it the first time around, but there will be a few who might ask you why you didn't write in a simpler idiom – an idiom well tried and exploited by past composers.

Tom: Well this is a question that is frequently asked and I think that it stems from misunderstanding. Art is about the present not about the past. If someone says to you, "Why don't you write like Brahms?" the answer is that I can't, even if I wanted to, because Brahms was a nineteenth-century man and I'm a twentieth-century man. Art is about the present, it illuminates the present, it reflects the present, and, if you like, perhaps also it is a comment on the present. But if you try to immure yourself in some previous style you are tantamount to living in a museum, it just won't do. And furthermore the result of all of that would be to produce a piece of counterfeit music – it would be a sham.

Malcolm: A pastiche.

Tom: That's right. And a sham of course never works. It's tantamount first of all to writing down to your audience, and when you write down to your audience I think you always fail as a result.

Malcolm: It would be attempting to do something as well as the great masters of the past, which is impossible to do, because they were pushing forward too.

Tom: Yes. If you look at the masters of the past they wrote in terms of the musical style that was current in their own day. It's the same for the twentieth century composers, as it always has been in that respect. You have to write in terms of what you find, and what you want to say, and in terms of the language of the present day.

Malcolm: Looking at the score you can see it's in one continuous whole, no division into movements, but there are five very obvious sections in which the slow first one corresponds to the last, and the second is a scherzo and so on, but what strikes me as unusual here, is that your meat, your meatiest stuff, comes shortly before the end.

Tom: This is something that I always thought was a wee bit odd about music. If you look at the symphonies of Beethoven, it tends to be as you say that the meat comes very near the beginning. But if you look at paintings, or if you read a novel, or if you go to the cinema the climax always comes about three-quarters of the way through – perhaps even further on than that. And what I wanted to do this time was to try to reverse the musical process and put the meat at the end, rather than at the beginning, build up to it in a steady acceleration to the point of climax being reached, because that corresponds more closely in a sense to the way you would normally expect these things to happen. As I say, they haven't happened like that in music in the past, which is an oddity. There's no criticism implied, but I wanted to see if, by reversing it, I could in fact make it work.

Malcolm: Perhaps the reason past composers haven't done it is they felt their audience's concentration might run out.

Tom: It might have something to do with that, it could be that it's the concentration factor that has prompted them to do this in the first place. But what I am doing here is, as I say, going for broke as it were. I'm hoping to take them with me.

These idiomatic innovations notwithstanding, musicians and audiences have responded extremely well to the *Fourth String Quartet*. It is one of Tom's most performed works. The pianist Claire Liddell wrote to Tom:

Dear Mr. Wilson,

I was most interested to hear your *Fourth String Quartet* on Spectrum last night.

It was a work of great clarity of texture and structure and you have done full justice to the transparency of the "quartet medium."

I cannot pretend to have taken it all in at a first hearing but I do wish you many more performances of it – Loved the poignant statements made by the 1st violin.

My best wishes,

Claire Liddell

Another interesting letter from a viewer read:

Dear Mr. Wilson,

It was a great pleasure to see you on TV and to hear the first performance of your latest quartet. It is difficult to swallow everything at an initial hearing (how's that for a well mixed metaphor?) but I for one, find that four strands are far easier to follow than the dozen or so crowded into my ears from a full orchestra. When I was involved in technical discussions during my working days, I always said "the smaller the committee the greater the progress". It is a pity the BBC gave us TV instead of 3rd programme VHF sound, but we must be thankful for small mercies.

Although the remarks you made during the interview regarding the need for modern composers to write in the 20th century idiom were apposite, I was none the less intrigued to note that you were particularly careful to follow the 18th century practice of Joe Haydn, in adjusting the overall length of the quartet to fit comfortably on to one side of a 33RPM LP!

Are any plans afoot in that direction?

Congratulations, and my wife joins me in sending our best wishes to Mrs. Wilson and your good self,

Yours sincerely

A. Johnson.

There are many such letters, from viewers, friends and fellow musicians, but I feel that I must quote one other, that from William Wordsworth, a friend, fellow composer and fervent golfer who was obviously more impressed by the music than the camerawork and set design.

Dear Tom,

We much enjoyed listening to your quartet on Friday, even if I found the tricks the TV people were up to somewhat distracting – and as having no relation to the music. I hope it will not be long before there is a chance to hear the work again and get a tape of it; I had the impression that you had broken new ground in it, and I should like to be able to concentrate on it without having my attention continually diverted by changes of colour or pattern. (The only time when these seemed appropriate was when the circles at the back of the players looked – to my prejudiced eye, like golf balls). (By the way how kind of the BBC to arrange that I didn't have to miss any of the Gleneagles match in order to see the Spectrum programme – or vice versa!)

With love to you both from both of us, Bill.

Following the broadcast on January 26 1979, Ian Robertson, the music critic for the Times Educational Supplement Scotland wrote enthusiastically in the Classical Music Magazine:

Unlike more fêted figures of his generation who have pursued transatlantic careers, Wilson has chosen to stay in Scotland and face up to the real challenge of thinking out the big traditional humanist and artistic problems in terms of a potentially unglamorous environment. For this he has earned the respect and gratitude of everyone writing here, and from this he has formed a powerful, uniquely eloquent idiom, which may not register a heat wave on more fashionable barometers, but is as insistent and un-ingratiating as the truth. This superb new quartet, his first in twenty years, plays continuously over contrasting sections in a beautifully clean form, and cells, whether developmental or static, are unfolded with economy and elegance.

In February 1979, hard on the heels of this success, Tom was commissioned by the Scottish National Orchestra to write a significant work for orchestra to be performed in their Musica Nova Series, the Fourth International Festival of Contemporary Music, to be held in September. Though it was not stated specifically, the suggested length of the work and the fee essentially meant that they were asking for a symphony. Having most recently completed the *Fourth String Quartet*, the opportunity to take his musical imagination to the other end of the spectrum and explore once more an extended palette was very welcome.

Ideally he would have preferred to have more than seven months at his disposal for a major work, but Tom hated to disappoint people and so he immediately set to the task of composing his *Third Symphony*. As always he spent the first weeks in contemplation, emptying his mind of everyday thoughts, and focussing on what was most important to him. He was always interested in the idea of rites of passage - birth, death and questions of destiny and fate. But whereas in the choral and operatic works he had concentrated on man's moral failings and our own part in our rise and fall, on this occasion he chose to approach this idea from a more physical and abstractly metaphysical perspective, to look at the idea of evolution, equilibrium, disequilibrium and circularity (or 'Rondeaux et Rituels/Cycles' as he wrote on the cover of his manuscript and all the parts). While Tom was writing his *Third Symphony* he talked to me about it, and this is the way he described it; the first movement would depict 'Birth'; the second, 'Growing and Building' (but here he said that he must avoid a *jeu d'esprit* feeling as the building must be of serious intent); the third, unexpected 'Degeneration'; and the fourth, 'Chaos'. And at the end a hint of 'Re-birth' that is better than the initial idea depicted in the first movement. Of course not all his works were constructed in this manner, but this is an example of one of his ways of thinking. In 1982 he would use a similar pattern for another orchestral work *Introit*.

The composition had to be put to one side in March since Tom had been invited to go to Berlin for ten days to attend the 7th Musik-Biennale as representative of the Composers' Guild of Great Britain. While there he met Gunmar Bucht, Carlos Farinas and Kane Kolberg and they all got on very well together.

It is a measure of Tom's development as a composer that he was able to take a break like this and return with such focus to his composition. Whereas the *Second Symphony* had been a real struggle in that it took him the best part of three years to complete, the writing of the *Third Symphony* proceeded smoothly without outward complication, with all the spiritual battles condensed into the music itself. The result was to be an assured, beautifully modulated and gripping life-journey from the momentous upheaval of birth, through confusion and complication, to eventual clarity and simplicity.

On the first page of his manuscript Tom had outlined the following framework including his estimates of the timing for each section:

Intro – 3 1/2 [minutes]	– Problem and solution 1	
A – 4 1/2	["]	– New problem (consequent on previous section)
B – 4	["]	– Solution 2
C – 4	["]	– New (catastrophic) problems (consequent on B)
D – 4	["]	– Vision of the "real" solution that man is capable of.
Total – 20	["]	

The finished piece is remarkably true to this original plan and philosophical intention (though the finished work is 28 1/2' not 20') and finds Tom once again pondering the true nature of creative consciousness to which we should all aspire.

In September the new symphony was to be the centrepiece of the Musica Nova Fourth International Festival of Contemporary Music at Glasgow University. On September 18 as part of the Festival, the strings of the BBCSSO gave the first performance of the recently written version for full string orchestra of *Ritornelli per Archi*. Writing about this performance in the Glasgow Herald, Malcolm Rayment declared that "*Ritornelli* is among Wilson's finest compositions."

Complementi was also included in this series of concerts, and the piece and performance earned these remarks from critic Ian Robertson:

> A fine work whose taut construction and dramatic gestures made a strong impact. It is a work which grows in stature with each hearing and it received a strongly characterised performance by the New Music Group of Scotland.

At the final concert of the Musica Nova series on September 22 1979 the SNO conducted by Alexander Gibson premièred Tom's *Third Symphony* which had been completed in mid August. Also on the programme was Robin Holloway's *Second Concerto for Orchestra*, along with Debussy's *Jeux*. This resulted in a dramatic clash of styles!

This in turn was reflected in the reviews, all of which had trouble judging the works solely on their individual merits and instead took the easier option of remarking on the obvious differences between the two contemporary works. Tom always said that "comparisons are odious" and on this occasion Malcolm Rayment's review was a bit harsh towards Robin Holloway:

> There could hardly have been a greater contrast than that between the works of Wilson and Holloway, the first being a creation by a

master of his craft, and the second one by a composer who is still experimenting.

Another felt that Tom's *Third Symphony* was "solid" but "perhaps not one of Wilson's most adventurous works". I felt and still feel that this criticism is rather unfair to a work that, though not as avant garde as *Ritornelli per Archi*, is a very seductive, eloquent and absorbing work, strung with brilliant musical ideas, many of which would be further explored in future works.

Looking back, I feel that Gerald Larner's review in the Guardian was possibly the most balanced. He found much to praise in Robin Holloway's work before going on to write about the *Third Symphony*:

> In another to all appearances excellent first performance, it emerged as one of the most impressive works written by a Scottish composer in recent years. It is particularly rewarding for its calculation of sound qualities, from the confused sub-Pendericki Genesis to its serenely linear Apogee in the centre of the construction. In fact, Wilson makes his long term point by stylistic allusion and is remarkably successful in sustaining the argument over a large span and with a genuinely symphonic effect.

In his review for The Scotsman, Conrad Wilson described the symphony as:

> ...a positive and dramatic piece of a kind which Sir Alexander Gibson and the Scottish National Orchestra will surely wish to keep in their repertoire.

Even though the work is dedicated to Sir Alexander Gibson and the SNO (now the RSNO), the orchestra did not take Conrad Wilson's advice and performed the symphony on only two more occasions. Indeed, for a national orchestra, the SNO has not been as supportive of Tom's work in recent times, as the BBC Scottish Symphony Orchestra, having performed only one work since 1992.

Over the years the *Third Symphony* has grown in critical stature. In *The Music of Thomas Wilson* published by *Musica Scottica* Professor William Sweeney wrote:

> In this work, Wilson's personal strengths of spiritual and emotional intensity, capacity for intellectual objectivity and professional

craftsmanship, are exemplified by the flow and balance of musical incident. The classical balance of expectations satisfied or surprised is sustained by the final pages, which in their tonal simplicity might, in other hands, be experienced as a disjunctive sentimental loss of direction."

Tom spent the months before Christmas working on a series of arrangements of Burns songs for a Radio Clyde commission. These included *Ca' the Yowes*, *Corn Rigs*, *The Lea Rig*, *Ye Banks and Braes* and *Ae Fond Kiss*. The programme, transmitted on Burns Night, was to be called *There was a Man*. Tom delivered the nine or ten songs for baritone, violin, clarinet and piano in January 1980. Hamish Wilson, the Head of Drama at Radio Clyde wrote to him saying:

Dear Tom,

...Just a wee note to say thank you very much for your very hard work on the music for 'There Was a Man'. It is a source of wonder to me that despite the incredibly short notice you were able to produce music which was not only of the highest order of quality, but completely relevant to the production and so constructed that there was not the slightest problem of marrying dialogue to music. The enhancement of our production by your music was considerable and I am very grateful once again.

I hope that there will be opportunities in the future for us to work together again and perhaps under slightly less hurried circumstances.

In the event, in less than a year's time, Tom did indeed work again for Radio Clyde. But prior to that second commission he had other projects to occupy him over the New Year.

CHAPTER 14 (1980 - 1983)

Symphony and Synthesizer

Tradition has it that women talk a lot, but when musicians of whatever sex meet it is hard to get a word in edgewise. Tom had many composer friends, but the one he would see most often was John Maxwell Geddes. They had a close friendship spanning thirty-five years, and Tom inscribed his copy of his *Third Symphony*, "For John Geddes, my alter-ego, with whom I have had so many moments of understanding of a clouded universe of music. Tom"

Every week John would appear, and most often their discussions would continue until the early hours. They were certainly on each other's wavelength, and the subjects were wide-ranging: philosophy, music, history, the arts and life in general. They discussed rather than argued, even though they approached things from different angles, Tom being deeply spiritual, while John is a humanist. One of the subjects discussed at length was how to achieve a situation of transcendental timelessness or *zeitlosigkeit*. In musical terms this is a sense of feeling that we are standing momentarily outside time rather than being swept along by it. Tom said that true timelessness is impossible to achieve in music. He believed that stasis could not be achieved without kinesis. Sometimes he used the simple perfection of plainchant as a device to simulate stasis by reducing the inner complexities of a work. At other times he wrote 'mobile-like passages' without linear development to achieve a dream-like state, and indeed one of his finest guitar works is called *Dream Music* while one of his *Three Pieces for Piano* is called *Reverie*.

He was fascinated by metaphors for physical and spiritual enlightenment. The metaphors he frequently explored in his more abstract works included the diurnal rhythm of life, evolution and decay, and even the motion of a mobile spinning in the breeze. One great problem that all composers face is how to diffuse tension after a climax, before reminding the listener of the initial musical ideas. Tom dealt with the problem using melodic simplicity, while John often resolved his dissonances and tensions harmonically.

196

Both were interested in using acronyms as did Bach, Schumann, Elgar and Shostakovich. Both of them used motivic devices and when John described these as his own fingerprints, Tom corrected him saying: "Not fingerprints John, hallmarks". In short, they bounced ideas off one another, as John described it to me after Tom died:

> Things that I suggested to Tom, he considered, and often to my delight adopted. I got a buzz from discussing ideas, both intra-and-extra musical, with him, and I was delighted that he valued my input. Tom's instinctual grasp of my work-in-progress was invaluable; things that he suggested about my work were so important to me, that I found that his thinking not only influenced what I was writing at any given time, but permeated my outlook and shifted my philosophical perspectives. Tom and I were often programmed together - for instance, the première of his Piano Concerto and the première of my Ombre. Tom was always a hard act to follow, but luckily I had written the overture piece before his symphonic work. But the point is this: over the years Tom and I were often at the same stage of composition of a work, and we had common, similar, parallel problems in the philosophy and craft of composition.

Throughout the 1980s Tom was invited each spring to deliver a lecture to the scientists who worked at the submarine base at Faslane. A car came to our home to take him there and bring him back, and the scientists always laid on an extravagant dinner. At this time, it was also Tom's habit to go with some members of his Tuesday afternoon class to a local pub for a pint of beer on his way home before dinner – lecturing could be thirsty work! So when the chauffeur turned up one Tuesday in February 1980 at 5pm to take Tom to Faslane – he was not at home. I asked the chauffeur to come with me to our local pub, Tennants, on the corner of Byres Road and Highburgh Road. Once there I marched in and said to Tom; "You should be on your way to Faslane." Before I could say another word the barman emerged from behind the counter to show me the door, saying: "Madam, this is a men-only bar". I was speechless but the barman indicated that he would stand no nonsense. Tom followed me out and, once he had recovered from his amusement at my loss for words (a situation that had not occurred previously in his experience), he replied; "No, Margaret, the lecture is next month." The chauffeur had turned up a month early. As a postscript to this event I should say that some years later, when 'Women's Lib' was at its height, a group of female students from Glasgow University went to Tennants pub and refused to be moved, and so the bar belatedly became open to both sexes.

Overall 1980 was not as busy a year as 1979 had been; however Tom did write *Dream Music* for the young virtuoso guitarist Phillip Thorne, who was already a tutor at the Royal Scottish Academy of Music and Drama. Phillip had long been an admirer of Tom's guitar works and believed Tom to be one of the pre-eminent composers for the instrument. Having obtained funding from the Scottish Arts Council, Tom and Phillip began talking about their hopes for the piece. They both shared the opinion that the guitar was a very lyrical instrument, though Tom expressed some surprise that some earlier performances, particularly of *Soliloquy*, had come across as more 'modern' than romantic. Phillip said that because he knew Tom well, he readily recognised the romantic element in Tom's writing for the guitar. However, he explained that the way Tom had composed for the instrument meant that some chords were difficult to finger, resulting in a more angular interpretation from some performers who did not know Tom's work so well. This did not mean that the alternative interpretations were less valid, but Phillip felt that this might explain the different approaches. When Phillip demonstrated this on the guitar, Tom was quite annoyed with himself for having made things more difficult for the performer when he thought he was making them easier. He was therefore determined to make sure that *Dream Music* would be as technically accessible as possible without compromising his musical intentions.

Working closely with Phillip, Tom changed the way that he wrote the chords to allow the performer to play quickly across the strings while simplifying the stopping along the neck of the instrument. Phillip said that he greatly enjoyed working so closely with Tom, though he was never in any doubt that he was the technical advisor. As Phillip put it, "The warmth of his compositions reflects the man. Tom was a great paradox. He knew exactly what he wanted but empathised with others' viewpoints without him losing his. He never had a cross word; he tried to accommodate but never shifted an inch. That collaboration gave me a real insight into the creative process, but also into what was negotiable and what was not."

Tom also talked to Phillip about the individuality and Mediterranean character of the guitar which lent itself so well to expressing emotion and the interior landscape: "During the early stages of composition we talked a lot about dream imagery, but Tom never really came away with the definite image. He did realise that music created images but didn't want to make these programmatic. He said that there were two phases in the dream world; the relaxed, lyrical time and the menacing moments. In composing *Dream Music*, Tom brought these contrasts very close together to create a series of fleeting moments."

Tom's insight into the nature and structure of dreams always struck me as amusing since he told me that he never dreamed. As I know this cannot be true, I just thought that he never remembered his dreams. Whereas mine were so vivid and offbeat that we often ended up in gales of laughter even before we had got out of bed.

Clearly Tom's dreams were far more 'serious' than mine since the resultant work was what Phillip Thorne describes as "the perfect work for solo guitar" with "only one chord that was difficult to play". The work was completed in June and Philip premièred it during a guitar recital that took place in St Andrew's and St George's Church Edinburgh as part of the Edinburgh Festival. It has since been played by many notable guitarists including Allan Neave, Stefan Grasse, Paul Gregory, Gerald García, Timothy Walker, Tuomo Tirronen and Anne Chaurand.

Tom first met Andy Park in the early 1960s when Tom and John Purser had invited Andy to become a member of the Scottish Society of Composers. Andy recalls that Tom and Martin Dalby were very supportive of his musical ambitions and that he admired both men greatly. When he was made the Head of Programming at Radio Clyde, and the opportunity came to commission works, he was more than happy to oblige. Though it may seem unusual today that a commercial radio station should commission original works from contemporary classical composers, the early eighties were an interesting time in the history of radio. As Andy remembers, commercial radio initially came about based on a political desire to counter the popularity of BBC Radio 1 and pirate radio stations, like Radio Luxembourg, and to be unashamedly 'commercial' not only in terms of making money but also in playing commercial music. The first two commercial radio stations were in London but the third was Radio Clyde, which began broadcasting on December 31 1973. Though the new stations had set out to play commercial music, the Musicians' Union was particularly powerful at the time and they were able to dictate that commercial radio stations could play commercial music only nine hours out of every twenty-four. Moreover the stations would need to remit 3% of their income to the union. However, Andy was able to negotiate a specific agreement between the Musicians' Union and Radio Clyde whereby part of this three percent could be spent on directly supporting musicians (rather than the union) through developing facilities, producing live performances, and commissioning new works across all musical genres. As a result Radio Clyde invested in two state-of-the-art 24-track recording studios, and supported a chamber orchestra known as Cantilena.

Although Tom did not write much music for radio plays, and now refused this type of work more often than he accepted because he was busy with other commissions, Andy was a very enthusiastic character, and Tom also had a soft spot for poetry. So Tom accepted Andy's invitation to write music for two literary programmes to be produced by Radio Clyde.

The first, named the *Splendid Silent Sun*, was broadcast to coincide with the summer solstice in June. The title was taken from a Walt Whitman poem read at the beginning and end of the broadcast. The central part was made up of a number of poems all accompanied by especially composed instrumental music. Some of the featured poets were Ted Hughes, D.H. Lawrence, and Percy Bysshe Shelley, whose famous sonnet *Ozymandias* had made a great impression on Tom. It echoed his feelings about the impermanence of glory so well. It is said that Shelley wrote this poem after seeing the remains of the statue of Ozymandias, another name for Rameses the Great, which had recently been acquired by the British Museum. In his notes on *Ozymandias* Tom divided his ideas into two parts. The first he refers to as the "desert" – "the invincible ease with which Time destroys human achievements; the impermanence of human affairs; the folly of pride and vainglory." The second part is split into "Desolation; Loneliness; Sadness". In the music for this poem he used the eerie sound effect obtained by stroking the outer rim of a cymbal with a cardboard tube covered in French chalk. When this sound was first heard, in the *Sequentiae Passionis*, the percussionist used the inside tube of a toilet roll covered in talcum powder!

Following a repeat broadcast, Kathleen Rantell's "Radio Review" in The Glasgow Herald reported that:

> LBC (local broadcasting companies) and the commercial radio companies broadcast a second hearing of the beautifully polished anthology of poetry and music *Splendid Silent Sun* that Radio Clyde had commissioned the previous year to mark the summer solstice. It has specially composed music by Thomas Wilson, professor of music at Glasgow University, and one of Britain's leading avant-garde composers, and it is one of those rare productions where every sound is significant and every evocative detail builds into a single complete sound picture.

The second programme, transmitted in November 1980, was based on the realist novel *The House with the Green Shutters* by George Douglas Brown. The novel depicts an ambitious, narrow-minded society motivated largely by greed and an obsession with money, which in his darker moments Tom felt was true of Britain in the 1980s.

In October a third commission came through Andy Park from Radio Clyde, this time for a piece of pure music, for transmission the following June. On this occasion, however, Andy specified that Tom should make use of the station's chamber orchestra, domestic-scale synthesisers, and multi-track recording studio. Otherwise as Andy puts it, "Tom had *carte blanche*". Tom had enjoyed the experience of composing for multi-track equipment when he was writing the Burns songs and now he was happy to accept the added challenge of using the synthesiser. He said it was "the duty of the composer to take risks and extend the range of their abilities."

As Tom had not used the Minimoog and Polymoog synthesisers before, this took him on a new learning curve. He went to Edinburgh to the home of David Pringle, (who was to play the synthesisers in the performance) in order to hear the sounds that the instruments were capable of making. After gaining a familiarity with the synthesisers' limitations and capabilities, he went on to choose the sounds and "special effects" that he wanted to use. These special effects included, in his own words, "Chattering glissando", "Wobbling (oscillating) drumming", "Decaying scream or howl (with initial 'attack'), "Didgeridoo + cymbal + random (preset) ostinato?", etc., etc.

While interviewing Tom in 1997 about this period in his life, Martin Dalby remarked, "I don't wake up in the morning and actually think of you primarily as an innovative composer in the field of electronic music, but there are in fact quite a few instances." Martin then went on to ask specifically about Tom's experience writing Mosaics, the work Tom had produced to fulfil the Radio Clyde commission. Tom replied:

> That was done using Moog Synthesizers (PolyMoog and MiniMoog) which are now, I think, non-existent. They produced a range of sounds which I found absolutely fascinating, and later models, such as the DX7 didn't quite manage to live up to that. They had greater sophistication in certain respects, but some of the sounds which the Moog was able to produce I could not find on the DX7. After I provided the music for Radio Clyde for the programme 'The Splendid Silent Sun', Andy Park said: "What about combining these two things? Write a piece which features the Synthesizer and also features Cantilena, and the fusion of baroque instrumental grouping and twentieth century instruments, and find a kind of connection between the two." And that's what Mosaics attempts to do.

Tom set out to create a piece that would bring about a convergence of these non-traditional instruments and more familiar modes of musical expression. It is in parts syncopated – effects that he knew I liked. In my opinion, *Mosaics* works wonderfully well.

He had reservations about talking about his own music and said about composers who spoke of their own compositions at length: "Why didn't they just write a book?" However in exceptional cases, he was sometimes persuaded. So it was in 1981, at the request of Andy Park, that he gave a series of six evening classes about the composition of *Mosaics* which reveal not only the musical construction of the piece but also the deeper philosophical ideas that lay behind it.

On a musical level this challenge was about how to bring about a synthesis of the "old" and the "new". Tom said that whereas he was known as a modern composer, Cantilena was famous for playing baroque music so the audience should have no preconceived notions about what type of music they were going to hear. In preparing the audience for discussions about the choices Tom made in composing this work he first talked more generally about the rôle and responsibilities of the composer.

> What is the composer's job? What is he supposed to be doing? Is he producing something that will entertain his audience? The answer to that is yes - always. But by entertain I would mean something wider than simply to produce a pleasurable sensation of a rather passing kind. I'm talking about entertainment in the sense of interesting people in something which stimulates them, which makes them want to think in some way differently perhaps, to any way they have thought before. So I would say that always the composer should be seeking to do that. The second thing that you might say the composer should do is in some way to enlighten the audience. That's very pompous sounding and indeed that will only happen if the piece in question is good enough for it to happen. There is an awful lot of music which is of good enough quality, without being good enough to enlighten anyone. It will simply entertain or please the senses. It just sounds enjoyable and lets it go at that. That's all it is any good for. I'm not for a moment going to suggest into which category this piece of mine will fit, it's up to you individually to make up your own minds about that. But in the case of this enlightenment question, the answer would be that the composer should try very hard to make it happen, but it will only happen sometimes and then only if it is good enough. The third possibility that you might say is that the composer is on some kind

of ego trip. He's doing something that is fundamental to himself. He's discharging some kind of personal obligation to himself. He's having a ball. He's doing his own thing. Now this is something that I have no doubt happens, and some composers may well be like that, but I'm not one of them. I feel that anything that smacks of self-indulgence of that kind is probably a black mark against the composer concerned. But there is a very strong part of the personality of the composer present in the music, there can be no doubt of that.

Tom then played the Overture from the *Magic Flute* by Wolfgang Amadeus Mozart.

My whole point in playing that to you, by of course a very great composer indeed, is that it is a very good example of what I mean by the answer to the question: What is the composer's job? He is there obviously being highly entertaining. He is writing music that is exceedingly pleasant to listen to; indeed beautiful would be a word that would spring to most people's minds. The actual piece of music is very funny in parts, quite hilarious in fact, so from that point of view it is also very diverting. However, the point that I want to get across about it is that Mozart's purpose here is a serious one. He may well present a smiling face to you, but what he is in fact doing is trying, in a sense, to change the world. He is presenting in the Magic Flute a philosophy of society, a kind of morality for society which he considers would be a better way for us to lead our lives than the way in which we go about things at the moment – and who can possibly disagree with that? Because we could hardly have got it more wrong than we have. Mozart is presenting his particular way of looking at things, and saying in a sense obliquely, because he can't speak directly about such things, that this is the way in which we should organise ourselves. It's full of all manner of things. It is a champagne piece in many respects; it bubbles along and it's got great verve and effervescence, but on the other hand it's full of Masonic symbolism. These three chords, each repeated three times is a symbolic element deriving from some aspect of Masonry. Though not being a member of the order, I am not able to say what it is, but this is well known. And in fact the nature of the musical material, though it might appear to be very direct and straightforward, is couched in a musical form that is really quite complicated and oblique. The sort of fugal patterns with which he places the music before you is of its nature rather complicated and labyrinthine. So all of these things are present in that piece and make it a very much more multi-layered affair than it might at first appear. So I am simply borrowing from the work of a greater man to indicate what I think that a composer should aim to cultivate.

Tom then went on to play a Cantilena recording of Vivaldi and subsequently discussed the specific challenges of composing for Cantilena and the synthesizer. Rather than try to somehow merge the baroque (for which Cantilena was known) and the modern in some sort of pastiche to satisfy both audiences, he instead explained how he chose to stay in his own field, set up a dialogue between the "orthodoxy of strings" and the "modernity of synthesised sounds", but with some sort of formal nod to Cantilena and the Baroque. He said that this would present a new challenge to himself, because he would not go back to established formal procedures, but would try to give them some form of new life. Since he had not done this in the past, Tom said it would present a "first" for him and; "I wondered what sort of success I could make of it if I took certain ideas from the Baroque period and combined them with my own contemporary style." This dialogue is accentuated by the stereophonic effects with the string sounds coming from the circular arrangement of the instruments and the synthesised sounds coming from the speakers around the hall. It is also pushed to a crisis and dissolution through the contrasting musical idioms, namely, the baroque use of strings and the "aleatoric, random effects for synthesisers." Later in the work he reconciled these differences by making the strings more modern in idiom, and by making the synthesisers more tonal in effect – more controlled in application, style and idiom.

On a deeper level, the challenge was to show the congruence of ideas and Tom's lecture notes reveal the true intention behind the reconciliation of this dialogue:

> – All passion spent – exhaustion, lassitude – new tendrils – new accords – new rapports – i.e. hope for some future fusion, synthesis i.e. "moral". Stylistic antagonisms appear to be real, fundamental, but they may only be external factors which disguise an inner accord, a mutual aim (SURFACE DIFFERENCES CAN DISGUISE ESSENTIAL IDENTITIES OF AIM) e.g. White vs. Black / Gentile vs. Jew / Roman Catholic vs. Orangeman ------ i.e. such conflicts spring from "superficialities" rather than essentials e.g. White and Black are both 'human'. Their source of discord is usually related to "superficial" and "changeable" factors such as economics, territorial disputes, vested interests, positions of privilege, etc.

– Their differences are real and certainly tragic, but their "brotherhood-as-human-beings" is the real factor which should be concentrated on – this is the ESSENTIAL UNCHANGING TRUTH about them – all else is transitory (POLITICAL DOMINANCE, ECONOMIC SUPERIORITY are factors which by their nature are impermanent and therefore unsatisfactory foundations on which to build.)

Overall the work is about the relationships between ideas, knowledge, experience and waywardness and comes in five stages of evolution, leading to a new beginning. Tom's notes sketch the work's structure.

Fantasia – ideas in conjunction which seem to have nothing to do with each other, but will develop relationships as the piece progresses – serves as an EXPOSITION

- Toccata ("Touch") – Knowledge through the sense [EXPLORATION] – innocent, thoughtless, wayward, changeable yet basically UNIFIED, basically CONSTRUCTIVE

- Aria I – Knowledge through the mind, emotions, sensibilities – the knowledge that comes from **EXPERIENCE** & CONTEMPLATION

- Capriccio – "irresponsibility", "waywardness" (like TOCCATA?) No – it is basically DESTRUCTIVE – leading to CRISIS, **DISSOLUTION**

- Aria II – **Lament** – "knowledge through sorrow"

- Fantasia II – Optimism – Knowledge through Faith, or **Intuition**

All of this was thought out before he committed a single note to manuscript paper.

While Tom was venturing into new territory in his music, I was charting a new course of my own. When the Adult Education Department of Glasgow University devised a one-year Access Course for mature students wishing to enter a degree course, I was enticed by this opportunity to do something for myself. Our sons were now grown men, and two of them lived away from home. After talking it over with Tom, who was wholly supportive, I enrolled in this preparatory course in English and Philosophy in October 1980. I completed one term but then events overtook me.

My father became ill in Newcastle upon Tyne, and in January 1981 the Victoria Infirmary telephoned to tell me that he had liver cancer and only weeks to live. He was eighty years old, and as my mother was eighty-four and unable to care for him, I went to look after him for the last six weeks of his life. After his death, my mother, who had outlived three of her four younger sisters, came to live with us in Glasgow.

Mosaics received its première in the SNO Centre on June 7 1981 and the concert was recorded for broadcast on July 12. The sizeable audience heard the piece twice, with a short interval in between. This is a practice that I find most commendable when a new work is introduced since it gives the audience a chance to really appreciate the merits and cadences of a new work. On the first hearing the colour and general character of the piece come to the fore, but on a second hearing one is more able to appreciate and focus on structure and form. Indeed upon hearing a contemporary work a second time I have often surprised myself by how much I have recognised and remembered from the previous performance. The audience response was very favourable; reviewing the concert in the Jewish Echo, Michael Tumelty wrote:

> The marriage of instrumental music with electronics is always a difficult union to effect with conviction. Wilson has met this challenge directly with the express intention of 'creating a musical meeting place between the traditional and the modern'. Integration takes place, in the composer's words, "at every structural and expressive level." Jazzy, syncopated, toccata-like sections of an exciting rhythmic drive, contrast with more meditative movements. The closing Fantasia contains a moving setting of a plainchant, which, presented on the synthesiser with a slightly delayed attack on each note, is of an ethereal glowing beauty. The work is highly attractive and immediately accessible. From the formal point of view the work is lucid in the extreme without conforming to any textbook pattern, while the content is as concentrated as it is gripping. Wilson is a master, and this is a very beautiful work whose sound world stems from *Canti Notturni*, with more of the gentle optimism which informed the recent *Third Symphony*.

Since Minimoog and Polymoog synthesizers are now almost museum pieces, it is unlikely that this piece (whose playfulness often reminds me of Tom's earlier work *Touchstone*) will ever be played again exactly as it was conceived though I do hope that one day I might hear it again live, perhaps using one of the newer synthesizers.

Shortly after the second performance of *Mosaics* in Edinburgh on June 21, my mother's youngest brother Harry, and his wife Peggy, came to our home to care for my mother while Tom and I went to Morocco for a holiday. For the past twenty years we had travelled extensively in Western Europe (apart from our one visit to Israel) and I was keen to explore a different culture. Morocco did not disappoint with its very different views on society, beauty and the arts. We spent the first week in Tangier and the second in Fez and we had a truly marvellous time. Here we visited the historic university, which was established in 859 AD and claims to be the oldest in the world, and the Roman ruins at Volubilis.

After hiring a driver and a guide we were taken to see a gathering of the different Saharan tribes. Bedouins were among those present, along with the Blue Men of the desert, whose womenfolk were tattooed on their faces, hands, and feet. The tribesmen had assembled to show off their horsemanship to each other. They raced round a track as fast as they could go, firing huge muskets into the air. It was an impressive display, though Tom scared me by running in front of the charging horde to take photographs. Later we were given comfortable seats in a capacious carpeted marquee, and we were as much an object of interest and speculation to the Moroccans as they were to us. Our guide prevailed upon us to visit his "uncle" who had a carpet-making business, and at the factory we saw children as young as six knotting carpets. Everywhere we went the poverty was quite startling – as was the wide gap between the many poor and the few rich.

Whenever we went on holiday or to a performance abroad, Tom would say to me when were halfway to the airport, "Have you got passports, tickets and money?" I always thought that it was a bit late if I hadn't. But there were four things that Tom was never without on these times away from home: his manuscript paper, a pencil, his pipe, and tobacco. That was as far as his interest in packing went. On the other hand his knowledge of Latin and Greek came in very useful on holiday when we looked at ancient buildings and statues and translations were needed.

After the summer holidays, Tom was supposed to start work on an orchestral commission for the BBC Scottish Symphony Orchestra. Though he had originally received the commission in 1980, he had been too busy with *Dream Music* and *Mosaics* to embark upon it immediately. Now that the time came to begin he spent many hours making notes on the composition but found it difficult to actually start writing the music. This was not because he was uninterested in the commission, but rather because of the abstract subject matter he had chosen to inform the composition – the nature of thought and the meaning of music. This meant that the pre-compositional stage took an unusually long time while he wrote exhaustive notes and sketches for this work – more than I can find about any of his other compositions.

On this occasion the conductor was to be Bryden Thomson, who had, as a young man, been a member of the BBC Symphony Orchestra when they had performed one of Tom's works. From their first meeting on July 14 1967, when Jack (as he was known to his friends) conducted the National Youth Brass Band in the first performance of *Sinfonietta* in St Andrews, Tom and Jack got on famously. This bond of friendship could have been tested when Tom, atypically, fell behind on his schedule for completing *Introit*, as the new composition came to be titled. Jack was not at all worried however; he knew that Tom would not let him or the BBC down. The score was delivered in sections as they were completed to Jack, who learned it in instalments. He did not get the full version of the work until ten days before the concert. It was a close thing, but Tom, in his usual unflappable way, just got on with it. However he never took things quite so close to the edge again.

Introit is the first prayer of the Mass Proper and it changes daily according to the feast; *Introibo ad altare Dei* (I will go unto the altar of God) is the beginning of the prayer said at the foot of the altar steps before the priest approaches the altar to begin Mass. Tom chose to interpret this, not in a strict Catholic sense (though he once again uses plainsong in the work), but as a journey toward enlightenment (Towards the Light). In his extensive pre-compositional and pre-performance notes, he begins by asking "What is the meaning of *Introit?*" In preparing his answer he then says that:

> The meaning of music is (obviously) musical, BUT if a more verbal answer is demanded, it suggests perhaps 1) That Intuition is a higher level of consciousness than Reason, 2) If this is true and the process of evolution is not yet complete for mankind, could it be that we will ultimately develop this "talent", and with it shed some of the greed, pride and other blemishes which have so far bedevilled our every attempt at real progress?

He elaborates further about the faculties of perception being 'Reason' and 'Intuition' and says that, "*Introit* is 'about' the disconcerting presence of both these faculties in our listening and in our lives." He goes on to say that:

The intellect has been predominant since the Renaissance and provides us with clarity, focus, sharp outlines, control and accountability. Intuition on the other hand is powerful (but hazy), undeniable (but unreliable), unclear and not so subject to control. *Introit* has both intellect and intuition, e.g. it has controlled form, shape, it has portions which are very precise, neat and orderly, BUT it also needs to jump out of these (in the early stages) or be transported to other areas which are less rational (e.g. the "refrains") and back into the rational again in an unaccountable and disconcerting way. It is a fusion of the conscious, controlled, professional and technical with the subliminal, unconcious, inspirational, intuitive faculties (which we all possess?), even though these have become suspect by being of their nature beyond the power of Reason to control.

For him intuition was a much more powerful, higher state.

I think our latent, undernourished, underused, inspirational and intuitive side is our GOOD side (whence comes compassion, altruism, virtue, self-denial). *Introit* is an optimistic work, one which recognises Man's capacity for divination rather than just his capacity to account for facts. All the great forward steps have been the result of this intuitive faculty (Gallileo, $E=mc^2$, Mozart, Michaelangelo, Goethe, DNA). Reason alone would never make these advances; it is incapable of a suficient degree of lateral (or even apparently contrary) thinking. It cannot deal with the paradoxical aspects of existence with which we are surrounded.

In these notes, he also lays out his own musical beliefs in no uncertain terms:

My Credo? I am only a musician and I do what I can with notes, my given language; music "must not only be good, it must also be beautiful." This does not mean <u>pretty</u> or <u>comfortable</u> or <u>soothing</u> or <u>acquiescent</u>. It means <u>True</u>!

On March 11 1982, the BBCSSO gave the first performance of *Introit* at the newly built MacRobert Centre, on the campus of Stirling University. The performance went very well and the orchestra as always did their very best for Tom. Malcolm Rayment pointed out the distinctive features of the work in his review:

When writing programme notes for his works Wilson usually speaks of several sections, but this is only part of the truth. His one-movement compositions have the contrast and emotional range we associate with works of three or more. Moreover their construction incorporates elements of variation and sonata form.

(In his pre-composition notes Tom described the work as a symphony in five continuous movements).

Later in the same review Malcolm summed up what I believe was the general feeling of the listeners:

> The work is undoubtedly one of the finest Thomas Wilson has so far given us. Not least of its virtues is that it is superbly written for the orchestra which, except during the climactic section, is treated on chamber music lines. Every note is essential, and many a composer has said very much less while taking twice as long doing so.

Praise indeed.

During the same month Tom revised his work for guitar, *Dream Music*. Then at the end of the month the BBC wrote to him commissioning incidental music for the TV production of *Cloud Howe*, part two of the Lewis Grassic Gibbon trilogy *A Scots Quair*. Tom had written the title music for the first part, *Sunset Song*, eleven years earlier so he readily agreed. However, *Cloud Howe* was written in four episodes, so producing the required music was quite an undertaking.

In June, Brendan graduated with a D. Phil from Oxford University, so the proud parents took themselves off to Oxford for the ceremony. Brendan had two degrees conferred on him that day so he was capped twice, and afterwards we all repaired to celebrate in one of the many local pubs selling 'real ale'.

Around the same time Glasgow University decided to cut down on its senior staff in order, I think, to save money on salaries. Tom was one of the professors approached by the Principal Alwyn Williams. All of the selected staff were offered the same deal: if they would work for three years for half pay plus pensions benefits, then the university would make up their pensions as though they had worked until they were 65 years old. The alternative was that they would be made redundant immediately and their pension would only reflect the years they had worked for the university. Tom had started late as a student, having had first to fulfil his three years of National Service. His honours degree took four years, and

210

his teacher training eight months, so his entry into the work force was later than is the norm. He was 54 years old when the offer was made, but his 55th birthday fell a few days after the start of the new academic year. Though not really happy with the terms, he did not have much option but to accept the offer. Tom enjoyed teaching though, and he continued to lecture in the Adult Education Department as an Emeritus Professor until prevented by ill health in 1997. Despite this reduction in salary, we weren't badly off as Tom was now firmly part of the musical establishment and commissions kept coming in - money that proved very useful to pay for such necessary tasks as preparing copies of scores and orchestral parts. A composer's life is all about scattering the bread upon the waters and hoping that some of it will come back as performances. Very few composers are lucky enough to have a publisher who will tirelessly promote their work, so most composers are now self-publishing, and it is an expensive business.

During the summer of 1982, Malcolm Rayment went to Europe to look for a place to buy his future home. He was suffering from arthritis and found the Scottish winters difficult. Eventually he settled on Sotogrande in southern Spain as the place he wanted to live. Since his Air Force days Tom had wanted to buy a holiday home in the south of France, but Malcolm persuaded him to come and look at Sotogrande. At the time, it was being developed and looked more like a building site than anything else. However, we climbed over planks that stood in for future steps and eventually chose the apartment that we felt was the best for us (or it would be when it had windows, doors, a kitchenette and bathroom).

The building of our block was completed in 1983. It was 150 yards from the beach and had views of the hills, and what are known as the White Villages to the north, and Gibraltar to the south. The climate was beautiful, and the golf course in Sotogrande is one of the nicest I know. We spent many happy days playing foursomes, but not as many as I would have liked, as Tom always had yet another commission to complete. We had also hoped to spend the winter months there, but university lectures in the Extra-Mural Department always took place between October and May. Tom enjoyed this teaching aspect of his life as it provided some balance to the loneliness of composition. So in the end we never carried out our plan to reside in Spain for an extended period.

In January 1983, David Dorward asked Tom to give a radio talk as part of a series called 'In Miniature' to be transmitted that month. During the talk to introduce a performance of Mozart's *Eine kleine Nachtmusik*, Tom recounted some formative memories from his early life:

I first heard that music when I was about five years old. My father was a passionate music-lover, and an ardent admirer of Mozart, and even though we weren't well off, his priorities required that the family should possess a good gramophone and a steadily expanding record collection. He was a man of wide tastes – anything ranging from chamber music to (Italian) opera, and from Paul Robeson to Stravinsky's 'Rite of Spring'.

Of course my father tried to pass on his love of music to me (without much success to start with). But one day he played *Eine Kleine Nachtmusik*. I remember it very clearly – the volume was turned up high; the day was warm, the windows of the room were open, and before the performance was over, our garden fence was festooned with absorbed passers-by who had stopped to listen. That was the first time that *Music* really got across to me – it wasn't a moment of great revelation or anything like that, just the kindling of a flame that has gone on burning ever since. However the path of true love, as they say, doesn't always run smooth.

Later on, in my middle teens, I had a more direct encounter with this same music. I was enlisted into the school orchestra. My parents provided me with a violin and lessons, but unfortunately my talent for the instrument was less than adequate. I found it almost impossible to play the thing in tune! Despite this drawback I was allocated to the back desk of the second fiddles – more or less to make up the numbers. And, lo and behold, our very first concert was scheduled to include the slow movement of *Eine Kleine Nachtmusik*. I well remember that concert – in fact I'll never forget it. The second violin part is burned into my brain. It was awful.

And again, much later, when I should have had more sense, I was persuaded against my better judgment to conduct a small band of amateur players who had the very laudable idea of honouring the 90th birthday of Mouland Begbie, a very celebrated Scottish violinist. *Eine Kleine Nachtmusik* was suggested, and I was daft enough to agree. Mind you, the result was closer to Mozart's intentions than the school concert, but that only made matters worse, because with Mozart's music everything has to be absolutely right. Nothing less will do. Well, we got it nearly right. The result was excruciating. In fact one of my friends, Tom Walsh, fled to the bar midway through the first movement. I felt like joining him.

The lesson of this little tale is simple. If great music looks, or sounds easy, it ain't necessarily so, in particular, the playing of music as transparent as Mozart's calls for the highest skills.

During March it seemed that the fates were getting at us. The publishing company called Scotus which had been started by James Douglas and for which we had had great hopes folded. For many years we were terribly concerned as to whether the parts for Tom's music would be returned safely; however, the issue was eventually resolved in 1991. The one positive effect of this episode was that Tom decided to found his own publishing house Queensgate Music, solely for his own music, that same autumn. And many composers have followed suit.

Lesser irritants also struck that month. While mentioning every other composer whose music would be performed in London during March, Classical Music Magazine omitted a performance of *Ritornelli* by the Priory Concertante in the Purcell Room. Even closer to home The Glasgow Herald in its "What's On" section, a column of details of concerts for the week, neglected to mention that Tom's *Sinfonietta for Brass* was to be performed in the Henry Wood Hall, Glasgow. Then just a day after he had come to the house and made plans to take on Tom's smaller works (vocal and chamber), publisher Kenneth Roberton telephoned to say that he had changed his mind. It was enough to make anyone feel paranoid; Tom though did not have time to brood, for despite its frustrations, March 1983 was a very busy month for performances.

Bird, Fish, Ring, Bell, Tree

At the beginning of April 1983 Tom completed *The Willow Branches* (for voice and piano) a work that had been commissioned by the mezzo-soprano Marilyn de Blieck. Marilyn had waited patiently for some years for Tom to be able to fit this in, but she reckoned it was worth the wait. When writing a piece for a single musician Tom always needed to hear the person play or sing first. Though he never compromised on his musical vision, he would take into account the performers' strengths. The seven poems he chose to set to music for Marilyn were taken from various ancient Chinese sources; The pre-Confucian 'Book of Songs', and a number of later T'Ang dynasty works by Li Po, Tu Fy, and Po Chu'I (8th and 9th century A.D). They tell the tale of an unhappy love affair, seen from the feminine point of view. As Tom described the work, "The intimacy of theme is a direct response to the nature of Chinese verse itself, which aims at perfection of form within simplicity of substance." Marilyn loved the tragic song cycle which was perfectly suited to the velvety quality of her voice. This epistolary song cycle about a woman looking for a fine lover starts with *Ripe Plums*, then proceeds in "a distilled, almost abbreviated way which suggests extracts from a personal diary". Soon she is in love (*The Moon, Love Song*) but already has misgivings. She then discovers that the man is married and falls into despair (*Storm, Despair, Drinking Song*). She finally comes to terms with her grief (*Spring Song*) and determines to start afresh. The première, which was also broadcast live on Radio 3, took place in September 1986 at the Purcell Room in London when Marilyn was accompanied by Roger Vignoles.

Having graduated with Honours in his Bachelor's Degree in Music in June 1983, our son Martin was job hunting. He knew exactly the kind of teaching work he wanted: a post as a lecturer in music. During his student years he had lectured in the Extra-Mural department of the University in place of Tom, when performances of Tom's works demanded his presence elsewhere. He also had his own series of lectures in the same department.

He had recorded several of his electronic pieces in the University's Electronic Studio as well as a number of others for acoustic instruments. He had worked in the Music Department of the BBC during his university holidays producing and promoting the orchestra, and he accepted a temporary post there after graduation. There he led a production team with the aim of delivering a series of six concerts featuring the BBCSSO. Eventually he accepted a lecturing post at Motherwell College in Lanarkshire. I had been involved with the promotion of Tom's music since we were married, and now Martin was able to help me with this. As a musician he is able to talk with local performers, and other musicians visiting Glasgow, on their own terms.

On July 20 1983, Tom completed *Incunabula* for piano, a commission from the pianist Richard Deering. *Incunabula* can be translated as 'from the cradle' or more freely as 'getting back to basics' and developed out of ideas considered for the piano accompaniment for *The Willow Branches*. Tom described it as "an unfolding series of musical ideas, (prisms?), that are almost dreamlike in that they are fleeting, apparently (though not really) disconnected, and incomplete in themselves." He regarded it as a "rethinking.... of the possibilities of musical form". He went on to write in the programme notes that, "Formal devices like recapitulation play very little part in the work's structure, the unity of the music deriving from the essential expressive coherence of the various ideas, which, (like prisms), offer different views of the same reality, and the way in which tensions generated between these conflicting images are developed and finally resolved." It's an inward looking piece perfectly suited to the intimate side of the piano as an instrument. He would later use one of the musical ideas from the melodic resolution of the piece in the *Piano Concerto* which he spent most of the next year composing.

Dimecres Musicals de Radio Nacional in Spain broadcast *String Quartet No. 4* from Barcelona on December 7. It is a well travelled piece having been performed in London, Jelenia Gora, Milan, Bonn, Vienna, Moscow, Rostov on Don, Taganrog and Dortmund as well as here in Scotland.

The first performance of *Incunabula*, played of course by Richard Deering, took place in the Purcell Room, London, on April 27 1984 to an appreciative audience. Richard was delighted with this reflective work which he played for many years in venues as far afield as Botswana, Malawi, Sydney and New Zealand; the piece has since been performed and recorded by a number of pianists including David Wilde, Johannes Wolff and Simon Smith.

1984 was another very busy year. Having written the incidental music for *Grey Granite*, the third part of the trilogy by Lewis Grassic Gibbon (which had begun with *Sunset Song*, eleven years before) Tom was asked to provide music for the radio-play *The Voyage of St Brandon* by George Mackay Brown about the Irish priest who is said to have discovered America in the Sixth Century, long before Columbus. At this stage in his creative life and career Tom had no great desire or need to take on incidental work; however he felt a loyalty towards the authors whose works he had set in the past and his integrity demanded that he give of his best. These were, though, some of the last requests to provide incidental music that he agreed to.

A few days after the radio transmission on Easter Sunday of *The Voyage of St Brandon*, we received an enthusiastic letter of thanks from the producer, the poet Stewart Conn, who said in part:

> Dear Tom,
>
> I have just had a letter from George [Mackay Brown], who has now heard the tape. He particularly asks me to let you know how much he likes and appreciates your music for the play which to him, seems "to fit the words perfectly – a quite excellent interpretation…those harp notes will linger long in my own mind". My own personal thanks to you, for the patience and professionalism with which you devoted yourself to the project – and for the finished results, with which I must admit I am delighted.
> Warm regards to you both,
>
> Yours sincerely,
> Stewart.

The next month, *Refrains and Cadenzas* was chosen as the test piece for the 1984 European Brass Band Championship and the winning performance was broadcast. Some of the musical ideas that Tom had incorporated in this work had derived from the names of the first performers, Geoffrey Brand and Black Dyke Mills Band. He hid allusions like this in many of his works. In compositions like *Introit*, there were quite a lot of them. When I asked him why he did not mention such references in his programme notes, he told me that they were there for those who wished to look. I think that these insider jokes appealed to his sense of humour. Such devices showed another side of the man whose thoughts were mostly deep. The publishers Boosey and Hawkes were kind enough to present Tom with a brass plaque to commemorate the occasion, with the first page of the piece engraved on it.

In August 1984 the BBC Scottish Symphony Orchestra, under its newly appointed conductor, Jerzy Maksymiuk, performed *Carmina Sacra* at a BBC Promenade concert in the Albert Hall. The tenor soloist was Neil Mackie.

Reviewing the concert, Hilary Finch wrote in The Times:

> What the evening did have was a quiet integrity, epitomized in the song cycle Carmina Sacra. Its direct simplicity of means and ends is its strength.

In an interview during the interval of the concert, commentator Geoffrey Baskerville asked Tom about falling attendances at concerts and Tom replied:

> Audience reaction is a mysterious business and one which has just to be taken as a fact of life. But one trusts that if a work is of sufficient calibre an audience will respond to its integrity in some intuitive way. Unfortunately the values people place on music have changed enormously since early times, when it was rather like magic or medicine: folk were in awe of these things and they occupied an integral place in society. Now, for many listeners, music has become an adornment to living – something that helps them get through the day like an aspirin.

Asked specifically about *Carmina Sacra* Tom said:

> I'm fond of it because in this age which has been so expressionistic and violent I have taken my full share in producing work of that kind. Carmina Sacra is quite tranquil. It carries an attractiveness just because it seems to be dealing in certainties rather than emotional grey areas: these poets are all expressing certainties of belief and, though it doesn't mean that I share this certainty with them, there is definitely something attractive about people who express this belief in a robust way. From a stylistic point of view, it's not particularly "advanced" but that doesn't trouble me because style is not my principal concern. It is a question of musical quality.

Tom was very pleased with the performance. Not only had he long admired Neil Mackie, but he found Jerzy Maksymiuk's effusive way of communicating with the orchestra unusual, (partly due to his halting command of English at that time) but very effective. Jerzy was also very funny and warm-hearted, if a little eccentric, and I even remember one time when he and John Ogden came to dinner and Jerzy had a nap between courses two and three. As a fellow composer, Jerzy also had a deep understanding of Tom's musical intentions and their artistic collaboration would be a key feature of the next fifteen years.

Throughout the year Tom had been working on the *Concerto for Piano* for his old friend Bryden Thomson, who commissioned the work with the support of the Scottish Arts Council for the soloist David Wilde. This immediately occasioned critical interest since Tom had always made extensive use of the piano in his work. Writing in The Scotsman, Conrad Wilson summed up the general consensus:

> Thomas Wilson seems to have spent much of his career resisting the temptation to compose a concerto. True in the 1960s, he produced a chamber concerto Concerto da Camera which was not what the general public would regard as a concerto at all. Then came his Concerto for Orchestra, which neatly avoided what audiences enjoy as the traditional conflict between the soloist and the other players. But in the end it happened.

Later in the article Conrad wrote:

> The 58-year-old Glasgow composer says he has had a love affair with the piano throughout his working life, as his body of chamber music testifies, and the new concerto is the natural outcome of all the other music he has written for the instrument. But though the ending is "ebullient, emphatic, even triumphant, giving the listener the impression the matter has been resolved," the most fascinating feature of this single-movement 30-minute concerto does appear to be its more ambiguous slow central section, inspired by a song cycle based on Chinese poems which Wilson had composed a year earlier. "The nature of the piano writing in that work was of such interest to me that I felt more use could be made of it. So I recomposed it and expanded it and metamorphosed it," he says. The resultant six little episodes are evidently linked with each other psychologically rather than formally, and the last of the six is the epicentre of the whole work.

In fact, Tom had written a *Piano Concerto* before, in the 1950s, but he withdrew this early effort a few years later. More significantly, however, none of the commissions he had received over the last twenty five years had afforded him this opportunity. He also knew that Bryden Thomson and David Wilde were musicians at the height of their powers which added to the excitement and the sense of serendipity.

In spite of this, Tom had his problems with the composition. These stemmed from the intimidating tradition of the piano concerto, a form he recognised was already replete with great works and sometimes "tyrannical" conventions. He said that he did not want to write a heroic whizz-bang piece that would have the soloist forever charging about grandiloquently trailing virtuosic sparks, while a dutifully low-profile orchestra panted along in his wake.

He therefore pondered the form for a long time before deciding that the piano should lead from behind as it were. I remember him saying, "The kind of structure I've aimed at is one which will be apparently simple, effortless and elegant to the person sitting in the stalls." He went on to say:

> I wanted to write a work which would be a worthy conflict between genuine contestants, the struggle for dominance swinging first one way and then the other before the issue was finally decided. What eventually emerged from that was the idea of standing the priorities of the "heroic" concerto on their heads – letting the orchestra rather than the piano dominate in the early stages, sweeping all before it by sheer impetus and aggression, while the soloist took on a quieter and more persuasive rôle, moderating and gradually transforming the orchestra's energies a little bit at the time. In other words the soloist would take on an Apollonian rôle – standing for poetry, restraint, humour, intelligence and so on, while the orchestra was cast in the more disruptive and turbulent Dionysian aspect. I liked this "reversed" approach. …The unfolding of the work would then resolve these antagonisms so that the orchestra's early forcefulness would gradually become more channelled, more Apollonian, whilst the soloist progressively adopted sufficient Dionysian characteristics to achieve the upper hand. In other words the piece would start with the participants at loggerheads, and then refine matters gradually, to the point where they would evolve into a unified, if not entirely equal partnership.

Tom completed this work on December 27 1984, so at least the New Year was a brief time of relaxation for him. For many years Tom had always felt confident about the musical integrity of his compositions, but on this occasion he also felt that he had written a work which would be immediately appealing to the general public. In the lead up to the première in 1985, Michael Tumelty of The Glasgow Herald interviewed Tom and John Geddes about their friendship and the background to the commission for an article entitled 'Composers in Harmony'.

Towards the end of this month new works by two composers will be premièred in Manchester by the BBC Philharmonic Orchestra. A remarkable sense of unity surrounds the occasions. Connections abound. "I suppose we're a kind of composers' co-operative society," said Thomas Wilson, whose new Piano Concerto will be launched on the 31st of the month. "We're completely different as composers, but we use each other as sounding boards," interjected John Maxwell Geddes, commenting on a perhaps unique relationship which started with discussions in a garage in Hamilton Drive, Glasgow, around 20 years ago.

The romantic notion of the composer as a solitary figure, secretive and deeply protective of his work, is refreshingly dispelled by these two men, who present their musical ideas for each other's scrutiny and criticism before the ink is dry. "Suggestions made at the formative stage can be crucial," says Tom Wilson. "There is no direct interference, of course, but in some cases the effect of the other's opinion has been quite fundamental."

John Maxwell Geddes acknowledges the senior composer's critical suggestions regarding formal layout in his new, 12-minute work for orchestra entitled Ombre (Shadows). "Tom's observations carried me a stage further in my thought," said Maxwell Geddes. Tom also sought John Maxwell Geddes's view during the composition of the piece. "Not about themes, harmony, style or anything like that," he said. "We know each other's music too intimately. We argue about both the larger and the detailed concepts. If John says 'You're wrong about that bit,' then I will look at it very seriously, and consider if John's right or not."

A further link in this relationship lies with Bryden Thomson, the Scottish conductor now based in Ireland, who commissioned and will direct both works. "He's not only one of the finest conductors around today, but he is a staunch champion of new works," said Tom Wilson. "He's done a lot of performances for us and many other contemporary composers too; performances at crucial times."

"Thomson was always, when teaching at the Academy, aggressively in favour of new compositions," said John Maxwell Geddes. "Most of the teachers were academics, and frankly, not particularly interested in what you were doing. If you were writing at all, Thomson was interested and wanted to see it. Now, years later, he's regularly commissioning and performing. It's all come together."

And so at the end of January 1985 we drove down to Manchester in the family Volvo to the studios of BBC Manchester who hosted the world première and live broadcast of Tom's *Piano Concerto*. This was performed by David Wilde with the BBC Philharmonic Orchestra conducted by Bryden Thomson. Though the performance went beautifully, my memories of the occasion are mixed, since as soon as the piano began – very quietly – I was overcome by the sudden desire to cough. I am sure almost everyone who has been to a classical concert has experienced this embarrassment at some time. However, this being a recording studio, transmitting a live broadcast, I simply could not give in to this impulse until three minutes and twenty seconds in, when the boisterous arrival of the full orchestra would give me the opportunity to hide my disruptive coughs.

The première performance was a tour de force and this is reflected in the review from Ian Robertson, writing in the Times Educational Supplement:

> In Manchester, Bryden Thomson has just conducted the première of a piano concerto from Thomas Wilson which I believe is the finest essay in the medium ever by a Briton and one of this most sparing and introspective composer's greatest achievements. Though not programmatic, like Nights in the Gardens of Spain (and much more disciplined), the Concerto shares a large tripartite, processional design, so atmospheric that the ear cannot but be beguiled by the subtext of a succession of ravishingly beautiful sound worlds. Never have Wilson's orchestral chording and his very personal sense of filigree ironies been better heard than in this quite magnificent performance by Wilde, Thomson and the BBC Philharmonic...

Michael Tumelty was equally impressed and wrote so passionately about the *Piano Concerto* in The Herald that when Bryden Thomson took the work on a tour of Scotland in January 1987 the venues were packed, which was unusual for classical music concerts at the time. I was also fortunate enough to hear the *Concerto* again without my ticklish cough.

Tom received two letters after the first broadcast of the *Piano Concerto*. The first of these was from his friend, the pianist John Ogden, who wrote:

Dear Tom,

Many thanks for your letter enclosing the tape and solo part of your new Piano Concerto. I think it is a tremendous piece, full of drive and inner poetry: I listened with a friend from the Birmingham School of Music (John Humphreys), and we both found it absolutely fascinating. We both thought David played the difficult solo part absolutely superbly, as he always does. The atmospheric beauty and structural logic and growth seemed to both John and myself to mark it as one of the very best British concertos for quite a number of years. I should certainly be most thrilled and honoured – very honoured – to play it, and when the period of exclusivity to Jack Thomson expires, would love to do so.

What brilliant piano writing the Concerto contains, and the balance with the orchestra is truly perfect. The concerts must I feel have been particularly happy and satisfying occasions for you.

I hope Margaret and Martin are in the best of health, and as always I look forward to seeing you before long.

With many congratulations on a truly magnificent concerto.

Much love as ever,
John

A second letter, from another celebrated pianist John Lill, read:

Dear Mr. Wilson,

It was so good of you to send me the score, together with the recording and information of your fascinating Piano Concerto. I find the work admirable in many respects and I feel sure it will take its place alongside the finest works for piano and orchestra from this country. I hope to learn this work before long. Thank you again for your great kindness.

Yours very sincerely,
John Lill

A reviewer in 1987 after a public performance and simultaneous radio broadcast from Dundee wrote:

> Another British Piano Concerto – that by Thomas Wilson – was tucked away late one night, in a BBC Philharmonic (not BBC Scottish) programme under Bryden Thomson, with David Wilde a seemingly commanding soloist. I found Wilson's work very impressive indeed, and if there's any justice this is a Concerto that John Drummond should immediately earmark (if he hasn't done so already) for next year's Proms.

Unfortunately, it didn't happen.

After the same performance in Dundee, another critic who is just identified in the Dundee Courier as 'Our Music Critic' wrote:

> A fairly smart arrival on the platform to acknowledge applause is normally recommended for composers of challenging contemporary pieces. Last night Thomas Wilson was able to indulge the rare privilege of getting lost behind the stage and still receive a warm ovation. Mr Wilson's work, convincingly presented by the dedicated David Wilde, has an immediately attractive final scherzo and some striking sonorities. The very angular melodies rang agreeably and the whole work was most engrossing.

Yet another critic wrote:

> Wilson's music presents a series of endlessly changing effects which merge into one another like the camera work of a film. Wilson has evolved a totally new approach to the concerto in which the relationship of orchestra and soloist is never static. The music is not always easy or comfortable but has its own valid structures and as in the slow movement is often deeply evocative. Wilde's performance of the piano part was filled with subtlety and conviction.

The recording of the *Concerto* onto CD from the Henry Wood Hall in Glasgow nearly didn't happen as David Wilde refused to use the piano there. So our son Martin approached David Dorward, a composer and music producer at the BBC in Edinburgh, who generously agreed to the SNO hiring the BBC's studio Steinway Grand.

On October 27 1985, the New Music Group of Scotland premièred Tom's new *Chamber Concerto* in the Queens Hall in Edinburgh. The ten players were directed by Edward Harper. Written in early 1985 this piece had been commissioned the previous July by the Group with the help of the Scottish Arts Council and the Hope Scott Trust.

When he began to write the concerto the previous year, Tom had the idea in mind of a hanging mobile twisting in a breeze. His intent, he said, was to explore "the idea of movement and stillness and how the two can co-exist and interrelate." He had discussed this idea many times before with John Maxwell Geddes over a glass of malt and was fascinated with the challenge of finding a way to represent these states of kinetic equilibrium through music.

Naturally, the music develops beyond the initial source of inspiration as Tom was keen to point out in his programme notes for the work:

> ...the idea of the mobile should not be taken too far. Mobiles depend upon random air currents around them to make them work – but elements of chance play no part in the musical structure of the piece.

> Musically the work plays as a continuous whole, but divides itself into three main substantial parts (fast: slow: fast) – the usual concerto layout. The main body of the work is preceded by a slow introduction and, at the end, is concluded with a slow coda based on similar material. However, implicit in this coda is the idea that there is no reason why the whole process should not go round for a second time, and by extension, continue to do so indefinitely.

The critics appreciated the point.

As Michael Tumelty wrote in The Herald:

> Wilson believes that music can never by definition achieve a condition of stasis. In the Chamber Concerto he seems to be questioning his own ideas on the subject with some remarkably effective results. The performances offered hypnotic and compelling listening.

Unfortunately, this piece with its syncopated sections has not received as many performances as I would like, but then I have always had a particular fondness for this kind of jazzy treatment, where appropriate. Naturally not all works allow the composer this freedom.

In addition to his work as a composer, Tom had long been active in the world of music, looking for ways to promote performances of new music and help the lives of composers. This did not change now that he was possibly the most successful composer in Scotland. So when, in 1984, the Scottish Arts Council was contemplating the withdrawal of support for the Scottish Music Archive as it was then, in favour of giving more money to recordings, Tom wrote to them in his capacity as a committee member of the Composers' Guild condemning the proposed move. He compared the support given to sister institutions such as the British Music Information Centre and the Welsh Music Information Centre:

> Far from withdrawing its support for the Archive, the SAC should increase it, bringing the Archive into line with these bodies. This would allow the Archive to tackle directly the problem of engaging more public interest in its work. It would allow the Archive to cast aside its underserved "passive" image, mounting exhibitions, giving lectures, and most important of all, arranging regular concerts consisting for the most part, or wholly, of all of the works which it houses. In this regard we can learn from the BMIC where similar policies are bearing fruit even now. The 'dead' music on the shelves would thus be brought to life and its merits made apparent to those who heard it.

He added:

> Doubtless these ideas will be dismissed as impracticable by those who are wont to invoke the present climate of financial restraint, but I am not convinced by such arguments... It is my belief that the composer is a vitally important factor in the musical health of any society. Any proposal which diminishes the effectiveness of this contribution for the want of what is, in the context of other grants, a trifling sum, is, in my view a deplorably retrograde step. It is indeed a sad irony that Scotland, which in setting up the Archive showed the rest of the UK the way, should now lose faith in that vision and endanger its continued existence.

Fortunately, the Scottish Arts Council listened and funding continued. Indeed, in view of Tom's letter I was rather surprised when two years later he was invited to sit on the Board of the Scottish Arts Council for the years 1986 – 1989. His appointment coincided with the arrival of a new Chairman, Sir Alan Peacock, although they did not see much of each other, as Tom was involved only with the music committee of the Council. From this seat he was able to argue on behalf of Scottish composers. He was a very polite, but very able fighter!

Later in the year Tom was elected Chairman of the Composers' Guild of Great Britain, a post he held from 1986 to 1989. As Chairman of the Guild, he was responsible for coordinating the activities of the Executive Committee in dealing with the Arts Council, the Performing Rights Society, Regional Arts Associations and the broadcasters. Though he carried out much of the work from home, the position required him to travel to London once a month for meetings, and occasionally to represent the Guild on visits to foreign capitals like Berlin and Moscow.

As Chairman of the Composers' Guild - he was the first Scot to hold the position - Tom fought for a rise in commission fees; for a distinction between 'title music' and 'incidental music'; for an end to coercion (whereby commissioned composers were obliged to assign their publishing rights); for an increase in the number of broadcasts of works by living composers; and for the Composers' Joint Council to be formally recognised by the BBC Copyright Department as the negotiating body on behalf of composers. Later in his Chairmanship, the Guild was to support the BBC through the consultation process which arose from the government's white paper, 'Broadcasting in the 90s'.

No sooner had he taken office than he had to grasp a very thorny nettle indeed and decided to discontinue the publication of *The Composer* magazine. It was a good magazine, but it had been losing money for years. Tom's predecessors had sidestepped the matter, but the problem could not be avoided any longer. As much as Tom would have liked to continue the magazine, he recognised that the Guild simply could not afford to support it any longer. Fortunately this was the only distasteful task that befell him during his years in office.

However, another duty was the annual chairman's speech, which he dictated to me while I typed away. There were no computers then so each time he made changes to words I had to do the whole thing again. When I had done it five times I rebelled. "This is the last," I said, "If you make any more amendments, you do it yourself". He fine honed his words as he did his music.

I remember sitting with Tom at breakfast one morning early in 1986 when the telephone rang. Whenever I was at home, it was somehow always my job to answer the telephone. The caller was Moira Meighan, the Joint Convener of the Friends of Glasgow Cathedral. She told me that the committee wanted to commission Tom to write a suite to commemorate the 850th anniversary of the cathedral. I handed the 'phone to Tom, who learned that the Friends wanted something on the programmatic side. He was hesitant at first but said that he would consider taking the commission. Tom's instinct always leant towards the abstract in his original compositions, and he did not like having to follow some extra-musical scheme or reflect pictorial imagery. Moreover, he particularly disliked the term suite which I had said was mentioned to me, and which always suggested to him something rather inconsequential - light background music of the type that used to be played in the tea rooms of large hotels before the war. These associations aside, this particular suite was for the Cathedral founded by Saint Mungo himself. As a child Tom had holidayed at Aberdour close to Culross where his imagination had been fired by his father's stories of the early Scottish saints. He therefore had a natural empathy towards the subject matter, and so it seemed natural to me to suggest that he use the symbols on the Armorial Insignia of the City of Glasgow, namely the bird, the fish, the ring, the bell, and the tree. They relate to the legendary miracles of St Kentigern (or St Mungo or "Dear Friend" as he is also known) so it could not really be classed as "light" or incidental. Tom approved of my suggestion, and so the programmatic requirement that might have seemed a superficial element became integral to the music's conception and structure. Each of the five symbols was taken as a movement that would reflect the miracles of St Kentigern.

BIRD   (Kentigern the Aspirant)
FISH   (The Christian Activist)
RING   (The Contemplative)
BELL   (The Proclaimer of the Word)
TREE   (Kentigern's Legacy)

I'll let Tom take up the story:

Our early saints were extraordinary men. They believed in an unknown God-Man and, by spreading His Word, changed history.

St. Kentigern (who died about 603), is a shadowy yet vivid figure and founder of Glasgow Cathedral. He comes down to us by way of a few rather random facts and many legends and stories. But the scanty evidence matters little. His real achievement is that he gripped the imagination, and continues to do so, in the symbols of The Bird, The Fish, The Ring, The Bell and The Tree which feature on Glasgow's Armorial Insignia to this day.

My music takes these five symbols as its starting point. Their original purpose was to remind us of episodes in the life of

Kentigern the wonder-worker. But they also lend themselves to deeper interpretations. Thus the first movement of my suite uses THE BIRD not so much as a reminder of a particular miraculous event, but rather as a symbol of Kentigern's aspiration to higher things - the conversion of the world, and the achievement of sanctity.

In the second movement the FISH is the activist, the messenger (as in the legend of the restoration of the Queen's missing ring). But the Fish also has another dimension in that it was one of the most universally known Christian symbols of early times.

The RING centres on the inner world of Kentigern the contemplative, the thinker. The circle is the perfect shape; it has no beginning and no end, and as such, presents a potent meditative symbol of perfection and eternity.

The fourth movement, the BELL is a straightforward evocation of Kentigern proclaiming his message. It is a solemn yet urgently joyous, even raucous carillon.

As the clamour recedes, the gentle fifth movement, the TREE follows on without a break. The Tree here is used entirely as a symbol of the growth, maturity, and longevity of Kentigern's achievement. An ancient plainsong melody "Ubi caritas et amor Deus ibi est" sets the tone for this serene meditation on the work of a man whose influence has been immeasurable.

The Scottish Ensemble (11 players) directed by Leonard Friedman gave the resulting work, the *St Kentigern Suite*, its first performance in Glasgow Cathedral in April. Though that particular spring evening was very cold, the work was warmly received by the audience who packed the Cathedral. Originally conceived as a chamber work, the Suite has become one of Tom's most popular compositions and has since been played by larger ensembles, including one performance in Toronto in 1988 by 150 massed strings.

In July, Tom and I were invited to accompany the Scottish Ensemble on a trip to France, where the players performed the *St Kentigern Suite* at the Troisième Festival Franco-Écossais and also at concerts in the Department of the Charente, in Thouars, and in Mortagne-sur-Sèvres. Most of the concerts were held in churches or monastic buildings, one of which - the Abbaye de Chartres, founded in 1077 - was in the middle of a field which itself seemed to be in the middle of nowhere. I wondered where the audience was going to come from. The souvenir brochure for Charente's Festival suggested that people would come early and picnic in the field before the concert, but I doubted that many would follow this advice. However, about two hours before the concert was due to begin, cars began to arrive from Cognac and Jarnac and from neighbouring villages and soon the field was full of people. To our surprise, we came upon a pipe-major from Dalkeith (which is the twin town of Jarnac), marching up and down the field playing Scottish tunes. Towards 9pm more and more cars arrived, while small planes landed at the nearby military airport. Steadily, the audience grew, and extra chairs had to be placed in every possible spot – to within a metre of the Ensemble. Finally, with no more seats available, people simply stood in the entranceway and in the field beyond that. The church itself was lit solely by candles, which produced a wonderfully atmospheric effect but couldn't have done the players any favours. Being the director, Leonard fared better since a fine candelabra was placed alongside him.

At another of the churches, Sant-Laon, in Thouars, a pair of tramps who had been sitting on the steps came in for the performance. At the end of the first movement, one tramp clapped vigorously and when shushed by his friend said in a loud voice "Mais, c'est merveilleuse!" Everyone smiled. During our visit we were lodged in the beautiful Courvoisier Chateau on the banks of the Charente. It was all very splendid and even more so for Tom as we had a bedside carafe of 60 year old cognac which was replenished each morning. To add one more touch to the ample hospitality already showered upon us, the owner of the Hennessy Company invited all of us to spend an evening at his nearby home. Those who wished were invited to enjoy a swim in the pool before supper. I was most impressed by the friendly relations between the representatives of the two seemingly rival companies. They seemed to operate under the assumption that there was room for all.

After we returned from this wonderful trip, Tom received a letter from Bonn, then the capital of West Germany, asking him to become an honorary member of the Deutsch-Englische Musikgesellschafte E.V. In his letter, the President of the Society, Georg Binzenbach wrote "Your 3rd Symphony, conducted by our honorary member Sir Alexander Gibson, belongs to the most impressive contemporary compositions we have listened to up to now. We were also captivated by your thrilling *Piano Concerto*. Shame on the record companies that there is no record yet!"

In September 12 1986, Marilyn de Bliek gave the first broadcast of *The Willow Branches* in a programme for Radio 3, accompanied by Roger Vignoles. Tom was so fired up after the performance that he finally made time to complete the requested orchestral version. Having waited three years for the first broadcast of the version for voice and piano, we had to wait until March 4 1988 for the première of the orchestral version in the Henry Wood Hall in Glasgow, when Marlilyn sang once more with the BBCSSO conducted by the Polish conductor Jerzy Maksymiuk.

Tom's music was played in nine countries during the year, and his international reputation received a further boost when the BBC Scottish Symphony Orchestra and their conductor, Jerzy Maksymiuk, took *Touchstone*, and John Geddes' work *Voyager*, on a tour of Germany in late September/early October. A strong advocate of contemporary music in general, Jerzy took every possible opportunity to give the music of Scottish composers a hearing. Tom and John were just two of many composers who benefited during his tenure with the orchestra.

In Bad Homburg the review in Taunus Zeitung read:

> The clearly orchestrated, capricious piece had an immediate impact. Touchstone is the fool in Shakespeare's "As You like It" whose bizarre and melancholy character in his colourful jester's costume inspired the music. The tone-language of the ten-minute piece, which is modern and rich in dissonances, is fragmentary, iridescent and shimmering. The Polish conductor Jerzy Maksymiuk and the orchestra committed themselves with precision and with conviction to this distinctive work.

The music critic of the paper Frankfurter Allgemeine wrote:

> The programme started with 'Touchstone' (1967) by the Scottish composer Thomas Wilson, born in 1927, which is a "Portrait for Orchestra" named after the fool in Shakespeare's "As You like It". This extremely colourful ten minute piece lives by way of contrasts which depict the bizarre nature and melancholy of the fool like the colourfulness of the jester's costume. Passages subtly sounded out, stood against pointed staccato passages; passages lit up chamber music-like, featuring solos for violin, flute, celesta and piano, appearing against the lightly ironic solemnity of the full orchestra. The beginning and end, corresponding to each other, open and close an imaginary curtain. "Touchstone" creates a scene which is moderately modern, set in clear colours and lines. The visitors from

Glasgow fully honoured the sub-title of this entertaining and volatile piece, as well as its likeable composer who was present. They adapted the Portrait for Orchestra as a demonstration of their own clarity of contours and colours.

Full Orchestras

Despite the proven connection between music and mathematics, it's a great shame that in modern education children are not taught from an early age how to listen to, and appreciate, abstract music. They never have the opportunity to become familiar with the instruments of the orchestra, and instead grow up feeling classical music is somehow distant and separated from them. If they do eventually develop a taste for classical music, it is perhaps unsurprising that it tends to be for the easy-listening, 'hooked-on classics' offerings of the commercial radio stations who these days seem frightened to present their audiences with anything too challenging. Tom was deeply concerned by the growing estrangement of audiences from new music. The issue came up in a pre-Proms talk he gave in one of the lesser halls in August 1987 before the performance of his orchestral work *Introit* at the Royal Albert Hall. In the course of his remarks he summed up his thoughts regarding the rapid development of modern classical music since the 1950s:

> The trends of musical composition themselves have gone through a period of change during my lifetime and a great number of influences have come forward – things like serialism, and aleatorism, which is a measure of chance elements in music. What one does is, one takes these things on board, one digests them, takes a personal view of them, and when you've had enough out of them you discard them and you move on to whatever lies in store for you. On the less technical side, on the more expressive side, those who know something about my music from my earlier days to my recent time will, I think, be able to discern a greater measure of optimism and a certain serenity possibly, beginning to develop in later pieces which was absent from the earlier ones. The earlier ones were rather more expressionistic and dramatic and pessimistic in character.

> The piece isn't programmatic; it doesn't tell a story other than the fact that I'm interested as a person in the way that we listen to music, and the way in fact we approach life generally. Introit was written in 1982 so it is fairly late in this sequence of events. We use

our reason to try to figure out things around about us. Musicians are no exception. But the higher plane for me is the intuitive plane where one simply responds, sometimes without knowing quite why one does, except to know in one's inner being that that is right as it were, that has a higher significance, and what I wanted to do in this piece was in fact, to start out by asking the audience to hear the music, shall we say, on the rational level, or whatever the appropriate adjective would be, and then gradually lead them through a various series of levels, which will ultimately come out on the intuitive plane.

One should remember also that music is always inherently dramatic, because it's someone playing one idea off against another, and there's a dramatic quality about that which can't be avoided. I have been lucky in that I've been asked to write pieces at particular junctures in my career that I would have liked to write anyway. Sometimes a degree of stage management is possible – you might drop the hint that you would like to write something and somebody will pick you up on it, but that is comparatively rare in my experience. It just seems to happen that after you have written a number of works, shall we say, for chamber music ensembles, string quartets, that kind of thing, someone will come along and ask you to write an orchestral piece, which is exactly what you want to do in these circumstances.

Feedback from an audience of course is a very precious thing for a composer; it is an exercise in communication, composition. There is in a sense no music unless there's someone there to listen to it.

The public tends not to like the unfamiliar first time round, so it's only when it becomes relatively familiar that they begin to understand how the thing works, and begin to respond to it. So I think one simply has to exercise a degree of patience, and a certain belief in oneself of course, and simply keep going and allow the audience to catch up in their own good time. This is a problem which has been much exacerbated in this present century, because the degree to which music has leaped forward has been so prodigious that the public is having a hard time catching up - but they are beginning to do so, and I'm really quite optimistic about the future.

I have thought long and hard about why Tom spoke at this time about his more recent music showing greater optimism and serenity than that written in his earlier years. I think this change showed itself most clearly in his choice of subject matter for his various commissions. So whereas in the late Sixties and early Seventies, he was writing *Threnody*, a song or hymn of mourning (1970), *Missa Pro Mundo Conturbato*, a *Mass for a Troubled World* (1970), *The Charcoal Burner* (1968) and the *Confessions of a Justified Sinner* (1974), from the late Seventies the subject matter became decidedly more hopeful. First came *Songs of Hope and Expectation* (1977), then *Introit* (1982), the *Piano Concerto* (1984), the *Chamber Concerto* (1985) and the *St Kentigern Suite* (1986). There were of course exceptions to this general trend, such as the more upbeat *Touchstone* in 1967 and the darker *Willow Branches* in 1983; however, I think that there were a number of factors that lay behind this trend. Our family life was much more settled in the late 1980s, we did not have parents to look after, two of our children had left home and were pursuing their careers elsewhere, Tom had the respect of the critics, he was offered more commissions than he had time to fulfil, and his powers as a composer continued to grow. This did not mean that his new music lacked any edge – far from it; nor that he stopped crossing his fingers whenever it came to a performance, let alone a première – but Tom was never one to tempt providence.

One of the later performances of *Introit* took place in August at a Henry Wood Promenade Concert. It went beautifully; the BBCSSO conducted by Jerzy Maksymiuk did their local composer proud. Tom always liked to hear his works from the auditorium, so when the time came to take his bow, he had to rush out of the hall, slip backstage, and find his way into the wings. Unfortunately he had not reckoned with the looking-glass interior of the Royal Albert Hall and he couldn't find the right door. This was bound to happen again sooner or later, in fact it had already happened earlier that year at a performance of the *Piano Concerto* in Dundee, but despite my many warnings he would not change. Since the conductor and orchestra had by now taken several bows, I sat wondering what on earth was keeping him. But the applause went on for another minute, then another, and another. By now the audience were looking around at each other wondering whether to stop applauding, but the orchestra remained on stage and so they kept clapping. Finally, Tom walked out onto the stage as if nothing untoward had occurred – to rapturous applause.

After the concert, Tom was besieged as always by fans wanting him to autograph their programmes. He was always happy to do this even though it could take up to half an hour – my shoulder was a convenient desk for him.

In 1987 the acolades came in thick and fast. In March he received a letter most cordially inviting him to become a Vice President of the British Music Society. This was a great honour; however Tom was frequently touched more by the personal compliments he received.

Following this triumphant performance and its live broadcast, Jerzy Maksymiuk and the BBCSSO took the work on tour to Poland. The London performance had gone so well that in October Tom received a very gratifying letter from Professor Lalage Bown, the head of the Department of Adult and Continuing Education at Glasgow University. It read:

Dear Tom,

One or two of us were fortunate enough to listen to your contribution to the Proms. I personally was delighted to hear the performance of your Introit – as you know this is a great favourite of mine and I very much treasure the recording of it which you gave me. We were enormously proud of the reception which you and your work got. I think you had the loudest applause of any contributing to the Proms, except of course the "last nighters." I mentioned your tremendous triumph at the last Staff Meeting of the Department and it was agreed that I should write formally on behalf of all members of the Department to congratulate you most wholeheartedly for your very well deserved success and for the appreciation which you gained. Some of us also heard the interview with you, which was recorded on Radio 3, and wanted to add congratulations for that too. It was a most interesting interview and very illuminative of your work and purposes.

All we can say is more power to your elbow!

With all good wishes,

Yours sincerely,

Professor Lalage Bown.

In September the management of the Scottish National Orchestra were thinking about the conductor that they would have to appoint the next year, following the resignation of Neeme Järvi. Tom and I were delighted when a member of the orchestra's board asked our opinion about appointing Bryden Thomson to the position. We both thought that Jack would be an excellent choice. First of all, he was a great conductor. In addition though, he had spoken to us many times of his wish to head the SNO. To him, we knew, such an opportunity would represent the acme of his career. Sadly, the appointment caused Jack a great deal of heartache, in part owing to clashes of personality over programming that could not have been foreseen.

Later that same autumn, Aberdeen-based Welsh composer and conductor John Hearne conducted the Festival Chorus (an ad hoc group of 80 singers drawn from 20 university choirs from Hungary, Austria, West Germany, East Germany, Poland, Turkey and Yugoslavia) at the Fourth International Festival of University Choirs in Budapest. One of the songs they included was Tom's *How Sweet the Moonlight Sleeps upon this Bank* (a very early work, one of the *Five Shakespeare Songs* from 1952). After the concert, each of the singers signed the back of a concertina of postcards of local beauty spots. Tom was so very touched and pleased to accept it, for whenever performers sent something personal like this, he felt that his wish to communicate via his music had been accomplished, and this gave him great satisfaction.

In November the BBC mounted a week of programmes 'Celebrating the music of Thomas Wilson' for his 60th birthday, which had taken place the previous month. Thirteen works were performed over three days including the première of his most recent composition, the *Viola Concerto*. As part of the celebration Michael Tumelty, who had succeeded Malcolm Rayment as music critic of The Herald newspaper, wrote a large article about Tom:

> By rights Tom Wilson ought to exhibit at least some of the symptoms of a composer under pressure. Just returned from London and a series of meetings of the Composers' Guild of Great Britain, of which he is Chairman, he was off to Edinburgh for a performance by the Scottish Ensemble of his St Kentigern Suite.

> The following day, straight from this interview, he was back there again for rehearsals with the Scottish Chamber Orchestra of the same work, which they will take to Japan later this month.

> The ink is almost dry on his *Viola Concerto*, a work which receives its world première on Friday as the climax to the four concert festival of his music that opens tonight at the BBC Studios in Glasgow in celebration of his 60th birthday.

Immediately afterwards he was faced with another major commission, this time for the SNO, to be performed in Paisley Abbey next year as part of the celebrations for the 500th anniversary of the burgh. The deadline is less than a year – sooner than he would like.

Yet the man radiates an almost saintly calm. Time was when Scotland's most distinguished composer would produce major works at the rate of two a year. Now he confesses, the rate is relatively slow – "and getting slower" – although he does not seem unduly perturbed.

In the considered depth of his conversation, and in his gently expressed philosophical wisdom, Wilson is a joy to interview. As someone working in the hothouse, interior, and essentially egotistic world of composition, he is positively refreshing.

Clarity is the touchstone of Wilson's thought and expression. It is a feature that characterises both the man and his world. It is interesting that while some observers have noted an increasing warmth and richness of expression in Wilson's recent music, the composer's essential criterion of lucidity has remained unclouded, a fact that was quite evidently perceived by the large audiences who gave such warm responses to his masterly Piano Concerto in the major Scottish cities earlier this year.

As he said:

> "I am very much in favour of the proposition that music, and all art should be as clear as possible, I think the nature of composition is to take an extremely complex problem and clarify it as much as possible."

It's a philosophy Wilson feels has served him well. In a catalogue of around sixty published works, including operas, symphonies, and a wide range of orchestral, choral, and chamber music, written over the past 30 years, the majority of his compositions are commissions, which suggests to the composer that he has been "extremely fortunate."

Not everyone agrees. Fellow composer John Maxwell Geddes has a unique collaborative relationship with Wilson – they peruse and criticise each other's works-in-progress. This started about 15 years ago, "in a double garage sound-proofed with about a million egg trays and an atmosphere more like a gang hut than a formal meeting place of composers."

"Tom has been cruelly treated," said Geddes, referring to separate periods of 10 years and 6 years when nothing of Wilson's was performed by the SNO, as well as to works performed once and never repeated. Wilson, who will not be drawn into a discussion of the personalities involved, again is more philosophical.

> "It's like the climate; there are periods of plenty and periods of drought. There is an undulating graph of activity and inactivity that you come to accept."

He has witnessed several fluctuations in the graph over the last three decades in Scotland. One of the reasons that he resisted the lure of the south some 30 years ago was that:

> "It was already becoming clear in the late 50s that something was brewing up here. When it did start to happen – with Jimmie Loughran, Alex Gibson, the SNO, Musica Viva and Scottish Opera – it felt like a Renaissance. It seems to be happening again today. It was just like that then, perhaps even a little more exciting because it was the first time."

The present trend includes the glimmering of a reawakening of responsibilities towards composers like Wilson, a trend he obviously hopes will continue.

> "But there is a lot of ground to make up after the "drought" of the 1970s and early 80s – fifteen years of vacuum. Not just me, not just local composers, but any modern music at all. All organisations seem to go through these periods of crisis, usually financial and connected with worries about bums on seats, they then exclude anything apparently risky and revert to yet another cycle of Brahms's symphonies."

While he sees a grain of optimism in the attitudes today of performing organisations, there are developments in other areas of the arts that Wilson finds "positively alarming." Tom Wilson spent almost thirty years as lecturer, reader, then professor in the Extra-Mural department of Glasgow University, and views the current developments of music departments throughout the country, closing and under threat of closure, with the utmost concern:

> "Stirling, St Andrews, now Aberdeen – the whole system is collapsing. The implications of these appalling developments will be felt in a generation. Building up some kind of artistic awareness, taking the arts as parts of life, naturally and spontaneously, is something that is hard won. Provision of musical education, general and specialised, is one of the essential planks that has made for a fundamental change in attitudes and awareness towards music since my own young days: What will have happened to those attitudes in twenty years?"

After this week's festival which Wilson feels includes 'a fair representation' of his music from apprentice works up to the new Concerto, he will launch himself into a busy schedule. After the new piece for the SNO, there is a chamber symphony to be written for the Paragon Ensemble and a new work for the Scottish Philharmonic Singers with the Scottish Chamber Orchestra.

It is a prospect he views with some alertness.

> "Technical facility gets greater as you get older, but the problem is always different. If you're a surgeon doing a heart bypass operation, the first time it's bloody hard, the next you know what to do. With composition you're dealing with different materials, all equally intransigent, and it's up to you each time, to find ways of disciplining them."

Although the celebrations for Tom's 60th birthday had begun earlier, the BBC presented a Thomas Wilson Festival lasting four days in November in his honour. The players involved were Leonard Friedman, The Edinburgh Quartet, the New Music Group of Scotland, and the BBCSSO who premièred the *Viola Concerto*. This work was commissioned and played by James Durrant. While Tom was pleased on occasions like this, (and what composer wouldn't be?) they did not turn his head. He never felt more important because of them, nor did he require that others should defer to him. He had not presumed that he would be asked to choose which of his works would be performed, nor did he feel slighted that he was not even consulted. He was happy to go along to rehearsals if invited, but, if not, he was content to let the professionals get on with it. With regard to his music, the thing that he wanted most of all was the respect of his peers, and I think that in his mature years he realised that he had that.

Jimmy Durrant had first asked Tom to write a viola concerto for him while they were playing golf on the Linn course in Glasgow. When Jimmy finally got it, many years later, he said that it was technically demanding but a tour de force. He told Tom that he practised the work for four hours each day while preparing for the première and felt that he could have done with more.

In this work the soloist has a particularly daunting task in that he must play more than forty bars before the entry of the orchestra. Although very nervous - after all it was a new work before a musically literate audience in Studio One of the BBC - Jimmy played with assurance and great sensitivity. Philip Dukes who later repeated the performance in the same studio remarked that it was a shame that players had to spend so much time learning a new work to play it only once.

In anticipation of the *Concerto's* first performance, Tom was interviewed by Kenneth Walton for an article entitled 'Great Scot' to be published in October's issue of *Classical Music Magazine*. In accounting for the work's long gestation, Tom said that he had noticed a certain slowing down while he was working on the *Viola Concerto* but added that, "It is a difficult medium to write for." Acknowledging that Jimmy Durrant had asked for the piece 15 years previously, Tom admitted:

> "I've been fending him off ever since. I didn't feel ready for it. Concerto implies domination and the viola in many ways is the least fitted instrument for the task because it is essentially gentle and lyrical. Some way has to be found to allow the viola to dominate. The orchestra has to be treated with circumspection and delicacy. Given the instrument's retiring disposition there were problems to solve. I hope that I have solved them."

Walton's interview continued:

> When I commented upon the fact that the solo writing seems to lie consistently high, Wilson revealed, interestingly, that this reflects James Durrant's personal feeling that "contrary to popular supposition, the viola sings best higher up."

Later in the interview Wilson said that he perceived certain changes that had taken place in his composition over the years:

"The technical equipment has changed. My later music is less involved in contrapuntal textures, whereas my early works were full of canonic and fugal devices. You have to look fairly hard to find them now. The expressive nature of my music has changed also, having begun in my early youth as a really quite fiery, at times expressionistic style, often experimental in character, now I have developed a stability and control, which were there in different ways before."

He observed that the most significant changes took place in the *Third String Quartet* (a McEwen commission written in 1958). He was, at this stage in his career, refining his compositional language. He always believed that music should communicate with the greatest possible clarity, and he found the musical aesthetic behind many of the musical styles of the time disturbing. He was disappointed at Scottish Opera's current policy of only rarely performing contemporary operas written by Scots. He thought that if the music was good enough, then there was no reason why the box office should suffer. Also opera audiences had to face up to modern music at some stage.

In November and December 1987, the Scottish Chamber Orchestra conducted by James Loughran took the *St Kentigern Suite* to Japan and played it in Tokyo, Hiroshima and Nara. Michael Tumelty's review in the Glasgow Herald on his return to Scotland read:

> The sensitivity of the strings in their polished and eloquent playing of Thomas Wilson's *St Kentigern Suite* was so laden with atmosphere that the breathless hush at the end of the work was almost tangible. And the extra round of applause it received might well be allocated to the organisation for bringing this masterpiece into its touring repertoire.

Conrad Wilson said in his review:

> In the hall's luminous open acoustics, Wilson's string writing sounded wonderfully subtle and elegant, and James Loughran conducted it with the utmost finesse.

To round off the year the orchestra of the Royal Academy of Music in London performed the *Chamber Concerto* and *Sinfonia for Seven Instruments*. In fact life was very busy - as usual.

Early in 1988, Tom began work on *Passeleth Tapestry*. This work, which became Tom's *Fourth Symphony*, was commissioned by Renfrew District Council and Strathclyde Regional Council, with assistance from the Scottish Arts Council, to honour Paisley's 500th anniversary as a Burgh of Barony. "Passeleth" is the name by which the town was known in the 12th Century, the period during which the Abbey was founded and the Stewarts rose to power. Indeed the first mention of the town itself occurs in documents of the time.

When he called me into the study to listen after the first few pages were sketched out, I said that I could hear an allusion to 'Hosanna in the Highest' from the *Missa Pro Mundo Conturbato*. Tom turned from the piano and agreed, saying that it was there as an ironic comment on the modern tendency to praise Mammon rather than God, something that is remarked upon again in the sour note at the end of the plainsong. But these were very private reflections on the state of modern society, and were meant to be hidden in the background of a work that is in every other respect a celebration of the history of Paisley. Tom's description of the work in his programme notes (written in 1988 and revised in 1996) is very detailed and revealing; so on this occasion I will include it in its entirety:

> The plan of the piece is based upon the broad pattern of Paisley's history from its earliest days to the present time. It is not a programmatic work in the usual sense, in that it does not describe individual events, but rather concerns itself with whole passages of history and the ideas, trends, and characteristics which underlie them. The work plays without a break.
>
> The music opens with a carillon of celebration. Throughout the work such bell-like patterns and themes form an important and constantly recurring feature. This opening carillon is founded on four notes which appear at the outset (A-Bb-E-Eb). These notes are derived from the name Paisley, the Abbey, and the Stewarts (the Royal dynasty with which Paisley and the Abbey are very closely associated). Thereafter they form the basis of the whole piece.
>
> After the opening carillon recedes the tapestry begins to unfold. Three linked musical statements outline in turn the major influences on Paisley's early history – the steady but restless growth of the town itself, the comparative peace and serenity of the Abbey (founded in 1163 and dedicated to St. Mirren, Paisley's patron saint), and finally fanfare-like ideas suggesting the Stewarts. This

section ends with an orchestral carillon which slowly dies away, allowing fading echoes of the Stewart fanfares to be heard.

These lead without a break into the second main part of the work which moves forward to the days of the Reformation, and is principally concerned with the religious upheavals of that time. Music based freely on the Protestant psalm tune 'Martyrs' vies for supremacy with the Abbey's music - though the original psalm tune itself is never heard as a whole. Eventually the 'Martyrs' music emerges uppermost and the section ends with reminders of the carillon and echoes of 'Martyrs'. Gradually a certain serenity is restored.

The third section of the piece moves on to the 19th and 20th centuries. Here the music reflects the energy and dynamism of the age of the machine. The 19th century was a time of opposites – great idealism and philanthropy, bounding drive and confidence, and unprecedented wealth. But on the other hand it was also a time of appalling inhumanities such as slavery, child labour, and the abject poverty of working people. Not surprisingly, this was a turbulent time in Paisley. Strong radical traditions came to the surface, and led to serious civil unrest amounting to near-revolt among Paisley's weavers (so seriously was this affair regarded that the ringleader was tried and executed in the 1820s). However this age of materialism had another side in that it also produced results of high quality in the arts in Paisley, perhaps the most famous of these being the Paisley shawl with its renowned pattern, which quickly became celebrated throughout the world for its beauty and excellence. While this high point in Paisley's fortunes was maintained for many years, it began to falter in this century, and especially after the Second World War. Decline began and economic recession took hold. The music attempts to assemble these bewildering contradictions. Mechanistic patterns abound, motor rhythms, energy and growing power drive the music on, a process leavened only by a gentler central passage in which Paisley's artistic achievements are recalled. Finally the music reaches a high point of grandeur, marked by a carillon for full orchestra. Gradually the intensity of the music declines, receding to an inert calm.

The final pages of the work briefly look to our own day and to the future. It begins by underlining the need for resolution of destructive tensions and conflicts – represented here by a newfound harmonious partnership forged between elements of the Reformers' tune 'Martyrs', and the Abbey's age-old melody 'Victimae Paschali Laudes'.

Lastly the opening carillon of celebration is briefly recalled, and the work ends on a note which is confident, and yet also speculative, as it looks to the future.

Passaleth Tapestry was completed on June 23 1988, six weeks in advance of the première. This did not give Jack Thomson much time to prepare, but he was not unduly worried. As Tom got older he seemed to enjoy the danger of a looming deadline more than in his early years and spent many more weeks ordering his thoughts before launching into the composition proper. I often had to remind him of the passage of time and the need to put some notes on the paper. However, in spite of his apparent reluctance to commit, my fears were never realised and the quality of the work was as assured as ever. At this stage in his career Tom had the absolute confidence to be open about his thoughts and emotions and this shows in the introspective and intuitive nature of many of the later orchestral works (from the early 1980s onwards). Though on the surface one might think it would be easier to compose in this more fluid way, I think that these surprising leaps of his musical imaginings required much greater forethought if a piece's inner integrity was to be properly revealed.

During this period the performances of Tom's other works continued unabated. In April Richard Deering took *Incunabula* to Africa and played it in Gabarone, Ratibor, and Lilongwe. Richard was always a staunch supporter of Tom's music and we received the following letter from him on his return to the UK:

Dear Tom,

Incunabula went well, particularly as it was the most abstract piece on the programme. Many people remarked on its peaceful sense of space. Several other people singled out the "modern" piece as the highlight.

So, yet again, it's passed the "little old lady on the back row" test.

Best wishes to everyone,
Richard.

In the same month David Wilde was performing it in Germany.

After the broadcast in May of *The Willow Branches*, performed by the BBCSSO and mezzo-soprano Marilyn de Blieck, and conducted by Jerzy Maksymiuk, Tom received a most amusing letter from Father Duffy, an elderly priest who had been the organist and choirmaster at Blairs. Here is part of his letter:

Dear Tom,

No reason in the world for writing except to say Hello. Every time I hear one of your compositions, or when I read articles in The Herald about you, I resolve to drop a line; but, till today, never do.

After your lovely – but for me difficult – oriental piece last night on Radio Scotland, I phoned my organist, who knows Marilyn de Blieck, to get your address.....so here I am.

As I said, I could only dabble in music. Even today "Rule Britannia" can knock me over by its sheer virtuosity....but I think I can recognise greatness when I hear it, and I can always hear it in you. I think I told you once before about the pious Dublin "shawlie" who was raving over a sermon she had just heard. It was given by an ascetic Oxford Jesuit, and was on the complementary nature of the inner workings of the Blessed Trinity! Asked what she had found so thrilling she replied; "I didn't get a single word; but the Holy Ghost was leppin' out of him." And the Holy Ghost leaps out of your music.

Every good wish to you Tom,

Sincerely,

Francis Duffy

The first performance of *Passeleth Tapestry* was conducted by Bryden Thomson in Paisley Abbey on August 6. Once again the SNO had been pressed into action for a Scottish composer, and I have to say they gave of their very best. The piece sounded fantastic in the slightly resounding acoustic of the Abbey, and the excitement that the work generated amongst the audience was little short of rapturous. After the concert a stream of well-wishers came to congratulate Tom on a fine work. At the reception after the concert in the Loggia of the Town Hall, Tom was presented with a bottle of whisky from Chivas Regal that had been specially blended for the occasion. It was a limited edition called Royal

Paisley; ours was no. 43 out of 500. I said that we should keep it as a memento, but I was persuaded that the whisky might "go off" and that we should be happy to keep only the bottle. So Tom enjoyed the fruits of his labours, and I got to save the bottle.

The reviews of the concert were as good as the audience response. Kenneth Walton wrote in The Daily Telegraph, August 9 1988:

> As the Burgh of Paisley reaches the height of its 500th anniversary celebrations, a significant musical event took place in Paisley Abbey, featuring the Scottish National Orchestra in a concert conducted by its principal conductor Bryden Thomson, which included a major new work by Thomas Wilson, commissioned for the occasion and appropriately called "Passeleth Tapestry".

> The title is particularly helpful besides its reference to the 12th century form of the town's name. Wilson has created a veritable musical tapestry throughout which are woven distinct motivic threads, the most significant of which being the opening symbolic carillon motifs, its flittering percussion sonorities ringing gloriously in the reverberant acoustics. Again and again it appears, as if to represent the affirmative and optimistic spirit of the townspeople throughout the ages, despite religious and social upheavals. These too, provide inspiration for Wilson's score: the regal association with the Stuarts, the turbulence of the Reformation, the consequences of the Industrial age.

> Relevant also is the fact that the composer had the Abbey in mind when composing the work. He uses the acoustics to great advantage, the rich string textures multiplied in warmth manifold, while he is careful to treat tutti passages with directness and clarity. Bryden Thomson's direction realised the powerful structural shape and the wide gamut of expression which, ultimately, counteracts any notion of longevity.

The Herald critic Michael Tumelty wrote:

> How does a composer react when given a commission like the one Thomas Wilson received to mark Paisley's 500th anniversary as a burgh? The orthodox response, I suppose, would be to produce a true Occasional piece – short, a bit of pomp, and a lot of ceremony. Wilson's solution, the Passeleth Tapestry, which received its first performance on Saturday night with the SNO under principal

conductor Bryden Thomson, is, in that sense, extraordinary. It is a huge piece, half an hour in duration, and broad in its scope and scale. It is a kind of descriptive abstract, weaving together several distinctive sound worlds suggested by various events and stages in the history of the burgh. Clarity of thought and expression is a perennial strength of this composer. But here he has surpassed himself. The individual materials of the work are clear in their presentation – without a trace of episodic construction – and pellucid in their assembly. (I cannot think of another recent work that has communicated such a structurally assured sense of self-confidence on first exposure.)

The materials themselves are striking and include some beautifully expressive music for strings, a typically defined and focused rhythmic character, and a dramatic clattering evocation of the machine age. And what an introduction! The great, jangling opening flourishes – an exotic array of tuned percussion, redolent of the gamelan – were absolutely unforgettable. It was an unusual sound from this composer, but one crafted – like the rest of this piece – with consummate skill.

Of a further performance in the Abbey, Janice Galloway wrote in The Herald:

Thomas Wilson's Passeleth Tapestry, a present for Paisley's 500th anniversary, is a marvellous invention: four closely-stitched panels of history with a coda to glimpse the future. More practically, its moody atmospherics could fight through the Abbey's hothouse acoustic with no apparent damage; playing full of colour, with perfectly judged extremes of dynamic shading, thick-textured strings, volcanic eruptions of brass and the excitement of a packed percussion section playing sterlingly well. And Edwin Paling's deliciously lyrical solo didn't do any harm either.

A few days later, one of our friends, the critic Ian Robertson, came over to the house and suggested to Tom that *Passeleth Tapestry* was really a symphony. After thinking about it, Tom agreed with him, and so he added the title *Symphony No.4.*

West and East

After the triumphant première of *Passeleth Tapestry*, Tom and I flew off with our son Brendan to Spain to our apartment in Sotogrande for a well deserved holiday. The holiday started very well; however, one very hot afternoon, while Tom and Brendan were playing golf, I was suddenly taken ill with stomach pains, and when they returned to the apartment they found me on my knees doubled up in agony. They quickly found a nurse who lived in the next apartment block and she thought I might have appendicitis. However the pain passed, and when we returned to Scotland I had a scan taken. The family doctor told me that I was living with a "time bomb" inside of me, a stone in the neck of the gall bladder.

This news was distressing in itself, but the worst part was its potential effect on the plans Tom and I had made. He had been invited to accompany the BBC Scottish Symphony Orchestra in October on a tour in Canada where they would be performing the *St Kentigern Suite*. Our plan was that I would go with him and we would then extend our trip into the USA to visit Tom's birthplace. The doctor, however, said that I could not fly as I might become a surgical emergency on board the plane. Apparently one's internal organs move about when one is in flight and the stone might break through from its original position. The only alternative was to remove the stone, but these were the days before keyhole surgery, and the surgeon, Alan Mackay, said that it would take seven weeks to recover sufficiently to travel. The orchestra was leaving in seven weeks and two days, so the very next day I had my operation, and, seven weeks later, and two stones lighter (one of them the gallstone), I was able to join Tom on what was to be the trip of a lifetime.

We flew with the orchestra and their conductor Jerzy Maksymiuk from Glasgow to Toronto where we picked up a flight to Halifax, Nova Scotia, where the North Atlantic air is so pure it feels like champagne. One of the things that surprised me about this part of the world is that almost all of the buildings – even the churches – are made of clapboard. It reminded me of the book *Little Women*. The BBCSSO gave concerts in Sackville, Fredericton, Pictou, Halifax, Montreal, Ottawa, Sault Ste Marie,

Kitchener, and Toronto. We travelled with the orchestra by bus and by plane to the various venues. After a few days on tour groups often start to feel like family and the jokes become that little bit more personally revealing, although without malice. The chat amongst the players was hilarious despite the fact that they must have been very tired at times. One comment I remember was directed to a male member of the orchestra about the state of his socks. His nonchalant reply was "I threw them at the wall and they did not stick so I put them on."

While we were in Toronto the string players from the orchestra went to Toronto University to deliver a master class on the *St. Kentigern Suite* to the string sections of the student orchestra. The Herald critic Michael Tumelty who accompanied them wrote of the event:

> What looked on paper a rather academic format turned out to be a highly successful afternoon of group music making. The composer's descriptive talk set the scene. The Scottish Symphony Orchestra with conductor Jerzy Maksymiuk then performed the piece, and after that the orchestra was joined by the student players.

> This looked a bit implausible – with a total of 86 strings playing, the suite looked destined to be weighty and inflated. Not so. Throughout the rehearsal and the subsequent performance, it became increasingly apparent that this superb piece – which has already worked successfully across a range of sizes and ensembles, was revealing new colours, new resonances. As the moment of great relief, which occurs in the last movement, came round, the composer's eyes were shining with delight.

For the public performance that evening in the Roy Thomson Hall, Toronto, the BBC strings were joined not only by the Toronto University student orchestra string sections but also by students from the Royal Conservatory of Music. There were about 150 players in all. It sounded like something from outer space and was greatly acclaimed. One of the Canadian reviewers wrote "this work should be taken up by orchestras all over Canada."

Jerzy proved to be a very entertaining travelling companion, although not always intentionally so. One evening at dinner he asked me if I liked the braces that he had just bought. He was obviously very pleased with them so I didn't have the heart to tell him that their scarlet colour didn't really go well with his green scarf, camel coat, and blue shirt. It must be said, though, that they were great braces. Another evening, when we went out to dinner, he left his seafarer's cap in a taxi, and only discovered his mistake when we were leaving the restaurant (Jerzy is very fond of denim caps and has quite a few of them.) Nothing could be done, so we hailed a taxi, got in, and to our amazement, there on the back seat was the cap. The taxi driver said that he had had three fares between dropping us off and picking us up again. The chances of hailing the same taxi in a city the size of Toronto must be minute, but obviously fate meant that Jerzy should keep his cap.

Another time we took him to a music shop and he asked to see a grand piano. He is a fine player who had won the Paderewski Piano Competition in his youth. The assistant said that the storage area was opened only by appointment, but when we explained that Jerzy was a very famous conductor, he found a key and took us to an upper floor of the building where he solemnly opened up. Jerzy immediately sat down at the piano, but, instead of playing a sonata or some such that we expected, he presented us with *I'm Dreaming of a White Christmas*, and asked us mischievously if it was not a "good tune?" After all our efforts to impress the shop assistant, I felt mortified.

When we left the orchestra in Toronto, we headed for Windsor to visit my brother for a few days before crossing the border into Detroit.

At home we had applied for visas to enter America, and though I was given one, Tom's application was refused. The consulate in Edinburgh said that Tom had to have a US passport as he had been born there. So Tom had two passports and dual citizenship, even though he had been asked when he was eighteen years old to make a choice and had chosen to be British. When we got to the U.S. border he was waved through, but despite my visa, I was taken into a wooden building and grilled by a very tough lady who eventually relented and allowed me entry.

Our first visit was to the Henry Ford Museum in Dearborn, Michigan, a huge museum dedicated to the history of transport. I was amazed at how small the landing craft was from the first flight into outer space and how big the transcontinental trains were – they must have been at least ten feet high. The next day we flew from Detroit to Las Vegas where we picked up a car to take us on our grand tour. We arrived in darkness with only sketchy directions as to how to get to our hotel. At one point we found ourselves going the wrong way up a one-way street with five lanes of traffic coming towards us – headlights full on! Fortunately there was a pavement with a piece of waste ground beyond it and I told Tom to head there so that we could consult a map. The next thing that we heard was the siren of a police car! American police with their holstered guns terrify me, but the two officers who approached just asked Tom politely if he had been drinking. After we explained our dilemma, they told us to follow their car, and they took us to our hotel. The incident was not to be our only brush with the law.

After a night spent in the Aladdin Hotel/Casino we set off to cross the Nevada desert to Utah and stopped at the roadside so that Tom could have his photograph taken in front of the Utah State sign. He was determined to have such a photograph taken as we entered each state. The scenery was magnificent – different from anything that we had experienced elsewhere. It was various shades of coral pink and the landscape had been weathered so that the rocks looked like giant fairy castles. When the sun shone through the apertures in these towers the sight was breathtaking. At one point the road was so high above sea level that there was snow. We visited Bryce Canyon and Cedar Breaks, invoked famously in the music of Messiaen, and also went to Zion National Park. We also went to see an Anasazi Indian village built around the eleventh century.

The wildlife we saw was known to us from books and television programmes, and it was thrilling to see a coyote close at hand. He was sitting quite quietly by the roadside in the shade of some bushes and we could have reached out to touch him.

Tom's father had often talked about the rattlesnakes sunning themselves on the roads in the area but fortunately we did not come across any on our travels. Everywhere we went people asked us where we were from. When we answered "Scotland", they all seemed to have an aunt or a grandmother from the 'old country'.

After three days driving through southern Utah, we crossed over the Sangre de Cristo mountain range, where prospectors and miners panned for gold in the 1860s, into Colorado. There we went to the Mesa Verde National Park to see more settlements that had been built into the sides of the mountains by Indians in the eleventh century. The caves that were the homes of the Indians, were virtually impregnable as the cliffs above and below them were almost vertical.

It took us another three days of travel through the south of Colorado, (including an evening lost in the San Isabel National Forest), to reach the little town of Trinidad, where Tom was born. It was then a very small town just off the main North-South Highway, though I understand its population has grown significantly since the 1990s. Most of the town seemed to be grouped around Main Street to the east of Highway 25. We spent three days exploring it and the surrounding hills and beauty spots, such as Simpsons Rest, trying to find the places Tom had glimpsed in family photographs and heard of in his father's stories. Nothing much had changed so he could easily relate the real thing to these mementos and memories.

We asked about his godfather George Doherty who had owned the local supermarket, only to find out that he had died two years earlier; however, we did visit the Church of the Holy Trinity where Tom was baptised and were shown the entry of his birth and baptism in the card index. It was telling that the complete card index of baptisms was comfortably housed in one drawer about eighteen inches long.

The house where he had been born was no longer there but this visit to his birthplace filled him with nostalgia for what was past, and the inevitable thoughts about what might have become of his life had his sister lived and his family stayed on in that isolated western town.

I was at a loss to know how anyone slept in Trinidad. The railway went right through the town centre, and as it was without any boundary walls or guard rails oncoming trains started to hoot about a quarter of a mile before they arrived. This they continued to do right through the town, and on until they were about a quarter of a mile on the other side of it. Fortunately they were not too frequent.

After we left Trinidad we turned south into New Mexico. Here we took the road to Taos, a little town that is now an artists' colony. This was where Kit Carson lived, and his home and the original shops are still there. They have hitching posts, but all that is parked outside the shops now are cars. Not a horse or cowboy in sight. On our way to Taos we visited the Taos pueblo which is two miles north of the town. It is probably the most famous of all the Native American pueblos in New Mexico and some of the structures date back to 1150 AD. The sculpted adobe homes, church and shops reminded me of the coral pink of the rock formations in Utah. Access to each room was by outside ladder from one floor to another. It has remained unchanged for several hundred years. Unfortunately while we were there we managed to lock ourselves out of the car. It was Sunday, and although it was November the heat was unbearable, but when we explained what had happened to the son of the chief he 'phoned the Reservation Police to report our difficulty to see if they could help. While we waited we looked at jewellery, pottery and other artefacts – anything to keep out of the sun. After we had waited three hours the chief's son went to find his father and they returned twenty minutes later. The chief was a very cultured man. In fact I have seldom met a man who appeared so totally at peace with himself. He had plaits but wore western dress. (I was, though, a bit saddened to see some of the Tiwa Indians wearing what they called the white man's moccasins – trainers.) The chief asked us where we were from and when we replied Scotland he said, "Ah yes I have read about Scotland, it is a land of peat." No mention of heather, haggis, or kilts, or even of whisky. He took us to the motel where we had spent the previous night and booked us back in. Then he telephoned for the locksmith who was of course out having lunch. Eventually the locksmith got our telephone message and took us back to the reservation where he had the car door opened in ten seconds flat. I had said to him "Wait until I get there to see how you do it," but it was done before my feet touched the ground. It cost us eighty dollars, which was quite a lot to pay, but Tom said that he would have gladly paid double just to have the problem solved.

The next small town we came to was Cimarron where we learned that there is a Wilson Mesa Trail in Cimarron Canyon. We went into the St James Hotel that was built in 1875 by Henri Lambert who was chef to Abraham Lincoln and General Ulysses S Grant. The rooms inside the hotel were tiny although from the outside the place looked quite modern. The name Cimarron means "wild" and "unbroken." Desperadoes wanted by the law often stayed there – they even had their names on the doors of bedrooms, and photographs of them were posted alongside. Jessie James, Clay Allison, Marc Bowman, and Doroteo Arango, alias Francisco "Pancho" Griego, were just a few of them. Buffalo Bill Cody and Annie Oakley also stayed there. The staff told us of ghosts who still regularly caused mayhem, overturning furniture and upsetting the cutlery. It was easy to imagine the dance-hall girls hanging out of the windows back in the 1870s. The seminal American artist and sculptor Frederick Remington visited the hotel in the days of the old west and the popular novelist Zane Grey also wrote a book while he stayed there.

At one point we did see cowboys bringing cattle down from the scrubby mountains, but as we got out of the car to take a photograph the cowboys waved us furiously back into it. Wearing guns and carrying rifles too, they looked really frightening, so we promptly did as we were bid. Then we realised that the reason they were waving was because these cattle had never seen a man other than on horseback and might well have charged at us.

Santa Fe was our next objective. The highway runs parallel to the old
Santa Fe Trail from time to time and the tracks of the wagons are still easy
to see. It is also very easy to imagine the old covered wagons rattling
through the landscape carrying everything that their passengers owned.
Travel along the trail stopped when the railroad opened in 1879. From
there we followed the road through Albuquerque, Gallup, and on to
Flagstaff, Arizona, where we spent the night. The following morning we
had our second brush with the law. Again it was a Sunday morning and we
were on our way to the Grand Canyon. Part of the road was being rebuilt
in Flagstaff and it was not easy to negotiate so Tom just put his foot down
and followed the van that was in front of us. Unfortunately the traffic light
turned to red just as we started to cross the intersection. I was beginning
to tell Tom what he had done when we heard the police whistle. We were
pulled to the side of the road and were told, "You may get away with that
sort of thing where you come from, but you don't get away with it here."
We felt about one inch high. Then our persecutor said, "I expect you are
going to the Grand Canyon" and when we replied that we were, we were
allowed to continue with our journey. After seeing the Grand Canyon and
some of the many canyons going into it we visited the Petrified Forest and
the Painted Desert. Then we drove to Las Vegas to return the hired car,
passing the gigantic structure that is the Hoover Dam on the way.

We flew next from Las Vegas to Los Angeles, to spend a few days with our
friends John and Anna Currie who could clearly see the HOLLYWOOD
sign from their garden. John had left Scotland early in the eighties to take
the prestigious post as head of the Los Angeles Master Chorale. The
Chorale consists of 75 professional singers and this was added to, as
required, by gifted amateurs. Sometimes it numbered as many as 150
choristers. One evening we attended a performance of Lutoslawski's
Stabat Mater in the Dorothy Chandler Pavilion of the Los Angeles Music
Center and after the performance we were introduced to some friends of
John and Anna. When these friends heard that we intended to return to
Scotland via Canada, they kindly invited us to spend some time with
them at their home in Victoria on Vancouver Island.

But before this Tom had another commitment to fulfil in California and
so we travelled by bus to Santa Barbara where he gave a lecture to the
music students in the University of California, Los Angeles, or UCLA as
it is more commonly known. After his lecture on contemporary Scottish
music, we had tea in the home of Peter Racine Fricker and his wife. They
were delightful people, and we got on well despite the fact that Peter had
had his larynx removed because of cancer, and our communication was via
the written word.

In Santa Barbara we hired another car and proceeded to travel north again, passing the home of William Randolph Hearst. We opted to take the coast road, and the scenery was truly magnificent. The weather was unusually warm and sunny for late November but we weren't complaining. We travelled on to San Francisco – a town that really enchanted us. Tom saw an African American there playing guitar on the quayside. The man was busking, but his mind was totally focussed on his music, and Tom was most impressed by his playing. He said to me "That man is an amazing musician."

Our journey then took us through Northern California towards Oregon where the redwood trees were so big and high and so very beautiful to see. One of the motels we stayed in had been completely made out of, and was furnished from, one tree. It was on our journey along this highway that we had our third brush with the law. This time I was driving as Tom had hurt his ankle. We were in opal mining country and came upon the superstore belonging to the collector, actor, and singer of folk songs, Burl Ives. It was tastefully built into the mountainside and of course I wanted to visit it, if only to look at the opals. I slowed down the car in order not to miss the parking lot that I was sure should be there. Suddenly there was a mighty voice. It was impossible to ignore it. The policemen in the car behind us boomed out, "You can't park here." I tried to look as though parking was the last thing on my mind as we continued up the road. Nevertheless we were followed for at least a mile in case we changed our minds.

It was our intention to stay overnight in Portland, Oregon with Dorothy Sermol, an opera singer friend of John Maxwell Geddes, but it took us a while to find her home. The first part of the street (which was parallel to the main road but quite a bit away from it) began behind the left hand side of the highway, and the second part continued behind the right hand side, with a gap of about 500 yards in between. The house number was higher than one thousand so we drove quite a way before we worked out what the urban planners had been up to. I don't know how many people we had to ask before we found it, but I do remember that we went for tea halfway through our search and had pumpkin pie as it was near Thanksgiving. The house was, as usual, made of clapboard, but it was beautifully furnished and had all mod cons.

Our last night in the United States was spent in a hotel in Seattle, where we had a great view of the overhead trolley as it was level with our window. At breakfast the following morning I asked for a fruit salad and was presented with a large platter with three bunches of different kinds of grapes, two kinds of melon (whole), an apple, pear, orange etc. all topped off with a banana. I didn't know where to begin. I remembered the blank look that I had got when I asked for a fruit salad in San Francisco and had to explain to the waitress what it was. Later that day we caught the ferry to Vancouver Island, but, disappointingly, we did not see any killer whales in the Juan de Fuca Strait. Our hosts from the concert in Los Angeles kindly met us at the ferry terminal; however, when we arrived at their home Tom was told that he had to go into the back garden if he wanted to smoke. He muttered to me in a rare moment of irritation, 'We won't be going back there.' That said, in every other respect our hosts were very kind to us, and we spent a very enjoyable long weekend with them. They took us up country to the river where the salmon spawned, where the waterway was about five inches deep. The sides of it were littered with hundreds of dead salmon and the seagulls were so sated with food that they just stood and watched the salmon floating by them. I was appalled by the waste and suggested that the dead salmon could be collected and used as fertiliser, but I was told that the river dealt with them within a week.

On our return to the Canadian mainland a few days later we finally saw snow at close hand. The forests of pine trees were heavy with it and they looked like Christmas card scenes. I was glad that we were in a bus and the responsibility for our safety lay in the hands of the driver. Our journey took us through British Columbia to Kamloops where we stayed overnight, and then on through the Rockies to Calgary in Alberta where we caught the plane to Toronto for our connection to Glasgow. Our American road trip had been even more wonderful than we had hoped, and the break from composition was good for Tom.

Once we returned to Glasgow Tom started work on *Amor Christi*, for chamber choir and orchestra, commissioned by the Scottish Philharmonic Singers. Though this was the first commission from this particular group of singers, *Amor Christi* is composed as a dialectical work based on antiphonies and responses. It is clear from his sketches that Tom was once again looking at opposite states: "Good-Evil, calm-agitated, sweet-acid, loud-soft, high-low, complex-simple, dark - light or bright, chromatic-diatonic, dense-pellucid". It features: "unisons, pairs, trios, quartets, quintets, sextets," etc. which are used "colouristically, harmonically, intervallically, in register, in dynamic, etc."

In his programme notes Tom explained his purpose in choosing the music's title:

This work is not a religious text. Nor is it a (cloud cuckoo) depiction of some sort of Utopia. Still less is it a lament for the good old days. Its concern is with the present, and even more important with the future. The world is in a bad way. The nuclear threat is still very real, and even if that never happens, Man's own greed and folly could soon turn the world into a sterile, uninhabitable waste unless he comes to his senses and behaves responsibly.

The theme of the work is Love, represented in its purest form by the mediaeval plainsong (*Ubi caritas et amor*), which appears at the start, and then throughout as a kind of refrain. Against this, various deviations are examined using the verses of more modern poets. These range from the negative and isolationist fear and shunning of the world of *Lucy Ashton's Song* by Walter Scott to the hypocritical gossiping malice of the *Old Women* by George MacKay Brown. Interposed are reminders of what real Love can achieve in the Gradual for Holy Thursday (*Christus factus est pro nobis obediens usque ad mortem*), and St Paul's famous description of Charity. Finally passages from Edwin Muir's *The Transfiguration* foresees a world in which evil, not eradicated, but nevertheless controlled, makes a better world a possibility. The work ends with the purity of the plainsong hymn reminding us again of the ideal we must try to achieve.

Like all programme notes, these two paragraphs can only give a partial description of the work. In this case Tom is taking a rather subject-driven view of his own work. My own interpretation of *Amor Christi* is quite different from the way Tom writes about it here. When I listen to it, I experience it as a quite exotic tapestry in which ethereal sounds of sections like the Transfiguration are balanced by deliberately down-to-earth sections, for example, the gossiping women – and plainsong weaves in and out like a thread of gold.

On completing *Amor Christi* at the beginning of April, Tom immediately started work on his next composition, a chamber work commissioned by the Paragon Ensemble and Glasgow District Council, with the support of the Scottish Arts Council and the Esmée Fairbairn Charitable Trust, as part of the celebrations during Glasgow's reign as European City of Culture 1990. This work would become Tom's celebrated *Chamber Symphony*.

Amor Christi received its first performance at a concert held on November 3 1989 at the Royal Scottish Academy of Music and Drama, where Jerzy

Maksymiuk directed the BBC Scottish Symphony Orchestra and the Scottish Philharmonic Singers. Among the glowing reviews, Neil Mackay writing in the Guardian called Tom the "doyen of Scottish composers" while the Independent critic Raymond Monelle said: "With darkly glowing lower strings, glints of muted trumpet and sonorous choral harmonies, this was in the mystical tradition of British composers, its rich incantations garlanded with the florid snake-charming of woodwind solos." Tom smiled quietly when he read this.

A few days later the Russian composer Professor Leonid Pavlovich Klinichev came to Glasgow. A Merited Artist of the Russian Soviet Federated Socialist Republics, Leonid (or Leo) was here to sign the Soviet part of a formal exchange agreement between the Scottish Society of Composers' and the Union of Composers of the Soviet Union. A gregarious outgoing man of considerable influence and power, for many years he was Chairman of the Composers' Union of Rostov on Don, a city that shares close cultural links with Glasgow. Leo was very impressed by Glasgow and following the signing we were formally invited to visit Rostov the next month for Christmas 1989 and New Year 1990. During this period some of Tom's works, most notably the *Piano Concerto*, were performed in public and transmitted on radio across the USSR. In all we would visit Russia five times during the next two years to hear performances of Tom's works.

In March 1989 Tom paid a visit to Moscow and Leningrad where he was representing the Composers' Guild of Great Britain at the signing of the Scottish part of the agreement. It was wide-ranging in that it embraced the exchange of composers, musicians, performers and researchers, as well as the mutual promotion of compositions. Tom knew that the Scottish Society could never match the facilities available to the Russian composers, but he felt that both organisations had a lot to learn from each other.

For the 1989-90 visit, my first and Tom's fourth to the USSR, we were met at Moscow's Sheremetyevo Airport by a huge black limousine. It was near midnight and minus 20 degrees Fahrenheit. The insides of the car windows were icing up, and the wind chill factor made the temperature seem even lower. Despite this the driver took us immediately to see Red Square. I must admit it was a magical sight. The snow and the frost made the scene look very Christmassy. We were expected to leave the car to see the Square, but I reckon our sortie lasted all of three seconds. I felt so sorry for the soldiers on night watch who must have been freezing despite their huge great-coats.

The next day, Leonid Klinichev took us to have tea with Tikhon Khrennikov, the head of the Composers' Union in Russia. His influence in the lives of Russian composers was enormous, and I quickly felt that he was not someone to warm to. After the opening pleasantries, he told me I laughed a lot, and asked me pointedly why, as though it was a sin. I think he expected me to be afraid of him and maybe I was naïve not to be. I can understand his puzzlement though, because people in Russia at that time had very little to laugh about, and many were apprehensive about the changes that were taking place politically. Nonetheless Khrennikov had great respect for Tom and was very interested to learn about the musical conditions and opportunities for the performance of new works in Scotland. Hearing us explain the difficulties, he was somewhat bemused, as were most of our hosts. They simply could not understand that contemporary classical music was not held in higher regard in the West.

Then we flew to Rostov on Don, a city known as the Gate to the Caucasus. We learned that because of the huge distances between cities in Russia and the lack of private cars, people tended to use planes as we would buses. Founded in 1749 Rostov is situated on the right bank of the river Don. After the construction of the Volga-Don Canal, Rostov became the 'port of five seas': the Black Sea, the Sea of Azov, the Baltic, the White Sea, and the Caspian Sea. When we arrived in Rostov airport, the music we heard over the Tannoy was from Leo's ballet *Tikki Don* whose story is taken from the book 'Quiet Flows the Don' by Mikhail Alexandrovich Sholokhov. The following May we met the author's son when we went to see a performance in the Maliv Theatre of Opera and Ballet in Moscow. This performance was given to celebrate Sholokhov's 85th birthday.

One of the objects of our visit was to hear the Rostov Philharmonic Orchestra perform Tom's *Piano Concerto*. The soloist was Olga Pavlovich and the conductor Semjon Kogan. As was typical for performances of classical music, the concert halls were filled to capacity.

Russian concertgoers were not provided with programmes. I do not know what the situation is now, but then there were musicologists who gave an introductory talk about the works and composers to the audience. This was their full time employment and they did the job very well. Tom had interviews with them and he found their questions very intelligent and searching. Of course it was a slow business because everything had to be translated. I hope that the following transcript will give an idea of the general pattern of these pre-concert talks:

Naturally we have a particular interest in the performance of the *Piano Concerto*. This work, written in traditional form, does not have a programme. The composer attempted to depict the eternal figures of Apollo and Dionysus, an aspiration to order, harmony, and to the ridding from life of disharmony and chaos. This has been fulfilled with surprising talent and mastery of the highest class by Thomas Wilson.

Leo then said:

This composition has been written with inspiration. Regardless of the fact that this composer uses modern musical language, it is accessible not only to the professional musician but to the ordinary, educated, aesthetically mature person.

The performance would then commence. Audiences in Russia were always extremely attentive and were not slow to show their appreciation. Many people approached Tom after the performances, to shake his hand and talk to the composer sometimes in halting English. After the performances our hosts would invariably put on a dinner at the hotel and the opportunity for toasts was properly taken.

It was then the custom for newspapers to be pasted up in public places, and the next morning those in Rostov on Don reported that:

In the opinion of Thomas Wilson the performance of his music was magnificent, distinguished by a full understanding of its spirit. When the last chords of music ended, for the first time being heard in the USSR, the Philharmonic Hall rang out in a long ovation.

Leo had told the Rostov String Quartet that they must learn Tom's *Fourth Quartet*, for performances in Rostov and Moscow during our visit. When Tom heard their interpretation a few days later his eyes lit up. He told me that it was one of the few times in his life when he heard one of his works exactly as he had imagined it while composing the piece. The *Fourth Quartet* was described there as a modern masterpiece, but the compliment for Tom was to feel that the performers had been totally in sympathy with his intentions.

The Quartet players were employed by the Philharmonia Society of Rostov, but, like most musicians, they needed more than one job in order to support their families. Lev Atlas, the viola player, played gypsy music at weddings, and the others taught in part of their spare time. The Society was a concert organisation that employed singers, actors, dancers, soloists, string quartets, chamber orchestras and symphony orchestras. It was funded by the state and arranged the concert life of the whole region.

After the performance we became friends with the Quartet. They told us they often rehearsed together for six hours, and as a result knew each other better than they knew their own families. Years later they revealed that before seeing the score they were quite annoyed that they had to learn a work by a composer that they had never heard of, from a country they knew only from books. But when they heard a cassette of the *Fourth Quartet*, performed by the Edinburgh Quartet, they recognised what a wonderful work it is. The following year they came to Scotland to play it again, fell in love with the country, and in the mid 1990s three of them came to live in Scotland. The first violin Yuri Yurasov played in the BBC Scottish Symphony Orchestra until his unfortunately premature death. The second violin, Leonid Aizenburg, went to America, but developed a problem with his bowing arm and ended up working in the computer industry. The viola player Lev Atlas is currently the leader of his section in the Scottish Opera Orchestra and he teaches at the Royal Scottish Academy of Music and Drama, while the cellist Alexander 'Sasha' Volpov is principal cellist in the Opera North Orchestra.

As in all societies, there were pluses and minuses in a composer's life in the USSR. Paper was in very short supply and manuscript paper could only be bought two or three sheets at a time from the Composers' Union. On the other hand, every work a composer had performed was automatically recorded on vinyl and could be bought in the shops. The Rostov State University enrolled many international students who were amazed at the fact that paper for writing lecture notes was in such short supply. On the rare occasions when the stationery shops had jotters in stock they had to queue for them. One of the students told me: "We are supposed to come from Third World countries but we do not have to do this at home." The fact that they were there at all, however, was due to the high quality of education in Rostov.

I had thought prior to our visit that perhaps I should not appear too 'dressy', but many of the women were very elegantly dressed. Many wore mink coats, and of course in winter everyone wore fur hats. It was so very cold that it would have been tempting fate not to wrap up properly. Most of the clothes in the markets were manufactured in China and were very well made as Russian women certainly had an eye for quality despite their many years of privations. When I asked what I should bring them on my next visit, they asked for French perfume.

Fruit and vegetables in the state shops were very poor, so wherever possible people grew their own on allotments and sold the excess produce in the local market. Fancy sponge cakes with lots of artistic icing were the only provisions in good supply in the state shops. This seemed very strange until I discovered that this was due to the fact that the USSR had such a close political alliance with Cuba and imported a great deal of sugar from there.

During our visit to Rostov we were taken to see a very old church in Novocherkarsk which stood in the middle of a bleak windswept square. It was not a place I felt happy to be in, and with hindsight I believe that the past history of the city still casts a shadow. Novocherkarsk was the capital of the Cossack country and was the headquarters of their ruler, the Ataman, who was head of the army. This very historically interesting area of southern Russia was ruled by the local aristocracy, who were served by - and who owned - the peasant population. Frequently, however, the serfs rebelled and ran away to the borders of the region where they became outlaws, so the area was in continual ferment. When Katherine the Great came to power, she gave the region tax-free status, and placed it under army rule, with peasants being enlisted to fill the ranks. The state provided a horse for every male child at the age of three, and during their formative years they were trained as soldiers. At the age of fourteen they were military horsemen in the White army and were used to defend the borders of Russia from the Caucasian invaders from the Steppes and the East. Before the revolution in 1918 the White Army was used to fight the Bolsheviks. They supported the monarchy, and so when the Red Army was formed, Rostov on Don became a very important centre in the battles between the White and Red Russians.

A mini-bus and driver were provided so that the local composers could take us to see places of interest. One of the performances of Tom's *Fourth Quartet* took place in Taganrog at the school that Anton Chekhov had attended. The school was scrupulously clean, and the pupils were most attentive. On the way back to Rostov, we visited the small cottage where Chekhov was born and I remember thinking that he must have been a little man as his bed looked no more than 5ft 6 inches long. However, I was later informed that he was 5ft 11inches so he obviously slept with cold feet. On another outing we stopped at a very bleak spot in the middle of a heavily misted landscape to see some primitive stone figures from the dark ages. One of our Russian friends opened her mouth wide and emitted a most primitive series of sounds which was apparently a song to the place.

We returned to Glasgow at the beginning of the second week of the New Year so that Tom could attend rehearsals for the upcoming première of his *Chamber Symphony*. The *Chamber Symphony* shared its première with a new work from the young composer James MacMillan.

Having caught 'flu before our visit to Russia, the completion of the work had been delayed, and so Tom offered to help Beth Mackay prepare the parts. The *Chamber Symphony* is not conventional in structure since it is cast in one movement with five sections. Tom had toyed with several titles for the work e.g. 'Movements', 'Anacrus', 'Labyrinth', 'Mosaics II', 'Jig-Saw', but it always came back to the fact that he felt that it had the scale of a symphony, and so it became the *Chamber Symphony*.

It is possible that the source of inspiration for this work came from the River Clyde, though Tom never said as much to me. However when he was dictating his programme note to me, he did say this:

> The work is not programmatic, but my early thoughts on the shape of the piece were about natural patterns of movement and their development, e.g. the bubbling spring which becomes the stream, then the mature river, then loses itself in the immensity of the ocean, finally suffering dramatic disintegration as the waves break on a distant shore. It was never my intention simply to <u>describe</u> this process, it is not Water Music in any shape or form, but it does have an organic flow that is transferable into music.

In his programme note, Tom provides an overview of the development of the piece:

> The work plays without a break and has five main sections (Slow Introduction: Fast: Very Slow: Fast: Coda). First a slow Introduction calmly uncovers various source materials which the work will use. This is followed by a fast movement, full of early energy and contrasts of texture, but not yet very coordinated. Three very different ideas confront one another (the first bubbling with energy but rather wayward; the second a "stammering" idea for trumpet; the third based on syncopated antiphonal chords). The last part of this movement then briefly establishes the common ground between these apparently incompatible ideas. The central section of the work is very slow and spacious. Like the keystone of an arch it is (almost) motionless, still. But the quick movement which follows is very different, showing an increasingly nervy and anxious quality which drives the music forward on an inevitable collision

course. Finally the crisis point is reached. Thereafter a Coda (getting slower gradually) records the break-up of the work and its ideas. But the mood is not wholly sombre or pessimistic. There are signs of fresh patterns emerging, a developing calmness and stability, with the implicit possibility that a new and different cycle is about to begin its course.

To those who did not really know Tom he appeared to be simplicity itself; quiet spoken, unassuming and humble. In fact he was a very deep thinker, whose complexity was very well disguised by a patina of straightforwardness, whose conclusions were reached after a lot of thought and soul–searching. He believed that intellectuals should avoid being obscure and should put clear communication above all else. He was very slow to judge people and preferred to leave any final judgement open. And this was so ingrained that it inhabited every aspect of his thinking - even decisions on everyday matters. He preferred to leave them to me, and when pressed would only take a stand if I suggested something so outrageous that he could not accept it. Only in his own music was he absolutely adamant about what he wanted, and in this area there was no room for manoeuvre or compromise.

The première of the *Chamber Symphony* was given by the Paragon Ensemble in the Stevenson Hall of the Royal Scottish Academy of Music and Drama in Glasgow on January 28 1990. The work is written for a chamber orchestra of thirteen players without percussion, harp or piano; the sound is rich and full of instrumental colour.

After the performance, Tom was delighted when Clio Gould, the leader of the Ensemble, said to him, "not a note too many." A compliment from a fellow musician meant a lot to him.

The newspaper reviews were also very positive, Neil Mackay wrote in The Guardian:

> The Paragon Ensemble premièred two remarkable Scottish commissions. These were the chamber symphonies by Thomas Wilson and James MacMillan. At 62 Wilson is an acknowledged leader and spokesman for contemporary composers here, and his modesty and kindness are a byword. His music, which can sometimes seem conservative, usually has a cutting edge, and is always craftsmanlike and elegant. His new five-movement *Chamber Symphony* has moments of drama, and its 'nervy and anxious quality' (to use the composer's words) communicates powerfully.

Michael Tumelty of the Glasgow Herald wrote:

> There is terrific continuity in Wilson's music at present. It's as though ideas from one work fertilise another – nothing new in that, history is full of such fluid developments. What is heartening is that these ideas (always recognisable, whatever their source) are pregnant with possibilities. The *Chamber Symphony* begins softly, with a little curling run-up figure, very expressive in its shape and subsequently threading through the work. It figures in at least one other Wilson piece, but is a basic building block here. The work is superbly constructed and played with marvellous control. There is a cool classical quality to Wilson's music.

Writing in The Scotsman Raymond Monelle said:

> Wilson's *Chamber Symphony* is a piece for 13 players, its lapidary motific shapes deftly transformed and combined. At first the music is still and ominous, the lines increasingly florid, the chords glowing smokily, later stepping out into a dance, firm-footed, with the bustle of a concerto finale. Not only is this composer lucid and economical with his themes; he is a precise distributor of instrumental colour.

The greatest compliment about the work however came only recently, when, after a performance of the *Chamber Symphony* at the Stevenson Hall in 2003, the world-famous trumpeter and dynamic current Principal of the RSAMD, John Wallace described the composition as "an iconic work of the last half of the 20th Century and a beacon for young Scottish composers".

CHAPTER 18 (1990 - 1991)

Chimes and Gongs .

I remember coming home from shopping one day in spring 1990 to find Tom with a letter in his hand and a look of consternation on his face, and as he handed it to me he said, "I don't want to accept this but you'll kill me if I don't." The letter was from Buckingham Palace offering him a CBE in the Queen's Birthday Honours List. His reluctance to accept the medal did not arise because he was a republican or anti-Royal, but because he didn't want to operate from a position of any kind of social privilege as he saw it. However, I persuaded him that he should accept the honour as it recognised that good classical music was being written in Scotland, and would, moreover, reflect well on all Scottish composers. On that understanding he agreed. So we went to London in June where we met our son Stephen whom we had invited to join us for the investiture, and who was curious to see inside the palace. We stayed overnight with Stephen in Crouch End before setting off the next morning, suited and booted, for the ceremony. The investiture takes place in a large hall with a low platform where the Queen stands, and before which those honoured receive their medals. The ceremony took several hours and I thought it must be quite an ordeal for the Queen. Tom was one of the first to receive his medal and afterwards he went off to smoke in the courtyard, while the rest of the audience was 'entertained' by a military band playing music from the shows like *Annie Get Your Gun* and *Oklahoma*. It was not quite what either Stephen or I were used to.

A few days after the investiture we left for a second visit to Russia. This time we were accompanied by our composer friends John Maxwell Geddes and William Sweeney, and the guitarist Anne Chaurand. Later David Wilde, who was to play Tom's *Piano Concerto* arrived from Germany where he lived with his wife Jane. Apart from our airfares all our expenses were to be met by the Union of Composers of the Russian Federation. Should extra funds be needed, we were told that we could rely upon the Rostov City Council and the Regional authorities. The Russian people have always had a great respect for the fine arts, and foreign composers were treated like visiting dignitaries. Unfortunately we did not have the same funds at our disposal to return such hospitality when the Russians came to Glasgow, but we took them to places that we thought would be of interest in the city, and to Loch Lomond and the island of Arran. They simply could not understand why it was so difficult for us to arrange performances of contemporary classical music.

The Russian state provided us with a daily allowance for incidental expenses, and the hotel in Rostov where we had a suite was basic but comfortable. It had the added advantage of a *berioska* (literally "birch-tree shop") where duty free foreign goods were sold, so we were able to buy goods not available to the ordinary Russian citizen. The ground floor also housed hairdressers, manicurists and chiropodists - all of which were well used by people from all walks of life. Foreign currency was in short supply so I was always very welcome when I paid with my German marks. On each visit my suitcase was full of Nescafé and other items that were in short supply, and I always took a good supply of hypodermic needles to give as gifts. They were particularly prized because having one's own needles (two sizes, one for teeth and another for blood samples, etc) was a protection against being infected with the HIV virus.

During our visit our hosts chartered a boat called The Meteor to take us across the Sea of Azov to Starocherkarsk. Here we saw the world famous iconograph made up of at least eighty icons. As all good tourists do, we stood under an enormous chandelier before the iconograph for the necessary count to ten that ensures good luck. If the chandelier had fallen, we would almost certainly have been killed. But it held, so the charm apparently worked.

Later in the week I was asked to speak to students in the Pedagogical Institute about life in Britain. After my talk I asked if there were any questions that they would like to put to me. A student surprised me by asking what I thought of Graham Greene. I had not expected that Graham Greene's novels would be known in Russia. Unfortunately, all that I could say was that I had read *Brighton Rock* when I was sixteen years-old and could remember very little about it. Later I learned that Greene had written the introduction to Kim Philby's book *My Silent War*, so perhaps that explained his popularity in Russia. I think that the main reason I had been asked to give a talk was to see how much spoken English the students understood. When some Norwegians had visited the previous year the students could not understand their English at all, so they were very worried. However they assured me that they had understood me very well, so from that point of view at least I got full marks.

We renewed our acquaintance with the composer Vitaly Hodush and his wife who invited us to their home for dinner. Here we were introduced to other composers who all, at various times, told me that my husband was a genius. I was especially pleased because the Russian people are not given to overstatement; I therefore knew that their remarks were both considered and heartfelt.

Whenever we visited the USSR I was asked where I would like to go. Not knowing southern Russia I was unable to suggest places and left it to our hosts to take us to places of interest. Two weeks before this visit, however, I had watched a TV programme in which Judith Chalmers extolled the Folk Festival held each summer in Vyezhinskaya. So when I was asked again what I would like to do, I said that I would like to go to the Folk Festival not having any idea of the great distance that was involved. Undeterred, however, our hosts chartered an aeroplane to take us there. We were then lodged in a hotel for the weekend and were entertained royally. Vyezhinskaya is famous for being the home town of Mikhail Sholokhov the only officially sanctioned Soviet writer to win the Nobel Prize for Literature.

On the afternoon of our arrival we were taken to a park where about five rows of seats had been reserved for us so that we could have plenty of choice. Folk groups from all over the USSR had come to sing, dance, and act in their beautiful national costumes. Each group stopped in front of us to give us a clear view of their various skills, then went on to perform before the crowd. I turned to watch the next performance just after one of the groups had passed when I heard the clatter of a lacquered spoon dropping at my feet. Thinking that the child behind me had dropped it, I turned and gave it to him. I later learned from our translator that the spoon had been thrown by a man 100 yards away who was part of the previous group. She told me it was a traditional gift, and that I should have accepted it! This was a cause of much embarrassment to me as the Festival was being televised nationwide. Of all the performances, I particularly remember the Cossacks and the Women on Wheels. In fact the women are not on wheels at all, but they glide rather than walk so that no steps are discernible.

Following the performances we went to a hotel on the riverside for a meal. After that we watched men parachuting to the far shore with coloured smoke streaming from attachments on their heels, choirs floating on huge rafts, and coloured searchlights turning the sky to stained glass. The finale was a firework display that depicted a scene from Sholokhov's *Quiet Flows the Don*. Then there was a lavish banquet at which many toasts were drunk. I don't think that I ever had a really hot meal in Russia as they were all interrupted by toasts – some of them rather longwinded. The women were expected to retire after the meal while the men stayed on for additional toasts. Most of them – Tom included – returned in the early hours much the worse for wear.

The next morning we went into the village streets to find that the local people had put out tables with food and kvas so that visitors could help themselves as they passed by. Kvas is a mildly alcoholic drink made from fermented bread and I would have to say that it is definitely an acquired taste. It was also available from vending machines in the main street of Rostov on Don. The visiting folk groups were dancing in the village streets and of course we joined in. Everyone had a good time for almost no cost at all. I was very impressed by the people who managed to make their own enjoyment when they had so little in the way of material goods. It was shameful that we were not able to provide such hospitality in Scotland.

That afternoon we were taken to an impressive wooden house close to the river which had been the home of Mikhail Sholokhov. We had tea on the veranda and were introduced to a smartly dressed lady who was Sholokhov's literary secretary who now seemed to be in charge of his museum. Tom and John asked her a number of questions, though I must confess I was too busy soaking up the atmosphere to remember her answers. Indeed, throughout our stay the Russian people were very kind to us and we were often presented with flowers in the street.

Our flight from Vyezhinskaya back to Rostov in a small nine-seat aircraft proved exciting to say the least. There was a strong crosswind and it was an extremely bumpy flight. Then, as we neared Rostov airport, we were told that we would have to land at Volgadonsk some eighty miles away. The pilot brought us down hard - but safely, in a field in the middle of nowhere. There was a small shack that housed an office and a hole in the floor toilet with no door. That was it. No facilities for even a cup of tea, and a ground staff consisting of just one middle-aged woman as far as I could tell. However after two or three hours, we were airborne again and touched down safely in Rostov.

At a party given for us in the Composers' Union in Rostov on Don that night there were 23 toasts. I know because I counted them! My little speech thanking our hosts for their hospitality was number seventeen. Fortunately, the ladies were served only champagne – not vodka, which was regarded as a man's drink, and not proper for a lady. The women, moreover, were free to take just a sip of their drinks whereas the men were expected to empty their glasses.

On one occasion one of our friends in Rostov said to me: "We do admire the way you treat your husband, Margaret". On enquiring what she meant, she replied: "You always say: 'Do you think it would be a good idea if...?'" To me this was just the best course to follow, since it involved Tom in the decision. Tom, as I have already said, was not the most decisive of men outside of his music, and I had found over the years that he invariably agreed with my suggestions. Indeed, the ideas often became his own if the subject came up with friends. I came to accept this and be amused by it, but I was surprised that it had been noticed.

During this visit our friends The Rostov Quartet again played Tom's *Fourth String Quartet* in the Philharmonia Hall, Rostov, and in the Gnesin Institute, Moscow. And we were informed that his *Chamber Symphony*, *Piano Sonata*, *Piano Concerto*, and works for solo piano and solo guitar were performed during the Don Spring Festival. On our way home we stopped off in Moscow to hear performances of some of his shorter piano works and the *Fantasia for Solo Cello* as well as the *Fourth Quartet*. Once again, all the performances were excellent, thanks to the extremely high standards of musicianship in Russia.

On our last night in Moscow, I was made aware of how sign language can get one into hot water in another culture. A group of Russian composers invited us to dinner one evening in the Composers' Union in Moscow. At one point the waiter who was standing at Tom's shoulder, asked what he thought of the Georgian wine. Tom put his thumb and forefinger together to form a circle to indicate that he thought it was perfect. Noticing the waiter's face fall, I asked our translator what was wrong. She explained that in Russia this sign means that a thing is worthless, and the correct sign is 'thumbs up'. Fortunately we were able to apologise and explain the situation to a very puzzled waiter.

In 1990 Glasgow was the European City of Culture and many musical events were arranged throughout the year.

The Glasgow Harpsichord Society arranged a series of concerts called a 'Concert Bonanza' in August. At one of the concerts the Glasgow Festival Strings performed *Pas de Quoi*, and then played the *St Kentigern Suite* at their Early Music Festival concert the following month.

During the summer Tom completed a six minute organ work, *Toccata Festevole*, which had been commissioned for the Paisley International Organ Festival in association with the European City of Culture. This work would form the centrepiece of a competition between 27 organists from all over the world. Having played the organ while at Blairs College, Tom was well aware of the challenges that needed to be overcome and was in the ideal position to compose this competition piece.

There were four stages in which players were gradually eliminated. Then each of the final three competitors performed a 35-minute programme in Paisley Abbey which included *Toccata Festevole*. Tom had purposely not put in any registration, giving the players room to use their own imagination, and so we heard some very different interpretations ranging from the conservative to the very modern. Since church organists often have to improvise as they wait for the congregation to assemble, this is a necessary adjunct to their musicianship. When asked to help judge the competition he reluctantly agreed, saying that "Enthusiasm and objective judgement are uneasy bedfellows." The Festival was very well attended and culminated with a performance of *Passeleth Tapestry* by the Scottish National Orchestra conducted by Alexander Gibson.

Toccata Festevole was not the only commission to come out of the year's celebrations. For most of the first half of 1990 Tom had been working on a major orchestral work for the Royal Gala opening of Glasgow's new Royal Concert Hall. Though nothing was specified in the commission letter, Tom knew from the outset that the piece, which he came to title *Carillon*, would be about Glasgow. He was also adamant, however, that the work would need to stand on its own and be understood musically even if one knew nothing about the source of inspiration. Though Tom had written the *St Kentigern Suite* about St Mungo, *Carillon* was the first piece that would be directly about the city he regarded as his home. He chose not to focus on the external features of the city but on the enduring spirit and resilience of Glaswegians.

In the programme notes that he prepared for the première, Tom described the thought process he went through in approaching this celebratory commission in some detail (to which I have added a few biographical comments in brackets):

> Celebration music can pose some problems for the composer. The most important of these is perhaps the danger of such a work degenerating into obvious "whoopee" music with lots of noise but little real substance. I was not interested in writing music like that.

So it was necessary to give the work a number of layers, which would give it enough body to avoid the possibility of superficiality, yet retain the celebratory quality that the occasion demanded. The music had to relate to Glasgow in a very direct way. Obviously the name GLASGOW itself offered a good starting point because it contains four musical notes which have interesting possibilities - GAS(E-flat)G. This motif provides the basis of the whole piece. Thereafter I decided that the music should look back over the periods of recent times that have led the city to this point. But at the same time I wanted the music to have a personal aspect that would allow me to say something about my own feelings for the place. And I wanted both of these levels to run in tandem throughout.

The opening quickly defines these two aspects. The music begins with a "fanfare" which establishes the 'public' nature of the work, but the mood soon subsides to become more personal and reflective. The introduction over, the tempo changes to fast, and the main part of the work begins with material reflecting the general liveliness of the place and its people. But it goes on to outline my response to the city's earlier heyday in Victorian-Edwardian times - the massive weight and clamour of heavy industry which made the city rich and powerful, albeit at great human cost, and resulted in the great wealth which can still be seen today in the opulence and grandeur of so many of its buildings.

This is followed by a more pointed, sardonic episode, (Glasgow people have a ready wit – it is usually good humoured, even kindly, but nevertheless often has an unmistakeable edge). This moment of light relief gradually dissolves and leads into the work's slow central part – a rather elegiac Nocturne, which recalls the sadness and inertia of the 1930s.

I saw unemployed men standing at street corners, with nowhere to go, nothing to do, no money to spend – damn all; empty; a terrible existence. And yet while it was a time of great misery, there was somehow or other, a sense in Glasgow of a triumph of the human spirit. So, while the music here is a kind of elegy for those days, it is not unalleviated gloom.

[Tom's childhood home was at the top of a hill. From his bedroom window he could see the lights of Colville's steel works brighten the night sky. So he was very aware even as a child of the heavy industry in and around Glasgow.]

But this music also has more personal moments. I remember as a youth seeing the city from Cathkin Braes one summer's night, the whole valley below filled as far as the eye could see with calmly twinkling lights. It was a beautiful sight and I have never forgotten it.

[When we were courting, Tom and I often walked in Cathkin Braes.]

The final part of the work moves on to the post-war years, which have seen the city gradually regenerate itself, and become again a place of world prominence. The music, now fast again, becomes increasingly exuberant and confident as it approaches the end.

The name of the work, '*Carillon*', obviously refers to the age-old use of bells to proclaim events of major importance to all the people. However, this does not necessarily mean that actual bell sounds are always used in the piece, but bell-like ideas, figures, and shapes dominate the piece from the outset. As it happens Glasgow still has a real carillon – it is housed in the Tolbooth at Glasgow Cross. Formerly this carillon was very famous. It was used not only on big occasions like the New Year, but also daily to play folk-tunes and popular melodies at different times of the day.

Besides being playable by hand, the bells were also equipped with a clockwork mechanism. The weekly programme was as follows: Sunday: a hymn; Monday: *Gilderoy*; Tuesday: *Nancy's to the greenwood gane*; Wednesday: *Tweedside*; Thursday: *The lass o' Patie's Mill*; Friday: *The last time I cam' o'er the muir*; and Saturday: *Roslin Castle*.

There is one other level to the music. Those quick on the uptake may spot the shape of the opening phrase of 'I belong to Glasgow' here and there, and I have also made several brief references to other works of mine. This is part-joke for those who like puzzles of that sort, but it also has a more serious side, in that I believe that music written in a place has something of that place embedded in it.

So the piece is not as straightforward as it might appear. But my main intention is simple enough – to say that Glasgow is a great city and I love it.

Hopefully in incorporating both personal and public levels, the music will have the extra body, which will make it not just a topical, throwaway piece for 1990, but something which might have some extra significance.

In late September, in the run-up to the première, Michael Tumelty of the Glasgow Herald published the following interview in which Tom gave a candid reassessment of developments in Glasgow's musical culture over the previous three decades.

> With three months of the year still to unfold, nobody could deny that the music scene in Glasgow during 1990 has exploded in a wave of creativity and productivity. It is tempting – and it has happened – to attribute that explosion solely to the catalytic phenomenon of the city being European City of Culture. From the outset of the annus mirabilis, siren voices of warning have raised questions about the aftermath. "Can the impetus continue," and "Is there life after 1990," are questions that have been implied, if not raised, suggesting almost that there was little or no life before 1990. "The way I see it, it's been a gradual progress rather than a dramatic sudden shift," said composer Thomas Wilson, who – with an important world première about to be unveiled in the SNO's gala opening concert next week at the Royal Concert Hall – stands at the prow of activity which will represent the final major thrust of the musical scene in 1990.

> Thomas Wilson, retired chairman of the Composers' Guild of Great Britain, honorary president of the Scottish Society of Composers, was awarded the CBE this year for services to music. He is also among the most distinguished of Scottish composers. And, though his innate, quiet modesty would compel him to decline the assessment, he is widely respected not only for his compositional abilities but also for his historical insight into, and philosophical understanding of, the Scottish music scene.

> "It is important" considers Wilson, "at this most significant point in Scottish musical history, with the long awaited replacement for the St Andrew's Halls about to open, to see 1990 not just as the phenomenon that it is, but as part of a historical continuum. Remember that the 1960s in Glasgow was a time of ferment too" he said, citing the remarkable proliferation of ensembles (many since 'passed away') and activities, particularly in the field of modern music, which burst upon the scene at that time.

>> "In a way that time was even more exciting than now because it was all happening from scratch. The big change

came at the end of the Fifties, and has been built on since, though not always with unfailing success. Much of the credit, of course, lies at the feet of Sir Alex Gibson. He was an initiator, and a notable contributor. But there were others too."

Wilson cited Watson Forbes, the BBC's head of music in the mid-sixties, and James Loughran, then chief conductor of the BBC Scottish Symphony Orchestra.

"When Wattie Forbes was here there was modern music in almost every programme and, very often, Scottish works too. Throughout that period there was an immense amount of activity, and the same sort of heady, exciting feel that there is now. Then there was a trough, a levelling out where nothing much happened. It was, I suppose, a decline of sorts, which then started building up again in the eighties. Throughout the eighties there has been resurgence in the performance of modern music – resurgence through persistence, and with some differences too; differences in the security of ensembles and in public perceptions. In those days," he said [referring back to the Sixties] "it was more common to put on odd concerts with a modern work in them, rather than a consistent series. Nowadays," he said, citing organisations like the Paragon Ensemble, the Edinburgh Contemporary Arts Trust, and the development policy of the Scottish Chamber Orchestra: "these organisations have administrators and offices – they have become securely established and are a major embellishment to the scene; and they had to fight for it. Audiences too have developed in their receptivity, partly through the firm establishment of such organisations and the fact that they provide a regular diet of modern music, thus offering opportunities for familiarity, but also because much modern music has come part of the way to meet these audiences. At a time when William Walton's First Symphony was deemed to be the unacceptable face of modern music, you can imagine how some of the other stuff - the serial and aleatoric - was regarded. The sixties was a time for revelling in new devices, and technical advances, rather to the exclusion of audiences. There was a danger then that the young composer wrote in this way because it was fashionable, and because there was real pressure on him to do so."

Was Wilson himself susceptible?

> "Everyone was. It was a matter of survival to be susceptible. But the way that music developed at that time was too conscious of how things were done, rather than why they were done. It was craftsmanship all the way. That has begun to adjust itself; and the old equation of craftsmanship and expressive content is beginning to come into a more desirable equilibrium."

Even with these developments, it still comes as a surprise – albeit a pleasant one for Thomas Wilson - to find new music, including his own, featuring in such an occasion as the opening of the new Royal Concert Hall. He continued:

> "After all, things haven't changed that much. There is still a resistance to programming modern music for certain occasions and certain types of audience. The "bums on seats" principle is much more firmly established now than it was 30 years ago. Then you had pioneers who said, 'To hell with bums on seats – this is what people should be hearing,' and went ahead and played it; and got scant thanks for their pains because audiences voted with their feet. But they persevered. And the result is the benefits we have nowadays: audiences seem to be able to live with this kind of music, are able to make the distinction as to what is good and rewarding, and indeed are able to enjoy it."

In October, some of our Russian friends came to Glasgow to be with us as our guests at the inaugural concert for the official opening of the Royal Concert Hall on the 5th. Work had been going on in the building for a few years and we were very anxious to see the end result. Since the St Andrew's Hall had burned down in the Sixties, Glasgow had been without a premier venue and hopes were high. While we were discussing the attributes of such a hall with Alex Gibson in 1972, I remember saying that I thought we should have one with a seating capacity of 2,500. He must have taken this on board, for so it was! At the time Tom and I had just returned from Israel, where we had been impressed by the beautiful Mann Auditorium in Tel Aviv, and the Hall of the Nations in Jerusalem, both of which had wonderful acoustics.

To open the long inaugural programme, Bryden (Jack) Thomson and the Scottish National Orchestra performed *Carillon*, followed by Vaughan

Williams' *Serenade to Music*, Liszt's *Piano Concerto No 2*, Thea Musgrave's *Rainbow*, and Beethoven's *Choral Fantasia*. It was a very grand occasion with Princess Anne in attendance, and the hall was filled to capacity with everyone in evening dress. To keep our feet on the ground, we took Jack and his wife Mary and our other guests to dinner in a Chinese restaurant in Byres Road afterwards. At that time Chinese cuisine was something of an exotic treat for our Russian friends.

In a review appearing the next day in the Glasgow Herald, Michael Tumelty wrote enthusiastically about the opening night's concert:

> In terms of last night's programme, the best of it – and it's not too often one can claim this – lay in the two new works, (Tom's and Thea Musgrave's) each receiving its première. Each was different, each highly effective, and each executed by the SNO with the lucidity of interpretation and communication that are the hallmark of Bryden Thomson's direction. In these two pieces I sensed the occasion of the night.

> Thomas Wilson's *Carillon* with its evocation of the hyperactivity of the factory floor – all that wonderful rhythmic clatter and rhythmic tension – was characteristically exciting and tension-ridden; and neatly complemented by the more poignant reflection of the inner section of the piece. The dazzling light towards the close, as the piece slammed into major mode, seemed to suggest the vibrancy of modern Glasgow.

Five days after the concert Tom celebrated his sixty-third birthday. I decided that we should surprise him with a birthday party, and I had a cake made in the shape of a grand piano. Because he was lecturing in the evening, the preparations could get underway without his knowledge. One neighbour kept the cake in her home and another kept the wine, and altogether there were more than sixty guests.

About half an hour before Tom was due home I asked the Rostov Quartet if they would play "Happy Birthday" in the front hall when he arrived. Alas, they had never heard of the tune, so there was a mad scramble as three of our composer friends and our son Martin wrote out parts for them. One quick run through and they were ready. We put out all the lights while I watched for Tom's arrival through the curtains of the front room. As he came up the front steps we put all the lights on, I opened the front door and the Quartet started to play. Tom was truly surprised but very happy, and we all had a wonderful night.

Then in November 1990, to complete a wonderful year, Brendan and Makiyo were married in a Protestant church in Tokyo, where they have lived ever since. Despite his DPhil from Oxford and three other degrees Brendan had been unable to find a post in a British University teaching philosophy, so he taught English in Biggar High School for eight years. In Tokyo, however, he quickly found himself head-hunted by two major Universities. He is now Professor of English at Tokyo University where he writes books on philosophy. Makiyo became Head of the Department of Japanese Language in the Shinjuku Education Institute.

Later in December Tom and I went to the USSR yet again. Tom had been promised further performances of some of his chamber works but this time he was disappointed in that for one reason or another, most of them did not happen. On this trip our son Martin accompanied us. Though we were once again well entertained in Rostov, I have to say that the highlight of this particular trip to Russia was a visit to the office of the Composers' Union in Moscow, when both Tom and Martin were permitted to play the piano that had been used by Shostakovich. I don't think that Tikhon Khrennikhov allowed many people to do that.

CHAPTER 19 (1991 – 1993)

Elegy for Jack

In March 1991 Tom flew to Nuremberg to hear Stefan Grasse repeat the guitar pieces he had played in February in Glasgow, while Phillip Thorne played *Dream Music* in Inverness at the International Guitar Festival ten days later. Kay Soteriou, who is the sister of our friend the composer Vivienne Olive, sang *The Willow Branches* while Tom was in Nuremberg, and Marilyn de Blieck sang it in London the next day. The same month *Pas de Quoi* was performed in Yerevan, Armenia, by the "Serenade" Chamber Orchestra. A few days later the Norwegian Romsdahl Orkestra in Molde, Norway, gave it another airing. On both occasions the conductor was Nigel Boddice.

A year after completing his time as Chairman of the Composers' Guild of Great Britain Tom also stepped down from the Executive Council. In a tribute that appeared in the Composers' Newsletter, fellow composer Les Emmans said of Tom's tenure:

> This year has seen the completion of seven years service by Tom Wilson on the Guild Executive, and this is the maximum term of office allowed by the constitution. Tom has served with great distinction as Chairman, and in his last year of office has made a valuable contribution as Past-Chairman. His gentle manner has concealed a 'firm hand on the tiller' and his wise leadership is greatly valued.

Tom had enjoyed the experience but in his sixty-fourth year he was glad to be relieved of travelling back and forth to London.

Over April 14-28 the Royal Scottish Academy of Music and Drama in Glasgow mounted a Prokofiev Festival to celebrate his centenary. The Festival was opened by Prokofiev's son Oleg, and every concert included, but was not confined to, Prokofiev's music. Tom's music appeared in two concerts. At one of them, the Russian cellist Alla Vassilyeva, and her fellow Muscovite, pianist Alexei Smitov, played Tom's *Cello Sonata*. At another, the Rostov String Quartet came to Scotland specially to perform his *Fourth Quartet*.

At this same time, Tom's acceptance of the commission from Richard Chester, Director of the National Youth Orchestra of Scotland (NYOS), to write a new work for them was deliberately made a very public occasion by BP Exploration, who provided the funds, and invited the press to the signing ceremony on April 19 1991. This was quite unusual, but the company clearly wanted to make an occasion of it and even organised a photo call for Tom on the roof of their offices. A company spokesman announced at the event that "The funding of this commission reinforces our commitment to the pursuit and discovery of talent and excellence in Scotland's young musicians." Tom, Richard and Jack Thomson had decided at the outset that the work would be a violin concerto to be conducted by Bryden 'Jack' Thomson with Ernst Kovacic as the soloist. In fact Jack had recommended that Tom write a work for Ernst many years earlier, but this proposal had lain dormant for some time while other musical obligations were fulfilled. As it turned out, two other commissions and ill-health would mean that the work would take a further two years to complete.

A few days later we flew from Heathrow to Moscow on what would be our last visit to the USSR. We were to stay for a month, and our purpose was twofold: to attend performances of some of Tom's works and to go to the wedding of Leo Klinichev's daughter, Madina. The trip did not, however, go as smoothly as we had hoped. In Moscow we ate some stale open sandwiches at the Composers' Union, and later boarded a train for Rostov on Don. During the night we both succumbed to gastric 'flu-like symptoms, and arrived the next day in a terrible state. We were put straight to bed in the home of Leo's sister, who nursed us for the next two weeks. Under her care we both improved, but Tom was still quite weak and his system never fully recovered. We would have caught the first plane back if our tickets had allowed. Unfortunately they were Aeroflot tickets and could not be changed, and so we soldiered on.

Our granddaughter Emma was born in Tokyo during the third week of our stay in Rostov on Don, and a great fuss was made of the new grandparents. We received the happy news by telephone while we were having dinner at the home of Leo's future son-in-law, and we were consequently overwhelmed with gifts for the new baby, including a giant teapot. However, in spite of this wonderful news, we still did not feel like doing much of anything at all.

When Tom's condition didn't improve, he was taken daily to the hospital in Rostov on Don for tests, and one doctor even felt the joints on his toes. When she reached his middle toe, she said: "You have high blood pressure." We were staggered, as Tom had been taking medication for this condition for some months, but no one in Russia knew this. Despite the doctors' diagnostic skills, the true cause of our illness was never determined. On top of this, medicines were in very short supply at the time, and to our intense frustration, few of the many prescriptions they did give us could be properly filled at the pharmacy.

To help us convalesce, Leo sent us by train to the spa town of Kislavodsk. There we were met at the small station by a local composer who took us first to our hotel, and then on to see the house of Feodor Chaliapin, the world renowned bass singer from the early decades of the twentieth century. Our volunteer guide told us that people could remember him standing on the veranda of his home, entertaining the local population with arias from popular operas. Over the next few days, we took short walks in the countryside but were still quite unwell. Kislavodsk, a most beautiful spa town, seemed quite out of place when I compared it with the poverty that I had seen elsewhere.

On our return to Rostov our health had improved a little and we felt physically able to attend Madina's wedding, but all we really wanted to do was to get home. However, a few days before our departure, the Aeroflot pilots announced that they intended to go on strike on the day we were scheduled to leave, so we were, thankfully, allowed to depart a day early.

We stayed overnight in Moscow on our way home as it had been arranged for us to go to hear the opera *The Snow Maiden* by Rimsky-Korsakov. When we arrived at the Bolshoi Theatre we were shown into the anteroom of the Tsar's box for drinks, and after this we were escorted to the royal box for the performance. Fortunately our seats were in shadow as we were both very tired, and I must admit I fell asleep. I just prayed that no one had noticed.

Despite having made many happy visits to Russia over the past two years this particular trip had been a nightmare from beginning to end, and we determined never to return. As the plane took off from Moscow to London we felt an enormous sense of relief.

When we arrived at the home of our son Stephen in London Tom had a temperature of 40.5°C. He was immediately taken to Coppett's Wood Infectious Diseases hospital and put into isolation where he stayed for two weeks. Like their Russian counterparts, the doctors there had no idea what Tom was suffering from. We had to put on gowns, gloves, and masks when we visited him, and had to wash on entering and leaving his room.

After two weeks he was flown to a hospital nearer home in Stirling. Tom spent a few days there, before he was finally allowed home at the end of May. Despite many further tests however, the true cause of his illness was never identified. This was the beginning of the poor health that was to trouble him for the rest of his life.

In June, the University of Glasgow conferred an Honorary Doctorate of Music on Tom. After the ceremony the custom is to hold a short service in the University Chapel. When Tom and the twelve other honorary graduands were processing out of the chapel after the service, the university organist, Stuart Campbell, played Tom's *Toccata Festevole* as a surprise for him. We were both moved by this kindness. On the 28th of the month the Royal Scottish Academy of Music and Drama also conferred a Fellowship on Tom. His sponsor was the conductor Sir Alexander Gibson.

In spite of his poor health, Tom still found the time to write *Chanson de Geste* in June and July 1991. This work for solo French horn had been commissioned in October 1990 by Redcliffe Concerts with funds provided by Yorkshire Arts but owing to Tom's ill-health was only completed a couple of weeks before the first performance. *Chanson de Geste* draws its inspiration from the epic romances and heroic ballads of the Middle Ages. In his sketches Tom's margin notes include words such as these:

ECHOES	ESCUTCHEON
(Chivalry, Romance, 20th Century Bias)	IRIS
JOUST	ORIFLAMME
LISTS	GONFALON
HERALDRY	~~CHEVRON~~
MOTTO	CIPHER
FANFARE(S)	MONOGRAM
	SIGIL
	PARAPH
	SHIBBOLETH

Ten minutes long, this work provides a perfect test piece for degree students in terms of both range and "lip endurance" as Tom put it. The whole piece is quite chivalric, magical, and mysterious, redolent with the sound of fanfares and distant battles. Tom's notes make specific references to the Horn of Roland, blown at the Battle of Roncevaux to call Charlemagne back to avenge his defeat and death at the hands of the invading Moors.

Chanson de Geste had its première in mid July at The Merlin Theatre (appropriately), Tintagel House, Sheffield. The soloist was Peter Francombe, who played the piece twice during the evening. Though still in fragile health, Tom gave an introductory talk before the performance. He was ever my "gentle, chivalrous, parfait knight".

On our return in November from a much-needed break at our apartment in Sotogrande, Spain, we were shocked to learn that our very good friend Jack Thomson had died at his home in Dublin from pancreatic cancer and that his funeral was to be held the very next day. Jack had first fallen ill in April at the same time as Tom became ill in Russia, but whereas Tom had slowly recovered, Jack had not. They had been good friends since 1967 when Jack conducted *Sinfonietta* with the National Youth Brass Band. Over the years the friendship had deepened and each had a great respect for the other's ability in their chosen field. So early the next day, Tom flew to Dublin for the funeral with Jack's other friends, John Maxwell Geddes and John Currie. I had passed on my ticket to John Currie as the flight was full when he tried to book. Jack's untimely passing in his early sixties was, and is, a great loss to Scottish music, for he was a true champion of contemporary Scottish composers. And here I would like to quote Karl Gwiasda:

> I was at the last one of Jack's performances (Prokofiev's Third Symphony) – on my birthday in fact – and I can confirm that the symphony was played with lacerating intensity. The concert was extraordinary. I had no idea that I was hearing a conductor with just a few days' life remaining, but I knew I was hearing a great musician.

His death also changed the direction of the work that he had commissioned for the National Youth Orchestra. Since Jack would no longer be able to conduct it, Tom now decided that the *Violin Concerto* (which his first sketches suggested he had been thinking would draw its inspiration from Biblical sources) would instead be about Jack. Tom now began making extensive notes, and sketching out his musical ideas. The note phrase B-D-E from Jack's name, Bryden, would become the first musical motif, but in addition Tom also set out to colour the piece with the qualities and emotional range of his friend who had conducted so many premières of his works, including the *Piano Concerto*, *Sinfonietta for Brass Band*, *Introit*, *Passaleth Tapestry*, and *Carillon*. Aptly for a piece composed In Memoriam, as Tom wrote on the title page, the *Violin Concerto* starts with an elegy on behalf of the mourners and then proceeds through seven more sections in various keys, each section representing different aspects of Jack's character. Section B reflects his quick temper (Bb); C his control and precision (in D); D his mischievous, irreverent humour (in E). Section E returns to the elegy which is a development of Section A but this time in the unusual key of B# (this is a theoretical key rather than a practical one, but I am told that conductors and performers will know what Tom meant); F honours the musician who enriched our lives (Eb); G is another elegy, a leave taking (in A and C from jACk); and H, which is the coda, is assertive and forceful, with a deliberate allusion to Jack's trademark foot stamp on the conductor's dais. Such a major reworking required much consideration, but since the concerto did not need to be delivered until 1993, Tom had the necessary time to do justice to what would become one of his most personal and heartfelt compositions.

In December 1991 our youngest son Stephen married Vanessa in London and we went down for the occasion. It was a happy day when everyday cares were put to one side and it was a good break for Tom.

When Capella Nova approached Tom in early 1992 to write an a capella work for them, he felt that the *Violin Concerto* would benefit from the additional distance that this interlude would provide. For this composition he went back to the Passion, a subject he had addressed more than two decades earlier in his *Sequentiae Passionis*. Taking his inspiration from the Holy Week processions that we had witnessed during our visit to Cadiz that spring, a spectacle that had deeply impressed him, Tom explained that his new work, *Cantigas para Semana Santa*, "presented a short and concentrated rather than a discursive version of the Passion" (you may well remember the problems he encountered surrounding the première of the *Sequentiae Passionis* in 1971). He completed *Cantigas para Semana Santa* on October 12 1992 while we were enjoying a break in our apartment in Sotogrande, Spain.

Michael Tumelty talked to Tom about the forthcoming work for an article that appeared on November 4 in The Glasgow Herald titled 'Inspired by Passion'.

> This weekend, Capella Nova, the choral group that, through a steady flow of commissions has inspired Scotland's leading composers to produce some of their finest work, launches its latest venture, a substantial commission from one of Scotland's senior composers, Thomas Wilson.
>
> The Cantigas para Semana Santa – Songs for Holy Week – was completed last month in Spain, and reflects two interests of the

composer: his love of plainsong and a deep fascination with the Passion story. To these, Wilson has added what he calls the "trigger" experience of having witnessed the large-scale and colourful Holy Week processions in Cadiz.

Interest in the Passion runs deep in Wilson's psyche – in 1971 he produced a full-scale version, Sequentiae Passionis, for Musica Nova.

He has selected three key points of the story, as it unfolds throughout Holy Week: Palm Sunday, where Christ is the darling of the crowd; Holy Thursday, where it all goes sour; and Easter Sunday itself, the mysterious element, the continually inspiring element for humanity.

Each of these key points is set as a musical movement, in a polyphonic idiom – that is, music of several or multiple simultaneous parts, and each movement is prefaced by a shorter movement of plainsong (in each case the original plainchant, not composed by Wilson), which, in textual terms, offers a different perspective on the same episode from the story. And it is in this juxtaposition of plainsong (single line melody) and polyphony (multiple choral lines) that the context of Wilson's new composition lies.

"The two musical styles may appear to be at odds." says the composer:

> They represent apparent and almost intransigently different points of view. More than that, the attitude of plainsong seems to be contemplative and mystical; whereas the opportunities offered by polyphony are much more dramatic, extrovert, and explicit in character.

But Wilson believes the two to have what he calls an inner congruence:

> I believe that the plainsong has, in fact, a great emotional charge, and the polyphony can have mystical qualities. So I thought it might be interesting to place them in context with one another and allow them to speak to each other.

So how does this work in the piece? Wilson describes it thus:

It is three episodes, or three chapters, from the Passion story. Each chapter has two halves, which contain the same events seen from different perspectives. A plainsong recounting the praises of the crowd as Jesus enters Jerusalem is followed by a composed movement, which gives an altogether more explicit version of the event. This is the adulation of the mob on Palm Sunday. It's a kind of empty enthusiasm, done with great gusto and punch I hope, but nevertheless, ultimately superficial. The musical style is spare and athletic.

The following plainsong reflects upon the plotting of the high priests and Judas to apprehend and dispose of Jesus. The corresponding polyphonic movement is a more dense texture, complex and conspiratorial.

The final movement, which follows a mystical and serene plainsong, goes back to the spare kind of writing present in the first episode. The irony is that this time, it's for real. This was difficult to do: how to capture the evanescence of the mob's enthusiasm, which quickly disappears, as against the abiding interest of humanity in the notion of Easter and regeneration.

He is naturally cautious about calculating the effect of the music before the first performance but says:

It's something you can't actually legislate for; we'll just have to wait and see if it works, but I think – I think – it'll come off.

Alan Tavener, director of Capella Nova, preparing his group for the first performances this weekend, is less circumspect.

There is general agreement in the group that this is one of the best commissions we've had on that scale. The final movement is thrilling; it keeps gathering in excitement right up to the end. And it is a superb, superb ending.

Which – with the superlative track record of compositions produced for this group – suggests that something special may be around the corner.

With Alan Tavener conducting, Capella Nova gave *Cantigas para Semana Santa* its first performance on November 6, 1992 in Greyfriars Kirk, Edinburgh.

Following the concert, Michael Tumelty wrote in The Herald:

> The *Cantigas* is a superb piece that embraces, in highly concentrated form, a range of moods from austere to extrovert from deeply contemplative to openly joyous.

Tom was also very gratified to receive a letter from Bar Purser, wife of the composer John Purser, whom we met frequently at concerts:

> I had to write to tell you how much I enjoyed *Cantigas Para Semana Santa*. John had said it was very fine, so I knew I was in for a treat, but I was totally taken by it and I am looking forward to hearing it again. Will it be broadcast? I have never before been so moved by a new work to write to the composer.

Congratulations.

During November and December, Tom returned to work on the *Violin Concerto* and we enjoyed a quiet Christmas at home, but early in the New Year we were off on our travels again. We were introduced to the German composers Stefan Heuke and Peter Wolf from Bochum, a town that is also twinned with Rostov on Don, during our final visit to Russia in 1991, and we also met some of the musicians from their hometown. On their return to Bochum they began to arrange a festival in Dortmund that was to feature contemporary music from Rostov on Don and from composers in their own area. They had admired the compositions by Tom that they heard in Russia so much that he was one of the first composers they invited to the four-day festival in January 1993. Though still not 100% fit, he was determined to attend, and I certainly felt more confident in the German healthcare system than that of Russia. We stayed at Stefan's flat in Bochum, a small town that was devastated during the Second World War but was painstakingly restored in accordance with the original plans.

The festival started with a composers' workshop, and this was followed by three days of concerts during which Tom's *Piano Trio*, *Fourth String Quartet*, *Piano Sonata*, and *Incunabula* were performed. We took the opportunity to renew our friendships with our Russian friends who also attended the festival. I was delighted that following the performances one of the reviewers called the "Scotsman the star...Wilson is in a class of his own."

Another commentator said:

> At the second KonTakte Festival the Glaswegian left all other musicians far behind.

Yet another added:

> It was none other than Wilson's composition which made yesterday evening a great success. Wilson's Trio was in a different league altogether. It is impossible to classify - free, atonal, but totally comprehensible in its expressiveness. It is truly great music.

In February 1993 Tom was invited by the Paragon Ensemble to accompany them on their visit to Iceland where they were to perform his *Chamber Symphony* in Akureyri, Reykjavik, and the Listasafn Islands. The *St Kentigern Suite, Dream Music for Guitar* and the *Fourth String Quartet* were also played during the six-day festival. Tom said that although the weather was very cold, his hosts were most kind and he had enjoyed the opportunity to take in the spectacular landscape. The concerts were very well attended and after one he was introduced to Vigdís Finnbogadóttir the first female President of Iceland.

Tom worked uninterrupted on the main compositional phase of the *Violin Concerto* between October 1992 and June 1993. He still taught four times each week for the Extra Mural Department, but he was fully focussed on ensuring that the *Violin Concerto* should be a fitting tribute to his friend. Many works have been dedicated to musicians or conductors, but few are written In Memoriam with the deceased dedicatee as the direct inspiration. This meant that Tom felt a special duty not only to the music but also to Jack's memory.

Following the death of Bryden Thomson, James Loughran was engaged to conduct the première of the *Violin Concerto*. Two weeks before the première, however, Jimmie sprained his ankle on the golf course and was forced to pull out. Fortunately, the British conductor Christopher Seaman, who works mostly in America but has a home in Glasgow, was able to step in at very short notice.

Between rehearsal sessions for the approaching première Tom found time to talk to Michael Tumelty for an article for The Herald (formerly The Glasgow Herald) suitably entitled, 'Seaman to the rescue':

There is no intention that the concerto should represent any kind of biography. It is not a picture piece. What the single-movement continuous work does is reflect some principal aspects of Thomson's character – both musical and personal characteristics. And that's a pretty rich source. Jack was quite a lad. As a person Jack was always affirmative, he was occasionally eruptive, and with a sense of humour that was only a hair's breadth away from sending things up. Jack was the kind of person you couldn't put down; there was a mischievous quality to him. These things were all meat and drink, translatable into musical terms. So it is a general reference to Jack and aspects of his character.

Tumelty went on to say that:

> While there are elegiac elements in the music, Thomas Wilson is keen to stress that the work is not funereal. Far from it; the music pushes towards an affirmative conclusion that, in tribute to the late conductor, is – in the composer's description – 'celebratory.'

I like to think that this buoyant finish was partly my doing. For many years I had been asking Tom to write a 'loud' ending and on this occasion he agreed. Many of Tom's longer works tend to fade away into infinity, intentionally leaving the audience with unanswered questions in their mind. In this instance, however, such an ending would have been wholly inappropriate.

Music critic Mary Miller had also talked to Tom about the work during its development. Her article entitled "Fine memorial to a much-loved musician" appeared on The Scotsman on the day of the première:

> Over a pint of beer, the story goes, the late Bryden Thomson, then conductor of the Royal Scottish National Orchestra, suggested to his friend Thomas Wilson, the composer, that he should write a Violin Concerto for the Austrian violinist Ernst Kovacic to play. It all sounds plausible – except for the pint. One can imagine Thomson and Wilson contemplating a musical future over a fine malt, but never surely, through an inch of froth.

> The concerto is premièred tonight in Aberdeen, by Kovacic and the National Youth Orchestra of Scotland who commissioned the work last year, nurturing a seed already taken root. It is a beautiful piece, not merely because Wilson unfolds his melodic skills with the kind of time-served spaciousness which real musical maturity has

brought him, but because without painting a portrait of Jack Thomson – Jack being the name by which all players knew him – the piece will surely make all who cherished him content.

Wilson insists that he wrote the music in Jack's memory as a gift, and not as an inventory of his personality traits. Wilson was not, in fact, familiar with Kovacic's particularly instinctive violinistic talents when the piece was written. The music, though, does emerge as a remarkable fusion of all three contributors' characteristics. There are long passages of melodic serenity – 'navel-gazing' Wilson says, with a smile, but not an apology – to which he, his soloist, and dedicatee are and were prone; there are passages of intensity which twist, to poke fun at themselves – a very Jack activity – and there is a forthrightness about the dramatic writing which reflects the directness of expression of all three.

There is too, 'an emphasis on contradictions', ostinati which bounce along for a few bars suddenly change character to a more plodding step, then stamp with insistence. And the piece ends in celebration. It erupts from a dreamy drift marked <u>calmo ingrantando</u> – enchantedly still – with a shout of mirth. "Jack's personality," says Wilson, "never could be held down." One might say the same of the composer and violinist.

Wilson did not write his concerto 'for those in the ivory tower of virtuosity'. As a composer, he is anti-cleverness and far from keen on the concept that intellect must be able to explain all complexity. "Music," he says, "must present some expressive reason for existing, must transcend mere order. There must be a conjunction of head and gut. It is fruitless to talk about technique, or about some processes. There must be a visceral quality, intoxicating moment, or music becomes a poor imitation of itself."

He writes constantly, realising his score on the piano, never satisfied with inner sounds. He says he needs to feel the colours, to satisfy himself that every inflection and texture is as he would wish. He found writing the new concerto extremely hard, and says he struggled to find the phrasing that would fulfil his needs, and battled to find an ending that would work not only structurally – for Wilson's writing is strongly shaped – but that would satisfy his own instinct. "When something is right, one feels a tick, a settling deep inside. I waited a long, long time for the concerto to close with that certainty."

Clearly it is within the canvas of a symphonic score where Wilson settles best. He likes time to develop his arguments, he says. A senior figure in a landscape of increasingly glamorous, young Scottish composers, he talks with enthusiasm of "the apprentices". He developed his particular skill of expressing himself precisely – his language is neither over-succinct, nor loose-lippedly effusive – as an incidental music writer for the BBC, in the days when the BBC Scottish Orchestra served the corporation as a flexible workforce. "One learned quickly what to develop, and what to leave to suggestion," he says.

He is not averse to learning now. With NYOS, he is much enjoying his concerto's rehearsals, relishing conductor Christopher Seaman's skill as he tailors the orchestral markings better to unveil the solo line. What Seaman, a musician with enormous rhythmic discipline, brings to the score is a sense, almost, of improvisation – with the musical scaffolding securely in place, the melodic surface can weave and soar.

And this, perhaps, will bring Jack's friends the broadest smiles. For few flew so freely over the spokes of constraint as he. Wilson's *Violin Concerto* may not purport to be a portrait, but neither is it a backhanded compliment. Wilson's gift in memoriam to Bryden Thomson is affectionate, expansive and effective. It's a great deal to have extracted from a pint pot.

Christopher Seaman and the National Youth Orchestra of Scotland gave the *Violin Concerto* its first performance on August 6 in the Music Hall for the Aberdeen International Youth Festival. The programme also featured Shostakovich's *Festival Overture* and Holst's *The Planets*. The soloist was of course Ernst Kovacic, who proved to be a fine exponent and a very sympathetic interpreter just as Jack had predicted. We greatly admired the way this lovely man gently led the young people in the string sections to the conclusions that he wanted. He had been studying the work longer than Christopher Seaman and was able to advise the string section during the latter stages of rehearsal. At the National Youth Orchestra, the different sections are taught their parts separately by individual coaches across Scotland before coming together as an orchestra – and it was at this stage that Ernst's encouragement of the string section proved so valuable.

Following the première, the orchestra toured the *Concerto* in Scotland and England, performing it five more times. Christopher and Ernst worked very well together throughout the tour, and Tom was delighted with the results. The last performance of the tour took place at a Promenade concert in the Royal Albert Hall in London. Jack's wife Mary, who came to a later performance in the Royal Concert Hall in Glasgow in 1993, was delighted with the work and told me that she could feel Jack beside her in the auditorium. Those of us who knew Jack could easily recognise his character and mannerisms in the music.

The reviews at the time were, as I remember, unanimously laudatory. After hearing the first performance, Mary Miller wrote in The Scotsman:

> Thomas Wilson's Violin Concerto premièred here by Ernst Kovacic compelled from its wistful, oboe-tinted opening, to its emphatic rhythmical final foot stamp. Kovacic, one of the most intelligent and imaginative soloists in new repertoire, brought to the concerto enormous affection, and a sense almost of wonder at his discoveries in the score. Listening, one felt as though one was being shown personal treasures. This is clearly an evocative portrait of a friendship.

Neil Butterworth wrote in the Times Educational Supplement:

> This deeply moving tribute must surely be Wilson's finest work to date. Few pieces in the past decade have made such a strong impression on me. From the opening elegiac oboe cadenza, through the percussion-propelled orchestral tutti, the poignant reiteration on the violin of three rising notes representing Bryden Thomson's name and the final orchestral outburst was an all-pervading logic which could be followed by eye and ear. The orchestra under Christopher Seaman was totally inside the music. Likewise the soloist Ernst Kovacic proved the ideal advocate for a concerto that must surely be taken up by other violinists. Its immediate impact should ensure international acceptance.

At the end of the Aberdeen International Youth Festival, Neville Garden reviewed the work in Scotland on Sunday:

> The highlight of the week though, was surely the concert on Friday night in the Music Hall by the National Youth Orchestra of Scotland under Christopher Seaman, which included the world première of Thomas Wilson's Violin Concerto.

> It is a work of rare quality, written in memory of the much loved conductor Bryden Thomson; a work full of atmosphere and

beautiful things but shot through with wit and mischief. If the much-missed Thomson was present in spirit he would have loved it as much as the audience.

I hope to write at greater length about this important addition to the repertoire at a later date. But we shall undoubtedly hear it again and again. Ernst Kovacic played the solo part as a man inspired while Seaman and the orchestra could not have provided more skilful or sensitive support.

The *Violin Concerto* has since been played very well by other violinists such as Edwin Paling, Dmitri Mahktin, and Kurt Nikkanen, but I was particularly pleased and touched when Ernst came back to Glasgow to play it for the BBC as part of Tom's memorial concert in 2002. The *Violin Concerto* is one of my favourite works. It is at once both introspective and overtly emotional, full of interesting tensions and insights. While the work feels comparatively simple on first listening, like the surface of a quietly flowing river, successive hearings reveal new depths and complexities. Indeed I often find myself feeling both tearful and elated during the same performance. Though in the beginning I would recognise Jack's presence in the work, I am now so familiar with it that my musical concentration is not interrupted or affected in any way by specific associations. Thus at the beginning of the piece I feel a more general sense of loss, and often feel myself transported to a bleak Northern European landscape, much like the bleak mountainous regions in the north of Scotland. Other people I have spoken to think of the work as a vision of man's odyssey through life and his quest for enlightenment and equanimity. Tom was a deeply philosophical man and he always said that there were many secrets to be discovered in his works beyond the puns, allusions, and use of signatures translated into musical motifs. If I were to advise anyone where to start their search, it would be here. The American violinist Kurt Nikkanen told me after a performance at the Royal Concert Hall in January 2008 that it was the best new work he had heard in the last ten years.

Tom's enjoyment of this celebration of the life of one friend was tempered by the news that another was seriously ill. In July Malcolm and Ann Rayment returned to Glasgow from their chosen place of retirement in Sotogrande because Malcolm was feeling very unwell. A scan revealed an inoperable tumour in his brain, and he was given three months to live. During the autumn we all got together many times and Tom and Malcolm spent many enjoyable hours together talking about music. In the end Malcolm lived longer than the specialists predicted and remarkably remained lucid until his death in December.

Despite the loss of these two close friends, Tom's faith in God did not waver. Though he had not been a regular churchgoer since the early seventies, when we felt the sermons in our local church were becoming overly political, his belief in the continuation of the spirit in some form was firmly in place, as is my own. Unsurprisingly, perhaps, the piece that he composed during this sad time was a hymn of praise to God, written to fulfil a commission that he had accepted in March 1993 from the Royal College of Organists, who wanted a work to celebrate the centenary of the granting of their Royal Charter. They asked to have it by the end of August, so Tom got down to composing *Confitemini Domino* as soon as he had finished the *Concerto*. As a result of the upheavals caused by Jimmie Loughran spraining his ankle on the golf course shortly before the first performance and the terrible news about Malcolm, Tom took the unusual step of asking for an extension, and the work was not completed until November 12 1993. I think this was the only time in his life when he failed to meet the commissioner's original deadline.

Like *Cantigas para Semana Santa* written the previous year, *Confitemini Domino* is a processional song, in this instance normally recited by the priests on Easter Sunday. *Confitemini Domino* is sung in praise of 'God the Creator': "*Confitemini Domino, quoniam bonus!* – Praise the Lord, for he is good!" It is made up of three movements for choir, brass quintet and organ, though the second movement is very challenging for the organist as he does not have the support of the brass. We attended the première on December 4 at a special celebration held in St Andrew's Church Holborn, in the City of London. John Scott directed the choir of St Paul's Cathedral, the organist was Andrew Lucas, and the brass ensemble came from the Royal Scottish Academy of Music and Drama. The performance was very well received by the knowledgeable audience of organists that included Tom's old teacher Fred Rimmer, who was then in his eighties. Tom later made a version of this work for organ and choir.

In an essay appearing in *The Music of Thomas Wilson - A Symposium (Musica Scotica, 2004)* the composer and conductor John Hearne offered these remarks about *Confitemini Domino*:

> This is some of Wilson's most forthright music. I conducted a performance of it to conclude a Whitsuntide concert in Stonehaven in 1997, and Tom travelled up from Glasgow to hear it. The rain poured down, but the direct appeal of the music brought warm applause from the audience like a ray of sunshine! I would encourage any choral conductor to consider this piece. It is short, challenging yet practical, and readily available. The brass parts are

within the scope of any of the young brass ensembles now emerging from the Academies, and there are several organists who would enjoy the colourful organ part. The middle movement would need careful rehearsal from the singers, but the rewards are considerable; and the final Alleluias, alternating between D flat and B flat majors, round off the piece with a splendid flourish. In a big church or cathedral, the rafters will ring.

It might seem from John's concluding comments that the work is transparent – it is anything but. There is an undercurrent of unease created by the harmonies that seem to be searching for a common chord which is only resolved as the work draws towards the final Amen. Belief in God for Tom was always more about faith than certainty.

CHAPTER 20 (1994 - 1996)

Two Significant Births

The year 1994 began happily with the birth of our grandson Hugo in Japan on January 21. Big sister Emma was bubbling with excitement when we spoke to her, and we couldn't wait for the summer, when his proud parents would bring him to Scotland for us to see him.

In March Tom learned that he had been elected to the Fellowship of the Royal Society of Edinburgh. He was the fourth Scottish musician to receive this honour, though he rarely attended the meetings of what is still largely a scientific society.

He continued to lecture twice each week in Glasgow University from October to Easter, with an extra six-week course after Easter lasting into May. I tried to persuade him to give this up, but he enjoyed it. Composing is a lonely business and meeting his classes was refreshing for him.

During the year there were of course many performances and broadcasts of his music both at home and abroad. Tom was, however, especially gratified when the Fife Youth Orchestra played the *St Kentigern Suite* at the 7th Glasgow Festival and at the 15th Edinburgh Festival of Youth Orchestras in Edinburgh. He was always happy to have youth orchestras perform his works as he felt that, though many of the players would not go on to pursue a career in music, others of this age group were important for the future of musical life in Scotland. He was also pleased to hear a foreign youth orchestra play *St Kentigern* as he did when the "Impromptu" Youth String orchestra from Helsinki came to perform it in the Mitchell Hall of Marischal College in Aberdeen on August 7 1995. Our own Scottish youngsters, The Hillhead Strings, repeated it in Glasgow ten days later. Then St Mary's Music School pupils played it in Greyfriars Kirk (made famous by the little dog Greyfriars Bobby), Edinburgh, in November 1995. This is Tom's most frequently performed work.

It had been our intention to spend the winters in our apartment in Sotogrande, but teaching commitments and performances always seemed to get in the way of this plan. However, Tom was able to compose while we were there during the summer months as he had bought a Yamaha keyboard and so was able to confirm his ideas. We spent our summer holiday in 1995 in Sotogrande as usual, enjoying the sun and the relaxed life of rural Spain. Here, Tom continued to work on the first draft of *Threads*, a work that he had been composing for bass clarinet and marimba/vibraphone. He reverted to writing in pencil on manuscript paper as he had done at the beginning of his career. It was not necessary to use symphax any more as it was becoming easier to employ others to put his works into print using a computer. It was also much easier for copyists to make amendments on the rare occasions when he had second thoughts.

The commission for *Threads* came from the Dutch-based Duo Contemporaine, an ensemble founded in 1981 by Henri Bok (bass clarinet) and Miguel Bernat (marimba), who had been introduced to Tom's music by the German composer Stephan Heuke. Tom liked the idea of getting to grips with this unusual musical combination and the Duo scheduled the British première for autumn of 1996. As usual, Tom had a problem finding an appropriate title for the work, but eventually he settled on *Threads*. There is a tantalising but inconclusive note amongst Tom's papers that suggests that the inspiration for the eventual title of this work may have been drawn from the dream sequences in Ingmar Bergman's final film "Fanny and Alexander", which he much admired. The piece lasts five minutes and Tom described it as a chain of "Rows" evolving into one another imperceptibly via "images" drawn from his previous works including the *St Kentigern Suite, Piano Trio, Piano Concerto, Chamber Symphony, Introit, Symphony No.3*, the *Fourth String Quartet*, and *Touchstone*. In the *Musica Scotica Symposium*, John Maxwell Geddes writes that the piece looked back to *Reverie*, and recast it in an unusually exotic sound world. He also said that he believed that the references to other works are fairly oblique in that they relate to signature sounds and 'trademarks', such as the summoning bell before a passage of plainchant in the *St Kentigern Suite* or the oscillating tonality from *Pas de Quoi*. John feels that these relate to threads in the tapestry of Tom's musical development and that the points of direct quotation could have some personal references beyond musical statement. Or, as John adds, 'perhaps Tom might just draw on his pipe and, with a twinkle in his eye, say', "Well, maybe......"

Shortly after Tom completed *Threads*, our holiday was interrupted by the news from neighbours in Glasgow that our second son Martin was almost immobile, suffering from a work-related back injury, and we were needed urgently at home. We took the first available plane back, to find when we arrived that he was in great pain, and flat on his back on the floor of the front room. It took him many weeks to regain any semblance of mobility.

While Tom's friends were often fellow composers and musicians, he did form a number of close friendships with people less directly related to his art. Among these were his school friend Jim Clayton, the art lecturer Martin Baillie, the music critics Malcolm Rayment and Ian Robertson, the Dumfries poet Kirkpatrick Dobie, and Ian Sneddon, who was Professor in Mathematics at Glasgow University. Late in his life Tom also befriended Karl Gwiasda, an American who twice came to Glasgow University as a visiting professor from Iowa State University where he taught courses in British literature and in science and literature.

Tom and I were introduced to Karl and his wife Barbara in the last part of 1991 through a mutual friend, Rosemary Eldridge, who was Chaplain to Overseas Students at Glasgow University. Karl's love of music and Tom's interest in literature were sufficient to establish a bond that developed through an exchange of letters after Karl returned to the U.S. When Karl and Barbara came back to Glasgow for a full year's stay beginning in August 1995, we all enjoyed more opportunities to meet. As I recall, our times together were filled with talk not just of music and books, but also of painting and politics because Martin Baillie was often in the company. As it happened, Barbara and Karl made a holiday trip to Glasgow in 2001 and Tom's last visit with them occurred the day before he died.

During autumn 1995 Tom began to work on the *Guitar Concerto* for Phillip Thorne. This composition had been placed on the back burner while Phillip sought to raise money from various people to fund the commission. Initially, Phillip had hoped that the funding would come entirely from the Scottish Arts Council, but they had changed their policy from providing 100% of commission fees to awarding only 50%. The change meant that musicians like Phillip, who were already busy teaching and performing, had to add fundraising to their schedules.

By this time Phillip had known Tom for more than eighteen years and had long been an admirer of Tom's pioneering compositions for the guitar, as is clear from an article he wrote about him in the *Guitar International Magazine* in May 1988:

> Thomas Wilson is perhaps Scotland's best known composer. His works have been performed all over the world and embrace all forms of orchestral, choral and orchestral, opera, brass band, vocal music and a wide variety for chamber ensembles and solo

instruments. To date, he has written five works for guitar. However, as far as most guitarists are concerned, he is only a name on the back cover of Berben Editions. This article aims to give an insight into Thomas Wilson the man and his music.

Well, for a start, no one who knows him or has worked with him has anything but praise for him and that includes this writer. Tom is a warm, friendly man, instantly likeable and with that rare commodity, integrity. All these qualities strike you on the first acquaintance and continue to grow as you get to know him better. Many an evening I have spent with him going over, note by note, the particular piece of his I was playing at the time. I learned a lot, Tom being very particular about his music, demanding very precise colours and dynamics. He is very, very perceptive, nothing escaping his notice. In saying that, his warmth of personality and sense of humour make these meetings a joint venture and an elevating experience.

Tom's music is essentially "European" in style, and he is surprised that his music is considered dissonant. However, he is quick to accept that his is not easy music. I put the old point to him regarding the rôle of music as purely entertainment, a view not held by myself but often encountered in the guitar world.

> "Music these days is used in much the same way as a convenience product, it's there for our pleasure so to speak and that is its sole purpose. I don't write music to simply give other people pleasure. I hope that they do enjoy it and are pleased by it and get a certain aesthetic reward from it. I don't see myself as an entertainer. A composer is someone who seeks to open a door and give an elevating experience – not simply showbiz."

> "As far as my music is concerned, I consistently find that 20 years after a piece of music has been written it stands a better chance of registering with an audience. This process of acceptance by the guitar-playing fraternity has not yet gathered full steam and I would look for it to get better and better because I think the pieces have certain qualities which recommend them to guitarists. My principal preoccupation as a composer is to write a good piece."

It is this writer's firm conviction that Thomas Wilson's guitar music does not get the exposure it deserves – notwithstanding the sterling work of players such as Tim Walker.

On the topic of guitarists' traditional repertoire, Thomas Wilson is of the opinion that the lighter, Spanish side is diminishing as the guitar grows in stature.

> "There is a kind of parallel with the brass band world with regard to repertoire – phenomenal players but a lollipop repertoire. A movement headed by Geoffrey Brand and Elgar Howarth has moved to playing contemporary music. They recognised that they were in danger of getting into a ghetto situation. The exciting thing about the guitar is that there is so much untapped potential. Everyone knows what a flute or a piano can do. The guitar is capable of an immense amount that has hardly been touched upon."

Tom Wilson's first work was composed nearly three decades ago in 1961. What prompted these early pieces?

> "A mutual friend knew a guitarist, Ron Moore (a well-known Glasgow guitarist) and suggested that I write a piece for guitar – *Three Pieces* were the result."

Surprisingly in that the composer knew little at the time about the guitar, they are very guitaristic. Tom puts this down to "a certain sympathy for the instrument" and to "checking that the chords were playable." This sympathy for the instrument permeates all his guitar works. There is a sort of serialism element in these early pieces reflecting an early influence, which in the end was never to convince him. The overall impression is one of real lyricism, a liquid languishing quality, which makes them immediately appealing."

Next came *Soliloquy*, composed in 1969, a work of substantial proportions and of serious intent. It is a bigger piece altogether than his first work, (the *Three Pieces*) and is a fairly massive single movement piece. It was commissioned by the Glasgow Concert Society for Julian Bream to perform in the City Hall, Glasgow. Of course the composer got to know Julian Bream quite well, and relates with his customary blend of warmth and humour, the "ups and downs of the rehearsal process", as Tom put it.

> "I don't know how much Julian will relish having details of those sessions revealed to the gaze of the public, but I well remember a particular session immediately before the

concert. I don't think Julian will mind me saying that he found it a fairly tough nut to crack; it was a difficult piece. He said that he spent about 70 hours practice on the piece before we met, and clearly some of it was still giving trouble. I remember one particularly troublesome passage which tended to elude him and I well remember the kind of purple language with which he used to greet each failure to get it quite right. But, we rehearsed and he went on to give a spell-binding performance at its première. Soliloquy is essentially a big essay in musical form and structure and in musical arrangement."

The composer's next work, colourfully entitled *Coplas del Ruiseñor* is very different in character. Written for the Italian guitarist Angelo Gilardino in 1971, he finds the work very Mediterranean in character. The composer in point of fact knows the Mediterranean very well, and at various points in his life has either lived there or stayed for extended periods, and responds to it, regarding it as his other home as it were. The title refers to the nightingale, a bird with poetic connotations, and the *Coplas* is a kind of Mediterranean musical form. Overall it is a night piece.

"*Coplas* is a dialogue between musical elements, which is broadly nocturnal and lyrical in quality, hence the reference to the nightingale. The title attempts to synthesise these elements."

The composer's affection for the work is obvious in conversation.

"Coplas is one of my favourite pieces, the one I respond to warmly. I like them all though – at least I haven't gone off any."

Coplas is, in the composer's view perhaps a reaction to the heavier *Soliloquy*, and as a result, is much more impressionistic and atmospheric:

"Whilst *Coplas* is musical atmosphere, and a view of night time, it is miles away from the nice comfortable 'kids-in-bed', 'sweetie box' scene; it is a dramatic view with disagreeable, dramatic and frightening episodes."

Rasqueados (i.e. arpeggio-like passages) shatter calm completely; very rapid note configurations which need to go on for quite a time and be played at great speed but quietly, create a sinister quality to the music. The work finally ends in a Mediterranean, almost folk tune, elaborately written in three or four parts, thus giving a tranquil ending.

On the same topic of night music, I asked him if Bartók's music in the same mood was any kind of inspiration – Bartók was one of Tom's first "turn-ons" as a composer.

"Bartók was one of the important figures for me. If you see any connection between the kind of night music that is implicit in Coplas and the night music that is celebrated in Bartók's music it is not entirely accidental."

Cancion, composed in 1977, is a beautiful miniature consisting of some 56 bars of music. It has an intentional Iberian dimension due not only to its title. Technically the easiest of Tom Wilson's music, it is however deceptively difficult to bring off musically.

"*Cancion* was written for a painter friend of mine, Martin Baillie, who was very keen on music but had a kind of block about reading music. I tried to encourage him by writing a nice simple piece. Of course it got rather out of hand and developed into a piece in its own right."

At the time of writing, the composer could actually play it on the guitar but that's not to say that it is technically straightforward. Tom actually took up the guitar to verify that it could be played by a beginner if need be. Asked about the beautiful sonorities created by his chordal writing, skilfully blending stopped and unstopped strings, he replied with not a little humour!

"From my experiences with the guitar I became conscious that it is easier to play open strings than it is to play stopped ones when you're learning the instrument, and I resolved to make plenty of use of them - they sound great, players like playing them as well as a purely musical event, so I made more use of them in this piece."

Tom Wilson's latest work for guitar, *Dream Music*, was written in 1980 at my own request. Having played many of Tom's earlier works and spent quite a few evenings collaborating with him on them, I felt I wanted a work that would be 'personal'.

When *Dream Music* popped through the letter-box it needed no editing whatsoever. It is a big piece by guitar standards and quite tricky. But the composer knows exactly what he wants and is not prepared to compromise the music in any way. I learned a great deal about the guitar during our sessions together, a non-guitarist composer's view of the guitar is sometimes different from a player's – both are listening from a slightly different view point.

As is the composer's custom, the player is given quite detailed instructions.

"Music is a very complicated art and the performer needs as much help as possible, even to the extent of complementary instructions to make it clear to the performer the particular quality of sound that's required by me. I try to help the performer to realise this."

Dream Music opens with a calm tranquillity and peacefulness which is new to the composer of *Soliloquy*. As you will see from the score, the fifth string is bent up a semitone and back down again, setting the mood of the piece. There is a melismatic quality to the next section which is intensely melodic. From time to time sonorous six-string chords appear "like pillars of the universe" culminating towards the end in a Bach-like chorale.

The "comfortable" music is counterbalanced with brittle, edgy, nervous and apprehensive music to be played brilliantly. These two opposing musical ideas initially have a clear identity – being contrasted in large sections of music. However, as the work progresses the sections become shorter and the two ideas become closer and closer. Tom explains:

"It is not programmatic however but an interest in what would happen musically if two quite different expressive states collide. The two ideas run into each other, interpret each other, in the kind of irrational ways that dreams happen. The attempt in the music is to convey this."

As I said earlier, Tom Wilson's music is extremely well conceived for the instrument and needs only to be fingered – no editing being necessary. I always prefer to have for reference, an original manuscript copy of any piece. The published version, by Berben, is printed and not a facsimile of the original.

Rounding off this article, a few general comments seem in order. Thomas Wilson's music is a great contribution to the guitar's repertoire. It is by no means easy music, either technically or musically. Like all good things worth having, it repays the effort invested. His music is, in my view, very melodic in an almost classical way. I leave the last word to the composer.

> "Rightly or wrongly, I always write in the implicit belief that the person I am writing for is the best. If I'm writing a violin piece, it's for Heifetz. I always take it for granted that the artist who is going to play it is top-notch."

Having raised the necessary funds to commission the *Guitar Concerto*, Phillip came to the house at regular intervals during the autumn of 1995 and spent many hours discussing the best way to produce the precise sounds that Tom wanted. Tom said that he wanted to write the perfect piece and was keen to work closely with Phillip as he had done on *Dream Music*. Phillip later described the process to me, saying:

> He sent me sketches over nine months of writing the Concerto - little pieces of manuscript. I would then come over to the house and play them. Tom was searching for what made the guitar "the guitar", to find its soul as it were. He didn't want to make the Concerto easier, but he wanted to make the music more 'guitarist'. He loved the Mediterranean influence (which he heard in Spain and the Carmargue in France), and he wanted to make the guitar sound most natural. All Tom's pieces use rapid articulation and dense note clusters that resonate, with lots of semi-tonal play across stopped and open strings. This gives his guitar music an unusually rich colouration and a deeply resonant sound.

Phillip further recalls:

> Tom played about a lot with registration to gain the right combination of resonance and melody. He asked a lot about colour, how to get this colour, that colour; I learned once more that when Tom wrote his music he was very meticulous, every 'p' and 'mp' is written to tell the player exactly what was in the composer's mind. However the paradox is, that this level of detail gives the player

great freedom to finesse their interpretation. Tom was not telling the performer what to do; rather these were clues, and he was delighted for musicians to interpret around them. In writing the Guitar Concerto, he wanted the singer's freedom of expression for the guitar, and we talked at length about how to create long resonant notes that would allow this.

It was agreed from the start that the guitar would be amplified, since Tom did not want to use strumming to gain volume. We both loved the same kind of composers, particularly Bartók, and the strings and percussions were built in to give the Concerto a Bartókian edge. The work could be described as having two contrasting styles of playing from two very different forms of stringed instrument, one bowed, and the other plucked, and added percussion.

Though the guitar picks a romantic, lyrical path through much of the Concerto the overall effect is almost Baroque. There is a lot of space. The singing quality of the piece is in the recitative-like sections which have Baroque connotations, and this gives the balance, the (singing) space wanted, against the virtuosic articulated fast sections where there is semi-tonal movement along the strings.

The guitar definitely leads and is supported by the orchestra. The relationship is not one of struggle; the guitar makes little responses to big gestures from the orchestra and percussion – it comments on the orchestra, it never really competes.

We discussed at length a cadenza. Tom didn't really want one but he put in a final solo recitative that quotes excerpts from his solo guitar works thus creating a short cadenza towards the end of the piece.

Though Tom had yet to be diagnosed with kidney problems, he was clearly not well as can be seen from press pictures at the time. After suffering from the 'flu-like illness in Russia, he had never fully regained his formerly robust constitution. By spring 1996, he had developed a pale grey pallor. Although he did not feel unwell, he did not look at all well, and I persuaded him that he needed to visit the doctor. Since he had suffered from irritable bowel syndrome for several years, the GP sent him for an endoscopy to test for coeliac disease. However, this proved negative, so Dr Dawes continued to prescribe Loperamide and for a time that was the end of the matter.

I was not the only one who noticed that Tom was ailing. Tom and Phillip continued to work closely on the *Guitar Concerto* right through to the completion of the first draft in the spring. Phillip later told me "Tom didn't want to write a piece and give it to me. He wanted to check it as he went along. I got the feeling that he knew his health was failing, and he wanted the concerto to be as perfect as possible. "

Having completed the *Guitar Concerto* Tom then began to revise *Threads* for the Duo Contemporaine, and when this was completed in July 1996, he posted it to Henri Bok. The next month Henri wrote from the Cote d'Azur commending Tom on his revisions saying, "The final version of your piece is excellent, we will start working on it in September". Although it was premièred that year in the Low Countries, it was not performed in Britain until 1999 in London. Later that year, they also performed the piece in Glasgow, on November 17 at the memorial concert for Tom's former teacher, Professor Frederick Rimmer, in Glasgow University Chapel.

On October 30 1996 Tom wrote to Karl Gwiasda in Iowa:

> We have just returned from a short sojourn in Spain, and are getting ready for the première of my *Guitar Concerto*. Early indications are good – Phillip Thorne, the soloist, is very happy with it – but the form is notorious as a breeding ground for problems of balance etc. so it remains to be seen whether I have succeeded in allowing the guitar to counter the 'orchestra' (in this case strings and limited percussion, mostly vibes). Time will tell....

Phillip Thorne and the Paragon Ensemble, conducted by David Davies, gave the première of the *Guitar Concerto* on November 10 1996 in the Stevenson Hall of the Royal Scottish Academy of Music and Drama, Glasgow.

The critic Kenny Mathieson wrote:

> A new work by Thomas Wilson is always a significant event, and his *Guitar Concerto* proved no exception. Commissioned by its soloist, Phillip Thorne, for the Paragon Ensemble, it is written for string orchestra, percussion, and guitar. It moved from a lyrical, romantic opening through a more forceful rhythmic momentum to a gentle coda. The music is as shapely and economically constructed as we have come to expect from this composer, and Thorne played the solo part with great conviction.

306

Mary Miller described the concerto as "a rich but utterly lucid work, with the solo instrument lyrical, shining and strangely un-percussive, a human voice conversing with its fellow instruments."

Phillip later recalled:

> After the performance Tom asked me to come to the house to listen to a recording of the concert. I didn't want to because I don't usually like to listen to a recording so soon after the event, and I feared Tom was going to point out any misinterpretations I had made. However, I couldn't have been more wrong, he hadn't heard any! Tom was really delighted with how it sounded, in every way. It was just how he had wanted it. It was a great compliment.

Phillip, for his part, was also delighted with this towering work and has remained so. "In the *Guitar Concerto*," he recently told me, "Tom captured the very essence of the Guitar."

CHAPTER 21 (1996 - 2001)

A Life in Symphony

In mid-November 1996 Mary Miller interviewed Tom for The Scotsman newspaper. The ensuing article entitled "A Life in Symphony," recounted both Tom's path to composing and his aims.

His is the voice of reason, of long spare lines and uncluttered harmony. Thomas Wilson, Scotland's senior composer, unfazed by fashion and delighted by the burgeoning of new music in his native land, sits in his sitting room where light plays on the grand piano lid, pictures hum from the walls, and where, as in his music, every object - a carefully chosen jug or cushion - has its place.

"If you ask me to talk about music," he says carefully, "I will become extremely nervous. I'll simply stutter and falter. The only explanation for music is the music itself. It must stand or fall on its own merits." In fact, he says, everything he writes is symphonic. It is true – string quartets, a solo horn piece, piano sonatas and symphonies – all have a sense of broad, unhurried sweep, of unfolding grandness.

So we drink strong coffee, peruse an enticing range of chocolate biscuits, and talk, obscurely, about small-town America, which has figured minutely in his past.

He was born in 1927 in Trinidad, Colorado, where his father had gone to join a mining company. The family returned to Glasgow with Wilson a toddler, and, pre-empting new age practice, his father raised him while his mother worked.

There were early games matching composers' names to letters of the alphabet, but the young Wilson loathed piano lessons, until a wet afternoon denied him football and he found himself at the keyboard amazed by its music. Thereafter life changed – bits and pieces of composition emerged, a passionate pattern of listening evolved – and his path was drawn.

National service, spent outside Marseille, allowed him the chance to study before exams, then followed Glasgow University and a lectureship. It was in 1956, he says, that his composition began to acquire some sort of gravitas – there was a Piano Sonatina which he still rather likes, then a *Third String Quartet*, the other two having been consigned to the dustbin. Wilson the fastidious, one understands, found that his Muse was tough to please.

His *First Symphony*, from 1954, had a first performance from the then BBC Scottish Orchestra, conducted by a young Colin Davis, one in a long line of orchestral assistant conductors to ascend to stardom – Andrew Davis and Simon Rattle were to follow. He remembers Davis as an engaging lad. "He would stop and say: 'what a ridiculous profession, waving your arms about to get money,' which did indicate some kind of basic humility." But the symphony met customary coruscating criticism from its composer and was withdrawn – "too long, full of a young man's excesses."

Its successor, more tautly drawn, has been allowed to remain in his catalogue, a work which he describes as "as close as I got to atonality – but I never fully engaged with that, because I don't entirely believe that it exists. When we hear sounds, we always erect some kind of hierarchy in what we are listening to – certain sounds will predominate, and that is the basis on which tonality is founded."

But the sixties in Glasgow saw the start of what Wilson describes as a golden period. The formidable Watson Forbes was head of music at the BBC – a weighty, florid character prone to loud bow ties and firm pronouncement.

Forbes, though English, was passionate about new Scottish work and commissioned fulsomely for his orchestra. Works by Wilson and his colleagues – Robert Crawford, John Maxwell Geddes, Robin Orr and John Purser – were played weekly.

He was, perhaps, the last Glasgow-based BBC head to be allowed such autonomy; his successors were to feel the chill breath of London dilute their best intentions. And Wilson's work had been taken up by James Crampsie in the BBC's radio department, where music was needed to accompany plays, some couthily parish pump, others European and eclectic. "That's where I learned to orchestrate – in 24 scores for radio."

The pipe is lit again and Wilson is smiling. "There's a hell of a lot I don't know," he says happily, and describes how a horn player bewildered him recently with instructions on hand-stopping. But he is fascinated by the current spirit of enquiry into this age's music. "As a listener, I can only operate on the basis that the music is performed on the platform, and that I absorb. If you show me pictures or tell me stories, I will simply not be aware of them."

But what about other attempts to engage a reluctant and conservative audience with the music of their time?

"It's a conundrum. We live in a world which is greatly influenced by music in some shape or other. People's ears function fine, but they are utterly uninstructed in matters musical. Perhaps we have to compensate in some way to meet that deficiency. Faced with modern literature, we all, to some elementary degree, have the basic equipment to sample it – with music, all most of us have is native intelligence. That is the dilemma for those who try to 'present' the concerts, and most fall flat – spectacularly so – in their attempts to make something profound seem easy."

But as a composer he is undaunted. "Music is such a potent force that we must trust it to fall onto fallow ground. We just have to write our very best and hope that the seeds germinate."

All this gravely spoken by Wilson who one knows to have a wicked sense of the ridiculous – who can forget the terrible black humour of his opera *Confessions of a Justified Sinner*, and who, as a lecturer, urged his students to accept music as an expression of real life and not something glass-encased, which demanded worship? So does he believe that musical jokes exist? Can a composer who delights in the farcical scatter his scores with rip-roaring nonsense?

His face, masterfully impassive, grows woeful. "It disturbs me considerably to see an audience sit through Haydn at his most hilarious [he does not mean the 'ho-ho' Surprise symphony, which is a deeply serious work, but Haydn the wicked, twisting and twitching in a scherzo] with expressions of devoted deference. But farce outside opera is not something which music does well. I suppose we must try to inject wit in a kind of pointedness of expression; a spareness. Whether the audience will be aware or not is debatable."

Wilson's *Fourth Symphony*, is to be performed on November 20 by the BBCSSO under the baton of Jerzy Maksymiuk, in a studio concert. It opens with a carillon of celebration, moves on to discuss religious upheaval, the energy and dynamism of the machine, abject poverty, the beauty of Paisley's renowned patterns, then recession, conflict, and goes on to consider coolly the future. We will recognise Wilson the elegant, the fair-minded, the individual and the steady hand of Scotland's elder statesman musician; his own man, and all our composers' wise friend.

Over the years Tom was offered many prestigious posts that he turned down saying, "I am a composer, not an administrator." However, he was frequently sounded out about his opinions of contenders for top jobs in the musical world, perhaps more often than people would believe. Unfortunately his endorsement did not always result in a happy outcome for the person involved. I am thinking particularly of Jack Thomson whose dearest wish in life was to be the chief conductor of the RSNO but who suffered greatly at the hands of a man of much lesser talent when in 1988 he was eventually given the appointment.

We spent part of February 1997 with John and Lily Maxwell Geddes in Winterthur, Switzerland. Here, Jerzy Maksymiuk conducted the Stadtorchester in a concert of music by Scottish composers which included Tom's *St Kentigern Suite* and John's *Voyager*. Evelyn Glennie, the deaf percussionist who hears through her feet, also appeared on the programme. She was very generous in her praise of *St. Kentigern Suite* and said it was the best contemporary piece she had come across in a very long time, which pleased Tom greatly. We all were very envious of the amount of funding that orchestras in Switzerland received from the state. Each canton, and there are twenty-three of them, has its own orchestra, so classical music has a prominent place in the country's culture. The orchestras also have enough funding to employ the top soloists to come to play for them - people that we have not been able to hear locally since the 70s.

From Switzerland we went on to stay with our friend the composer, Stefan Heucke in Bochum, Germany. At a concert in Dortmund during this visit Johannes Wolff performed Tom's complete works for solo piano, and in June he played the *Piano Sonata* in Berlin. He later recorded all of Tom's piano works, apart from the *Concerto*.

After Tom's spring lectures were finished, we spent a few weeks at home so that he could rest and then we went to Spain. However he was becoming increasingly tired and less and less able to enjoy golf. He would still play the first few holes at the Sotogrande course but would then walk back to the clubhouse, while I would complete the eighteen holes. Otherwise we would read books and take walks along the beach, drink coffee in the port, or meet friends for drinks. Since his years in France with the Royal Air Force, Tom had always enjoyed siestas but somehow he needed to be abroad to indulge in them. His days at home were structured so that afternoons were a time for work, but in Spain he felt he could relax – though even here his thoughts would turn towards the next commission. This was never an easy process as he explained to Martin Dalby for an interview printed in the Scottish Music Information Centre publication *Music Current* that autumn:

Martin: What about starting a piece?

Tom: A natural reluctance to face up to the long task that's involved. Once the ideas are flowing then I can't get enough of it, I can't leave it alone until it's finished.

Martin: But before you sharpen the pencil do you consider the content of it, possibly the musical material, "I'm going to base it on Ubi Caritas" – something like that?

Tom: The method of procedure between one composer and another may differ widely, but in my own case, I've tried to arrive at a kind of hypothetical view of the piece that I'm going to write before I've written it. I start with an overall shape which I then, like a piece of plasticine, remould and reshape, and if it started out being, shall we say, circular in shape, it may well end up being square. So, the original conception is not the final result. It is, in fact, simply the starting point from which you will finally arrive at the final result. I always try to think in orchestral terms, the kind of colouristic wash of the piece, and how I'm going to use the colours, whether they are primary or mixed or whatever. These things are all very vividly present and should provide the stimulus from which the ideas flow. You might say the colour comes first, or the imagining of the colour comes first, and is followed by the actual musical ideas which are appropriate to that colour.

The piece I have been asked to do is the piece I want to do. Music is a huge universe of possibilities. I never feel constrained by the circumstances of a commission in the sense that I have to go down that narrow path. The circumscription of a commission may be the forces to be employed, but even they are capable of a huge range of options and possibilities.

At the very beginning of my career I wanted to write in every acknowledged formal set-up that there was. I wanted to write quintets, quartets, sextets, septets, octets and so on – and I've done all that. So there are certain areas where I am going round for the second and third time now and my idea is to do it better the next time, or do it differently. There are certain things that I would like to do. It may well be, for example, something in the electronic field where I am comparatively under-represented. I haven't used it very much so I might possibly do something on those lines. I'm conscious of the fact that I've gone a fairly long way to realising the ambition that I had to begin with, to write pieces of various kinds for all sorts of ensembles. I've written ballets, operas, the lot, so I feel that I have to address myself to the major problems in so far as circumstances allow.

On our return to Glasgow in July, Tom wrote to Karl Gwiasda about his plans for what would become his *Fifth Symphony* - though we did not realise it this would also be his final work.

"Spain involved lots of relaxation (those siestas!) but also allowed me to start on a new work for the Scottish Chamber Orchestra for their 25th anniversary season in 1998 (in general terms, a piece of 20-30 minutes for classical-sized orchestra [double woodwind, 2 horns, 2 trumpets – but no heavy brass and minimal percussion]. So a certain amount of conceptual scaling down is involved (though I suspect I may call on some extras, a harp? Some tuned percussion? We'll see."

This commission, from the Scottish Chamber Orchestra, was the first that Tom had received from them in a quarter of a century. He decided fairly early on that it would be a reworking of ideas from two earlier works, the *Fourth String Quartet* and to a greater extent *Mosaics*. Tom revised and reconceived musical ideas throughout his musical career as he explained to Martin Dalby in that same interview for *Music Current* in 1998:

Martin: You say that Mosaics sprang from the Radio Clyde commission for music for the programme 'The Splendid Silent Sun'....so, is *Mosaics* a recycling of the Poetry programme?

Tom: I think it was Mahler who thought of each of his Symphonies as a kind of universe in itself - a sort of complete entity. I've never been able to see music like that. I suppose what one does is write the same piece from different points of view, of perspective, both from the material that you use and from the age at which you write it. You see things differently when you are seventy than you did when you were thirty. So that the thing that makes *my* music *mine* is the use of certain common factors. You could turn the argument on its head and say that you're writing the same piece through different lenses throughout your entire life. This is not intended to be cynical. It's intended to be honest and to let the cat out of the bag. It arises out of a predilection to write certain intervallic patterns, construct harmony in a certain way and so forth. These things may remain common but the formal disposition, the aesthetic impact of the constructions which one places upon these materials at various points in one's career, produces entirely different results.

In a break from the interview, Dalby comments:

Wilson's philosophies always appear simple and benign, but as their impact dawns, you catch your breath while he innocently and disarmingly leads you gently round the corner into a world of utterly new perceptions. He smiles as he does it but the dagger he might plunge into your back shines with a bright enlightenment. Here he is describing one life with only one piece – itself a vast construction of all the works that an individual may have ever written.

Martin: Is it possible to consider that you only write one piece in your life, which consists of all the pieces you have ever written? In other words you start with opus one and you end with the last movement of the last piece you write – the last song?

Tom: In a sense that is what I am saying. It's a kind of continuing process. You start out on a certain path and formulate....I mean, how do we choose what we like? I don't know the answer to that. I may have a preference for certain melodic leaps, or rhythms, or harmonies and so forth, which I just happen to like. I don't justify it beyond that point. It's then my job as a composer to integrate these likes and dislikes within a convincing overall pattern which has some sort of meaning when strung together.

Tom with conductor
Sir Alexander Gibson
after the première of his
Te Deum (1971)

"Music is Magic" Tom at rehearsals of his opera
Confessions of a Justified Sinner (1973)

Father and Son, Tom and Martin (1984)

A typical photograph of Tom

Playing chess with fellow composer John Maxwell Geddes (1985)

Relaxing in the Botanical Gardens after a performance
of the *Piano Concerto* in Dublin (1987)

Tom in the Cloisters of Paisley Abbey at the première of the
Fourth Symphony: Passeleth Tapestry (1988)

With conductor Bryden Thompson the same evening (1988)

Discussing *Toccata Festevole* with Professor George McPhee in Paisley Abbey during the International Organ Festival (1990)

Tom and Margaret on holiday in Sotogrande, Spain (1990)

"Mutual Congratulations"
with the opera singer
Dame Janet Baker.
Conferment of
Fellowships at the Royal
Scottish Academy of
Music and Drama (1991)

Honourary DMus conferred by
Glasgow University (1991)

Tom after the completion of his *Violin Concerto* (1993)

Martin: Is part of that pattern, or could part of that pattern be the inclusion of music that you don't like?

Tom: I think this is comparatively seldom. I think one tends not to revisit one's failures.

Knowing Tom, I think that one of the reasons he decided to revisit *Mosaics* was that this work had been written at the express wish of Andy Park for Cantilena and Moog synthesizer. As technology had moved on, and the Moog was superseded, *Mosaics* was no longer performed, and as Tom was a practical person the ideas begged to be reused. Of course these would be reworked in such a thoroughgoing way that the sources would be unrecognisable to all but the most discerning, as Tom explains in his programme note:

> Whereas a piece like *Mosaics* is deliberately episodic in structure (as its name suggests), the present work aims to achieve that special, 'symphonic' unity which derives from the fusion of dissimilar, ambivalent or even conflicting materials. There is no 'story' behind the music, other than the musical drama which unfolds: the drama is musical, not narrative.

During our summer holiday in Sotogrande, Tom's physical stamina continued to deteriorate and on many days I would find myself going around the golf course on my own while he continued to compose. In August we were invited to the Bath International Guitar Festival, where Alan Neave was to play the *Three Pieces for Guitar*, which he then took on tour, and afterwards recorded on a CD called "…The Isle is full of Noises…" We managed to see quite a lot of the city in between listening to rehearsals and attending recitals and Tom – ever the teacher – enjoyed talking to the students who were attending a summer school that ran concurrently with the Festival.

Pas de Quoi was given an airing in Yerevan, Armenia in September, at the Second International Chamber Music Festival, when Nigel Boddice conducted the Yerevan State Chamber Orchestra. We were especially pleased about the performances in Armenia and in Berlin during the year, as they helped make his music known to new audiences.

During October, Richard Deering came to Glasgow University to play all of Tom's works for solo piano in a lunch hour recital, as a seventieth birthday tribute. At the same time, the BBCSSO was rehearsing *Introit* in

St Andrews for a performance that evening. On the previous day, the Romanian conductor Nikolai Moldoveanu, who was to conduct the orchestra, discovered that his work permit had run out, forcing him to go home. Frantically, the BBC turned to Jerzy Maksymiuk who agreed to step in to save the concert. Though Jerzy had conducted the work eight times, the last time was nine years earlier. Now having only a few hours to refresh his memory of it, he needed some help. So, although we had intended to hear Richard's recital and then motor to St Andrews in time for the evening performance of *Introit*, Tom decided he would have to prioritise the radio broadcast and make his apologies to Richard. Fortunately this sort of clash happened rarely, because Tom felt uneasy if he could not be present at a performance.

On November 2 the BBCSSO conducted by Jerzy Maksymiuk performed the *Viola Concerto* in Studio 1 at BBC Glasgow. Afterwards, soloist Philip Dukes lamented having to spend so many hours learning an interesting new work only to play it once – but then there are very few soloists who can choose what they wish to play.

We went to Nuremberg in March 1998 for performances to hear Stefan Grasse play Tom's *Cancion* for solo guitar. At another concert he appeared with the Neue Pegintzschaffer Ensemble as soloist in the *Guitar Concerto*. Stefan had been an admirer of Tom's music since his days as a student of Phillip Thorne, and he was one of eight musicians who performed in December 1990 for Carlos Bonell when Bonell visited the RSAMD in Glasgow to give a guitar masterclass to the students. On that occasion Stefan played *Dream Music.* He went on to win the Governors' Prize in January 1991, when he performed *Cancion* and *Dream Music.* Then in February he played *Cancion*, *Dream Music*, and *Three Pieces for Guitar* in a post-graduate recital.

During our visit to Nuremberg we also attended a lecture by Dr. Vivienne Olive at the Konservatorium on "The Music of Thomas Wilson." Our hotel was at the top of a small rise that Tom sometimes found difficult to negotiate because he became breathless, so we would stop to have coffee halfway up. I put this down to the fact that he smoked a pipe - which was supposed to be healthier than cigarettes, but since he inhaled deeply, I think that the supposed benefits were lost.

Shortly after our return from Nuremburg the hot water boiler in our house burst, flooding the basement and causing a great deal of damage. We did not have heating for a couple of days and Tom came down with 'flu. However I did not interpret this as being anything ominous, although with hindsight perhaps I should have, as Tom rarely succumbed to seasonal infections. Fortunately the chaos in the house did not affect his ability to work in his study on the first floor as is clear from a letter he wrote to Karl Gwiasda on April 15:

I have been bedevilled somewhat by a bout of 'flu' (or something similar), accompanied with impeccable timing, by a breakdown of our boiler and heating system, just as the winter showed its teeth again by slipping to sub-zero readings. So I'm sitting in my anorak writing this with teeth trembling on the edge of chattering. Ah well, mortification is doubtless good for the soul.....?

The SCO piece is both a scaling down, and also a scaling up, of an earlier piece called '*Mosaics*' which was written for strings, flute, oboe, harpsichord, & synthesiser about 10 years ago. It's a good piece (and it will remain in its original form), but for present purposes I have written out the synthesiser/harpsichord element, re-written the beginning and the middle (about 50% of the whole), and carried out major overhauls on the rest, including the re-scoring of the whole lot for full chamber orchestra (double woodwind, 2 horns, 2 trumpets, percussion and strings). This sweeping rethink was brought about by the fact that people seemed to be a bit reluctant to use the synthesiser (or anything involving electrical or electronic gadgets), and, as a result, the piece [i.e. *Mosaics*] was seldom done. I hope what I've done will be a valid extension-rethink and will open it up to a wider audience. I think it will work, but time will tell. Wish me luck! At present, time is pressing and I must get on with completing the score (the present bout of 'flu is highly inopportune) but no doubt I'll get there in the end. But it will be a question of 'heads down' and go-for-it!

Tom's spirits received a much needed boost in March when Edwin Paling, Leader of the Royal Scottish National Orchestra, was the soloist in a performance of the *Violin Concerto* conducted by Gary Howarth in the Henry Wood Hall. Edwin was the third soloist to take up the work since its creation five years earlier. He gave a very good performance, so Tom was of course pleased.

In April we were invited to the Isle of Arran for an Easter Music Weekend during which Tom's *Fourth Quartet* was to be played. We travelled to Arran, but in the end Tom felt too unwell to go to the performance. As a result, when we got home I made Tom see the family doctor, who took a blood sample. Apparently Tom's creatinin levels were high, but this did not mean anything to us so we were not unduly worried. We thought that maybe a course of treatment would solve the problem. The doctor referred him to the local infirmary for more tests, and it was a shock when, in the autumn, the hospital doctor said that Tom was suffering from glomerulunephritis – an inflammation of the kidneys. In time, the doctors explained, he would probably need dialysis. Tom was knocked back by the news for a couple of days; however, having never really been ill, apart from his experiences in Russia he fully expected to get better with time. I do not think he really understood what dialysis would entail; however, on a more profound level, I don't think he was really interested in thinking about it. Tom had always had the ability to stick his head in the sand when there was anything 'trivial' to be dealt with, and I think he thought that if he did the same this time, the unpleasant problem would probably go away.

The *Fifth Symphony* was completed in August 1998 and had by now evolved away from its original sources, as Tom remarked in a letter to Karl Gwiasda written December 10:

> It changed a lot in the writing – so much so that in my mind the connection with '*Mosaics*' no longer holds, even though certain passages are used. But the whole thrust of the structure is changed. So I marked this transformation by giving it the title of Symphony No.5. It is longer than Mosaics was, and the notion of setting aside the jumbo orchestration (without any flavour of neo-classical resurrection), struck me as an interesting notion.

The *Fifth Symphony* was scheduled to be performed on October 8 1998. Prior to the concert, Conrad Wilson interviewed Tom for an article in the Herald entitled, "The fifth milestone - Conrad Wilson beats the drum for a striking symphony from Thomas Wilson." The article served as great publicity for the première:

> Superstitious composers know all about ninth symphonies. These are works which need to be written with caution, in the fear that they might not lead to a tenth. But what about fifth symphonies? The Scottish Chamber Orchestra will be performing a pair of these this season, reminding us that five is also an emotive number in symphonic terms, which (albeit for different reasons) demands to be treated with similar respect. Beethoven's Symphony No. 5 in C Minor is the work we shall hear alongside that of Thomas Wilson.

Getting rid of the weight of a full orchestra was what, in the first place, prompted Wilson to accept the SCO's invitation to write a major work for about 36 players. Having already produced four symphonies for large orchestra, he welcomed the chance to create something entirely different as his fifth. It would be in keeping with the revolutionary spirit of previous fifth symphonies, even if, as he says, he felt not particularly 'bothered by' the shadow of other such works lying over him while he was writing it. "I might," he adds, "have had stronger feelings if it were my ninth."

Nevertheless, it can hardly fail to seem a milestone in his progress as Scotland's leading modern symphonist. At the very least it should consolidate his position as our most experienced orchestral thinker, unafraid to tackle what remains one of the most challenging and alluring of musical forms, however often people claim it to be moribund.

Though Wilson has composed successful operas – finding convincing music for the schizoid neurosis of Hogg's *Confessions of a Justified Sinner* – it is in the abstract drama of symphonies, string quartets, and sonatas that his heart seems mostly to lie. At the age of 70 – his 71st birthday falls the day after the new work's Glasgow performance on October 9th – he knows that a symphony does not need to tell a story to make itself understood by an audience. The drama is in the music, and when it is expressed by the sharp, clear, timbres of a chamber orchestra it can sound all the more potent.

Yet he is not so puritanical that he would try to prevent listeners from seeking something pictorial in his fifth symphony. Even though he himself had nothing like that in mind. "Anyone who wishes to erect a story round the music is welcome to do so," he says. Certainly the major rôle for the kettledrums seems likely to emerge as its most immediately theatrical feature, and the one most likely to provoke people into searching for a storyline.

Much more than the drumming at the start of Haydn's Drum-roll symphony, Wilson's timpani part is an extensive and expressive element in the music's structure, recurring at key points in its progress. Its contours (long, muffled drum-rolls, soft glissandi, rising and falling chromatic lines) are meticulously annotated with a wealth of dynamic markings. Its initial appearance – "shadowed and ominous," as Wilson puts it – forms the first 22 bars of the symphony's opening section, implying that a spacious drama

(Wilson times it at about half an hour) is about to be enacted. Some of the material derives from an earlier work entitled *Mosaics*, which, says Wilson, he had wanted to employ again "in a different way."

When the resources of a brilliant modern chamber orchestra were made available to him, he knew he had found the medium he was looking for, and became 'increasingly intrigued' by the idea of a symphony written without the traditional backup of heavy brass. Yet nobody needs fear that the result will lack ballast. Symphonic form, it will remind us, is about organic growth, unity of opposites, truth arrived at by argument. Laid out in four connected sections, the music reaches a climax which Wilson describes as a "gridlock," where the entire orchestra underpinned by now ferocious drums, tries to batter its way out of an apparent impasse. The escape route, in a quiet epilogue, comes via the strains of an old plainsong already hinted at, and leading back to the muffled drumming with which the symphony began.

The première took place in the Queens Hall, Edinburgh on October 8, when the Scottish Chamber Orchestra was conducted by Joseph Swensen.

In her review following the première Susan Nickalls wrote:

Thomas Wilson is a great uncelebrated treasure of Scottish music so all credit to the SCO for commissioning his *Symphony No. 5* as part of its 25th anniversary celebrations. In it, groaning timpani and a keening cor anglais establish a moody, unsettled atmosphere, and Wilson's scoring has a wonderfully light and transparent touch. Individual instrumental figures are frequently silhouetted in chiaroscuro against a finely shaded orchestral ground. The emphasis is not so much on melody as on rhythm and texture – lots of pizzicato and muted trumpets – with all the thematic fragments coming together in the violent and dynamic central section. ....
This was a triumphant performance confirming that the potent relationship between Swenson and the SCO has lost none of the magic of its auspicious beginning.

In his review of the second performance in Glasgow the following day, Conrad Wilson wrote in the Herald:

Behind Thomas Wilson's *Fifth Symphony* there is the repeated sound of distant thunder. You hear it at the start, where kettledrum rolls and glissandi disturb a slow cor anglais melody, creating a combination of timbres evocative of Berlioz's Symphonie Fantastique.

There are many desolate passages in Wilson's latest symphony, as its first Glasgow performance revealed last night, those on cello and flute, in particular, emerging from the mostly restrained but always expressive and luminous textures of the work as a whole.

Unlike Beethoven's Fifth however, the septuagenarian Glasgow composer's is not a progress from darkness to triumph. The music ends much as it began, with the murmur of muffled drums, not exactly menacing but adding their own disconcerting sound to an often disconcerting score conducted by Joseph Swensen in a manner that bound its interplay of slow and quick passages into a terse and cogent drama.

The *Fifth Symphony* was described in a broadcast for German radio by Wolfgang Graetschel, retired Professor of Music at Nuremberg University as "the Mount Everest of European music in the 20th century". This, once again, shows how greatly Tom's music is respected abroad.

For my part I thought that I could detect a change in this piece - a development. With hindsight I would say that the *Fifth Symphony* was a culmination of all that had gone before. Tom did say to me when it was completed that he wondered if he had anything more to say musically. I responded by saying that if that was the case then I would be very happy to have my husband back. As I had told our Russian friends many years before: "Tom has a wife and a mistress, and as his mistress is not human I cannot compete with her."

Our last trip abroad for a performance was in October 1998, to Aarhus in Denmark. The purpose of the visit was for Tom to hear the Aarhus Symphony Orchestra, conducted by James Loughran, perform his *Violin Concerto*. The soloist was Dmitri Makhtin. Tom had deteriorated quite a lot by this time, and he was really most unwell. When he walked down the aisle to take his bow I was very worried whether he would make it to the platform. The next morning we did not go down for breakfast, so one of our friends Marjory Dougal came to see what was wrong and was visibly shocked to see how ill Tom looked.

The doctors had hoped that they would be able to postpone dialysis until November 1999, but Tom became ill with pneumonia in February and his kidneys failed. After discussing the situation with his doctors, we opted for CAPD (Continual Ambulatory Peritoneal Dialysis), which is a much gentler procedure than haemodialysis. An operation was performed to insert a catheter into his peritoneum. This meant that he was dialysed at home four times each day and so our lives revolved around this. Before the hospital staff would allow Tom to come home, they had trained me for one week to make quite sure that I knew how to dialyse, and they were rigorous. I had to prove to the medical staff of the department that I knew exactly what I was doing. Cleanliness was of the utmost importance.

John Maxwell Geddes was a great help to me at this time. He offered to learn how to dialyse Tom so that I could have time to attend to things that I needed to do outside of the home. He was as scrupulous regarding the hygiene of the dialysis as I was, and treated Tom with loving care, and I had no qualms about entrusting him with the process.

On June 8 1999 Tom wrote to Karl:

> Healthwise, slow but steady progress continues. Getting back to former energy levels is still far in the future though. But nice things continue to happen. John Wallace, the trumpeter for whom the Trumpet Concerto was to be written, phoned to persuade me to keep the project on the back burner for the indefinite future, which is nice. The other day an obscure brass band from Yorkshire wrote to me telling me of recent successes they had had playing my '*Sinfonietta*'. We have never met or corresponded in the past – the only point of contact has been that particular work. Enclosed was a 'Get well' card signed by all the members of the band with their personal reactions to '*Sinfonietta*', and best wishes. Very touching – quite amazing really…!"

At this stage Tom's mood was still very positive and his spirits where lifted when the BBC Scottish Symphony Orchestra decided to record his *Fifth Symphony* with Jerzy Maksymiuk conducting. Though very frail Tom attended both the rehearsals and the performance, after which the following review by Kenneth Walton appeared in The Scotsman:

> Listening to Thomas Wilson's Symphony No.5, it is easy to forget he wrote it two years ago at the age of 71. Underpinning every minute of its half hour duration is an effortless, naturally flowing energy. Not the kind of fired up angry insistence you would expect from a younger man, but one nonetheless gripped by a life giving

pulse that is urgent, alert and dynamic.

Despite the symphony's modest forces – it was originally written for the Scottish Chamber Orchestra – and its rather comfortable, sometimes unchallenging musical language, Wilson's experienced hand sets out a score that is ingenious in its application of colour and texture, and sound as a bell when it comes to formally developing his ideas. Maturity informs every bar, and when Jerzy Maksymiuk conducted the BBC SSO with his usual unbounded energy and explosive grunts, he applied his own elder statesman vision to a performance that was bold and persuasive, but adventurous too.

The gathering of tension, from the mysterious opening dialogue between timpani and cor anglais to the expansive string writing which polarises much of the symphony was handled with remarkable judgement and insight. But there was a ruggedness in the SSO's playing, which gave this performance an added spark, making all the more poignant that magical closing moment when the airy flute hovers contentedly over a mood of stasis and tranquillity in the strings.

There were a number of performances and broadcasts of Tom's works that year, such as the *St Kentigern Suite* in the Queens' Hall, Edinburgh and *Ave Maria* in Greyfriars Kirk, Edinburgh, but as his condition was deteriorating Tom now had to decline more invitations than he accepted. Indeed, over the next years Tom was hospitalised many times with peritonitis. The doctors explained to me that the infection was internal and it was nothing to do with the dialysing I was doing at home, and nothing could be done except to treat him with antibiotics each time. I offered to donate one of my kidneys for a transplant, but the doctors declined saying that the other internal organs were also failing so his body would not be able to withstand the trauma of major surgery. I spent many days in the hospital with him and must say that the staff were very good about allowing me time with him outside of the visiting hours. Another musician friend who was taken into the Western Infirmary for a relatively minor complaint told me that he found himself lying opposite Tom in the corridor on their respective gurneys. Apparently Tom looked across to him and joked: "So they are bumping us off in pairs now!"

We left Glasgow for a holiday in our flat in Spain in October 2000. A lot of arrangements had to be made by the hospital to make sure that the bags of dialysis fluid - 56 were needed for our two week stay - had been delivered a few days before our arrival, along with the attendant sterilising equipment and the paraphernalia that accompanies dialysis. We managed to enjoy our stay, despite the hazards of a plane that landed in Amsterdam too late for us to catch our direct flight to Malaga. So we had to go via Barcelona. On the way home there were no facilities in Heathrow to dialyse Tom, and we had to perform the procedure in a lavatory for the handicapped.

We were both fortunate that between 2000 and 2001, our son Brendan and his children Emma and Hugo came to live in Glasgow while Brendan was on sabbatical leave from Tokyo University. Unfortunately Makiyo was still teaching and could not come with them. They rented a flat in Observatory Road just around the corner from us in the West End, and their presence was a great support to us both. Tom particularly enjoyed his developing relationship with his grandchildren.

While Tom was at home he also had regular visits from people like John Geddes, Allan Neave, Nigel Boddice and Martin Baillie that cheered him up. He even dictated changes to the *Fifth Symphony* to our friend Pat Holmes – small things like dynamics. During these days it was difficult to persuade our visitors to leave – they all seemed to realise that it might be the last opportunity they would have to speak with Tom and couldn't bring themselves to go, even though he was tired.

Jim Clayton's cousin Moira Buchanan had been a friend of Tom's since childhood, although there was a break of about 20 years when she took up a nursing post in England. For the last years of her career however, she returned to Glasgow, and became a regular visitor to our home - and to the hospital, on the frequent occasions when Tom was incarcerated there. Four weeks before Tom died she brought his childhood friend Father Martin Sweeney to see him, and Father Martin decided that he would celebrate Mass in our home for Tom. Then our parish priest Monsignor Ryan came to visit, and Tom and he talked. Tom and I had not been to church for many years, but he was pleased that he was able to take the sacrament again. So in his final days Tom came back to the faith of his childhood, and he told Monsignor Ryan that he was very glad that he had done so.

As his bouts of illness continued through 2001 the doctors decided it was time for him to change to haemodialysis. The infection causing the peritonitis was travelling internally, so there was nothing we could do to prevent it while he was on CAPD. The doctors explained to me that his immune system had turned on itself. I believe that it was only at this late stage that Tom came to realise that he was not going to get better. The operation to allow a shunt in his arm to be used for the haemodialysis was never a success and so he was dialysed from his neck. He never complained during his illness, although he grew weaker and weaker, and I knew that at times he was very uncomfortable. Nausea and lack of appetite and the resulting lack of energy played a big part in it. I'm sure that at times he got tired of me trying to persuade him to eat though he never complained and never got angry.

Two weeks before Tom died he said to me: "They are speaking as though I am about to die and I am not ready to 'pop my clogs yet'." I knew that he hadn't long to live but I made a joke of it saying: "Don't you dare die! I'll tell you when you can die." Around that time, he also surprised me by saying, quite out of the blue, that he had sympathy for Judas Iscariot: "Did *he* have a choice? The prophecy had to be fulfilled."

I regret that I did not pursue this conversation, but felt that I did not want to discuss it in case it upset him, so I just took note of what he said. He was so very ill, but still felt compassion for others; yet again I was reminded of what a remarkable man Tom was. After all, it was not a statement that I had ever heard from anyone else.

He was quite animated when John Currie stopped by a few days later and they talked together of a possible future performance of *Sequentiae Passionis* but it was not to be. They agreed that if it should take place then the plainchant after the opening bars of percussion would have to be re-recorded.

Martin and Pat Baillie, and Karl and Barbara Gwiasda, came to visit Tom on the day before he died and once again he rallied for the occasion. He was a good actor, but eventually he had to give in and tell them that he was tired.

That evening he looked at a spot near the corner of the room for quite some time and I wondered what he was seeing. Eventually he looked up and saw me watching him, and he gave me a most beautiful smile and his eyes twinkled.

The following morning he was taken to the hospital for four hours of dialysis. Pat Holmes, who was helping me with printing scores and making a list of past performances of Tom's compositions, came to the house at lunchtime, and then John Geddes called.

When Tom didn't return home, I telephoned the hospital to see what was keeping him. Sometimes dialysis patients had to wait for hours for an ambulance, without food or even a cup of tea, and often feeling nauseous. (An ambulance was necessary as Tom had to be carried up the steps into the house in a wheelchair). The hospital asked me to come in, and Pat and John came with me. The doctor took us into a side room and said that my husband was very seriously ill and what did I want to do. I knew that he was asking if they should try to keep him alive. I was so distraught that I didn't know what to say, so I asked John. John said to me: "Margaret where there is life, there is hope." And I agreed. I will always be grateful to John for his support at that time. However Tom's hold on life gradually weakened, and three hours later at 5.25pm on June 12, 2001, he died peacefully.

CHAPTER 22

Tributes

Tom's funeral was held on Saturday, June 16 in St Aloysius Church, Garnethill, Glasgow. Before the priests came to the altar, there was taped music from his *Sequentiae Passionis* which merged into the plainchant *O Vos Omnes*. The John Currie Singers sang Tom's *Ave Maria* during the Eucharist, and Mozart's *Ave Verum* during the communion. These choral pieces were followed by extracts from Tom's *Violin Concerto* and as his coffin was carried out of the church a recording of one of our favourite pieces, Faure's *In Paradisum*, was heard.

Though the service was beautiful, I went through the requiem mass in a blur.

As Tom's widow, I stood to thank the mourners as they left the church, as did Brendan, Martin and Stephen. I remember my poor grandchildren waiting outside in the bitter wind, and I remember seeing Fred, my cousin Sylvia's husband, at the bottom of the steps alongside the hearse and hearing him say that he was "keeping Tom company".

Tom's childhood friend Father Martin Sweeney gave a second shorter service at the crematorium and before I knew it Tom's coffin had slipped away. Afterwards, at the reception in the University Club, it was all I could do to keep myself together, but having our three sons and two grandchildren there was a great help.

Over that week several of Tom's fellow composers along with various reviewers and music lovers wrote or broadcast obituaries, extracts from which appear at the end of this chapter. I also received hundreds of letters of condolence from his friends and colleagues all of whom remarked on his kindness and generosity of spirit and many of whom went much further. Here is a very small selection:

> "In the few years of what I consider a friendship, Tom's humanity, integrity, and kind nature registered ineradicably upon me. At our meeting the day before he died, there was some talk of music and

of past times, but above all there was wit and laughter. Illness could sap Tom's energy but was powerless against his quick and keen sense of humour. Tom never flinched at the fact of mortality; neither, though, did he surrender to its sway. He tempered life's rigours with grace, met its severities with compassion. As with his art, he took life seriously but never sombrely. Tom's compositions are not a memorial, they are instead his gift to a world in need of understanding, succour, and faith. The music is not a monument but a testament." Professor Karl Gwiasda

"He was someone I had the most enormous respect for – a fine composer and a fine man." Edward Harper, Composer

"Tom was such a wonderful man with such a noble character. He was one of the most distinguished composers I know." Peter Manfred Wolf, Composer

"His music I'm sure will live for a long, long time. It took me a long time to realise that impeccable technique owes as much to honesty of spirit as well as craftsmanship." David Dorward, Composer

"Tom was one of the most lovable people I have ever met." John Wallace, Principal of the RSAMD

"Professor Wilson's music means a great deal to me; St Kentigern alone is a masterpiece." Stephen Broad, Head of Postgraduate Progammes and Research, RSAMD

"To quote Ralph Vaughan Williams one could justly say – 'Great teacher; great composer: great friend'. Tom was all of these things and surely posterity will claim, as time goes on, that here was Scotland's greatest son." Bernard Barrell, Composer

"When I first came to Glasgow it was exciting to have someone of Tom's great talents on the staff of the department, and I found him a creative and imaginative colleague – no one anywhere could beat the teaching of Tom Wilson and Martin Baillie!" Professor Lalage Bown, erstwhile Head of the Department of Adult and Continuing Education, University of Glasgow

"Tom was an inspiration to all composers in Scotland who came after him. His beautiful music will survive and live for ever." James MacMillan, Composer

"Tom will always be with us through his music." Janet Beat, Composer

"He always spoke through his works, with absolute sincerity, conviction and expressive expertise. We shall all miss him so much." Richard Chester, Director of NYOS

"As a composer he taught me much. He listened patiently, commented wisely and charitably and, above all, represented in himself the true dignity of a man who practised his art with fervour, dedication and uncompromising self-discipline." John Purser, Composer

"I always admired Tom's music and I would go so far as to say that he was far and away the greatest Scottish figure in the second half of the Twentieth Century." Bobby Crawford, Composer

"There is a sense in which composers do not die, in that their work remains with us, to be serviced with every performance. But of course it behoves the rest of us to make sure that happens!" John Hearne, Composer

"Tom once gave me a score of his 3rd Symphony (dedicated to Sir Alexander Gibson and the SNO). He inscribed my copy with:

> "For John Geddes, my alter-ego, with whom I have had so many moments of understanding of a clouded universe of music."
>
> Thomas Wilson (Tom)

"It is, of course, by his works that he will be remembered; this is his legacy. But for me, he was unique; he was my model, my mentor, my friend." John Maxwell Geddes, Composer

We also received a very poignant letter of condolence from Thomas J. Cardinal Winning that was written on the eve of his own death;

> "I remember him well and I should like to say that I felt rather proud when he became such a fine musician and composer, bringing lustre to his native Glasgow and Scotland. He will be remembered in his music."

In 2002 Scotland's musicians organised four concerts to celebrate Tom's memory. The first of these was a Tribute concert given by the John Currie Singers who had a long professional connection with Tom. Director John Currie, who had also written the libretto for *The Confessions of a Justified Sinner*, chose to perform Tom's *Missa Pro Mundo Conturbato* and his *Ave Maria*. Coming in March, so soon after the terrorist attacks on the World Trade Centre, and with the winds of war blowing once more in many parts of the world, Conrad Wilson considered it "the appropriate, if uncompromising, composition with which to remember Tom's musical contribution."

On the afternoon of June 26 2002, 'A Celebration of the Music of Thomas Wilson' was held at the RSAMD. Featured were four of his early works: *Pas de Quoi*, *Piano Sonata*, *Cartoon*, and *Four Scottish Songs*. That evening James Loughran conducted the Academy orchestra in a thoughtful reading of *Touchstone*. In December the BBC Scottish Symphony Orchestra under the baton of James Loughran performed Tom's *Carillon* and *Violin Concerto*. Ernst Kovacic who had premièred the work in 1993 was once again the soloist.

These nine works form a small but representative selection of Tom's extensive musical repertoire, ranging as they do from the playful to the profound, from the contemplative to the festive, and from the romantic to the abstract. Throughout 2002, others of Tom's compositions were performed by musicians who delivered their own tributes to him.

Tom's work continues to be performed in Scotland and across the world. John Maxwell Geddes has called him a "national treasure". I am thrice blessed in that he is my treasure too. Our life together was not compartmentalised, but love was by far the greatest part of it. I think that the greatest contribution that I made to Tom's musical life while he was alive was to give him the space that he needed to compose. Since his death I have found great solace in his musical legacy and the continuing promotion of his works. James Reid Baxter recently told me that he asked John Purser his opinion of Tom and the reply was "In many ways he was the father of us all!" I think that Tom would have liked that.

An early retrospective of Tom's work was prefaced by the words of the Spanish writer and philosopher Miguel de Unamun: "There is nothing more universal than the individual, for what is the property of each is the property of all. Each man is worth more than the whole of humanity, nor will it do to sacrifice each to all, save insofar as all sacrifice themselves to each."

Those who knew my husband know how much these words typify his thinking. Those who have only known him from his music can be assured that the vision of the music reveals the man.

Catalogue of Works

Orchestral

Toccata	1959	3222/4231/Hp/Timp/Sts.	8'
Variations for Orchestra	1960	3222/4231/Hp/Timp/Sts.	18'
Symphony No. 2	1965	3222/4231/Perc/Hp/Pf/Cel/Sts.	23'
Concerto for Orchestra	1967	3333/4331/Timp/Perc/Cel/Pf/Sts.	18'
Touchstone	1967	3333/4331/Perc/Hp/Cel/Pf/Sts.	10'

Commissioned by the BBC for the Henry Wood
Promenade Concerts.

Threnody	1970	3333/4331/Timp/Perc/Hp/Cel/Pf/Sts.	18'
Symphony No. 3	1979	3333/4331/Timp/3Perc/Hp/Pf/Cel/Sts.	25'

Commissioned by Musica Nova.

Introit *(Towards the Light)*	1982	222/423/Timp.Anvil.SC/2Perc/ Hp/Pf/Cel/Sts.	25'

Commissioned by BBC.

Piano Concerto	1985	3333/4331/Timp/Perc/Hp/Cel/Sts.	28'

Commissioned by Bryden Thomson for David Wilde
and the BBC Philharnomic Orchestra.

Viola Concerto	1987	2222/4321/HP/Pf/Timp/Perc/Sts.	25'

Commissioned by James Durrant with assistance from
the BBCSSO Trust.

Symphony No. 4 *(Passeleth Tapestry)*	1988 3333/4331/Timp/Perc/ Hp/Pf/Cel/Sts.	28'

Commissioned by Renfrew District Council together
with Strathclyde Regional Council to mark Paisley's
500th anniversary as a Burgh of Barony.

Carillon	1990 3333/4321/Timp/Perc/ Hp/Pf/Cel/Sts.	15'

Commissioned by Glasgow City Council in 1990 as part of its
European City of Culture celebrations, as the inaugural work
to celebrate the opening of the city's new Royal Concert Hall.

Violin Concerto	1993 2222/4331/3Perc/Timp/ Pf Cel/Hp/Strings	26'

Commissioned by the National Youth Orchestra of
Scotland and BP for Ernst Kovacic.

Guitar Concerto	1996 Solo guitar Sts. 33221(minimum)/ 1Perc,Vibes,Bongos	20'

Commissioned by Phillip Thorne.

Symphony No. 5	1998 2222/2Horns/2Trumpets/Timp/ Perc/Strings	27'

Commissioned by the Scottish Chamber Orchestra.

Chamber Orchestral

Mosaics	1981 F1(AF)/Hpschd/ Polyphonic synthesizer/Sts.	20'

Commissioned for Cantilena by Radio Clyde.

St Kentigern Suite	1986 For 11 solo strings or full string orchestra	20'

Commissioned by the Friends of Glasgow Cathedral,
on the occasion of the Cathedral's 850th anniversary.

String Orchestra

Pas de Quoi	1964	Six little dances for strings *Prelude, Valse, Rigaudon,* *Sarabande, Polka, Gavotte.*	11'
Ritornelli per Archi	1972	For 11 solo strings or full string orchestra Commissioned for the Edinburgh Festival by the Scottish Baroque Ensemble.	19'
St Kentigern Suite	1986	For full string orchestra or 11 solo strings Commissioned by The Friends of Glasgow Cathedral, on the occasion of the Cathedral's 850th Anniversary.	20'

Chorus & Orchestra

Missa Pro Mundo *Conturbato*	1970	Chamber Choir. 2 Perc/Hp/Sts. Commissioned by the John Currie Singers.	22'
Sequentiae Passionis	1971	Large Chamber Choir. 222/4231/Timp/Perc/Hp/Tape/Sts. Commissioned by Musica Nova.	55'
Te Deum	1971	Large Chorus. 2233/4231/3 Perc/Timp/Hp/Pf/Sts. Commissioned by the Edinburgh Festival for the opening concert on the occasion of its 25th Anniversary.	17'
Songs of Hope *and Expectation*	1977	Chamber Choir. Pf.EO. Hpschd. (1 player)/Sts. Commissioned by the John Currie Singers.	16'
Amor Christi	1989	Chamber Choir. 2222/22/2Perc/Timp/Hp/Sts. Commissioned the Scottish Philharmonic Singers.	23'

Confitemini Domino	1993 SATB/Brass Quintet/Organ	11'

Commissioned by the Royal College of Organists to
celebrate their 100th Anniversary.

Opera

The Charcoal Burner	1968 3222/4331/Timp/Perc/Hp/Pf/Cel/Sts.	60'
Libretto: Edwin Morgan.	Commissioned by the BBC.	

The Confessions of a	1974 2222/323/Timp/Perc/Hp/Pf.Cel.	135'
Justified Sinner	EO.(1 player) Tape/Sts.	

Commissioned by Scottish Opera.

Ballet

Embers of Glencoe	1973 Percussion	35'

Commissioned by Scottish Ballet.

Vocal

Three Orkney Songs	1961 Sop/Bar/Fl/Ob/Vln/Vc/Pf.	10'

Commissioned by the BBC.

Six Scots Songs	1962 Arrangements for voice and Pf.	14'

Carmina Sacra	1964 High Voice/Hp/Sts.	18'
	Version for voice and keyboard	
	also available	

One Foot In Eden	1977 Mezzo sop./Fl/Clar/Hp/Pf/	27'
	Eo.(1 player)/Perc/Vln/Vla/Vc.	
	Version for voice and piano	
	also available	

Commissioned by Josephine Nendick.

| *The Willow Branches* (*Seven Songs from the Chinese*) | 1983 | Mezzosop./2222/2Hns/Hp/Cel/ 2Perc/Timp/Sts. Version for voice and piano also available. | 21' |

Commissioned by Marilyn de Blieck.

Unaccompanied Choral

| *By The Waters Of Babylon* | 1951 | SATB.Tenor/Bar/Bass 2 Versions | 5' |

| *Mass in D Minor* | 1956 | SATB | |

Broadcast by BBC Chorus
Conducted by Leslie Woodgate

| *Missa Brevis* | 1964 | SATB | |

| *A Babe is Born* | 1967 | SATB (and organ) | 5' |

| *Night Songs* | 1967 | SATB | 12' |

Commissioned by the John Currie Singers

| *Ave Maria/Pater Noster* | 1967 | SATB | 5' |

| *There Is No Rose - Carol* | 1974 | SATB | 4' |

First performed at King's College Cambridge,
Festival of Lessons and Carols

| *Ubi Caritas Et Amor* | 1976 | 2Tenor/2Bar/Bass | 18' |

Commissioned by the Baccholian Singers for the
City of London Festival.

| *Cantigas Para Semana Santa* | 1992 | Chamber choir | 21' |

Commissioned by Cappella Nova

| *My Soul Longs For Thee* | 1992 | SSA | 5' |

Chamber

String Quartet No. 3	1958 2Vln/Vla/Vc. McEwen Composition Prize.	21'
Violin Sonata	1961 Vln/Pf. Commissioned by the University of Glasgow.	19'
Sonata for Clarinet and Piano	1962 Clar/Pf.	9'
Concerto da Camera	1965 Fl/Ob.Vln/Vc/Pf. Commissioned by Bernicia Ensemble.	16'
Piano Trio	1966 Pf/Vln/Vc. Commissioned by the Scottish Trio.	17'
Sinfonia for Seven Instruments	1968 Clar/Fag/Hn/String Quartet Commissioned by the University of Glasgow.	17'
Sonata for Cello and Piano	1971 Vc/Pf. Commissioned by Glasgow Chamber Music Society.	22'
Ritornelli Per Archi	1972 11 solo strings (See also String Orchestra) Commissioned by the Scottish Baroque Ensemble for the Edinburgh Festival.	19'
Canti Notturni	1972 F1(AF)/Clar(BC)/Vln/Vla/Vc/Pf. Commissioned by the Clarina Ensemble.	18'
Complementi	1973 Clar(BC)/Vln/Vc/Pf. Commissioned by the Clarina Ensemble.	18'
String Quartet No. 4	1978 3Vln/Vla/Vc. Commissioned by the Edinburgh String Quartet. (Première BBC TV).	20'

Mosaics	1981	Fl(Picc.AF)/Ob/(CA)/Hpschd. Polyphonic Synthesizer/Sts. (See also Chamber Orchestra)	20'

Commissioned by Radio Clyde.

St Kentigern Suite	1986	For 11 solo strings	20'

Commissioned by the Friends of Glasgow Cathedral,
on the occasion of the Cathedral's 850th anniversary.

Chamber Concerto	1986	F1(Clar)/Hn/Tpt/Trom/2Perc/ Pf/Vln/Vc.	22'

Commissioned by the New Music Group of Scotland.

Chamber Symphony	1990	Fl/Ob/Clars(BC)/Fg/2Hns/Tpt/ 2Vlns/Vla/Vc/Cb.	26'

Commissioned by Paragon Ensemble and Glasgow
District Council as part of the celebrations during
Glasgow's reign as European City of Culture 1990.

Threads	1996	Bass Clar/Marimba/Vibraphone	5'

Commissioned by Duo Contemporain.

Instrumental

Sonatina	1956	For Piano	8'

Sonata	1964	For Piano	18'

Three Pieces	1964	For Piano *Reverie* *Tzigane* *Valse Viennoise*	7'

Fantasia	1964	For Cello	8'

Soliloquy	1969	For Guitar	12'

Commissioned by Glasgow Master Concerts for
Julian Bream.

Three Pieces	1971 For Guitar	7'
Coplas Del Ruiseñor	1972 For Guitar Commissioned by Angelo Gilardino.	10'
Cancion	1982 For Guitar	3'
Dream Music	1983 For Guitar Commissioned by Phillip Thorne.	10'
Incunabula	1983 For Piano	12'
Toccata Festevole	1991 For Organ Commissioned by the Paisley International Organ Festival.	7'
Suite for Piano	1957 For Piano	
Chanson de Geste	1991 For Solo Horn Commissioned by Redcliffe Concerts.	11'

Brass Band

Sinfonietta	1967 Commissioned by the Scottish Amateur Music Association for the National Youth Brass Band.	13'
Cartoon for Cornet	1969 Available in versions for Cornet and Brass Band; Brass Ensemble and Optional percussion; and Cornet and Piano Commissioned by Robert Oughton and the Scottish CWS Band (1969)	5'
Refrains And Cadenzas	1984 Commissioned by the Cheltenham Festival (Test piece for the European Championships 1984)	11'

Incidental Music

The Face of Love	1954	BBC Radio
Witchwood	1954	BBC Radio
Glencoe	1955	BBC Radio
Susannah and the Elders	1955	BBC Radio
Storm	1956	BBC Radio
Oggs Log	1956	BBC Radio
All in Good Faith	1957	BBC Radio
A Nest of Singing Birds	1957	BBC Radio
The Boy David	1957	BBC Radio
For Tae Be King	1957	BBC Radio
The Great Montrose	1958	BBC Radio
The Wallace	1959	BBC Radio
Enquiry	1960	BBC Radio
Brush Off the Dust	1964	BBC Radio
Checkpoint	1965	BBC Radio
Charles Rennie Mackintosh	1965	BBCTV
Robert Burns	1965	BBCTV
A Season for Mirth	1966	BBC Radio
A Spell for Green Corn	1967	BBC Radio
Ships of the '45	1968	BBC Radio
The March of the '45	1969	BBC Radio
Sunset Song (Part 1 of A Scots Quair)	1971	BBCTV
The New Road	1973	BBCTV
There was a Man	1980	Radio Clyde
Summer Solstice	1980	Radio Clyde
The House with the Green Shutters	1980	BBC Radio
Cloud Howe (Part 2 of A Scots Quair)	1982	BBCTV
Grey Granite {Part 3 of A Scots Quair)	1983	BBCTV
Voyage of St Brandon	1984	BBCTV
Murder Not Proven	1984	BBCTV
Gaudi	N.D.	BBCTV
The Castle of May	N.D.	BBCTV